VANNES AND ITS REGION

VANNES AND ITS REGION:

A STUDY OF TOWN AND COUNTRY IN EIGHTEENTH-CENTURY FRANCE

BY

T. J. A. LE GOFF

CLARENDON PRESS · OXFORD
1981

Oxford University Press, Walton Street, Oxford OX2 6DP
OXFORD LONDON GLASGOW
NEW YORK TORONTO MELBOURNE WELLINGTON
KUALA LUMPUR SINGAPORE JAKARTA HONG KONG TOKYO
DELHI BOMBAY CALCUTTA MADRAS KARACHI
NAIROBI DAR ES SALAAM CAPE TOWN

Published in the United States
by Oxford University Press, New York

© Oxford University Press 1981

British Library Cataloguing in Publication Data

Le Goff, T J A
  Vannes and its region.
  1. Vannes, France – Social conditions
  I. Title
  309.1′44′13   HN438.V/   79–41667

  ISBN 0–19–822515–6

Phototypesetting by Parkway Group, London and Abingdon.
Printed in Great Britain by Lowe and Brydone, Thetford.

PREFACE

This book began as a doctoral thesis under the direction of the late Professor Alfred Cobban, who supervised two years of its preparation until his untimely death in 1967. It was Professor Cobban who first turned my attention to the social history of western France by suggesting that I might like to do a study of the seigneurial system in Brittany and Normandy. My own inclination, at the beginning, was rather to work on the problem of the resistance to the Revolution in Brittany, but I soon became aware that so little was known of the social structure of old-regime Brittany, and especially of Lower Brittany, the Breton-speaking half of the province, that it would be more interesting to make this the focus of my research; Professor Cobban and Professor Douglas Johnson, who later took over supervision of my work, agreed and encouraged me in this direction. In the thesis which I eventually submitted in 1970, I tried to take a region of manageable size, containing both an urban centre and its surrounding countryside, and examine, within that framework and over a limited period of time, a certain number of problems which students of societies past and present might consider to be significant. Since then, I have expanded and re-cast some of these questions, explored a few others, and stretched the period covered to the space of three generations, from about 1730 to 1793, with occasional excursions beyond these limits where the subject seemed to require and the sources allowed.

The choice of these questions and of the period studied was to some degree arbitrary. Of course, the events of the Revolution made a suitable ending, and an occasion to explore the conflicts which sprang from, but also masked, the cleavages in the society of the region before 1789. The starting point of 'about 1730' was partly determined by the relative shortage of sources before that date, and partly by the general impression held by many economic historians that a recognizably distinct 'economic eighteenth century' began for France somewhere around the mid-1720s. More than the dates chosen, the questions asked naturally involved some rather arbitrary decisions, but in social history, as in all research and writing, choices inevitably have to be made. The problems I decided to explore were of three sorts. The first might be summed up as 'What were the economic relations of these people, artisan and bourgeois, landless peasant and substantial *laboureur, laboureur* and landlord, bourgeois and noble, town and country, and so forth?'. The second was 'What did these people think of each other and the world around them?'; the third, 'What was changing in this society and the economy which supported it, and what was permanent?'. It might have been possible, had I been so inclined, to use large models drawn from the social sciences to explore and explain the Vannetais in the eighteenth century, but I did not find it very practical to advance into the *bocage,* or even inside the town limits of Vannes, armed with a battle-plan for which the outcome was predicted in advance, and so preferred to draw up my campaigns in short stages, as long as I was in such unfamiliar terrain. Not all would agree with this method, but I found it more congenial to spend some time acquiring, in a fairly empirical fashion, a feeling for the behaviour of a relatively small group of people, rather than to proceed, as is so often the case with social scientists, from general theory to the particular case.

Many people helped me in the course of this exploration. Professor Douglas Johnson of University College, London, gave me the benefit of his good sense, patience and criticism. Professor Jean Meyer, of the Université de Haute-Bretagne was unstinting with advice and encouragement on my many passages through Rennes; Monsieur Pierre Thomas-Lacroix, now retired Archivist of the Morbihan, received an awkward and ignorant foreign student into his archives in 1966 with kindness and good counsel, as did his successor, Mademoiselle Françoise Mosser, and their assistants, especially Monsieur and Madame Alain Fougeray and Monsieur Jean-François Decker. Monsieur J.-L. Debauve allowed me to use documents from his private collection. The directors and staff of the Archives départementales of the Ille-et-Vilaine, the Archives nationales, the Service historique de la Marine and the British Library gave me special assistance at various times.

My research was made possible by a Commonwealth Scholarship for study in London in 1965–7, and by a Doctoral Fellowship from the Canada Council in 1967–9, as well as a grant for a summer's research in 1972. Subsidies from the Central Research Fund of London University and from York University helped pay for research and microfilm in 1966–7 and 1971.

Drafts of the original thesis and the revised manuscript owe much to the criticism and suggestions of Professor Johnson's weekly seminar at the Institute of Historical Research in London, and also to the meetings of the Toronto Social History Group and the Research Group of the Department of History of York University. Particular thanks are due to John Bosher, Ian Drummond, Roger Dupuy, Joseph Ernst, Olwen Hufton, John Hurt, Maurice Hutt, Michael Katz, and Alison Patrick, who read the manuscript at various stages, and to D. M. G. Sutherland and Claude Langlois, who shared with me their knowledge of eighteenth-century Brittany. Neil Arnason assisted me in some of the original statistical work which now appears in Chapter XI, Terry Mahoney of the Institute for Behavioural Research at York University helped me prepare the computer files used in Chapters II and III, while Jacques Pauwels put in many hours with me in coding that material. Valerie Bruce, Hilda Dworkin, Laura McPhail and Esther Melia did an excellent job of typing a difficult manuscript. The editorial staff of the Oxford University Press have been most encouraging and patient during its long preparation. Finally, I should like to thank my wife, Judith, who by her sensible criticism and encouragement was most responsible for bringing this work to a close.[1]

1978   *T. J. A. Le Goff*

---

[1] The manuscript of this book went to press before I was able to consult C. Bertho's beautifully detailed 'La Presqu'île de Rhuys au xviiiᵉ siècle' (Thesis, Ecole des Chartes, Paris, 1977), which carries the treatment of that highly original part of the Vannetais much farther than was possible here, though with a different emphasis. It is summarized in *École nationale des Chartes, Position des thèses soutenues par les élèves de la promotion de 1976* (Paris, 1976), 17–26. O. Jurbert's thesis for the École des Chartes, summarized as 'La région de Bignan sous l'ancien régime (1660–1789)', *ibid.*, 123–33 (Paris, 1975) confirms, for a region immediately to the north, the description of the structure and evolution of rural society on the mainland examined here.

CONTENTS

MAPS

ABBREVIATIONS

ARCHIVES AND LIBRARIES:

A.C.	Archives communales
A.D. Finistère	Archives départementales du Finistère
A.D. Gironde	Archives départementales de la Gironde
A.D. I.-V.	Archives départementales d'Ille-et-Vilaine
A.D. Morbihan	Archives départementales du Morbihan
A.N.	Archives nationales
A.N. Colonies	Archives des Colonies
A.N. Marine	Archives de la Marine
B.L.	British Library
B.N.	Bibliothèque nationale

PERIODICALS:

Annales: E.S.C.	*Annales: Économies, Sociétés, Civilisations*
BSPM	*Bulletin de la Société Polymathique du Morbihan*
MSHAB	*Mémoires de la Société d'Archéologie et d'Histoire de Bretagne*
RHES	*Revue d'Histoire Économique et Sociale*
RHMC	*Revue d'Histoire Moderne et Contemporaine*

DATES:

Dates are cited in an abbreviated form giving the number of the day, the month and the year, e.g. 18-9-1740 = 18 September 1740.

WEIGHTS AND MEASURES

SURFACE:
1 *journal* = 80 *cordes* = 0.4862 hectares

VOLUME/WEIGHT: GRAINS:
1 *perrée* = 1.717 hl
1 *tonneau* = 10 *perrées* = 17.17 hl

BURTHEN (SHIPS):
1 *tonneau* = 2,000 livres (979 kg) in a volume of 1.44 metres^3

PART I

CHAPTER I

VANNES AND THE *PAYS VANNETAIS* IN THE EIGHTEENTH CENTURY

A traveller in the eighteenth century, coming up the coast of south-western Brittany on the road which led from Nantes to Quimper, passed, after the rather flat and barren plains between Savenay and the river Vilaine at La Roche-Bernard, into a more gently undulating countryside, marked by the alternation of fertile grain-fields and wasteland dotted with pine-thickets and coarse weeds, stretching on his left southward to the ocean and, on his right, rising upwards into the more densely wooded uplands of the *landes* of Lanvaux. A few miles farther north towards Vannes, he would have noticed that the inhabitants of the towns and villages he was passing through—Ambon, La Trinité, Theix—spoke Breton rather than French, and that the hills on the right had become somewhat steeper and more sharply marked. This was the *pays vannetais;* it began at the Vilaine, extended northward to the watershed of the heights formed by the *landes* of Lanvaux and ended in the west in the foothills of the Montagne Noire, somewhere between Auray and Quimperlé. But if the boundaries of the Vannetais remained somewhat diffuse, stretched and compressed in turn by the political, judicial, ecclesiastical, and administrative limits imposed by centuries of rulers and officials, its geographical centre was the gulf of the Morbihan, a small inland sea within the peninsulas of Rhuys and Locmariaquer. At the head of the gulf stood the ancient fortified city of Vannes, the chief town, at least according to tradition, of one of the ancient tribes of Gaul and still in the eighteenth century the political and religious centre of the region, the 'capital of Lower Brittany', as its inhabitants flattered themselves in calling it. [1]

---

[1] The boundaries of the Vannetais are vague. In 1913, André Siegfried considered that it included the area enclosed by the river Vilaine, the boundaries of the cantons of Vannes-Est, and a line stretching through Elven, Grand-Champ, Pluvigner, [*p. 5 for n. 1 cont.*]

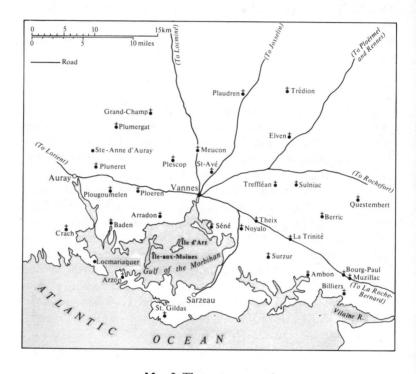

Map I: The *pays vannetais*

Although Vannes dominated and still in a sense dominates this entire region which today occupies most of the area covered by the Department of the Morbihan, its immediate influence was somewhat more limited, for as one advanced farther up the coast, other centres—Auray, Hennebont and the young and active port of Lorient—each in its own way exercised its own attraction over the surrounding countryside. This study is mainly about the more immediate sphere of influence of Vannes, the inner ring, as it were, of a series of concentric circles; it is concerned with the area comprising the *sénéchaussées* and *subdélégations* of Vannes and Rhuys under the old regime and the District of Vannes during the Revolution. But its conclusions are in general valid for the whole of the Vannetais and serve to illuminate in some way, at least by comparison, conditions in other regions of Brittany and the rest of France.

Within this region of immediate influence, there was a surprising degree of diversity, so that the Vannetais included most of the various elements, social, cultural, economic, geographic, which characterized the Breton peninsula and more particularly its western, Breton-speaking half, Lower Brittany. Geologically, the area is dominated on the mainland side by the alternation of barren granitic strips with more fertile gneiss–micaschist bands laid out on a northwest–south-east axis, a pattern which determines in turn a flow of watercourses parallel to the coastline. On the coast, the peninsula of Rhuys is divided into a gneiss–granitic border along its northern coast and a wider micaschistic belt in the south and south-eastern part. Soil fertility is not, of course, strictly dependent on the quality of the geological substrata, but in general, the quality of the land and its productivity did tend to diminish as one penetrated further into the interior, where granulitic and granitic terrain predominated. On the peninsula of Rhuys, wheat (*froment*) was grown almost exclusively, on the northern shores of the gulf of the Morbihan rye (*seigle*) and wheat were cultivated on an equal basis, but on the lighter soil of the interior, rye predominated over wheat. Partly explained by the variations of the geological strata, partly attributable

Plouay and Arzano; see *Tableau politique de l'ouest de la France* (Paris, 1913), 113, 151. A boundary based on the limits of the Breton dialect of Vannes would place the entire eastern frontier too close to Vannes, excluding such areas as Questembert, which most consider part of the Vannetais. On the other hand, the northern linguistic frontier along the summit of the *landes* of Lanvaux also corresponds to most administrative and judicial boundaries. Cf. P. Vidal de la Blache, *Tableau de la géographie de la France* (Paris, 1903), 328–38.

to variations in climate, the relative poverty of the soil in the interior was also the result of the advantage enjoyed by the coastal parishes, which were able to use seaweed (*goemon* and *varech*) as fertilizer while the parishes farther inland depended almost exclusively on the wild scrub vegetation of the uncultivated *landes* mixed with animal manure to supplement the resources of their soil. As a consequence of this dependence on the *landes,* the proportion of uncultivated surface in the interior was much greater than on the coast, reaching a maximum of 53 to 59 per cent of the surface in the 1840s in the communes of Meucon, Plaudren, Grand-Champ and Monterblanc.[2]

But men have a way of adapting themselves to ungrateful soil by spreading out their settlements and turning to more extensive cultivation on poorer land. Thus it is not surprising that the poverty of the population and the poverty of the soil did not necessarily coincide, despite the impressions held by men at the time, like Arthur Young, and by many historians since. If we were to draw a map of the distribution of the per capita assessment of the *capitation*, a tax on total wealth, by parish, as it appears in the inquiry of the *Commission intermédiaire* of 1778, we would find that people living in the Vannetais did not necessarily grow poorer proportionately to the distance from the seacoast, but rather that the region was split between a poorer section running east and north from the town of Vannes, and a more prosperous area in the western half of the region. Understandably enough, much of the richer land nearer the coast was able to support and attract a larger and poorer population, which found additional means of eking out its income in the wider opportunities offered by work in or about the town of Vannes, or by going to sea.[3]

[2] A.D. I.-V., C 1666: Bertin, bishop of Vannes to intendant, 4-2-1758; C 1690: De Glavignac, *subdélégué* in Vannes, to intendant, 4-4-1752; J. Letaconnoux, *Les Subsistances et le commerce des grains en Bretagne au xviiie siècle* (Rennes, 1909), carte hors texte; J. Ogée, *Dictionnaire historique et géographique de la province de Bretagne*, ed. A. Morteville and P. Varin (Rennes, 1843–53), *passim;* J. Kuntz, *Monographie agricole du département du Morbihan* (Vannes, 1937), 7–48; A. Choveaux, 'L'Influence des engrais marins sur les rives du golfe du Morbihan', *Annales de Géographie*, xxix (1920), 417–25; F.-M. Cayot-Délandre, *Annuaire du Morbihan*, (1833–56) *passim;* T. J. A. Le Goff, 'A Social and Economic Study of the Town of Vannes and its Region in the Eighteenth Century' (Univ. of London Ph.D. thesis, 1970), 400.

[3] Ogée, *Dictionnaire*, ii, 884; 'Réflexions sur les pétitions des colons à domaine congéable', [anon., n.d.], cited in L. Dubreuil, *Les Vicissitudes du domaine congéable en Bretagne, à l'époque de la Révolution* (Rennes, 1915), i, 246; Cayot-Délandre, *Annuaire du Morbihan* (1833), 102; A.D. I.-V., C 3982; and note 18 below.

The diversity of the Vannetais thus resulted from both the unequal distribution of Nature's bounty and the transformations which generations of men had worked on the region. It reflected the traditional opposition and interpenetration of the sea and the land; the contrast between the exclusively agricultural environment of the interior, on the one hand, and the maritime character of fishermen's settlements such as Séné and Billiers and the seamen's parishes of Arzon, Baden and the Île-aux-Moines on the other. In these latter, agriculture sometimes formed only a supplement, if that, to the normal occupation of the inhabitants, and often a separate task for the women. Opposed to the landlocked culture of the peasant of the interior, where permanent migration beyond the limits of one's own parish was rare and were few but a minority of well-to-do peasants knew much French or could write,[4] was the commercial civilization of the coast and the town, looking out to the great world, to the ports of the bay of Biscay, Spain, Portugal and the Midi, to the North Sea and the Baltic, and beyond the western horizon to the Antilles, where the local sailors travelled in the ships of the merchants and shipowners of Vannes, Auray and the islands of the gulf, those of the great *négociants* of Nantes and Lorient, and of the King. Town and country, coast and interior, commerce and agriculture, French and Breton: all of these oppositions, sometimes intersecting, most often reinforcing each other, gave to the region a peculiar richness which makes the Vannetais in the eighteenth century a particularly fascinating subject for the social historian.

What had given the Vannetais a geographic and human unity had been the action of man through the steady extension of the economic, political and cultural influence of the port town of Vannes over the surrounding area. This process had been begun by the Romans, who made of a tribal settlement the strategic crossroads of six highways leading to Corseul, Locmariaquer, Hennebont, Rennes, Nantes and Auray, and was continued and strengthened by the establishment of a bishopric in the town in the fifth century. Under

---

[4] According to J. Guyot, 'Étude démographique de la paroisse d'Allaire de 1693 à 1789' (Mémoire for the Diplôme d'études supérieures, Faculté des Lettres, Rennes, 1966), in a rural parish 49 kilometres from Vannes, only 20 per cent of husbands and 5 per cent of wives married in the parish came from outside that parish, and nine of ten of these outsiders came from within 10 kilometres. None were from places more than 100 kilometres distant. On literacy, see A. Cariou, 'L'Instruction dans le département du Morbihan à la veille de la Révolution de 1789', *MSHAB*, xxxv (1955), 39–50, shown as a map in Le Goff, 'Vannes', 485.

the dukes of Brittany, as under the Romans, ecclesiastical power was supplemented by military; in the sixth century Vannes became the seat of a county which, in the tenth century, was united to the domain of the duchy. During the Middle Ages, the administrative, religious and military influence of the town continued; at the same time, the commercial activity of the region, apparent even at the time of Caesar's invasion, seems to have expanded. By the fifteenth century Vannes was exporting on a large scale grain, leather, wool cloth, salt and butter, and importing wine.[5] It appears that this development reached a high and probably unprecedented level during the sixteenth and early seventeenth centuries, the 'golden age' of the Breton economy when the expansion of the population of the peninsula had not yet outweighed its production.[6] At the end of the seventeenth century, the town council of Vannes claimed proudly that

la d. ville assisse et plantée au lieu où elle est, approvisionne et fournist beaucoup de pais circonvoisins, tant en la terre ferme et le plat pais qu'en la coste de la mer, des plus grosses denres et marchandises. Le plat pais, comme tout le duché de Rohan, le compté de Porhoet, Jocellin, Malestroit, Ploermel, la Trinitté, Loudéac, Lachèze, Uzel et jusques à Moncontour, de vins, laynes, draps, fil, rousines, moullages, chauff, ardoises et aultres qui se deschergent au d. port. Les vins d'Anjou, Gascogne, Saintonge, de Espagne, nantois et aultres. Les materiaulx de Nantes pour tous, Rouan et autres endroits de Normandye, comme le cherbon d'Angleterre. Les denrées quy y sont aportés laines d'Espagne, poillieurs de Flandres, poix, goutron, rousines, matz de navires, bois et planches de sappins, le bois de la coste . . . par cette commodité se construissent au dict port de Vennes . . . des vaisseaux de touttes sortes . . . tellement qu'il se peult dire avesque quelque veritté quil ni a port dans la province ou il ne se construise plus de vaisseaux qu'en celle [*sic*] de la d. ville . . .[7]

In the eighteenth century, Vannes retained its predominant position over the surrounding region, a hegemony the extent of which can only be realized when we take into account the conditions of com-

[5] P. Thomas-Lacroix, *Vannes* (Paris, 1949), 5–8; A. Bourde de la Rogerie, *Inventaire sommaire des Archives départementales antérieures à 1790. Finistère. Série B* (Quimper, 1902), clvii, clx; J. de la Martinière, 'Vannes dans l'ancien temps. La coutume de la grande et de la petite croix', *BSPM* (1913–14), 20–32; É. Martin, 'Vannes aux xviie et xviiie siècles', *BSPM* (1917–18), 32–7; H. Touchard, *Le Commerce maritime breton à la fin du Moyen Âge* (Paris, 1967), 68–86.

[6] J. Tanguy, *Le Commerce du port de Nantes au millieu du xvie siècle* (Paris, 1956), especially 63–6 and J. Meyer, *La Noblesse bretonne au xviiie siècle* (Paris, 1966), i, 596–605.

[7] 'Remontrance faite par le sindic de la communauté de Vannes', 7-8-1609, cited in A. Guyot-Jomard, 'La Ville de Vannes et ses murs', *BSPM* (1887), 84–7.

munication at that time. Vannes was probably the only town which the overwhelming mass of the population of the region had ever seen, and it served as their link with the outside world. To travel by road the hundred-odd kilometres to Quimper or Nantes took six hours in a fast (and expensive) coach; only seven or eight people made this trip each week. The journey to Rennes, equally distant, but across the rugged interior of the province, took over twenty-four hours under ideal conditions at the end of the eighteenth century and considerably longer in the 1750s.[8] By river, the trip up the Vilaine from La Roche-Bernard to Rennes lasted ten to twelve days and until 1789 could be made only by boats of less than 10 *tonneaux* burthen above Redon to Messac. Even then, the river route was open only six months of the year.[9]

With the isolation of the region, and despite some improvement in the system of trunk roads in the later eighteenth century, the cheapest, and often the fastest, method of transport for freight and people was by sea. The situation of Vannes, with its port at the junction of the main roads from Brest and Quimper, Ploërmel and Rennes, Redon, Sarzeau, and Nantes, meant that through it and through the hands of its merchants, the products of the region were channelled to the outside: grain—wheat and rye—which travelled southward to Nantes, La Rochelle and the gulf of Gascony, to Spain and Portugal, even to Marseilles, or, less frequently, to the northern Breton ports and Normandy; livestock, which merchants from Normandy, Rennes and Nantes came to buy in the market place of the town; honey, beeswax and iron, drawn from the interior of the province and shipped to Holland; stave-wood and butter destined for Bordeaux, sardines and conger-eels for the Midi and the Atlantic ports; and salt from Rhuys and Séné for the fishing vessels of the coast. In return, through the port came the sheet and pig-iron and the oranges, lemons and sugar of Spain and its colonies, the balsam

---

[8] J. André and P. Thomas-Lacroix, 'Les Grands itinéraires de la Bretagne méridionale (de la Vilaine à la Laita)', *BSPM* (1953–4), 23–55; J. Letaconnoux, 'Note comparative sur la distance en temps entre l'intérieur de la Bretagne et la mer, aux xviiie, xixe et xxe siècles', *Annales de Bretagne*, xxiii (1907–8), 305–21 and *Les Subsistances*, 260–2; H. Sée, 'L'Enquête sur les messageries en Bretagne de 1775', *Mémoires et documents pour servir à l'histoire du commerce et de l'industrie en France*, ed. J. Hayem, 12e série (1929), 222–32. The journey from Rennes to Lorient via Vannes, Hennebont and Quimperlé took eighty hours in mid-century.

[9] J. Letaconnoux, 'Les Voies de communication en France au xviiie siècle', *Vierteljahrschrift für Social-und Wirtschaftsgeschichte* (1909), 118 n. 1 and *Les Subsistances*, 250–2.

oil, resin, clay, tar and whale-oil of Bayonne, wood, wines and
liqueurs from Nantes, Bordeaux and La Rochelle and the brass and
metal products of Holland.[10]
Not unnaturally, Vannes played a predominant role in organizing
the commerce of the hinterland in exchanges beyond the region.
True, it was not the only market centre: there was a small weekly
grain market at Sarzeau, and there were occasional rural fairs in the
larger parishes round about, but the nearest important markets
were almost all further than a day's journey on foot: Redon (57
km), Ploërmel (46 km), Josselin (41 km), Locminé (28 km), Auray
(18 km) and Muzillac (25 km).[11] It was in Vannes that the middlemen
and the shippers gathered, and where they found the funds, ships
and legal talent necessary for their dealings with the suppliers of
rural produce and their purchasers elsewhere in France.

With this commercial domination, Vannes continued to be the
religious and administrative centre of the area. In the eighteenth
century, the bishop with his see in Vannes ruled over a diocese
which retained virtually the same boundaries which it had possessed
at its foundation, corresponding roughly to the area of the present
Department of the Morbihan. Vannes was the centre of the *séné-*

---

[10]   B.N., fonds français 8753: Mémoire de l'intendant des Gallois de la Tour, 1731;
A.N., H¹ 419: Mémoire sur la ci-devant province de Bretagne [n.d.]; A.N. Marine,
C⁴ 175: Visite de M. Chardon, 1781, 852; A.D. I.-V., C 1712: Procès-verbal de
l'expédition de grains, 5, 6, 13-12-1787; C 1669: États des soumissions faites pendant
le mois de juin 1763 and letter (anonymous), 13-5-1763; C 1691: État des blés sortis
de la province, 1743; C1680–2: Enregistrement des acquits à caution, 1773–4; A.D.
Morbihan, 9 B 82: Amirauté de Vannes: rapports des capitaines, 1780–6. See also J.
Bérenger and J. Meyer, *La Bretagne de la fin du xviie siècle d'après le mémoire de
Béchameil de Nointel* (Paris, 1976), 132–6; J.-A. Piganiol de la Force, *Nouvelle
description de la France . . . seconde édition* (Paris, 1722), v, 196–7; H. Sée,
'L'Industrie et le commerce de la Bretagne dans la première moitié du xviiie siècle,
d'après le mémoire de l'intendant des Gallois de la Tour', *Annales de Bretagne*, xxxv
(1921–3), 187–208, 433–55. On the lack of trade relations with north-western French
ports, see J. Delumeau, *Le Mouvement du port de St-Malo 1681–1720* (Paris, 1966),
P. Dardel, *Navires et marchandises dans les ports de Rouen et du Havre* (Paris, 1963),
335; T. J. A. Le Goff, 'An Eighteenth-Century Grain Merchant: Ignace Advisse
Desruisseaux' in J. F. Bosher (ed.), *French Government and Society 1500–1850.
Essays in Memory of Alfred Cobban* (London, 1973), 92–122. On the salt trade, R.
Durand, 'Le Commerce en Bretagne au xviiie siècle', *Annales de Bretagne*, xxxii
(1917), 447–69 and J. Savary des Bruslons, *Dictionnaire portatif de commerce* (Paris,
1770), iv, 422–6.
[11]   A.D. I.-V., C 1276, 1571 cited in Letaconnoux, *Les Subsistances*, 75–82.
According to Letaconnoux, there was not even a market at Sarzeau as late as 1772,
but A.D. I.-V., C 1712: intendant to *subdélégué* of Rhuys, 2-12-1785 mentions one
there at the latter date.

chaussée of Vannes, which dated from the twelfth century and which included the town of Vannes and thirty of the surrounding mainland parishes. The same *sénéchaussée* court, sitting as the Présidial of Vannes, constituted the immediate appellate jurisdiction over the *sénéchaussées* of Auray, Rhuys, Hennebont, Ploërmel and Quimperlé. If in the eighteenth century the Estates, Parlement and Chamber of Accounts of Brittany no longer held their sessions in the town, it had nevertheless acquired a *maîtrise des eaux et forêts*, whose jurisdiction corresponded roughly to the boundaries of the Présidial, and an *amirauté* court, which after 1692 had jurisdiction over cases involving maritime law within the whole diocese. To these was added, in the eighteenth century, a *juridiction des traites*, which dealt with infractions against the administration of the tobacco monopoly, and a commercial tribunal (*consulat*), set up in 1710 with jurisdiction extending over the whole diocese. About this time, when the royal administration made a serious effort to take over the administration of the province, Vannes was chosen as the headquarters of a *subdélégation* which extended as far inland as Locminé, Grand-Champ and Trefflean. It was also the seat of several seigneurial jurisdictions and the base for a brigade of the *maréchaussée*. And when the Revolution attempted to give some order to this eccentric patchwork of jurisdictions, Vannes was made the seat of a Department, the Morbihan, and of a District, the District of Vannes, which corresponded roughly to the old *subdélégations* of Rhuys and Vannes; the redrawing of the administrative map by the new regime thus consecrated the historical dominance which Vannes had exercised over the region during the previous centuries.

Within the twenty-six parishes around Vannes which later formed this District lived about 50,000 people. Vannes, with an urban population of around 9,000 and a total population of around 10,000 ranked among the larger French towns in the eighteenth century and dwarfed all the neighbouring rural parishes, none of which had the character of an urban agglomeration.[12] The evolution of this population probably followed fairly closely the general movement of the Breton population in the seventeenth and eighteenth centuries. After an apparently quite remarkable rise during the first half of the sixteenth century, the upward movement was broken, then began again around 1600 if not before. However, towards 1670

---

[12] For a list of these parishes and their populations, see Le Goff, 'Vannes', 341–8.

the population of the peninsula, at least in rural parishes, where immigration did not cancel the effects of mortality as it did in the larger towns, seems to have reached a kind of level of saturation, and the upward trend was never really resumed, despite a tentative recovery in the 1750s and 1760s. Extensive research into the movement of the population in Brittany and Anjou during the eighteenth century shows stagnation during most of the period, followed by a series of demographic disasters in the 1770s and 1780s.[13]

It appears that the region of Vannes fitted into this pattern. A demographic study of the parish of Allaire, close enough to Vannes (49 km) to have some validity for the area, showed a pattern of rather slow growth during the eighteenth century hampered by a late marriage age, but above all by the frequent demographic crises— seventeen in all, covering 24 out of the 94 years studied—due to food scarcities, but especially to recurring epidemics which together rendered life so hazardous that a child, once born, had only an even chance of reaching the age of twenty. Dominating the demographic evolution of the parish was a series of great crises recurring at intervals of thirty years (around the years 1710, 1740 and 1770).[14]

Whether or not the demographic pattern of Vannes and its region resembled that of Allaire in the first three-quarters of the eighteenth century, it is certain that in the last two decades of the old regime, Vannes, and most of the surrounding area, underwent a profound and prolonged period of demographic crisis. It has proved possible to trace the extent of this crisis for the whole period of 1770–87 (and occasionally up to 1789–90) in ten rural parishes and the four urban parishes of Vannes, thanks to the calculations of the rectors and clerks of the Présidial who after 1770 were required by the intendant to count up the number of births, deaths and marriages in the registers kept by the rector of each parish.

[13] Meyer, *La Noblesse bretonne*, ii, 596–605; Y. Blayo and L. Henry, 'Données démographiques sur la Bretagne et l'Anjou de 1740 à 1829', *Annales de démographie historique* (1967), 91–171; H. Sée, 'Les Essais de statistiques démographiques en Bretagne à la fin de l'ancien régime', *Études sur la vie économique en Bretagne, 1772–an III* (Paris, 1930) 5–48; J.-P. Goubert, 'Le Phénomène épidémique en Bretagne à la fin du xviiie siècle (1770–1787)', *Annales: E.S.C.*, xxiv (1969), 1562–88 and *Malades et médecins en Bretagne 1770–1790* (Rennes, 1974), 11–51; A. Croix, *Nantes et le pays nantais au xvie siècle. Étude démographique* (Paris, 1974); J. Tanguy, 'Les Révoltes paysannes de 1675 et la conjoncture en Basse-Bretagne au xviie siècle', *Annales de Bretagne et des Pays de l'Ouest*, lxxii (1975), 427–42.

[14] Guyot, 'Allaire', 62–7, 103–4, 131. The years of crisis were 1699–1700, 1704, 1709–10, 1712, 1720, 1725, 1729, 1740, 1743, 1748–50, 1752, 1756, 1766, 1770–1, 1776–7, 1780–1.

The pattern that emerges from these figures is even more grim than that hinted at in the overall figures for Brittany.[15] Of the ten rural parishes for which complete figures for the period 1770–87 have been worked out, six show an excess of deaths over births. But not even those which could count in 1787 more births than deaths over the preceding eighteen years had escaped without three, four or five years of crisis. The crude mortality rate in the parishes of the region appears to have varied between 36 and 45 per thousand in rural parishes and reached 47 per thousand in the town of Vannes— rates higher than the figures calculated by J.-P. Goubert on the basis of mortality figures for the years 1781–3 only.[16]

Here, as elsewhere in Brittany, the immediate causes of these disasters were epidemics, the 'fièvres putrides et malignes' (typhoid, for the most part), which ravaged the whole of Brittany in the later eighteenth century, the great dysentery epidemic, and smallpox epidemics which, on the peninsula of Rhuys, found their victims chiefly among children. But it is impossible to isolate these immediate causes from the wretched sanitary conditions of the mass of the country and town dwellers, the reinforcement of local epidemics by troops continually shifted about the province either to new garrisons or overseas in wartime and by seamen constantly on the move. To these factors must be added the progressive impoverishment of those who had to purchase their bread, both in town and country, in a time of sharply rising and wildly fluctuating grain prices, and the inevitable thinning of their diet; a steady regime of buckwheat gruel and *crêpes*, the staple of the rural classes, is not the best preventive, for example, against dysentery.[17] Poverty and death were close companions: all of the parishes in the Vannetais which had a negative natural increase between 1770 and 1787 were also those in which the

---

[15] Only partial figures from this great statistical enterprise survive in the intendants' papers; they have been used by J.-P. Goubert in *Malades et médecins*, 11–51 and elsewhere. I have taken my figures for the entire period from the calculations made in the flyleaves and bindings of the copies of the registers submitted to the Présidial with a view to this enquiry.

[16] Le Goff, 'Vannes', 19 n. 23.

[17] A.D. I.-V., C 1423: États de la population dressés par les subdélégués, 1780 [remarks of the *subdélégué* of Vannes]; A.C. Sarzeau, GG 23: 1777 [remarks of the rector] cited in M. Rozenzweig and C. Estienne, *Inventaire sommaire des archives départementales antérieures à 1790. Morbihan. Archives civiles. Série E Supplément, 2ᵉ partie* (Vannes, 1888), 291; Ogée, *Dictionnaire*, ii, 902. On diet, Meyer, *La Noblesse bretonne*, i, 445–74 and A.N., F²⁰ 229: Essai statistique sur le Morbihan, an IX [1800–1]; on diseases and epidemics, Goubert, *Malades et médecins* and 'Le Phénomène épidémique en Bretagne' replace earlier work.

proportion of inhabitants assessed at less than three livres *capitation* tax was greater than the average for the diocese[18]; all those in which the demographic balance was positive had less than the average in this category.

The result of all this was almost certainly a fall in the overall population of the area during the last two decades of the old regime. The figures of the intendants reproduced by Sée and J.-P. Goubert show a marked preponderance of deaths over births and seem to hint at a fall in the birth-rate in the *sénéchaussée* of Vannes. It is possible that the deficit was compensated by an influx of immigrants from outside the area. But this seems unlikely. Most of this immigration, if it existed, would probably have been towards the town of Vannes, and we know from a study of the origins of the parents of newly-baptized children that in its largest parish, St-Patern, the one in which rural immigrants were most likely to take up residence, the number of parents coming from outside the area of the present department of the Morbihan was only about 10 per cent of the total number of parents.[19]

Although the dominant impression which emerges from a study of the demography of the Vannetais is one of stagnation and crisis, it remains true that the region, or more particularly, certain groups within that region, did enjoy a kind of prosperity which appears to have increased at times throughout the eighteenth century. This prosperity was, however, built on a precarious footing; essentially, the Vannetais in the eighteenth century provides an example of the 'one-crop' export economy characteristic of many developing countries today; and, again, as in many of these countries, it tended to benefit the more prosperous sort of merchants, those who, as landlords, prosperous peasants or rentiers, held large stocks of grain and, more generally, the mercantile town over the agricultural countryside.

For the region of the Vannetais, despite a somewhat ungrateful soil, usually yielded a considerable surplus of grain which formed the staple of exports through the ports of the region. The grain which was exported was almost always of two types: wheat, or more

---

[18] Elven, Meucon, Plaudren (without its *trèves*), Theix, Surzur and Sulniac; the figures, almost certainly negative, were not worked out for the parishes of the peninsula of Rhuys. For the *capitation* figures, A.D. I-V., C 3982: Évêché de Vannes, État des articles employés dans chacun des rôles de la capitation des villes et paroisses dudit évèché pour l'année 1777 et de ceux portés au-dessous de 3 livres . . .

[19] Le Goff, 'Vannes', 372–4.

specifically *gros froment* (occasionally mixed with small amounts of *guen blevec*, a smaller species), which was grown along the coast and around the gulf of the Morbihan, and rye, the main cereal crop of the parishes of the interior.[20] In 1698, the intendant Béchameil Nointel reported that an average of 9,000 *tonneaux* (155,000 hecto-litres) of rye and 6,000 *tonneaux* (103,000 hectolitres) of wheat were exported annually from the three ports of Auray, Hennebont and Vannes. His estimate continued to be repeated by administrators throughout the eighteenth century and, given the lack of progress in agricultural techniques and the failure to improve the wasteland in the region during the eighteenth century, they were probably not far wrong in doing so.[21]

The overwhelming proportion of this grain passed through Vannes, which was second in Brittany only to Nantes in the quantities of grain handled. In an average year, it was estimated, 4,000–5,000 *tonneaux* of grain passed through its port. In 1734, 6,039 *tonneaux* were exported through Vannes to foreign ports alone; in 1735, about 5,000 *tonneaux;* in 1736, 4,513 *tonneaux,* and in 1765–6 (over an eighteen-month period), 24,660 quintals of wheat and 14,840 quintals of rye. The total exports from the great port of Nantes represented about four to five times this figure in 1734–6 and twice the amount in 1765–6, but Vannes led by far the rest of the Breton ports in the volume of its grain exports.[22]

The bulk of the export grain trade was carried on separately from the ordinary provisioning of the markets for domestic consumption. The more prosperous peasant who held stores of grain, and those proprietors who collected rents in grains or those who could claim tithes in kind, sold their grain in bulk at a price slightly above the going market rate, on the basis of samples, directly to merchants in Vannes such as Dubodan, La Rive, La Motte, Delourme and Desruisseaux, who had sufficient capital to pay for the cost of the

[20] A third species, *petit froment,* was grown in the interior and used only for local consumption; see A.D. I.-V., C 1690: De Glavignac, *subdélégué,* Vannes, to intendant, 4-4-1752; Bibliothèque municipale de Rennes, MSS. 309–11: Mémoire du président de Robien [c. 1730], iii, 6–8.

[21] A.N., H¹ 419: Mémoire sur la ci-devant province de Bretagne [n.d.]; B.N., fonds français 5463: Mémoire sur l'état présent de la province de Bretagne [n.d.]; Béchameil's text has been edited by Bérenger and Meyer, *La Bretagne de la fin du xviiᵉ siècle.* An estimate of the changes in production during the eighteenth century is contained in T. J. A. Le Goff, 'Autour de quelques dîmes vannetaises (xviiᵉ–xviiiᵉ siècles)', paper presented at the Colloque d'histoire rurale, Collège de France, 2 July 1977.

[22] Letaconnoux, *Les Subsistances,* 297, 370–2.

purchase and maintain granaries to store the grain. In turn, these merchants undertook to find a market for the grain at their own risk, or else bought up stocks on commission for dealers outside the region. From the granaries of the merchants, the grain was shipped either from Vannes or occasionally from the little ports of the peninsula of Rhuys, chiefly to the coast of Gascony, but also to Spain and Portugal, and into the Mediterranean. The success of those engaged in this larger trade depended on four variables: the volume of regional production, the level of local prices, the existence of sufficient shortages outside Brittany to make exports profitable, and the varying attitude of the royal government which granted, or refused, permission to export, in principle according to the ability of the area to provide for the subsistence of its inhabitants, but also in response to the interplay of pressure groups within the Parlement and Estates of Brittany and within Breton society in general.[23]

Grain production in the Vannetais showed an almost continual surplus, to judge from the annual reports drawn up by the intendant's *subdélégués* each year just before the harvest was in and based, it seems, on tithe-collectors' estimates.[24] To be sure, these reports do not measure the exact volume of production: they are given in terms of a 'common year' equal to two years' normal consumption within the region.[25] Nevertheless, as a guide to general conditions, these reports are sufficient. In 22 of the 27 years listed between 1754 and 1789 there was a surplus of wheat available for export, and in 23 a surplus of rye.[26] But a surplus did not automatically mean prosperity, and could even be disastrous for producers and merchants alike:

Quand les débouchés manquent [wrote a *subdélégué* in 1758] les plus riches se trouvent souvent dans une espèce d'indigence . . . car quoique le plus ou moins de production doive s'influer sur le prix de cette denrée, c'est moins

[23] A.D. I.-V., C 1692: Réponses aux questions . . . contenues dans la lettre de M. le Contrôleur-général du 28 7bre 1773. In the *subdélégation* of Vannes, 'tout se vend au marché pour la consommation journalière, les gros propriétaires vendent dans leurs greniers'; in that of Auray, 'presque tous les grains s'achètent dans les greniers et non au marché'. See also A.N., F12 555 Bretagne: Notes sur la position, les établissements, et le commerce de plusieurs villes de Bretagne [1778]; Letaconnoux, *Les Subsistances*, 86–8, and Le Goff, 'An Eighteenth-Century Grain Merchant'.

[24] Meyer, *La Noblesse bretonne*, i, 296.

[25] 'Tout cela n'est . . . qu'un à peu près, et je crois qu'il est très difficile de savoir au juste la qualité des productions, et le nombre des consommateurs les variations là-dessus sont continuelles et influent nécessairement sur la valeur des prix.' A.D. I.-V., C 1653: Dubodan, *subdélégué* in Vannes, to intendant, 28-9-1776.

[26] Below, p. 299 n. 12.

cette circonstance qui y contribue que le plus ou moins d'exportation et quand elle vient à manquer, les grains sans former des récoltes abondantes tombent à vil prix.[27]

The problem was not only to find markets because even when there was a demand elsewhere for grain, it was not always possible to export. The government of the old regime, aware of the dangers of social unrest which popular fear of famine and dearth caused, had at least a theoretical commitment to regulating the grain trade during most of the eighteenth century. In practice, however, this control was rather less than effective. Permission to ship grain, even to the rest of France all the time, legally or surreptitiously. In any sometimes enforced, sometimes winked at, then repealed, only to be introduced again. Without going into the tangled history of this legislation in the eighteenth century, it seems safe to conclude that in fact at least the most powerful of the Breton merchants exported to the rest of France, all the time, legally or surreptitiously. In any case, after 1763 exports to the rest of France were allowed on a permanent basis, except during Terray's brief term as Controller-General (1770–3) and even then the merchants of Vannes appear to have obtained special permission for exports on a large scale to the domestic French market. The shipping of grain beyond the French frontiers was somewhat more stringently controlled, but here as well, considerably more grain went abroad than the texts of the legislation would seem to indicate. This was especially true of the region around Vannes, where in normal years there was no great need to worry about the creation of local shortages. Where the pleas of the Parlement and Estates—who acted in this case as the spokesmen of the landed proprietors and the grain merchants—failed to change the government's attitude and where the intendant refused to grant export permits, there always remained the simple expedient of fraud.[28]

In contrast to the grain trade, local industry in the area around Vannes never developed to any great extent. Wool spinning and the preparation of woollen cloth was given a certain impetus in the region at the beginning of the century as a part of the government's plans to reduce French dependence on English goods. There were, according to the records of the *inspection des manufactures*, 40

[27] A.D. I.-V., C 1652: État des récoltes, 1758.
[28] Letaconnoux, *Les Subsistances*, 228–36; Le Goff, 'An Eighteenth-Century Grain Merchant', 101–2.

looms in the area around Vannes in 1704, 62 in 1719–21, but only 12 in 1779. Roughly as many looms were also operating in some of the *bourgs* to the south-east of town: in Theix (12 looms in 1720), Noyalo (8 looms in the same year) and Surzur (40 looms). The material produced, dyed and finished in the district was chiefly a heavy, crude cloth called *drap de Groutel,* made of yarn spun locally from mainly Spanish wool, but also from some local supplies. This cloth although made of good woollen strands, suffered from its wool being poorly fulled and trimmed.[29]

Each of these looms was reckoned to employ one weaver, three carders and an equal number of combers. In 1779 it was calculated that one loom kept busy an average of 48 spinners, presumably working at home. At that time the total number employed in Vannes, Theix, Surzur and La Trinité–Surzur was 164; by 1794–5 it had fallen to 142. In this latter period there were in all 10 weavers (all men) and 132 other people employed in preparing the wool: 63 men and boys, presumably carders and combers, and 46 women, 10 girls and 8–10 old women. The market for their products was almost exclusively regional, and the enterprise was strictly artisanal, without even the limited degree of centralization implied by a putting-out system. The total production of the area was as unimpressive as the number of people employed. According to the figures of the *Inspection des Manufactures* in 1779, the total value of production in the Vannetais was 54,000 l. While this is not insignificant, it hardly compared with the transactions recorded in regions further inland which specialized in weaving woollen cloth: Josselin (247,200 l. in 1779), Ploërmel (175,440 l.), Malestroit (180,000 l.), Rochefort (163,200 l.).[30]

Even less impressive was the production of linen textiles in the region, limited as it was to artisans scattered among the towns and *bourgs* of the region who worked almost entirely for local needs. Indeed, the output of the area was so small that the *bureau de*

[29] A.N., F^{12} 1347, 1370; H. Sée, 'Études sur le commerce en Bretagne: I. La draperie au xviiie siècle', *Mémoires et documents pour servir à l'histoire économique du commerce et de l'industrie en France,* ed. J. Hayem, 10e série (Paris, 1926), 95.
[30] Sée, 'Études sur le commerce en Bretagne', 95; A.N., F^{12} 1347: Questions sur . . . la fabrication des étoffes de laines, An III; F^{12} 1344: Manufactures: enquête sur les fabriques de draps, etc., Ans II–III; États de métiers et des ouvriers employés . . . An III; F^{1}C^{III} Morbihan 7:4e semestre 1811; Cayot-Délandre, *Annuaire du Morbihan* (1834), 100–1; Bérenger and Meyer, *La Bretagne de la fin du xviie siècle,* 135.

marque operated there only intermittently. Between 1760 and 1769, the total number of bolts registered annually in the bureau of Vannes hovered between 450 and 650. Two kinds of cloth were produced: *toiles fortes*, also called *toiles d'usage*, and *toiles bretagnes étroites*. This compared badly with the production of the great cloth-producing area of Brittany such as Quintin and Uzel, St-Malo and Loudéac–Moncontour, each of which produced around 20,000–25,000 bolts annually.[31]

Finally, there were a certain number of tanneries in the town of Vannes, and also in nearby Questembert. Before 1750, there had been sixteen tanneries in Vannes, but the tanners claimed to have been hurt seriously by a tax imposed by an edict of that year and, by their own account, the number of tanneries had declined by a third when they petitioned Turgot in 1775 to have it removed. It seems that after this tax was abolished in 1786, a certain prosperity returned to the industry until it was upset by the wars of the Revolution. However, it was only a very small set of artisanal enterprises (there were nine masters in 1794) and was far overshadowed in Brittany by the production of areas such as that around Pontivy.[32]

The evidence we possess on manufactures then, although neither abundant nor complete, does seem to point towards a kind of stagnation in both the wool and textile trades, and to the total insignificance of the tanneries. In the wool cloth industry, a decline in the quantity of wool cloth and in the number of workers and looms is clearly discernible, while in the textile industry, as grain prices rose, the market for cheap cloth such as was manufactured around Vannes fell, as wage-earners and people of small means found an increasing proportion of their budget taken up with food purchases, and as workers left their looms in response to the fall in

[31] A.N., F¹² 1418: États de la recette et dépense des bureaux de visite, 1760–9; F¹² 555: États de visite, 1767–9. The production by bolts has been calculated from the total duties charged, at the rate of 1 sol a bolt. See also F. Bourdais and R. Durand, 'L'Industrie et le commerce de la toile en Bretagne au xviiiᵉ siècle', *Comité des travaux historiques et scientifiques. Section d'historie moderne et d'histoire contemporaine*, vii (1922), 1–48; J. Tanguy, 'La Production et le commerce des toiles "Bretagnes" du xviᵉ au xviiiᵉ siècle. Premiers résultats', *Actes du quartre-vingt-onzième congrès national des Sociétés savantes. Rennes, 1966 Section d'histoire moderne et contemporaine*, i (Paris, 1969), 105–41.

[32] A.N., F¹² 1464: Tanners of Vannes to Turgot, controller-general, 9-5-1775; F¹² 1596: circular, 25-11-1811; F¹² 1370: État de la tannerie de la commune de Vannes, 1–10 frimaire, An III.

consumer demand for their products in the last two decades of the old regime.[33]

There was one other reasonably important source of local revenue independent of the grain trade; this was fishing, which provided part of the livelihood of the small ports scattered around the shores of the gulf of the Morbihan and on the peninsulas of Rhuys and Locmariaquer. Conger-eels, plaice, and *fouanne* were caught in the area, and there were quite extensive mussel and oyster-beds in the gulf of the Morbihan, the latter off Séné and Locmariaquer. These shellfish, together with congers and a certain amount of herring caught off Rhuys and Penerf, were exported, but it was sardine fishing which occupied the most important position in the local fisheries. Though sardine fishing had been important in the seventeenth century, it was in the eighteenth century that it began to take on something of its present proportions in Brittany. What encouraged this development was apparently the creation of a market for Breton sardines in Languedoc by the migration of the Mediterranean schools of sardine towards Catalonia at the beginning of the century, which in turn led to a decline in the Languedoc fisheries. This market, and the outlet provided by the ports of the northern gulf of Gascony, were reserved almost entirely for the Breton fishermen by the royal government, which excluded cheaper Spanish sardines from all but the ports of Hendaye, Bayonne and St-Jean-de-Luz. Fish caught off Belle-Île were taken either to Belle-Île itself, or to Vannes or Port-Louis to be pressed and packed in barrels for shipment to these markets, or were rushed 'green' (fresh) in luggers to nearby ports such as Nantes for immediate consumption.[34]

The Belle-Île sardine fisheries were large, occupying all the sailors

---

[33] See the comments of the inspectors on the general situation of the cloth industry in Brittany in A.N., F^{12} 555: 1767, 1769 and F^{12} 1418: e.g. 'le commerce . . . a été languissant pendant toute l'année . . . le prix excessif des grains avant la dernière récolte a fait consommer à plusieurs fabriques l'objet de leur travail, quelques-uns avaient quitté leurs métiers pour mendier.'

[34] A.N. Marine, C^4 170: Amirauté de Vannes: état d'inspection, 1734, fols. 53–119^v; C^5 35: Mémoire concernant la pêche qui se fait sur les côtes du ressort de l'Amirauté de Vannes, 1747 [Verdier]; C^4 175: ii, 864–72; C^5 36: Mémoire sur l'exemption des droits pour le hareng pêché en Bretagne [1758?]; A.D. I.-V., C 1595: Dubodan, *subdélégué* in Vannes, to intendant, 16-11-1773, 17-11-1778 and Mémoire [by M. Le Nain, intendant of Languedoc] concernant l'introduction des sardines d'Espagne [1751]. See also Savary des Bruslons, *Dictionnaire portatif*, i, 1086, iv, 393–6; A.N., H^1 419: Mémoire sur la ci-devant province de Bretagne, which repeats Savary; H. Sée, 'Le Commerce maritime de la Bretagne au xviiie siècle', [*p. 21 for n. 34 cont.*]

and ships that could be spared during the fishing season, which lasted from May to October. Each boat employed four to five fishermen, who pooled their nets and resources, obtained a boat, and worked together as partners. Like the fishermen farther up the coast, they too must have been subject to the manipulation of the price of bait at and around Belle-Île by the richer merchants of the port towns; because *gueldre*, a local fish useful for sardine bait was over-fished, by the later eighteenth century its use had been forbidden and fishermen were obliged to buy codfish eggs (*rogue*), imported in Norwegian ships and bought up by local merchants either by pre-arrangement in Norway or on board the ships when they arrived, to be re-sold at exorbitant prices.[35] Despite these and other difficulties, there appears to have been some growth in the fisheries. Remains of official figures suggest that the region extending from Le Croisic to Plouharnel saw its annual catch quadrupled, the total revenue increased ten- and twelve-fold, and the number of fishing boats perhaps doubled. It is likely that they exaggerate the growth of the fishery, but there probably was some real growth, and although the total production of the area was not as large as that of the great sardine ports of Camaret, Quimper and Lorient, it was nevertheless considerable.[36]

The export of these articles of primary consumption, chiefly grain and fish, brought a livelihood to the captains, shipbuilders and sailors who lived in the small ports around the gulf, on the peninsula of Rhuys, and on the two largest islands of the gulf, the Île-aux-Moines and the Île-d'Arz. These people made up a sizeable proportion of the population of the region; the rolls of the *bureaux des classes* of the French navy recorded some 850 officers and sailors on

Mémoires et documents pour servir à l'histoire du commerce et de l'industrie en France, ed. J. Hayem, 9e série (Paris, 1925), 236, 266; Bourde de la Rogerie, *Inventaire sommaire . . . série B*, ccxxxii and Meyer, *La Noblesse bretonne*, i, 458–60.

[35] A.N. Marine, C⁴ 175: ii, 864–72, 1781; C⁵ 35: Mémoire au sujet de la pêche de la gueldre dans l'évêché de Vannes, 1745; C⁵ 21: Procès-verbal sur la pêche en mer, 1778; A.D. I.-V., C 1594: Sartine to intendant, 28-1-1775, Terray to intendant, 29-10-1770 etc.; C 1595: duc de Praslin to intendant [1770], etc.; A.N., F¹² 1838: Mémoire sur la rogue, 7-2-1788; J. Savina and D. Bernard (eds.), *Cahiers de doléances des sénéchaussées de Quimper et de Concarneau pour les États généraux de 1789*, i, xxvi–xxxvii; ii, 301–10; see below, p. 330–1.

[36] Bourde de la Rogerie, *Inventaire sommaire . . . série B*, ccxxvii–ccxxxii. In 1787, Vannes had 76 boats engaged in the trade, which brought in 163,400 l. worth of sardines. Lorient had 247 boats and a catch worth 970,216 l., Quimper, 494 boats and a catch of 1,366,076 l. and Camaret, 200 boats but only 194,400 l. worth of fish.

the coast and in the interior between Billiers and Ploeren in 1786. With their families, these would have represented about 3,500 people, concentrated mainly in Vannes and Séné, the islands of the gulf, Arradon and, especially, on the peninsula of Rhuys. In addition, there were 96 craftsmen and masters engaged in shipbuilding in Vannes.[37]

At the end of the old regime the merchant fleet based in Vannes itself numbered 181 vessels in 1775 and 197 in 1786. Most of these, as was also the case with coasting vessels in the other nearby port, Auray, were smaller single-decked two-masted luggers (*chassemarées*), 30–50 feet in length with a 10–14 foot beam and a burthen of 30–50 *tonneaux*. Only about 27 were of more than 100 *tonneaux* burthen in 1786, and, of these, only one was greater than 200 *tonneaux*.[38]

By the end of the old regime, the region around Vannes was also one of the most important shipbuilding areas in France. The Breton peninsula as a whole produced by far the largest number of merchant ships and the bulk of the French tonnage on the eve of the Revolution, and the region included in the *amirauté* of Vannes contributed in no small measure to this preponderance, with a total tonnage in the years 1762–87 greater than that of the *amirautés* of Toulon, Brest, Honfleur and Marseilles and surpassed only by the *amirautés* of Nantes, Bordeaux, Bayonne and St-Malo. However, the type of ship produced in the region tended to be the smaller coasting vessel rather than the triple-masted merchantman. The shipyards were concentrated in the gulf of the Morbihan, which produced the smaller sort of vessel, and Redon, where fewer vessels were constructed, but of more considerable tonnage. A few heavy vessels were also built at Lorient.[39]

Nevertheless, Vannes was a long way from being the most active maritime region of Brittany, and its activity did not compare with

[37] A.N. Marine, C⁴ 208: 1786.
[38] A.N., F¹² 1680ᴬ, An III; A.N. Marine, C⁵ 51, fol. 258–99v; C⁵ 53, fol. 36–47v, 1775–86; Letaconnoux, *Les Subsistances*, 247–8. The figure of 50 coasting vessels in 1759 given in Letaconnoux dates from a period when the French commercial fleet had been seriously reduced by privateering.
[39] P. Thomas-Lacroix, 'Les Constructions et les ventes de navires dans les amirautés de Vannes et de Lorient au xviiiᵉ siècle', *MSHAB*, xlix (1969), 71–111; T. Le Goff, 'La Construction navale en Bretagne de 1762 à 1788', *Annales de Bretagne*, lxxv (1968), 345–69; T. Le Goff and J. Meyer, 'La Construction navale en Bretagne de 1762 à 1788', *Annales de Bretagne*, lxxvi (1969), 433–43, and 'Les Constructions navales en France dans la seconde moitié du xviiiᵉ siècle', *Annales, E.S.C.*, xxvi (1971), 173–85.

flourishing commercial centres like Nantes. As was often the case elsewhere in France, most of the economic expansion which took place in eighteenth-century Brittany came from the development of colonial commerce, but here the record of Vannes was not brilliant. The beginning of the end for the commercial expansion of Vannes could have been forseen as early as the 1580s, when it was noted that the port was beginning to be silted up,

ce mal . . . a lieu à la mer bassée de plus de deux brasses au d. port . . . et les vaisseaux quy avecq toute facilitté venoient au d. port demeurent à demy lieu dicelle quil fault alléger avecq gobarres et batteaux par une grande despance qui rancherit les marchandises.[40]

But a shallow port alone did not necessarily mean the end for a city; at Nantes, for example, the larger slave ships and other commercial vessels which had made its success in the eighteenth century were forced to unload far downstream at Paimbœuf. Nor did the lack of a prosperous hinterland inevitably determine the failure of a port, for Lorient in the eighteenth century suffered just as greatly as Vannes in this respect. Rather it was the combination of both these factors, plus government policy, which condemned Vannes and its smaller satellites of Auray, Sarzeau, Billiers and the like to a secondary role. The gulf of the Morbihan had been Richelieu's first choice as the site for a great new western commercial port. But Colbert wisely judged it impractical because of its shallow waters and treacherous currents. Instead Lorient was chosen, while Nantes, already established, built on the growth of Lorient at the beginning of the century and at the same time obtained for itself the privilege which was to provide the basis of its prosperity in the eighteenth century, that is, the exclusive right to export freely 12,000 *barriques* of colonial sugar each year.[41]

To be sure, the merchants of Vannes participated to a certain extent in colonial traffic, but the degree of their participation remained small. In 1728, they obtained from the Conseil de Commerce the privilege of trading in the 'islands and colonies of America' on the same basis as the ports of Marseilles, Dunkerque, Calais, Dieppe, Le Havre, Honfleur, St-Malo, Morlaix, Brest, Nantes, La Rochelle, Bordeaux, Bayonne and Sète, and sent out a couple of

[40] 'Remontrances faites par le sindic de la communauté de Vannes', cited in Guyot-Jomard, 'La Ville de Vannes et ses murs' (1887), 84–7.

[41] Gaston-Martin, *Nantes au xviiie siècle. L'ère des négriers (1714–1774)* (Paris, 1931), 181–2; Guyot-Jomard, 'La Ville de Vannes et ses murs' (1887), 164–5.

ships to the West Indies in most years. But in comparison with the great ports, the part of Vannes in this grim and risky business remained quite small—0.5 per cent of the total of negro slaves brought into the Antilles from 1725 to 1741 came from ships originating in Vannes, and the trade seems to have declined, except as an appendage to the activity of the port of Nantes, after the close of the War of American Independence. As for privateering, that vastly overrated compensation for the fall in maritime trade in wartime, the record of the ports of the *amirauté* of Vannes, was farcical; one privateer was sent out by a few local merchants during the War of the Austrian Succession only to terminate its career as soon as it had begun by an attack on an abandoned French vessel; and its single successor in the Seven Years War fared hardly any better.[42] The judgement of the merchants of Lorient in 1781 was harsh, but not far from the mark; the commerce of Vannes, they said

n'est autre que celui des denrées que ses environs fournissent . . . quelques barques qui en sortent chargées de grains et quelques autres qui y entrent avec des vins de Bordeaux et de Nantes . . . Son port . . . ne pourra jamais devenir important . . . puisqu'il est plein de vases. . . . Voilà la ville qui prétend assimiler son sort à celui de Lorient qui reçoit les vaisseaux de guerre de 80 canons et qui a expédié des vaissaux de commerce, de 1300 tonneaux. Quels sont les grands vaisseaux qui ont relâché ou qui se sont armés à Vannes? . . .[43]

Thus, the whole of the Vannetais, and particularly the region under the direct influence of Vannes, although geographically and economically diverse, was given a kind of unity by the political, administrative, cultural and commercial extension of the influence of the town of Vannes. Situated in the dominant position of a port town on the fringe of an otherwise isolated agrarian hinterland, like many ports in developing countries today, Vannes resembled them in another way, for through it was channelled the main marketable crop of the area, grain, on which the prosperity of the whole region

[42] Dardel, *Navires et marchandises*, 403; H. du Halgouet, 'Commerce de Vannes avec les Isles d'Amérique', *BSPM* (1940), 1–12; E. Raut and L. Lallemand, 'Vannes autrefois, la traite des nègres', *BSPM* (1933), 53–74; J. Meyer, 'Le Commerce négrier nantais', *Annales: E.S.C.*, xv (1960), 120–9; L. Lallemant, 'Le Corsaire l'Hermine de Vannes', *BSPM* (1892), 47–61 and P. Thomas-Lacroix, 'La Guerre de course dans les ports de l'amirauté de Vannes et de Lorient', *MSHAB*, xxvi (1946), 159–215.
[43] A.D. Morbihan, 12 B 2: Mémoire des députés de la ville et du commerce de Vannes, 1-10-1781.

and, *a fortiori* of the town, depended. True, there were other sectors in the local economy besides agriculture: coastal shipping, fishing, some 'manufactures' and the artisans and shopkeepers of Vannes, but those basically unaffected by the evolution of the rural economy were few. The fragile and rather stagnant demographic pattern of the area seems to hint at this dependence on the whims of nature, and to suggest that nature was not favourable to the majority of the population. How the people of Vannes and the surrounding countryside worked out their destiny in these conditions forms the subject of the rest of this book.

CHAPTER II

THE TOWN OF VANNES: (1) AN URBAN PROSPECT

Vannes held few attractions for the visitor in the eighteenth century; the medieval aspect of the town, its twisting, narrow streets and overhanging houses which tourists find so attractive today were seen then as just so many marks of barbarism. Few of the travellers who recorded their impressions of Vannes could find much praise for it. Babin, *trésorier de France,* in 1663 complained that the plainness of mind and body of the local women drove the Vannetais to drink; the engineer Mignot de Montigny in the middle of the eighteenth century wrote that the streets were so rough they might have been built by savages. Verlac, the frustrated English master of the École de la Marine, driven out of town by a student riot in 1790, thought the townsmen ignorant and unsociable, the climate dangerous, the air and water unhealthy; and La Vallée, ardent writer of republican travel literature, damned the Vannetais for their superstition and the nobility for snobbery, and found the architecture, except for the cathedral, undistinguished. Only Arthur Young, who stayed for a couple of hours before pushing on southward to 'the great commercial city of Nantes' had a few kind words for its port and promenade. Much of what these observers wrote about Vannes was warped by personal experiences or the aesthetic blindness imposed by a century of neoclassicism, but there was more than a little truth in their reports. Like most French towns of the old regime, Vannes had kept at least in its centre much of the appearance, and all the inconvenience, of a medieval city. Though virtually surrounded with streams, lakes and marshes, the town was poorly supplied with water for everyday use, and twice a day, when the tide fell, the black mud on the bottom of the port lay exposed, giving off a powerful and unpleasant odour, especially nauseating in summertime.

There were four principal quarters in the town. The first was the walled town, the *ville close.* Its nucleus had been built on the top of a

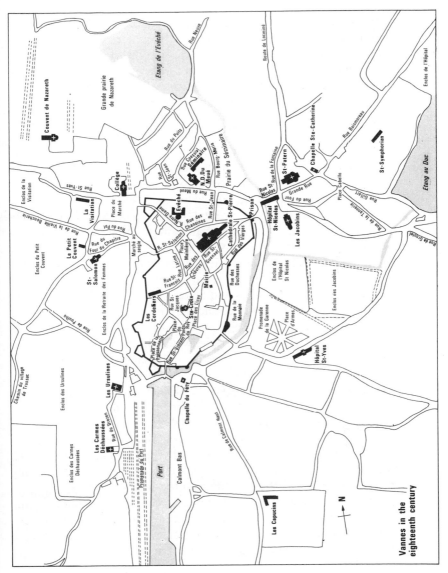

Map II: Vannes in 1785

slope rising from the end of the channel which served as a port. By the seventeenth century, the original enceinte had been extended to the edge of the port, taking in what had once been mud flats at the foot of the hill. This reclaimed area within the walls was where the houses and apartments of the local nobility were to be found; next to it, still at the foot of the hill, were the fish market, the public weighing-station and the place des Lices, on which were the residences of administrative officials, the contractor of the tobacco monopoly (*entreposeur des tabacs*), the officials of the royal *domaine* and the post office. Further up, the hill was crowned by the cathedral and Town Hall where the local courts held their sessions and the municipal officers deliberated. Around these two landmarks were clustered the dwellings of the lawyers, a few professional men and prebendary canons, and the bishop's palace. The Cathedral served as the parish church for the walled town. Outside the walls were the faubourgs, built-up areas covered by three parishes: Notre-Dame-du-Mené, to the north, and St-Salomon, to the west, were pocket-sized parishes surrounded by the biggest parish, St-Patern, which completely enveloped these enclaves and the walled town itself, and extended over part of the nearby countryside.

Outside the walls, lakes and fields and the enclosed grounds of monasteries and convents cut across the town's periphery, giving each of the faubourgs a separate geographical identity: there was the Boucherie to the north of the walls, the market quarter to the north-west, and the large cluster of buildings about the parish church of St-Patern. Finally, in contrast to the walled town, dominated by nobility, ecclesiastics, legal men and office-holders, the area around the little port was the site of the merchants' quarter. Here were the houses of the *négociants* Danet, Desruisseaux, Dubodan and others, who shipped the grain of the Vannetais down the Atlantic coast. Unlike the showy Île Feydeau in Nantes, which mirrored the wealth of eighteenth-century shipping and slaving magnates, most of the buildings on the port of Vannes were the product of more modest seventeenth-century speculation. The architecture of the port, like its economic foundations, changed little during the eighteenth century, except for the spread of shipwrights' yards along the banks of the narrow channel.[1]

[1] Bibliothèque municipale, Rennes, MS. 309; J.-P. Leguay, 'Vannes au xve siècle', *BSPM,* ciii (1975), 45–120; S. Canal, 'La Bretagne au début du gouverne-
[*p. 29 for n. 1 cont.*]

The four neighbourhoods which clustered about the port and the hill which ran down to it differed considerably in wealth and in the sort of people who lived in them. If we leave aside the nobility and the clergy for the moment and restrict our analysis to the Third Estate, looking at the professions of the male household heads who paid the *capitation* in 1704 (the patterns changed later in the century, though not much) it is evident that the preponderance of prestige lay within the town walls. With only 35 per cent of the taxpaying population, the *ville close* had 74 per cent of the royal officials, 61 per cent of the members of the liberal professions, 71 per cent of luxury trades, 54 per cent of the leather workers. Food and hostelry trades tended to concentrate, not surprisingly, around the Boucherie, but they were also present in almost equal numbers about the church of St-Patern, as were the building trade and metal workers. St-Patern and its adjoining faubourgs, as Table II-4 shows, were predominately artisan and shopkeeper quarters and had in addition the largest share of simple day-labourers and other unskilled workers—38 per cent of them were in St-Patern alone, and another 56 per cent in the other peripheral quarters. Along with the geographical distribution of trades went a differential topography of wealth. In 1704, the mean *capitation* payments in the walled town and on the port were 16.8 and 17.5 livres, or more than three times the mean in the three popular quarters.[2] The segregation of trades and fortunes by neighbourhood, often thought a mark of the modern town, was not perfect (it never is), but it was certainly a reality by the beginning of the eighteenth century in Vannes.

But if each quarter of the town preserved a distinct atmosphere of

ment personnel de Louis XIV', *Annales de Bretagne,* xxii (1906–7), 393–441; H. Bourde de La Rogerie, 'Les Voyageurs en Bretagne: le voyage de Mignot de Montigny en Bretagne en 1752', *MSHAB,* vi (1925), 225–302; L. Desjobert, 'Notes d'un voyage en Bretagne effectué en 1780 par Louis Desjobert', *Revue de Bretagne,* xlii (1909), 190–200, xliii (1910), 146–52; A.D. Morbihan, K 1553: J. La Vallée, L. Biron *père,* L. Biron *fils, Voyage dans les départemens de la France* (Paris, 1794), 7–9; Ogée, *Dictionnaire,* 940, 961; Guyot-Jomard, 'La Ville de Vannes et ses murs' (1888), 80; A. Young, *Travels During the Years 1787, 1788 and 1789* Bury St Edmunds, 1792–4); i, 87; J.-L. Debauve, 'Verlac et l'école de marine de Vannes', *BSPM* (1951–2), 66–8; S. Jouvin, *Le Voyageur d'Europe* (Paris, 1672), i, part 1, 285–7; Piganiol de la Force, *Nouvelle description de la France,* v, 232–6; Cayot-Délandre, *Annuaire du Morbihan* (1834), 97.

    [2] The *capitation* rolls used for the study of the Third Estate in this chapter and the next were A.D. Morbihan, C (unclassified): Commission intermédiaire de Vannes: 4 paroisses de Vannes, 1733, 1760, 1765, 1783; A.D. I.-V., C 4134: 1738; C 4141–3: 1784–9; A.C. Vannes, CC 1–2: 1703–9.

its own, the presence of the Church as an institution weighed heavily on the whole. Church property occupied large tracts on either side of the town and was given over, not only to places of worship and dwellings, but also to spacious gardens and meadows. The town itself was dotted with chapels and convents in every quarter, and continually overrun by the students of the college of Vannes. The latter, 500 or so undisciplined, rowdy, untrained lads off the farm for the most part, lived an austere life in boarding-houses run by pious old landladies, who engaged their tutors and in general ruled over them with an iron rod; it was not surprising that they sought relief from their studies and this regime in the occasional riot:

C'est un spectacle curieux [wrote one witness] que de voir cette pépinière de latinistes au sortir des classes, en vestes, en sabots, les coudes percés, les habits rapetassés, les cheveux épars, le teint halé, une pile de livres sous les bras, le père étudiant avec le fils, l'enfance à côté de l'âge mûr et dévançant le vieillesse.[3]

Less immediately apparent, but also important to the economy of the town, were the girls' boarding schools, run by the Ursulines, and the technical school established by Bishop Bertin, which had about 300 pupils.[4]

Table II-1: Mean *capitation* payment, by quarter (livres)

Year	Intra-Muros	Marché	Boucherie	Port	St-Patern	Total
1704	16.8	5.5	5.2	17.5	4.7	10.3
1733	9.0	4.8	3.2	9.8	3.2	6.5
1760	10.6	6.2	3.8	11.9	5.4	8.6
1783	11.6	5.9	3.3	15.3	3.8	8.5

[3] Debauve, 'Verlac et l'école de marine'.

[4] J. Allanic, 'Histoire du Collège de Vannes', *Annales de Bretagne,* xviii (1902–3), 59–105, 234–75; E. Raut and L. Lallemant, 'Une Page peu connue de l'histoire du Collège de Vannes, actuellement "Collège Jules Simon": l'École de la Marine', *Revue de l'enseignement secondaire et de l'enseignement supérieur,* vi (1889), 383–410; A.-F. Rio, *La Petite Chouannerie ou histoire d'un collège breton sous l'Empire* (London, 1842), 1–61; H. Marsille, 'Vannes', in *Les Établissements des Jésuites en France depuis quatre siècles,* ed. P. Delattre, v, 15–22; Cariou, 'L'Instruction dans le département du Morbihan'; A.D. I.-V., C 694: Freneau to intendant, 4-12-1787; C 692: Freneau to intendant, 23-6-1785.

Vannes was typical of a certain sort of old regime town. Its population was about the same as that of Chartres, Bayeux and Saumur; with about 10,000 inhabitants, it was about twice the size of Elbeuf and one-third of the size of Rennes: large enough to be included in the list of the 'principal towns' of the kingdom in Calonne's report to the Assembly of Notables in 1787, but small enough to be in the least considerable quarter of the towns on that list. Among the towns of north-west France, it came far behind centres like Angers, Rennes and Nantes, but nevertheless remained the biggest place on the southern coast of Brittany between Nantes and Lorient.[5]

Vannes was representative in another way, too. Although the population of the built-up part of the town did not vary a great deal across the century, its fluctuations are significant in that they followed a pattern common to most towns in southern Brittany, and perhaps in the greater part of France. The number of households established in the town, as measured by the number of *capitation* assessments, gives a rough indication of population change across the century. These figures indicate a fairly abrupt drop at the beginning of the century, followed by a levelling-off between 1733 and 1760, and another decline in the last decade of the old regime.[6] Much of this story is common to the smaller and middling towns throughout north-west France: Bayeux, Angers, and eight of the ten towns of the *comté nantais* to the south of Vannes experienced a fall in population in the first third of the century, followed by only a modest recovery, if that, around 1750.[7]

This simple tale of falling numbers does not go very far towards explaining either what urban society in Vannes was like or the

[5] E. Levasseur, *La Population française* (Paris, 1889–92), iii, 227; E. Martin, 'La Population de la ville de Vannes au début et à la fin du xviiie siècle', *Annales de Bretagne*, xxv (1921–3), 610–25 gives an estimate of 14,000 for 1701, but this includes about 2,000 in the rural part of St-Patern. A summary of estimates for the period 1702–1831 is given in Le Goff, 'Vannes', 344–7.

[6] The *imposition mobilière* of 1792 in A.D. Morbihan, L 462 and the list of citizens not inscribed on the roll gives a total of 1,315 men and 667 women but these rolls were not strictly comparable with those of the old regime (they included, among other new categories, ecclesiastics and former nobles).

[7] For the figures of the *comté nantais*, see Meyer, *La Noblesse bretonne*, ii, 851; also M. el Kordi, *Bayeux aux xvii et xviiie siècles* (Paris, La Haye, 1970), 162; F. Lebrun, *Les Hommes et la mort en Anjou aux 17e et 18e siècles* (Paris–The Hague, 1971), 162; J.-C. Perrot, *Genèse d'un ville moderne: Caen au xviiie siècle* (Paris–The Hague, 1975); C. Nières, *La Réconstruction d'une ville au xviie siècle: Rennes 1720–1760* (Paris, 1972); J. Meyer et al., *Histoire de Rennes* (Toulouse, 1972), 258–60.

reasons for the town's plight. To do these things requires us to begin at the beginning with a view of the population in 1704. At that time, there were probably over 12,000 people in Vannes, of whom about 300 were nobles and 360, clergy.[8] The economic activities of the remaining population could be described as pre-industrial, even medieval. About 13 per cent of the male tax-paying population belonged to what might be termed, anachronistically, the 'public sector' and the professional classes, and another 5 per cent were merchants of some importance. The 'public sector' counted 62 judicial officers, 29 financial officials and 6 men whose tasks might be called purely administrative. The reason for the presence of so many judicial officers was the existence in Vannes of the Présidial, the Admiralty Court, the jurisdiction of the *eaux et forêts,* and two substantial seigneurial tribunals, the court of Largouet and the Régaires of Vannes. Twenty-seven of the judicial officers were judges, counsellors, *procureurs du Roi* or procurators-fiscal in these courts: seven ran their chancelleries (*greffes*) or inspected their operations for the government; twenty-eight did the less genteel work of delivering summonses, keeping order in the town, taking prisoners, and so forth. The financial officials consisted of eleven men who took in, managed and distributed revenues from harbour dues, the registry offices, the royal domain, the clergy's self-imposed income tax (*décimes*), provincial sales taxes and funds deposited with the courts (*consignations*); the rest were their clerks. There was also a mayor, a postmaster and their various underlings. The liberal professions were represented by fourteen barristers and forty-one notaries and attorneys, thirteen doctors, surgeons and apothecaries (seven surgeons, three of each of the others), a couple of midwives, a surgeon's mate, an architect, and a score or so of men in odd trades still considered as liberal professions at the time: billiard and tennis-court keepers, a dancing master, a couple of fencing-masters, writing and school-masters and a half-dozen musicians employed in the cathedral. Such was the basis of the town's official and professional cadres; when we add to it the seventy men and twenty-five women who carried on extensive trade, or were believed to do so, we have all of the active population which did not have to work with its hands, about one-fifth of the total of heads of households.

---

[8] Martin, 'La Population de la ville de Vannes', 613.

The remainder of the active population fell into three groups: the artisan, shopkeeper and labouring part of the town, who supplied the needs of the wealthiest 20 per cent of the Third Estate, of the 600· or so resident nobles and clerics, and those of each other and the surrounding countryside. Fifteen per cent, or 271 individuals, were in the hostelry or food trades: 11 innkeepers, not less than 60 tavern-keepers—one for about every 156 men, women and children in the town—and another 10 boarding-house keepers; the rest were butchers, bakers, grocers and candlestick-sellers. The artisanal part of the town accounted for about a third of the active population.

Table II-2: Number of personal *capitation* assessments, 1704–83

	1704	1733	1760	1783
Men	1428	1245	1108	1057
Women	349	326	478	377

The largest single group among these was in the textile or clothing trades (13 per cent), but a little less than one-half of this group were in the textile trade properly speaking: 30 drapers, 5 *toilliers,* 12 *sergers,* 9 carders, 7 *texiers en lange,* 44 weavers. The rest were tailors (67), wigmakers and the like. Vannes was a far cry from proto-industrial towns of the old regime like Beauvais, where in 1696 something like 25 per cent of the total population was employed in the textile trade, or Elbeuf, with about half of the active population in textiles at the end of the eighteenth century.[9] In Vannes, only 6 per cent of the total active population was included in this proto-proletariat. The other 'industrial' sector was the tannery, but all leathercraft together only employed another 6 per cent of the active population in 1704, and of these only a dozen were tanners. The remainder of the artisan population was what might be expected in such a town: enough people in the building, wood and metal trades to supply the needs of the town and its region.

Finally, a high proportion of the active population was composed of day-labourers and other unskilled workers—23 per cent of the

[9] P. Goubert, *Beauvais et le Beauvaisis de 1600 à 1730* (Paris, 1960), 257; J. Kaplow, *Elbeuf during the Revolutionary Period: History and Social Structure* (Baltimore, 1963), 65–9.

male population or 26 per cent of men and women combined. This relatively high concentration can be explained only by the presence of the port and also the chance of finding employment on the estates and in the gardens of convents and monasteries surrounding the town and in the market-gardens just outside the walls, to the east and west. In addition to the quarter of the population classed as unskilled workers, we should add domestic servants. There were 410 domestics in the service of 296 heads of households in the Third Estate in 1704, plus another 51 working for 31 clergy and religious establishments and 62 who served 16 various privileged people and absentees. Some of these had a specialized trade, but most did not, and there were more women among them than men. The majority probably came from rural families, but it seems likely that domestic service in towns like Vannes did not offer even the limited opportunities for social advancement that it did in the countryside. In

Table II-3: Occupations of taxpayers in 1704

	Men		Women		Total	
	number	%	number	%	number	%
Royal officers	97	6.8	—	—	97	5.5
Liberal professions	120	8.4	5	1.4	125	7.0
Commerce	70	4.9	25	7.2	95	5.3
Food & hostelry	205	14.4	66	18.9	271	15.3
Luxury trades	21	1.5	3	0.9	24	1.4
Textile & clothing	205	14.4	18	5.2	223	12.5
Leather trades	113	7.9	1	0.3	114	6.4
Building trades	57	4.0	—	—	57	3.2
Wood trades	46	3.2	—	—	46	2.6
Metal trades	73	5.1	1	0.3	74	4.2
Labourers (unskilled)	329	23.0	126	36.1	455	25.6
Agriculture	48	3.4	2	0.6	50	2.8
Unknown professions	39	2.7	102	29.2	141	7.8
Retired	5	0.4	—	—	5	0.4
	1428	100.1	349	100.1	1777	100.0

Clergy, institutions and privileged taxed for servants	50
Minors	3
	53

Table II-4: Percentage of occupations in each quarter according to *capitation* roll of 1704 (men only)

	Intra-muros	Marché	Boucherie	Port	St-Patern	?	Total
Royal officers	74.2	5.2	2.1	14.4	4.1	—	97
Liberal professions	60.8	12.8	7.2	5.6	12.0	1.6	125
Commerce	53.7	17.9	0.0	13.7	14.7	—	95
Food & hostelry	17.3	19.2	26.9	5.9	30.6	—	271
Luxury trades	70.8	20.8	—	4.2	4.2	—	24
Textile & clothing	41.3	11.7	3.6	5.4	38.1	—	223
Leather trades	54.4	15.8	3.5	4.4	21.9	—	114
Building trades	14.0	24.6	10.5	3.5	47.4	—	57
Wood trades	54.3	10.9	—	10.9	23.9	—	46
Metal trades	32.4	18.9	12.2	8.1	28.4	—	74
Labourers (unskilled)	16.3	26.6	9.9	19.2	38.0	—	455
Agriculture	6.0	56.0	16.0	—	22.0	—	50
Unknown professions	59.6	16.3	1.4	12.8	9.9	—	141
Retired	100.0	—	—	—	—	—	5
Total							1830

towns there were few eligible young *laboureurs* or daughters of prosperous tenant farmers and no chance either to pick up by experience the primitive but none the less complex technology needed for the intensive agriculture practised in the Vannetais. Looked at from the point of view of its economic activities, then, Vannes was an administrative and commercial centre, and even an industrial town, in a 'pre-modern' sense, but it did not have that concentration of activity in any one industrial sector which characterized towns of a superficially more 'modern' sort, such as the great cities of north-eastern France.

Nor was the concentration of ownership or control of the means of non-agricultural production as pronounced as in some other parts of France. It is difficult to draw an exact line between the owners of the means of production and those who had only their labour to contribute to increasing the wealth of the town. The traditional distinctions between master, journeyman and apprentice were capriciously applied by contemporaries in Vannes; the assessors responsible for the roll of 1704, which lists no masters at all for any trade, only very parsimoniously distributed the prefix 'marchand-' to a trade to indicate that a man sold goods that he made, had made for him or bought: only seven tradesmen were so qualified. Only two received the prefix 'garçon-' (one woodworker, one saddlemaker), and only one was qualified as a 'journalier-' with reference to a trade. This probably reflects the indifference or inertia of the assessors rather than a reality of daily life. At any rate, in the *capitation* roll of 1733, the distinction appears clearly, although the terms used are not the classic division between masters, journeymen and 'prentices, but rather between 'garçons'—hired men, mates—and the rest. One was a *charpentier* or a *garçon charpentier,* but never a *maître charpentier.* In general the use of the term 'master' was very rare, but a few of the manufacturing trades came to use it with time: one tailor in 1733, then four shoemakers in 1760, then four cabinet-makers (*menuisiers*) in 1783. But the real distinction was between the *garçons* and the others. In most cases there were fewer *garçons* than simple tradesmen; only among the nail-makers were there consistently nearly as many mates as tradesmen, probably because the nature of their craft demanded a larger labour supply. Among the textile trades, hiring a skilled helper was virtually unknown after mid-century, although there were 15 drapers' boys (*garçons drapiers*) in 1733 for 25 drapers. In all, the wage-earning 'industrial' proletariat amounted to about three-score people down to 1760, and dropped to 48 in 1783.[10]

It was supplemented to some extent by domestic servants. The

---

[10] The *vingtième d'industrie,* in A.D. Morbihan, C: Commission intermédiaire de Vannes: 4 paroisses de Vannes, does not seem to have been levied exclusively on masters, as was the case in Le Mans. No one is really sure what was the criterion for the levying of this tax in Brittany; in Vannes it appears to have been related to the prosperity of the enterprise and the presence of servants, but it was also levied on persons with no apparent 'industrial' occupation. In the 'industrial sector', the following were the figures in 1783:

	On the vingtième d'industrie	Employing servants, according to the capitation
Luxury trades	8–11	7
Textile & clothing	8	24
Leather	5–7	10
Building trades	0	0
Woodworkers	1	2
Metallurgy	3–5	6

See P. Bois, 'Structure socio-professionelle du Mans à la fin du xviiie siècle. Problèmes de méthode et résultats', *Actes du quatre-vingt-septième congrès national des Sociétés savantes. Section d'histoire moderne et contemporaine. Poitiers 1962* (Paris, 1963), 688; A. Rébillon, *Les États de Bretagne de 1661 à 1789* (Paris–Rennes, 1932), 572, 591–2, 599.

'productive sectors' (excluding food) maintained about a fifth of the servants in the town across the century, nearly all of these in the leather and textile trades, though a goodly number of the latter must have been mere shop assistants.

However, servants were practically unknown in the woodworking, building and metal trades: one nail-maker who did have one complained in 1758 that his man 'souvent ne travaille pas huit jours chez lui [et]quelquefois même ne travaille un jour que pour avoir des avances qu'il n'a pas plutôt reçu qu'il disparaît'.[11] Some of these domestics must have been apprenticed boys, but apprenticeship contracts, and the specific mention of apprentices in tax rolls,[12] are rare.

Considered in this light, the 'proletariat' of Vannes was small, probably about 100 people and their families at the beginning of the century. But it is possible to raise this figure if we look at the realities of the old regime economy, instead of modern categories designed to describe fundamentally different societies. It is legitimate, for example, to add almost all the building trades (masons, roofers and most of the carpenters as well) to the working people since there were almost no masters or mates in this trade: most were employed at day wages and the directing role in construction projects of any size seems to have been taken by 'entrepreneurs', architects and engineers.[13] This gives us another 70 or so heads of families. If we add to these the 450-odd day labourers, the size of the 'working class' comes to more than 600 heads of families, or about a third of the total. And if we add to this the remainder of all the servants, we can swell the figure to more than 1,000; if we use the eighteenth-century term 'ouvrier' as it was used in Vannes to designate anybody who worked with his hands, it would leave us with a majority of workers in the town. So if there was not a modern working class in Vannes, or even the sort of pre-industrial proletariat found in some of the other French provincial towns, there was a majority of the population directly dependent on its labour for a living.

The distribution of wealth in town conformed to what such an occupational pattern as this might suggest. For purposes of description, it seems best to use the method by which taxpayers are divided into

---

[11] A.D. Morbihan, C 273: Commission intermédiaire de Vannes: Petition of Yves Pourchasse, master nail-maker, Vannes.

[12] Two in 1704, 1 in 1733, 1 in 1760, 7 in 1783.

[13] É. Martin, *Une Grande Fortune bourgeoise à Vannes au xviiie siècle. Olivier Delourme (1660–1729)* (Vannes, 1921); in 1702 there were two architects; in 1733, 1 *ingénieur;* in 1760, 2 *ingénieurs* and 1 *sous-ingénieur;* in 1783, 2 *ingénieurs*.

a hierarchy whose echelons are defined by a geometrical progression based on the mean tax payment.[14] In 1704, 82 per cent of taxpayers from the Third Estate paid less than the average *capitation* assessment; 62 per cent paid less than half the average assessment and 36 per cent, less than one-quarter. The distribution of wealth among the different occupations in the town as measured by the *capitation* made a pretty sharp distinction between those who laboured and those who did not. Of all the men in the official, professional and commercial groups together, only 21 per cent paid less than the mean tax; of all those in the food and hotel trades and artisanal occupations, 95 per cent paid less than this amount. Among the more favoured professional groups, the judicial, administrative and especially the financial officials stood out by their wealth: 44 per cent of this group of officials paid more than four times the mean in tax and another 28 per cent, that is, 72 per cent in all, paid more than the mean. The commercial men came next, with 23 per cent paying more than four times the mean, and another 51 per cent paying more than the mean. The professionals came a comfortable third; very few of them paid more than four times the mean, but all in all, more than half paid over the mean. The largest and most prosperous group among these professionals were the lawyers of various sorts (57 of 121 men) and although society drew a nice distinction between barristers and the less genteel but more numerous attorneys and notaries, they were all endowed about equally in wealth.

With less than a dozen exceptions, none of the remaining people in Vannes reached these heights of riches. Among the remaining occupations, about a third of the score of artisans in the luxury trades paid over the average tax assessment, and one-tenth of the food and hostelry trades, but the centre of gravity in these groups was below the mean. There was a hierarchy of wealth even here, though: proportionately more of the woodworkers and metal trades paid taxes in the range between the mean and half the mean than in the other groups, and the lowest, predictably, were the day-labourers, who were the only group to have a sizeable share (15 per cent) in the category paying less than one-eighth of the mean. Women, as a general rule, appeared in the *capitation* rolls only if widowed or

[14] J. Dupâquier, 'Problèmes de mesure et de représentation graphique en matière d'histoire sociale', *Actes du quatre-vingt-neuvième congrès national des sociétés savantes, Section d'histoire moderne et contemporaine, Lyon 1964* (Paris, 1965), ii, v. 1, 77–86.

single, except for married women with independent incomes or fortunes: for this reason some historians prefer to leave them out of general descriptions of socio-professional structure based on fiscal documents, since their presence inflates some categories and deflates others. It is interesting, however, to note that in almost all categories, they appeared to lose in the competition with men; they were assessed at a lower average rate in almost all professions. In so far as women are represented on these rolls, they were (in 1704) predominantly unskilled labourers (36 per cent of women), with a few more representatives in the textile trade (5 per cent); another 16 per cent had no recorded profession, but paid less than the average assessment. Only 18 per cent of all women taxpayers paid more than the average; of these privileged 65 women, 44 had no profession and presumably lived from *rentes* or estate incomes.

Table II-5: Percentage of each occupational group at each tax level, 1704

Tax assessment*	0	e–c	b–a	A–B	C–E	Total number in group
Officers	—	7.2	22.7	27.8	42.3	97
Liberal professions	1.6	9.6	36.8	50.4	1.6	125
Commerce	—	2.1	29.5	46.3	22.1	95
Food & hostelry	—	8.9	81.2	10.0	0.0	271
Luxury trades	—	12.5	58.3	29.2	0.0	24
Textile trades	—	40.4	54.7	4.9	0.0	223
Leather trades	—	34.2	64.0	1.8	0.0	114
Building trades	—	5.3	87.7	7.0	0.0	57
Woodworkers	—	13.0	84.8	2.2	0.0	46
Metal trades	—	12.2	79.7	8.1	0.0	74
Labourers	—	91.6	8.4	0.0	0.0	455
Agriculture	—	22.0	72.0	4.0	2.0	50
Unknown	—	12.1	42.6	29.8	15.6	141
Retired	—	20.0	40.0	20.0	20.0	5
Total	0.1	36.1	45.5	13.3	5.0	1777

* Explanation of symbols: e–c = between $1/32$ of the mean and $1/4$ of the mean; b–a = $1/4$ mean to mean; A–B = between the mean and 4 times the mean; C–E = between 4 and 32 times the mean.

It might be wondered what these different levels of tax assessment represented, and whether the *capitation* gave a true representation of the scale of wealth. Unfortunately, there are not many other reliable sources to compare it with, and none gives as complete a view of the local population as the *capitation*. The *vingtième* was levied only on the real or potential revenue of property owned in the city and, in any event, many people did not own their lodgings: in 1783 there were 1,435 *capitation* assessments for the Third Estate, but only 709 people on the *vingtième* roll. Marriage contracts were rare, more the affair of the upper ranks of urban societies than the lower, and plagued with special provisions and inflated dowries offered in instalments or *rentes* on which the principal was probably never paid.[15] A more useful source are the *inventaires après décès*, post-mortem inventories of goods and chattels (*meubles*). They, too, are imperfect: they appear to under-represent the wealthiest and the poorest, do not usually give evaluations of real property and paper credits, and, in the town of Vannes at least, seem systematically to undervalue the resale worth of personal property. Nevertheless, it is possible at least to compare personal wealth with the tax assessments of the deceased.

When the comparison is made, there appears to be a rough correspondence between the scales of tax assessments and the value of chattels but the distance between rich and poor seems much greater when measured by the value of their personal possessions than it does when measured by tax assessments. No doubt this means that the *capitation* was a regressive direct tax, but this is not sufficient to justify abandoning the *capitation* in favour of the *inventaires*, because the *capitation* has a decided advantage in that it took account of all forms of wealth, including revenue from outside the town. The comprehensive nature of the *capitation* in fact explains some apparent anomalies between tax payments and the value of personal possessions. In 1783, the average tax assessment was 8 livres 10 sols. Anne Le Ret, widow of Jan Le Blouch, a baker on the rue St-Yves, paid 8 l. in *capitation,* but had personal property valued at only 523 l., even though many people with more valuable

---

[15] A.D. Morbihan, C: Commission intermédiaire de Vannes: 4 paroisses de Vannes: vingtième, 1783. On marriage contracts, Meyer, *La Noblesse bretonne*, ii, 1143–4; an examination of the papers of the notaries Perrigaud and Jarno in A.D. Morbihan, E^n 692–6 and 772–8 yielded only about thirty contracts for the period 1726–62 and 1781–3.

personal property paid less tax. This is because she appeared to be poorer than she was; in the papers listed in the inventory were documents showing that she and her late husband had a mortgage on a tenure held under *domaine congéable* in Surzur and owned their own house in Vannes. Jean-Marie Loher, a tanner near the church of St-Patern, had personal property valued at 2,121 l., but of this sum, 1,423 l. were in hides or leather, the articles of his trade. He owned the buildings of a tenure under *domaine congéable* in St-Nolf, but only rented his house in town; he was assessed 5 l. in *capitation,* or 3 l. less than Anne Le Ret, though his property was worth more than four times more, but it seems likely that the *capitation* assessment was a more accurate representation of the place these two people held in the hierarchy of fortunes.[16] It is for this reason, and also because of its completeness, that the *capitation* in Brittany is the best single document for the study of urban social structure and economic hierarchy.[17]

In that hierarchy, the employment of domestic servants was another sign of prosperity and power. In fact there was a direct relation between the wealth possessed by household heads and their employment of servants. Once again, in this, the professionals, the officials and commercial men led the way. In 1704 these groups, although representing only about 18 per cent of the active population, employed 201 of the 296 servants maintained by the Third Estate. Only the luxury trades came close to this (29 per cent of their households had servants); the food and clothing trades and those in agriculture (chiefly gardeners) had servants in about one household in ten, while only one in twelve of the people in the leather and metal trades had one. Women, proportionately, had slightly more servants than men, almost all of them employed in the food and hotel trades and commerce or by women whose professions were not given. Most of these servants probably attended to personal and housekeeping needs; only 50 or so were listed as having trades, even though some of the others must have had some specialized occupation, or waited in the shops of their masters. The total number of servants seems high—500 or so throughout the century, not including the servants of the nobility—but is no greater than that found in

[16] A.D. Morbihan, B: Régaires, minutes and B 648–52, 751–6: 1730–4, 1783–5.
[17] An identical conclusion was reached by A. Lespagnol in his work on St-Malo: 'A propos des élites urbaines dans l'Ancien Régime: l'exemple de Saint-Malo au xviiie siècle', *Bulletin de la Société d'histoire moderne*, 15e série, lxxiii (1974), 2–12.

Bayeux, with 686 domestics for about 9,000 inhabitants in 1768.[18]

At first glance, the society of the town appears to have changed little over the course of the eighteenth century, but on closer examination, there emerge the signs of a long qualitative decline which matched the fall in the number of inhabitants. The least promising change for the future of the town occurred between 1704 and 1733, when the strength of the legal and administrative sector, some 15 per cent of the active male population in 1704, was amputated by over one-third. Probably as a direct result, the 'food and hotel' sectors and the leather trade declined by one-fifth. This loss seems to have set the tone for the rest of the century. Why had it occurred? A local historian, Étienne Martin,[19] blamed the fall on the departure of the Parlement of Brittany, which, he claimed, had brought

Table II-6: Change in number of household heads, by quarter

(a) Men

Quarter	1704	1733	1760	1783
Intra-muros	491	308	310	299
Marché	274	260	188	189
Boucherie	143	101	118	60
Port	118	112	91	95
St-Patern	402	436	369	379
Officers (listed separately)	—	28	32	34
Unidentified	—	—	—	1
Total	1428	1245	1108	1057

(b) Women

Quarter				
Intra-muros	151	147	194	145
Marché	70	68	89	76
Boucherie	23	23	39	23
Port	23	22	51	33
St-Patern	82	66	105	100
Total	349	326	478	377

[18] El Kordi, *Bayeux*, 69.

[19] Martin, 'La Population de la ville de Vannes', 613–15; A.D. I.-V., C 3982: Morin, Mallet and Bocou, Vannes, to commissioners of the Estates, 2-3-1737; A.D. Morbihan, 47 G 5 (374), January–May 1721; A.C. Vannes, BB 16: 5-1-1742.

Table II-7: Evolution of taxpaying population by profession (both sexes)

	1704	*1733*	*1760*	*1783*
Officers	97	72	73	69
Professionals	125	72	49	58
Commerce				
('marchand', 'négociant')	95	62	55	64
Food & hostelry	271	240	244	217
Luxury trades	24	20	19	25
Textiles	223	227	189	190
Leather trades	114	90	93	79
Building trades	57	57	63	55
Woodworkers	46	52	83	72
Metalworkers	74	73	65	57
Labourers	455	268	217	152
Agriculture	50	49	55	61
Unknown professions	141	283	377	324
Retired	5	6	4	11
Total	1777	1571	1586	1434
Privileged, absentees, ecclesiastics, minors, institutions	53	57	76	58
Total	1830	1628	1642	1492

prosperity to the town during its exile there after the Breton revolt of 1675. But the Parlement had left fifteen years before the roll of 1704 was drawn up, and the real decline seems to have taken place after that date. The town council of Vannes put the responsibility (as they did in many things) on the town of Lorient, whose quick rise, they alleged in 1738, was depopulating all the towns of the diocese. According to another version, the rapid inflation and subsequent financial crisis during John Law's administration had some disastrous effects on the local holders of *rentes*. The absence of most notarial archives for the early eighteenth century around Vannes makes most hypotheses tenuous, but it does seem that the region was adversely affected by the decline of some sectors of the Breton economy, most notably the misfortunes of the cloth industry.[20]

[20] Bérenger and Meyer, *La Bretagne de la fin du xviie siècle*, 62–3; F. Le Lay, *Histoire de la ville et communauté de Pontivy au xviiie siècle* (Paris, 1911), 30–57; Tanguy, 'La Production et le commerce des toiles'.

After 1733, there were few signs of industrial activity beyond what had already existed at the beginning of the century; regression was the rule for the textile and clothing trades and metalworkers. The only sign of renewal was a significant increase in the number of woodworkers, probably a reflection of the rise of the one 'industrial sector' where Vannes experienced real growth by the end of the century, the shipbuilding industry.[21] Undoubtedly, too, the various shifts in the town's population bore some relation to the depressed state of the region's agricultural economy at the end of the seventeenth century, its recovery in the 1750s and 1760s, and subsequent difficulties in the last two decades of the *ancien régime*, questions which will be taken up in detail in Chapter XI.

But the decline of so many French and Breton towns in the eighteenth century suggests that more general causes were also at work. Indeed, it seems that only in the larger cities of Brittany and France, or in those with some new form of economic activity, was there more marked population growth, as was the case in Rennes, Caen and the conurbation of Nantes–Paimbœuf. The eighteenth century was a time of urban growth for the greater centres in France, but for Vannes and scores of other middling and small towns, it was the beginning of a decline which, for some, was to prove permanent.

The effects of this long-term stagnation were felt differently in each neighbourhood of the town. The amputation of the professional and business classes hit the walled town first; its male taxpaying population fell by about a third[22] between 1704 and 1733. This fall was matched by a drop in the number of people in the clothing trade within the town walls. The other quarters declined only slightly in the first third of the eighteenth century, except, significantly, the Boucherie, where there was a fall of about 30 per cent of its male taxpaying population, mainly butchers dependent on the tastes of the richer inhabitants. By 1760, the contraction of activity in Vannes had begun to have an effect on the market quarter and the area around the church of St-Patern, where the number of male taxpayers

---

[21] See Le Goff, 'La Construction navale en Bretagne'; Thomas-Lacroix, 'Les Constructions et les ventes de navires'. There were 52 woodworkers in 1733, 82 in 1760, and a small reduction in 1783 was probably owing to wartime requisitioning of shipwrights.

[22] Thirty-seven per cent according to these figures, but the loss is exaggerated since several of the office-holders are listed without their residences on rolls of 1733 and subsequent years.

Table II-8: Per cent of each occupational group in various tax categories

	Officers	Profnls.	Comrc.	Food & hostelry	Luxury trades	Textile	Leather	Building trades	Wood-workers	Metal-workers	Labrs. etc.	Agri-culture	Unkwn.	Retired	Total number in group
(1) Per cent paying less than mean assessment (both sexes)															
1704	30	48	32	90	71	95	98	93	98	92	100	94	55	60	82
1733	33	39	31	82	60	89	94	95	77	86	100	76	65	50	77
1760	27	37	42	70	53	85	83	97	82	77	99	76	74	25	75
1783	24	36	61	73	68	92	90	95	88	90	98	77	66	82	75
(2) Per cent of men paying less than ¼ of mean assessment															
1704	7	11	0	6	14	39	35	5	13	12	75	23	5	20	34
1733	6	12	0	15	5	48	36	59	35	31	83	20	36	0	40
1760	11	6	3	14	22	32	30	42	27	25	69	37	31	33	32
1783	11	11	15	26	12	64	53	58	46	37	86	46	29	50	44
(3) Per cent of men paying more than 4 times mean assessment															
1704	42	2	23	2	0	0	0	0	0	0	0	2	13	20	5
1733	28	7	29	2	0	0	0	0	0	1	0	0	14	0	5
1760	30	13	30	4	0	0	0	0	0	0	0	8	7	67	5
1783	27	30	12	4	0	0	1	0	0	0	0	0	15	0	6
(4) Per cent of category of men paying more than 4 times the mean assessment represented by each group															
1704	62	3	24	0	0	0	0	0	0	0	0	2	26	0	66
1733	34	9	24	5	0	0	0	0	0	2	0	1	26	0	58
1760	38	10	17	10	0	0	0	0	0	0	0	7	14	3	58
1783	30	23	7	10	0	0	2	0	0	0	0	0	28	0	60

fell by 29 per cent and 15 per cent respectively. The decline in the market quarter was felt in all the trades there, while in St-Patern, it was due to a fall in the number of people in the clothing trade and, especially, in the number of day-labourers. Unlike the rest of the town, the quarter around the port showed little change at all, except for a long-term decline in the number who called themselves *négociants* or merchants—there were thirteen of them in 1704, but only three in 1783. The increasing activity of shipbuilders around the port and in the gulf nearby, who sold their products to captains often working for merchants in the larger commercial towns, was a poor compensation.

Not only did the social composition of the various parts of the town change in a way that reflected its growing economic stagnation, but the relative distribution of wealth and the social composition of the affluent groups in the town, as measured by the *capitation,* also changed characteristically between 1704 and 1783. At the beginning, it was marked by a considerable gap between wealthy and poor, with 82 per cent of the active population paying less than the mean assessment; the wealthiest fifth of the active population thus possessed 72 per cent of the wealth of the Third Estate in the town, to say nothing of the share held by the nobility and clergy. Throughout the eighteenth century, this disparity remained virtually unchanged; by 1783, 75 per cent of the population paid less than the mean assessment, but the wealthiest fifth possessed 79 per cent of the wealth. The apparent stability in the scale of wealth, in fact, conceals the overall impoverishment of the town and an increasing disparity between rich and poor. There were simply less rich folk, and therefore the tax burden had to be spread more evenly; the proportion of people in the lowest class of taxpayers grew. Table II-8 shows the increasing proportion of male taxpayers who paid less than one-quarter of the mean tax payment. And when this category of taxpayer is broken down by professional groups, the true range of the increasing gap between rich and poor appears. At the beginning of the century, 39 per cent of men in the clothing trades paid less than one-quarter of the mean; in 1783, 64 per cent. In 1704, 35 per cent of leather workers paid less than one-quarter of the mean; in 1783, 53 per cent. Among all the labouring and shopkeeping groups, only the unskilled workers and people in the building trades escaped this movement, because they were always doomed to remain at the bottom of the jagged pyramid of wealth. Only the liberal professions and royal officials seemed to have been relatively unaffected by the general trend.

In the meantime, the composition of the class of highly-taxed members of the Third Estate shifted. Throughout the eighteenth century there were always about sixty men in the group paying greater than four times the mean assessment, but at the beginning of the century it had been dominated by office-holders of all sorts and the businessmen, with 62 and 24 per cent of the total. By the 1730s, the proportion of rich office-holders had declined to 34 per cent, and the rich professional men began to emerge. By 1783, the royal officials were still only one-third of the richest taxpayers, but the businessmen had declined to 7 per cent of this group. The latter had been replaced by the professional men, who now represented 23 per cent of the total and, to a lesser extent, by people in the hotel and food trades (10 per cent). At the same time, the proportion of rentiers, which had declined by the 1760s, now went back up again. At the beginning of the century, the town had been dominated by royal servants and businessmen, but as the possibilities for profit disappeared,[23] the wealth of the Third Estate tended to concentrate in the hands of placemen and professionals, left in the position of middling-sized fish in a shrinking pond. The rich were not getting richer, but they were no longer the same sort of rich men, and the numbers of the poor were rising.

The number of people employing servants remained pretty much the same across the century and most of them were employed by men, though there were a few less of these at the end of the century than at the beginning. On the whole, less of the total number of servants employed by the Third Estate worked for officers, professional men and merchants at the end of the century than before (27 per cent as against 47 per cent); the only groups which appeared to be taking on significantly more help were the hostelry and food trades and the rentiers. The stagnation of the middle classes and the tendency of the town to fall back on its rural economic basis by the end of the old regime is thus confirmed by the pattern of servant employment. Finally, the disastrous economic effects of the first few years of the Revolution (as well as of the new-fangled progressive tax on domestic servants) are reflected in the fall of the number of servants by over a quarter between 1783 and 1792,

[23] See Chapter XI, pp. 293–8 below.

despite the inclusion of nobles' domestics in the figures for the latter year.

A comparison between the post-mortem inventories for the period 1730–3 and 1783–5 gives the initial impression of less change than the tax rolls suggest; in the 1780s as in the 1730s, the goods and chattels of the one-quarter of the people whose inventories were the most valuable were worth about 80 per cent of the total of all inventories. The proportions of artisans and shopkeepers at each level of the pyramid of wealth did not change either. Judged by the exterior signs of wealth, nothing seems to have altered. However, closer examination of the contents of the lists of private papers, inventoried by the court officers but not included in the total evaluation, shows a tendency for the town to invest less in general, and to invest less in the countryside. In the period 1730–4, five of the twelve artisans, shopkeepers and tradesmen with chattels worth more than the median evaluation had land in the countryside, either owned outright or held under *domaine congéable*. Thus Olivier Phelipot, a master-joiner with chattels worth only 583 livres on his death in 1733 nevertheless had acquired land in Sérent and St-Nolf, and another parcel under *domaine congéable* in Elven through his first marriage with a country girl early in the century, as well as some city property. René Chassebœuf, a merchant beltmaker with only 584 livres worth of possessions on his death in 1730 had a tenure under *domaine congéable* in the countryside for which he had paid 2,800 livres in 1724. One nailmaker-merchant, one master coppersmith (*maître chaudronnier*) and one merchant-butcher also had country property. In the 1780s, rural investment of this sort was less common among tradesmen: only two of twelve inventories, and only among the very richest tradesmen, mention rural property: one tanner and one baker who held lands under *domaine congéable*. Though these numbers are small, it should be remembered that they represent all the people whose personal property was evaluated in the town during these years. It looks very much as if the ability of the whole middle rank of townsfolk in the Third Estate to save and invest had been seriously shaken.[24]

The real stagnation and decline of Vannes and its fortunes during the eighteenth century suggests that the town was a sleepy place where no change ever occurred. But this stability is in a way illusory,

---

[24] Sources as in note 16, above.

for the population of the town was in constant renewal throughout the century. This process can be measured, at the cost of a little tedious work, by taking random samples of taxpayers from each of the *capitation* rolls of 1704, 1733, 1760 and 1783, and checking their presence on subsequent and preceding rolls.[25] The initial results are somewhat surprising. At the end of five years, on the average, no less than 43 per cent of the active citizens had disappeared from the rolls, to be replaced by others. This represents an extraordinary rate of mobility, comparable to and indeed greater than what historians have discovered in nineteenth-century North American cities. Most of this turnover took place within a year of each tax listing; thus, the group assessed in 1704 was reduced by 24 per cent between 1704 and 1705, and that assessed in 1783 fell by 12 per cent in 1784. Similarly, these groups grew by 18 per cent between 1703 and 1704 and by 19 per cent between 1782 and 1783. So dramatic are these changes that one is forced to look for a bias in the data to explain them.

Biases do exist. One was caused by death-rates, which in Vannes, as in nearby Auray, were of the order of 40 to 50/1000, or somewhat larger than in nineteenth-century North American towns.[26] Some difficulty is caused too by the unknown proportion of residents present, but too poor to pay the *capitation*. This problem is of course not particular to Vannes, since virtually all students of urban history recognize the existence of a shifting group of marginal, usually impermanent, residents. In Vannes, this group was variously estimated between 400 and 1,000 people, but many of these were

---

[25] The method was pioneered by P. R. Knights, *The Plain People of Boston, 1830–1860* (New York, 1971); see also P. R. Knights and S. Thernstrom, 'Men in Motion; Some Data and Speculations about Urban Population Mobility in Nineteenth-Century America', *Journal of Interdisciplinary History*, i, (1970), 9–35; M. B. Katz, *The People of Hamilton, Canada West* (Cambridge, Mass., 1975), 94–175, which has an abundant bibliography. The sample sizes were: 1704, 375 (of 1830); 1733, 344 (of 1628); 1760, 315 (of 1662); 1783, 276 (of 1492); these sizes give a confidence level of 95 per cent with a reliability of ± 5 per cent (± 4 per cent in the case of the 1704 sample) in the most conservative hypothesis: see A. Arkin and R. R. Colton, *Tables for Statisticians* (New York, 1963), 145. This is the same level used by P. R. Knights in his study of Boston; it has been criticized, somewhat unfairly, by M. A. Vinovskis in the *Journal of Interdisciplinary History*, iii (1973), 781–6 as being too small, but the amount of time required if a larger sample had been used would have made it impossible to treat the subject at all.

[26] A. Le Goff, 'Bilan d'une étude de démographie historique: Auray au xviiie siècle (vers 1740–1789)', *Annales de Démographie historique* (1974), 187–229; cf. a rate of 25/1000 in Boston for 1850–60 in Knights, *Plain People*, 164 n. 2.

truly 'floating', seasonal migrants. The most reliable estimate of residents paying no taxes, made in 1790, put their numbers at 236 'individuals', presumably adults, and not all of them household heads. By slipping into the ranks of the completely insolvent, a person could thus be left off the tax rolls and still remain a resident. However, the municipal authorities, in Vannes at least, were quite reluctant to absolve any potential taxpayers from their obligations, and kept insolvent taxpayers on the rolls for several years at a nominal assessment, even though they paid nothing, so it is not likely that much of this quite low rate of persistence can be explained by citizens slipping into penury.[27] The most likely bias is caused by the presence of a higher proportion of women on the Vannes rolls than on comparable records.[28] Men could disappear from the Vannes rolls in two ways: by dying or by emigrating; they could appear on it by coming of age or moving into town. Women had a third way of disappearing and appearing: by marrying and becoming widows. For this reason it is safer to look to figures for male taxpayers alone as an indication of mobility into and out of Vannes. But even then, the results are impressive; they indicate an annual rate of decay or growth of the order of 8 to 11 per cent a year over a five-year period and 16 to 19 per cent a year over a one-year period. The rates for Boston, one of the great entry-points for American immigration in the 1830s, ran at 8.8 per cent a year over a five-year period and 15.6 per cent a year over one year.[29] If Vannes was in any way typical of eighteenth-century French towns, the axiom 'one family in five moves every year', true of nineteenth- and twentieth-century North American societies, was also true of eighteenth-century France.

This generalization, if statistically correct, is nevertheless open to misunderstanding, since in reality some groups tended to stay in a locality longer than others. It is interesting to speculate on the reasons why some people stayed in Vannes and why others left,

[27] Below, Chapter III, p. 96, n. 93.; A.D. Morbihan, L 357: État-civil, 16-12-1790; Katz, *The People of Hamilton*, 19–20; Goubert, *Beauvais*, i, 249–56; Le Goff, 'Vannes', 43.

[28] Twenty-six per cent of taxed persons in 1783, 20 per cent in 1704; cf. Boston, where women formed only 13 per cent of family heads in 1830–60 according to Knights, *Plain People*, 83.

[29] Knights, *Plain People*, 57; similar patterns in Hamilton, Canada West, between 1850 and 1861 described in Katz, *The People of Hamilton*, 123; at Quebec in J. Hare, 'La Population de la ville de Québec 1795–1805' *Histoire sociale/Social history*, vii (1974), 30.

Table II-9: Per cent of men and women in sample present on *capitation* rolls of selected years

	Base − 1	Base year	Base + 1	Base + 5	Base + 6	Number in sample
Base year						
1704 Men	84	100	81	56	—	302
Women	73	100	55	38.4	—	64
Total	82	100	76	53	—	366
(Others)						(9)
1733 Men	—	100	—	57	—	266
Women	—	100	—	44	—	61
Total	—	100	—	55	—	327
(Others)						(17)
1760 Men	—	100	—	61	—	207
Women	—	100	—	47	—	97
Total	—	100	—	57	—	304
(Others)						(11)
1783 Men	81	100	90	66	56	195
Women	83	100	83	49	37	63
Total	81	100	88	62	52	258
(Others)						(17)

and, indeed, why men and women went there in the first place. No simple answer can be given; if poverty and a lack of abundant cultivable land in the countryside undoubtedly were behind the immigration of the unskilled workers, the same can not be said of the artisans, shopkeepers, businessmen, professionals and office-holders, for whom it was, in varying ways, a stage in their careers, and for whom Vannes was one of perhaps two or three towns they would move to during the course of their lives. Similarly, it is difficult to demonstrate any one predominant characteristic of those who disappeared in comparison to those who stayed. Tables II-10 to II-14 show what can be said of the different occupations, wealth and status of those members of the sample who stayed and left. There is evidently a rough correspondence to the ladder of wealth and prestige here. Thus, among the occupational groups, the most permanent were the officers and professional men, followed, however, not by merchants, or men in the luxury trades, but rather by woodworkers, the building trades, and those in the hotel and food trades. Perhaps the necessity of building up and keeping a clientele of regular customers was a reason why these people did not move on so readily. After them came the various other tradesmen, then those engaged in agriculture and, predictably, day-labourers, the least permanent of all. One can also detect a certain tendency for the wealthy, and those employing servants, to stay on. Of those who had servants, only about 38 per cent disappeared after five years, while 44 per cent of those without servants had vanished.

Table II-10: Per cent of men in sample who stay, who disappear, and who move to other quarters

Interval	Per cent remaining	Per cent disappearance	Per cent internal migration	Number of men in sample
1704–9	41	44	15	302
1733–8	49	43	8	266
1760–5	48	39	13	207
1783–8	60	34	6	195
1703–4	71*	16	13	302
1704–5	58	20	22	302
1782–3	78*	19	3	195
1783–4	88	10	2	195
1783–9	50	44	6	195

* Per cent of sample of 1704 present in 1703; per cent of sample of 1783 present in 1782.

The general trend across the century was towards greater stability of population in Vannes. At first glance, this might seem to contradict the general French experience, since it is known that in all areas of France in the eighteenth-century where the phenomenon of migration to towns has been studied, mainly by counting the origins of marriage partners, the proportion of outsiders whose names appear on records was on the increase,[30] but this is not really incompatible with a greater tendency for immigrants to become

[30] Perrot, *Genèse d'une ville moderne*, ii, 717–20; M. Garden, *Lyon et les Lyonnais au xviiie siècle* (Paris, 1970), 79; el Kordi, *Bayeux*, 156. A decline in adult mortality might also explain some of this increased permanence.

Table II-11: Per cent of men in sample from each quarter remaining in Vannes after five years

Quarter	Period			
	1704–9	*1733–8*	*1760–5*	*1783–8*
Intra-muros	64	63	60	65
Marché	43	57	54	70
Boucherie	48	55	46	73
Port	68	62	81	60
St-Patern	55	52	62	61
(Officers)	—	(75)	(80)	(100)

permanently established in towns; it means merely that decisions to move led to more permanent displacements than had once been the case, and it is natural that more of these previously temporary migrants' names should appear in parish records as long-term moves become more common. As to why greater permanence in this town should have been the case, no easy answer can be given. For migrants of rural origin, it may be that the modest general rise in population down to 1770 made it increasingly difficult for the country to re-absorb larger numbers of young adults. For people of higher standing who came of age in the town or moved to it from comparable circumstances, it may signal an increasing lack of opportunity elsewhere in the province in the last generation of the old regime.

These results are suggestive, but not all of them are statistically significant, and this is not surprising, considering that there were many factors which could not be accounted for, such as varying death rates, imperfections in the documents and different patterns of age, education and migration peculiar to certain occupations. Altogether, the factors which were measured by the tax rolls— wealth, occupation, sex, the absence or presence of servants, the place of residence—accounted for about 13 per cent of the variance in the persistence of household heads by the end of the old regime, and 10 per cent at the beginning. Within these limits, it is possible to establish statistically an order of importance among these factors. When wealth, as measured by tax assessments, was held constant, it turned out that the neighbourhood a person lived in had virtually no consistent relation to a person's persistence in the town. Under the same conditions, the difference in sexes counted for something, but not a great deal, and less at the end of the century than at the

Table II-12: Per cent of men in sample remaining after five years, by level of tax payment in base year

Tax level*	Period			
	1704–9	1733–8	1760–5	1783–8
0	—	—	67	64
e–c	38	52	55	61
b–a	63	60	63	64
A–B	69	61	60	71
C–D	62	58	83	100
All	56	57	61	66

* See Table II-5 for an explanation of this classification.

Table II-13: Per cent of men in sample remaining after five years, by profession in base year

Profession	Period			
	1704–9	1733–8	1760–5	1783–8
Royal officers and professional men	57	65	63	86
Commerce and luxury trades	75	53	58	50
Food & hostelry	71	55	64	65
Artisans	61	58	62	69
Labourers	32	49	62	63
Agriculture	44	70	58	50
Unknown	50	59	54	55
Total	56	57	61	66

beginning. The occupational group to which people belonged counted for something at the beginning of the century, perhaps twice as much as a person's sex, but not at all by the end of the period. The only factor of some importance throughout (wealth still being held constant) was the presence or absence of servants, though even this was less important at the end than at the beginning of the period. Although the employment of servants and the possession of wealth were quite closely related all through the century, the tie between wealth and persistence was not strong at all at the beginning of the century: holding the variable 'wealth' constant did not alter the relationship between the presence of servants and persistence after five years. However, by the end of the period, wealth itself was much more closely tied in a direct way to persistence; the relation between employment of servants and persistence after five years was diminished by almost half.[31] When measured by simple correlation, persistence in the 1780s was linked to wealth almost as closely as it was to the employment of servants. When we consider everything else we know about the town, this suggests that such wealthy people as there were in Vannes became more settled and, as a corollary, that the place was attracting little new wealth by the end of this period. In any event, the presence of servants, itself closely tied to wealth, and the possession of means, meant the most in determining the permanent core or urban society,[32] those who 'defined' the town for the rest of the population; Vannes was apparently less of an undifferentiated way-station for people from all sorts of background at the end of the century than at the beginning.

[31] These measurements were made by the statistical technique of Multiple Classification Analysis; the best values (roughly equivalent to correlation coefficients) of these factors in explaining persistence after five years were as follows (figures for statistical significance according to an F-test are in parentheses; they give the probability that these differences were purely the result of chance—5 per cent is usually taken as a good risk):

Factor	Whole sample (weighted)	1704	1733	1760	1783
Sex	0.10(0.000)	0.12(0.033)	0.12(0.085)	0.12(0.072)	0.05(0.394)
Presence of servants	0.08(0.000)	0.11(0.037)	0.11(0.078)	0.05(0.436)	0.19(0.001)
Quarter	0.08(0.088)	0.11(0.435)	0.09(0.818)	0.14(0.250)	0.16(0.332)
Occupation	0.07(0.341)	0.19(0.063)	0.14(0.596)	0.08(0.996)	0.21(0.229)
Multiple r^2 (Proportion of variance explained)	0.05	0.10	0.05	0.06	0.13

[32] The possession of wealth and the employment of servants suggest of course several other related attributes such as age and the ownership of a house or apartment, which might explain permanence on the town. The ownership of a residence, indeed, has been said to be 'in some sense equivalent (to a decision to stay), for undoubtedly the decision to buy a house very often represented a commitment to remain within the city' (Katz, *The People of Hamilton*, 131–2). Unfortunately, the sources available for Vannes do not readily permit the measurement of these phenomena, but the importance of the related characteristics of wealth and employment of servants in explaining permanent residence suggests that, in Vannes too, they were equally significant.

Table II-14: Per cent of men in sample remaining after five years who do and do not maintain domestic servants

Interval	With servants	Without servants
1704–9	74	53
1733–8	65	56
1760–5	65	60
1783–8	85	60

But it would be unwise to put too much weight on these differences. Clearly, both rich and poor, prestigious and humble, moved into and out of Vannes in considerable numbers, each for their own reasons, whether to seek employment much as they would in the countryside, or to advance their career or standing. It is evident that there were more of the former than the latter, given the relative numbers of rich and poor in the town, and it is not surprising that most of the new arrivals should have been from the surrounding countryside. The tax rolls used for this study do not make this clear, although they suggest it, but the priests of St-Patern, the parish which received most of the migrants at the end of the century, took the trouble during the 1780s of writing down the native parish of the parents whose children they baptized. Only about 45 per cent of parents came from Vannes or the rural part of St-Patern parish: the rest were mainly from places within 25 kilometres of the town by road (34 per cent); another 13 to 16 per cent came from other localities in what was soon to become the Department of the Morbihan, 3 to 6 per cent came from the rest of Brittany, and another 2 per cent from the remainder of France. This pattern among permanent, married people is much the same as has been observed in an extremely thorough demographic study of the little town of Auray nearby.

Where did the newly arrived go? All things being equal, the appearance of men on tax rolls gives an idea of the proportions in which they chose to go to different quarters. At the beginning of the century, no particular quarter was preferred, but by the end of the old regime, St-Patern tended to be the first choice of newcomers, since it got 50 per cent of the new assessments but contained only 36 per cent of the population. Oddly, although the peripheral quarters of St-Patern, the market and the Boucherie had also been the ones from which people disappeared more readily at the beginning of the century, by the end of the old regime, the differences began to break down. Within the quarters themselves, there were still no doubt 'transient' zones where temporary citizens took up a fleeting residence, but they are difficult to pin down on the basis of a sample; at the most, the figures suggest that neighbourhoods such as the Croix Cabello, behind the church of St-Patern, and the long rue St-Yves had more than their fair share of transients.

Movement into and out of the town was not the only form of population instability either, since a certain number changed their residence each year within Vannes. The town council was perfectly aware of this, and directed that the draft of the tax roll should be prepared each year before Michaelmas, the traditional moving day.[33] It is impossible to measure precisely how many people changed residence after one year, because the tax assessors did not always assign exactly the same street name to the same houses, but one can at least measure the movement between quarters during the intervals between two assessments. Measured over a five-year period, the average annual percentage of movement for the remaining male population was 3.1 per cent in 1704–9, 1.7 per cent in 1733–8, 2.7 per cent in 1760–5 and 1.2 per cent in 1783–8. Those who moved within Vannes did so no doubt for a wide range of reasons, some to mark or attempt their social ascent, some because they were forced to seek cheaper lodging, some because of the needs of their trades. At the beginning of the century, the market and the port were the areas one left the most readily for the other parts of the town: in 1709, they had only 54 per cent and 62 per cent respectively of their 1704 male populations, while St-Patern and the Boucherie had 87 per cent, and the walled town, 74 per cent (exclusive of disappearances from rolls). By the 1730s, population movement within the town slowed down in general; the port itself became one of the most stable zones, while the market continued to be the zone of least stability. This pattern lasted into the 1760s. By the end of the old regime, people who stayed, stayed put much more in all parts of the town than they had in any earlier period.

The people who stayed behind did not remain fixed in their occupations any more than they remained completely immobile in their dwelling places. For the whole period running from 1704 to 1788, 22 per cent of the men remaining in Vannes after five years

[33] A.D. I.-V., C 4364: Diocesan commissioners, Vannes, to *Commission intermédaire*, Rennes, 2-9-1779, 12-6-1780.

had changed their occupational groups. But for nearly 5 per cent this change represented a shift into the category of those who were noted on tax rolls without any occupation at all.[34] This could imply either retirement, a retreat from active life, or simply absent-mindedness on the part of the assessor; because of this last possibility, the real rate of change was probably a little higher. Though it is difficult to make a direct comparison, the rate of professional mobility appears to be remarkably close to that observed in nineteenth-century America.[35]

It is possible to discern certain patterns of professional mobility in these statistics, but less easy to determine what they meant. Measured by the total moves out of or into each of these professional groups,[36] the liberal professions and office-holders were among the most fluid professions, but their high rates of mobility in and out—of the order of 25 per cent each way—probably indicate only that the same people had decided in each year to call themselves by a different one of the several titles which they possessed, or, if they did indeed change their function, that they were moving to a rather similar group. Thus 11 per cent of the office-holders passed to the liberal professions, but 11 per cent of the professional men became office-

[34] Based on the combined samples for all four *capitation* rolls, weighted to take account of population changes and different sample proportions in each of the sample base years (see note 25 above). The total sample in this case included 1,310 cases before weighting and 1,485 after weighting; the total population from which this was drawn numbered 6,612 cases.

[35] Knights, *Plain People*, 99; Katz, *People of Hamilton*, 143–4; but their figures include both men and women.

[36]

	Moves out of professional group (per cent) after five years	Moves into professional group (per cent) after five years
Officers	27.8	23.5
Professional men	25.7	35.0
Commerce	32.8	45.0
Food & hostelry	20.3	23.3
Luxury trades	20.1	0.0
Textile	12.5	14.2
Leather	3.1	9.0
Building trades	14.0	6.8
Woodworkers	21.0	13.2
Metalworkers	5.7	13.7
Unskilled	22.5	17.7
Agriculture	25.8	25.4
Undesignated	63.5	61.1

holders. One-fifth of the commercial men, apparently the most mobile group of all, tended either to lose all professional title, which could mean any of a variety of choices, or else to go into food and hostelry trades.

At the lower end of the scale, certain patterns of professional mobility do emerge. Men in 'agriculture', for example, tended to become simple labourers, perhaps, again, merely a change of designation rather than of activity, but it does seem significant that there was no corresponding change in the other direction on the part of unskilled workers: 21 per cent of the 'agriculture' group became labourers, but only 1 per cent of the 'labourer' group went into agriculture. Changes in this sector do therefore seem to demonstrate the process of absorption of the rural labouring poor into the urban proletariat. Below the level of the commercial men, the most stable occupations were the leather and metal trades; the least, labourers, woodworkers and the food and hostelry trades. Labourers had nowhere to go but up, and those of them who shifted occupations tended to go into the food and hostelry trades and, less frequently, woodworking, building trades and commerce; the latter shifts can only barely be termed improvements. Woodworkers were apt to turn into labourers or join the 'agriculture' sector or the leather-crafts; this was no improvement at all. It was chiefly the food trades which, next to commerce, provided the greatest avenue of change, though it was hardly a broad highway: 7 per cent of these men went into the lower liberal professions or building trades; 1 per cent into the metal trades, but 3 per cent dropped back to the estate of labourer. The recruitment of the food and hostelry sector did include members of inferior groups: 4 per cent of its members came from the textile trades, 7 per cent from the labourers. Though this may appear as a form of 'mobility' to modern eyes, such changes were more likely a sort of sideways movement, an optical illusion caused by people choosing to be designated alternately by two or more occupations they were carrying on simultaneously, or with their spouses, or between which certain tradesmen traditionally shuttled. This occupational double life even shows up in the tax documents themselves, when people are occasionally listed with two of their professions, and where the close kinship between, for example, tavern-keeping and the building trades or baking, or between inn-keeping and blacksmithing is evident. A historian who is aware of the way poor townsmen tried to turn to account any opportunity in order to scrape by[37] would be reluctant to put too much weight on the evidence, limited as it is, of professional mobility. Vannes was hardly a town of unlimited opportunity.

[37] Cf. O. Hufton, *Bayeux in the Late Eighteenth Century* (Oxford, 1967), 81–112.

CHAPTER III

THE TOWN OF VANNES: (2) URBAN SOCIETY

Whether they stayed for a lifetime or a few weeks, whether they succeeded or failed, the individuals and groups who found themselves in Vannes had somehow to make a living and to live with one another. The income of the entire town depended heavily on revenues provided by the surrounding countryside. The dominant classes drew their incomes from it either directly, from rents and dues which they collected, and from the sale of products received as rent in kind; or indirectly, by collecting rents and tithes, buying and selling grain, handling the financing of commercial operations, levying taxes, administering justice, legalizing the transfer of property and capital and dispensing the benefits of religion. To the extent that they provided goods and services for country people, the artisans, shopkeepers, labourers and poor of Vannes also made their living from the countryside, though much of it came to them indirectly from the wealthy and the propertied of the town.

When eighteenth-century observers said anything about the society they encountered in Vannes, they almost invariably alluded to the presence of a numerous and rich nobility, and this was one of the characteristics which made Vannes distinct from, say, Auray or Lorient. The nobles of Vannes were the most noticeable single group among the propertied. Twenty-eight noble families were reported resident in Vannes for tax purposes in 1783, and with all their members, they probably represented a total of a hundred or so people. The number had changed very little across the century. Of all the towns of the diocese, Vannes had the largest share of nobles resident (about 10 per cent of all noble heads of families in the diocese), and shared with Hennebont the distinction of having the greatest concentration of noble wealth.[1] In fact, the tendency of

[*p. 62 for n. 1*]

nobles to gravitate towards Vannes was rather greater than the tax rolls suggest, because so many nobles practised 'double residence', spending the growing season on their estates, away from the noxious summer air of Vannes, and only the winter in their *hôtels* or rented apartments in the town, when it had become more habitable. For some families, such as those who sat in the Parlement of Rennes, an even greater mobility must have been necessary.[2] One of the requirements for a noble to have voting rights on the town council of Vannes was that he own a house and be resident in the town with his family. Of the seven nobles who voted at one time or another in the meetings of the council in 1782 and 1783, only one, Gibon de Keralbeau, was listed on the *capitation* rolls as resident in Vannes; the rest paid the *capitation* elsewhere. Only three of these owned property in Vannes in those years; the rest probably rented apartments. In 1789–90, when the tax collectors had suddenly to include the nobles and other privileged persons in the same *capitation* roll as the commoners, fifty-eight new noble heads of families suddenly appeared on the records; of these, only twelve had owned property in Vannes in 1782–3; the remainder, once again, must have rented apartments. To be sure, some of the nobles who appeared on this later roll probably had been driven by fear of general insecurity to take refuge in Vannes, but surely not all fifty-eight families.[3] The number of noble families living at least part of the time in Vannes was thus undoubtedly much larger than indicated by the *capitation* rolls.

	Male heads of households in Vannes	Total families in Vannes	Total number of assessments in Vannes	Total number of assessments in Diocese	Total value of assessments in Vannes (livres)	Total value of assessments in Diocese (livres)
1694	20	—	—	—	—	—
1735	17	21	29	282	1,843	16,519
1760	21	31	35	301	1,789	13,068
1783	20	28	38	338	1,298	15,359

A.D. I.-V., C 4272–4: Capitation de Messieurs de la noblesse, 1735, 1760, 1783; 'Rolles des gentilshommes sujets au Ban de l'Évêché de Vannes', 1694, in Guyot-Jomard, 'La Ville de Vannes et ses murs', *BSPM* (1887), 68–75.

[2] Meyer, *La Noblesse bretonne*, i, 190–2; ii, 1220–4.

[3] A.D. Morbihan, C: Commission intermédiaire de Vannes, 4 paroisses de Vannes, vingtième, 1782–3; A.C. Vannes, CC 7: ci-devant privilégiés [1789 or 1790]; Le Goff, 'Vannes', 47 n. 15.

With this constant movement of noble households, it is not surprising that there were few families who stayed on to dominate the town for long periods of time. Roughly speaking, about one-half of noble families disappeared from the *capitation* listings for the town in every generation. By 1783, of the score of noble families from Vannes whose heads had appeared for Louis XIV's *arrière-ban* of 1694, only one can be identified for certain as still paying the *capitation* there. The other noble families had not all disappeared; many simply moved over the course of two or more generations, following the changing lures of marriage alliances, inheritances and careers. In fact, it is almost impossible to speak of the town nobility apart from the other nobles of the region. Like many of the common folk of Vannes, the local nobility moved easily from country to town and back again.

Yet if they resembled so many of their fellow townsmen in this, they were set apart from the mass of the population by their wealth, though they were not the only wealthy folk in Vannes. In a town where the mean *capitation* payment for people of the Third Estate was about 9 livres in 1783, the average payment of nobles was 34 livres; it had been considerably higher earlier in the century (and the *capitation* was generally criticized for treating nobles more leniently than commoners). In comparison with the nobles of the rest of the diocese, those in Vannes and its region had tended to have rather more 'poor' and wealthy nobles than in the diocese as a whole, though by 1783, this pattern had been reversed, and there were less extremes of noble wealth and 'poverty' in and around Vannes than in the diocese as a whole.[4] But these figures probably do not mean much. Many of the richer nobles paying taxes in the countryside were permanent absentees, either in Paris, Rennes or elsewhere, while the ranks of the 'poor nobility' were swollen in Vannes by widows and *pensionnaires* of convents, dependent for support on families who were taxed elsewhere.

It is a more interesting task to try to compare the wealth of the nobles with that of the bourgeoisie, but the task is not easy. Only one tax was levied on noble and commoner on a supposedly equal basis; this was the *vingtième,* but the *vingtième* measured only the value of income from property, and for some bourgeois engaged in trade, landed wealth constituted only a small part of their riches; in

---

[4] Cf. Meyer, *La Noblesse bretonne,* i, 15–16 for figures from 1710.

any case, *vingtième* rolls list only the property held in each parish. The *capitation*, the principal tax on overall wealth, was assessed on a different scale for nobles, non-noble townsmen, and the people of the countryside. Tables of *partages*, which should give the value of all successions[5] are inadequate in Vannes because of the negligence of the bureaux. However, two documents from the revolutionary period do give at least a hint of the relative riches of nobles and bourgeois. The first is the record of the forced loan of the Year II, based in theory on the overall wealth of the sixty-five most prosperous individuals of the commune. Of the 16 individuals taxed in the upper quartile (the upper 25 per cent), 12 were former nobles, but below this point, nobles become much less frequent, so that the total number of nobles paying the tax was only 29 out of 65 and the total amount of declared revenue in noble hands was only 54 per cent of the total.[6] Of course it is possible that the revolutionary authorities may have tried to victimize nobles, but on the other hand, several local nobles had emigrated by the time of this loan, so that nobles are probably underrepresented in this list.

A second source for the wealth of the local nobility is a list drawn up in 1791 by the barrister Jollivet, who estimated annual revenues from lands held under the system of tenure known as the *domaine congéable*.[7] This enumeration was supposed to serve as a basis for contributions towards the expense of lobbying the National Assembly for the defence of this system of landholding, which was then under attack from the more radical revolutionaries. Here, the assessment was on the basis of landed wealth alone, and of landed wealth of a particular kind. Nevertheless, as the *domaine congéable* was the most prevalent form of leasehold in the area, this estimate of revenues by a man who, as a notary, knew intimately the wealth of the local landlords is of some interest. The pattern was again the same. Of the highest assessed quarter of the names, at least 16 of 19 were nobles (though not all were residents of Vannes), but below

[5] M. Vovelle, 'Structure et répartition de la fortune foncière et de la fortune mobilière d'un ensemble urbain: Chartres, de la fin de l'ancien régime à la Restauration', *RHES*, xxxvi (1958), 385–98.

[6] A.D. Morbihan, L 1469: Matrice du rôle de l'emprunt forcé ordonné par la loi du 3 septembre 1793, reproduced in Le Goff, 'Vannes', 361–2.

[7] A.D. Morbihan, E 1072 (fonds Jollivet): Répartition de la somme de sept mille six cent soixante quatorze livres montant des avances qui ont eu lieu pour la défense de la propriété foncière des domaines congéables . . . [1791] reproduced in Le Goff, 'Vannes', 363–5.

this level, the local bourgeoisie appears again in force. In the quarter of persons immediately above the median assessment, only 9 (of 19) were nobles. The total number of nobles reported on this list, which includes 75 names, was only 35. The conclusion from this is, that if some of the nobles in the area formed the bulk of the wealthiest part of the local population, there were many more on the same economic level as the wealthier commoners who, indeed, outnumbered them in the 'second rank' of fortunes. This is especially true when we consider the nature of bourgeois fortunes, a larger proportion of which were likely to be tied up in commercial and financial investment than among the nobility.

Although nobles and bourgeois were sometimes equal in wealth, the gulf between them, in legal theory and popular belief, was great. Perhaps the most significant trait of the Breton nobility in the eighteenth century was its fierce pride of caste, reinforced by a sense of confidence created by its domination of the political and administrative institutions of the province, and by an economic situation in which their fortunes were, on the whole, prospering. What established an individual's right to be accepted as a peer by this group? The principle followed through the eighteenth century was that laid down at the great *réformation* of the nobility in 1668: proof that a family had been one of those mentioned in the *réformations* of the fifteenth and sixteenth centuries or that a family had divided successions 'nobly' (two-thirds to the eldest son) for three generations.[8] A family which had succeeded in establishing its titles in this way when the *réformation* of 1668 took place was sure of acceptance, and the decisions of the commissioners who directed that inquiry had the effect of fixing the boundaries of the nobility of Brittany for the next century, confirming it as a tightly defined group, conscious of its privileges and sure of its lineage.[9]

The nobility, if it presented a united front against the pretensions of commoners, was by no means a homogeneous group, but there is no sign that their internal differences mattered very much to them. It is possible to trace the 'quality' of the noble titles held by thirteen of the twenty-eight nobles taxed as residents of Vannes in 1781.[10]

[8] Meyer, *La Noblesse bretonne*, i, 107.
[9] Ibid. i, 164 and H. Bourde de la Rogerie, 'Étude sur la réformation de la noblesse en Bretagne (1668–1721)', *MSHAB*, iii (1922), 237–312.
[10] The sources for this study were, in addition to the tax rolls mentioned above, R. de Laigue, *La Noblesse bretonne aux xve et xvie siècles. Réformations et montres.* [*p. 66 for n. 10 cont.*]

Four had been judged 'noblesse d'ancienne extraction de chevalerie',[11] by the inquiry of 1668; four, 'noblesse d'ancienne extraction',[12] which meant that they had titles dating from before 1550.[13] Another two of the fourteen remaining families were in all probability possessors of noble fiefs or reckoned as nobles in the course of the fifteenth and sixteenth centuries.[14] It has sometimes been said that the nobility of the 'sword' were an economically declining group, eclipsed by the wealth of the more recent 'robe' nobles, but in Vannes at least there was no obvious distinction in fortune between different kinds of nobles in the eighteenth century, probably because the old nobility was so well represented in the Parlement of Brittany. The wealthiest nobles in the town, the brothers Le Charpentier de Lenvos and Le Charpentier de Keronic (who paid 380 livres in *capitation* between them in 1781) were both *conseillers* in the Parlement of Brittany and their nobility was fairly recent, dating from 1648, but the next most highly taxed was Roscanvec de la Landel, the head of a family without any close *parlementaire* relations (who paid 205 livres in *capitation* in the same year). Somewhat further down the scale of wealth were Jean-François-Ignace Dondel and his son Jean-Jacques-Hyacinthe (120 livres in *capitation*), descendants of rather recently ennobled stock, with former *parlementaire* connections, once important in the local courts, but whose only visible occupation was now soldiering. Paying a little less than the Dondels was de Langle, scion of a former *parlementaire* family as well, but a family whose nobility went back to the fourteenth century. In short, there was no necessary connection between the particular occupation of a noble, the age of his title, and his wealth.

A noble's chances of bettering his economic position through professional and economic activity in and about Vannes were rather limited. Most noble revenues came from tenants holding land under *domaine congéable*, a complicated local form of leasehold. The necessity of marketing these rents, paid for the most part in grain,

Tome I: Evêché de Vannes (Rennes, 1902), 2 t.; R. Kerviler, *Répertoire général de bio-bibliographie bretonne . . . livre 1: Les Bretons*, i–xvii (Rennes–Vannes, 1886–1908); F. Saulnier, *Le Parlement de Bretagne 1554–1790* (Rennes, 1909), 2 vols; Meyer, *La Noblesse bretonne;* H. Frotier de la Messelière, *Filiations bretonnes 1650–1912* (St-Brieuc, 1912, rpt. Mayenne, 1965).
[11] Du Plessis-Grénédan, Lescouet, Langle, Porcaro.
[12] Gibon (3 families) and de Lesquen.
[13] P. du Puy de Clinchamps, *La Noblesse* (Paris, 1962), 14–15.
[14] Roscanvec de la Landelle and Du Pallivart.

tied the local nobles closely to the fluctuations of the old regime commercial economy. Nobles and other landed proprietors usually sold their grain for hard cash to merchants acting on their own account or as commission agents for the larger *négociants* of Bordeaux, Nantes and the Spanish ports of the Atlantic; only rarely did nobles participate directly in commercial speculation on grain exports.[15] In a year when there was strong external or internal demand, they stood to profit, and displayed little reluctance in doing so. The correspondence of Ignace Advisse Desruisseaux, one of the most important of the local grain merchants, is full of complaints against the 'rentiers', as he called them. 'Vous savez par expérience', he wrote to his Bordeaux correspondent in 1779, 'la dureté, de traîter cette branche [of trade] avec nos propriétaires, il n'y a encore que ceux pressés d'argent qui vendent leurs seigles par petites parties.'[16] Desruisseaux, who had spent almost fifty years in the trade, claimed in the 1770s that the proprietors had become harder bargainers than ever before, and perhaps one can see reflected in his remarks the difficulties caused by the price recession of the 1770s and 1780s:

Il serait avantageux [he wrote] au commerce et aux peuples que les grains restassent chez vous à Bordcaux et ailleurs sans agitation pour ramener à la raison nos proprietaires aiguillonés il y a plusieurs années . . . il n'est plus possible d'entrer en marché avec nos rentiers, les plus modestes exigent aujourd'hui 150 [livres par tonneau] peut-être demain ne les voudront-ils pas et la plus grande partie ne veulent vendre que cet hiver.[17]

The strong position of the nobles and other landed proprietors had only one weak point, hinted at by Desruisseaux in these letters—the shortage of cash. In a year with good harvests and no external demand, or when the royal administration was forced by fear of riots to close off the export of grain, 'ceux pressés d'argent' stood to lose heavily, or at least to be forced to tighten their belts. The apparent security of the nobles' landed incomes was not as unshakeable as one might think.

Besides collecting their revenues from the land, most of the

[15] The only example I have found is in A.D. Morbihan, 11 B 23 and 11 B 53 (8) both *c.* 1754. This was an association between the grain merchant Desruisseaux, Provost and the noble G.-R. de Talhouet de Keraveon for shipment of wheat and rye to Faro in Portugal. Talhouet lost money on the venture.

[16] A.D. Morbihan, 11 B 56: Desruisseaux to Guérin de Malagué, Bordeaux, 31-1-1779; to Gibert, Bordeaux, 3-10-1778.

[17] A.D. Morbihan, 11 B 56: Desruisseaux to Vignes, Bordeaux, 1778.

nobles of the Vannetais also followed careers, although few were very exalted ones. None served the King as 'administrators' in that group of nobles which historians have called retrospectively the 'noblesse d'état' or 'de service', although the La Bourdonnaye-Coetcandec family had intendants in other branches of their family.[18] Of the 27 families in the region around Vannes paying *capitation* taxes in 1781 on the roll of the nobility, only 11 had representatives serving on the Parlement at one time or another during the century. The number of nobles serving in lower courts in the region was also small. One noble of an old family, R.-R. de Kermoizan, a former *conseiller ordinaire* of the Parlement of Brittany, was an *avocat du roi* in the Présidial of Vannes from 1765 to 1773 and *procureur du roi* of the *maréchaussée* of Brittany in 1774. A half dozen *anoblis* drifted in and out of the higher positions of the Présidial of Vannes: thus F.-H. Dondel, J.-A. Senant, Symon-Joseph Borie and Charles-François Le Gros, all sons of *anoblis,* helped gild their titles by holding the offices of *sénéchal* and *président.* A noble, probably a recent one, from Ploërmel, Pierre-Toussaint Houet de Chênevert was *procureur du roi* in the same court. If it was theoretically possible for a Breton to become a notary without losing noble status, none of the nobles of the Vannetais ever sank so low in the legal hierarchy and their own esteem as to assume this office, although most of this little group of *anoblis* accumulated offices in the other royal jurisdictions in the town, the Admiralty Court and the *traites.*[19] One or two *anoblis* also specialized in financial posts, but no financial officers—with possibly one exception[20]—were of families ennobled before 1700.

The Church was an outlet for some nobles, but less than might be imagined. It has been claimed that the Breton nobility shunned ecclesiastical careers increasingly as the century went by.[21] Some

[18] Meyer, *La Noblesse bretonne,* ii, 909.

[19] Le Goff, 'Vannes', 366–71, for lists of officers. On Kermoizan, see Saulnier, *Le Parlement de Bretagne,* ii, 550–1; Frotier de la Messelière, *Filiations bretonnes,* iii, 284–6; on Houet, P. Thomas-Lacroix, 'La Vie économique et sociale à Ploërmel avant la Révolution', *MSHAB,* xliv (1964), 153. According to A.D. Morbihan, K 1535: *Extrait du registre des délibérations de la ville et communauté de Vannes, en Bretagne,* 23-1-1789, Houët was only recently ennobled.

[20] J.-F. Laurens de Kercadio, who succeeded his father as receiver for the *fouages extraordinaires* of the diocese in 1742 and held office, with some difficulty, to 1764. According to Meyer, *La Noblesse bretonne,* i, 159, 396, Kercadio was of the 'petite noblesse'.

[21] Ibid. ii, 1151–2.

may, of course, have emigrated to serve in other dioceses, but it is certainly true that in the diocese of Vannes the number of nobles in the lower clergy was infinitesimal. Many nobles who entered the priesthood (one only has to look at the thumbnail biographies of the canons of the cathedral reported in the abbé Luco's *Pouillé historique*) received their training outside the diocese, especially in Paris; but as the proportion of all 'outsiders' in the diocese holding livings had shrunk from 26 per cent of the rectors in 1730 to 6 per cent in 1789, the number of nobles who entered the ranks of the lower clergy in this way could not have been significant.[22]

Where the nobility did continue to survive in the Church in the diocese of Vannes was in the ranks of the upper clergy. Most of the fourteen canons of the cathedral of Vannes were nobles. Certain local families, indeed, seemed to have an almost indecent prominence there. Thus the de Langle family in the persons of Augustin de Langle (1709–29) and Anne-Michel de Langle (1729–43) held two prebends in the eighteenth century, like the family of Du Clos Bossard, with Jean Bossard, sieur du Clos, canon from 1662 to 1716 and M.-C.-A. Bossard sieur du Clos, *scholastique* from 1743 to 1775. The record accumulation of cathedral stalls in the period, however, was held by the Boutouillic family, with four canons, Jean-Joseph (1718–41), Vincent-Jean-Louis (1741–81), Philippe-Jean (1760–90) and Jean-Louis (1781–90). Two local families provided bishops in the late seventeenth and early eighteenth centuries: Daniel Francheville, bishop of Périgueux (1694–1702) and Jean-François Dondel, sometime canon (1710–49), treasurer (1721–34) and archdeacon (1734–40) of Vannes, a resolute ànti-Jansenist who ended his days as bishop of Dol (1748–67).[23] The normal prebend of a canon, 2,700 to 3,000 livres at the end of the old regime, was not large. Those who held subsidiary benefices, like P.-J. Boutouillic, whose living from the abbey of Hyverneaux, near Paris, brought his annual revenue up to 11,337 livres, could survive on their ecclesiastical incomes alone. Other, such as his nephew J.-L. de la Boutouillic, may have had to rely in part on their own fortunes.[24] Perhaps for this

[22] *Pouillé historique de l'ancien diocèse de Vannes, bénéfices séculiers*, 2nd ed. (Vannes, 1908), 50–68. On the origins of the lower clergy see Chapter IX, pp. 249–54 below.

[23] Luco, *Pouillé*, 50–68 and J.-M. Le Mené, *Histoire du diocèse de Vannes* (Vannes, 1889), 129–30, 155, 194.

[24] A.N., D xix 17 (260): Traitement du clergé séculier et régulier, 12-1-1791. One
[*p. 70 for n. 24 cont.*]

reason, the local nobility was also deserting the dignities of the choir stalls, for while at least a half dozen of the fourteen canons of Vannes had been local nobles in mid-century, there were only three (including the two members of the Boutouillic family) left in 1789.

For women of the nobility, as for those of the upper bourgeoisie, there were places in the 'better' convents, such as that of the Ursulines or the convent of Notre-Dame de Charité, or the Hospitalières de Saint-Nicholas. The dowry was relatively small; the grain merchant Desruisseaux paid some 2,500 livres for each of his two daughters who entered the nursing order in the 1750s, and a minor colonial official on St-Pierre and Miquelon got his daughter accepted by the Carmelites in return for surrendering his pension of 150 livres a year.[25] Once established, sons and daughters were maintained for the rest of their lives, and their shares of any inheritances would never be permanently lost to the family. Convents and monasteries, as the local Jacobin and anticlerical, J.-M. Le Quinio said, rather uncharitably, 'sont, dit-on, une ressource pour les nombreuses familles; c'est-a-dire, qu'elles sont le grenier de l'État, où l'on relègue les meubles inutiles.'[26]

Other possibilities existed. The first was to engage in colonial trade, hanging up the sword, like Chateaubriand's father, until the family fortunes were re-established. Others, with sufficient money, could invest directly in commerce. None from Vannes did either, as far as I have been able to determine. Heavy investment in the colonial trade was in any case the prerogative of certain 'new men' and of the upper nobility, and the most extensive investments of this kind made in the Vannetais were small outlays of capital entrusted to merchants or sea-captains for the purchase of *pacotilles* (small cargoes of trading-goods) taken privately by owners, masters and officers of ships on overseas trade.[27] The *président* of the Présidial of Vannes, F.-H. Dondel, the son of *anoblis*, was particularly given to this kind of trading. In the 1750s and 1760s he helped finance several shipments of cloth to South America and the West Indies from

of the peculiarities of the canonical prebends was that a portion of the revenue came from rents charged for the use of salt-marshes.

[25] Ibid., État des religieux et religieuses en communauté au premier décembre 1790; A.D. Morbihan, E 2259³; A.N. Colonies, E 159: Dossier Dupleix Silvain, pc. 51, 18-3-1784.

[26] B.L., F 108 (6): J.-M. Le Quinio, *Suppression des religieux, extinction de la mendicité* (Rennes, 1789), 13–14; see also Meyer, *La Noblesse bretonne*, i, 128–34.

[27] Ibid. ii, 833, 1223.

Spain and Brittany, made by the St-Malo merchant Magon and his Cadiz associates, as well as one or two fishing ventures to the Grand Banks.[28]

In so far as the nobles of Vannes and its region in the eighteenth century sought employment, it was chiefly in the army or navy. To prove this systematically is impossible, but of the eldest sons of the eight noble families whose genealogies were traced by Frotier de la Messelière, two served in the Parlement of Rennes,[29] two in lesser jurisdictions,[30] fourteen in the army,[31] three in the navy,[32] and six were untraceable, or else did nothing but collect *rentes*.[33] The predominance of the military career is immediately evident, although the preference given to soldiering over the sea is rather surprising. In any event, the historian is far from the sophisticated world of the Parlements, not to speak of the salons of Versailles and Paris, among these sturdy *militaires* of the old regime.

It was the relative concentration and wealth of so many of these noble families in Vannes, and their existence there side by side with representatives of a bourgeoisie, some of whose members at least were just as wealthy as they, which seems to have given a distinctive character to the town, setting it apart from the other towns of the region such as Auray and Pontivy where there were few nobles, and Lorient, which had scarcely any at all. According to one outside observer, La Vallée

Une espèce de rivalité a amené cette nuance aimable que l'on ne retrouve pas également dans les autres petites villes du département. La fierté de la *noblesse bretonne* était extrême, et l'emportait sur tout ce qu'on rapporte de ridicule à cet égard des autres contrées de la France.

Jamais ce que l'on appellait alors bourgeoisie n'était reçue dans la société des personnages *blasonnés* et *écartelés*. Les *nobles* de ce pays s'étaient condamnés à s'ennuyer augustement. L'homme ou la femme les plus aimables n'eussent jamais été admis; les plaisirs, même les besoins indiqués par la

---

[28] Sée, 'Le Commerce maritime de la Bretagne au xviiie siècle, I: Le commerce de Saint-Malo au xviiie siècle, d'après les papiers des Magon', *Mémoires et documents*, ed. Hayem. 9e série, 67, 84, 94, 99, 103.

[29] De Langle (2).

[30] Dondel (2).

[31] Then from the families of Dondel (3), de Langle (1), de Lesquen (2), Le Maignen de Kerangat (2), Du Plessis-Grenédan (3), Francheville (1), Gibon (1, served subsequently in the navy), Lantivy (same remark).

[32] Gibon, Lantivy and Francheville.

[33] La Bourdonnaye, Le Charpentier, Derval, Descartes, Francheville, Le Gouvello, Kermoisan, Lantivy-Trédion, Gibon du Pargo, Le Prestre de Châteaugiron, Robien de Camezon.

nature, ne pouvaient les réunir; et le *noble* que l'on aurait convaincu d'avoir mangé avec un *bourgeois*, ou dansé avec une bourgeoise, *ipso facto* eut été rejeté du sein de la *matricule chapitrale*. D'après cet usage absurde, ce qu'il était de bon ton d'appeler *bonne compagnie* se divisait en deux castes, la société des *nobles* et la société dite du port; c'etait la bourgeoisie; et en vérité la plus agréable.[34]

Exclusiveness is a characteristic which, almost by definition, is usually associated with nobility, and particularly the Breton nobility. In real life, the links between nobles and commoners, in Vannes and elsewhere, were rather more complex than in La Vallée's caricature; the barriers between them no less real, but more subtle. In their choice of marriage partners, for example, the nobility of Vannes were by no means restricted to the offspring of their peers in the town and to those of a few aspiring *bourgeois gentilshommes* of Vannes; they had all the province to choose from. It is the mobility of the eighteenth- century Breton nobles which makes it so hard to assess the degree to which commoners were marrying into their order. Certainly, such marriages did take place, but it is difficult to say how representative they were and what they meant. Marriage contracts were drawn up and marriage ceremonies were most often held in the bride's parish, so that the records of a family's marriages were scattered through the parish registers of the whole province, and even beyond its boundaries. Genealogies, if they were complete, would be an invaluable help. Unfortunately, even the best collections by Breton antiquaries have the failing that they are concerned mainly with tracing the lineages through the eldest male; the marriages of the younger sons and daughters are not always mentioned.

With these qualifications in mind, it is nevertheless interesting to ask, on the basis of those marriages of local nobles recorded in the least unreliable of the genealogical collections, how easy it was to marry into the nobility. One test is to take the marriages of those twenty-seven families resident in Vannes in 1781 whose marriages are recorded between 1700 and 1789 by the genealogists Frotier de la Messelière, Saulnier and Kerviler. The total number of marriages is rather low—twenty-four in all—but of these, nine were with the daughters of bourgeois, fifteen with the daughters of nobles. A second test is to take all the marriages of *parlementaires* from the entire region in the eighteenth century recorded in Saulnier's excel-

---

[34] La Vallée, Biron and Biron, *Voyage dans les départemens de la France*, 9–10.

lent genealogical survey. Out of a total of twenty-two marriages of the sons of eleven families,[35] three were to the daughters of bourgeois, ten to nobles, seven to *parlementaire* nobles, and two were untraceable. The number of marriages examined is small, yet it bears comparison with Jean Meyer's figures for the whole of the *parlementaire* nobility in the eighteenth century: 46 per cent to the daughters of nobles, 30 per cent to those of *parlementaires,* and 21 per cent to those of bourgeois and *anoblis.*[36]

It would probably be wrong, however, to conclude from this evidence that the nobility of Vannes was an 'open' class. As far as the bourgeoisie of the town was concerned, only five of their daughters married into the noble families studied in this group, and only two into families ennobled before the seventeenth century—and of these five fortunate ones, all came from families living 'nobly'.[37] It seems, moreover, rather misleading to speak of a *bourgeoise* who abandons her class as an example of social mobility; unless the nobility was moving into 'bourgeois' professions and ways of life, which by and large they were not, it appears rather to be a means of perpetuating the existing situation.

Social mobility in Vannes took rather the classic form of the old regime, in which families rose gradually and almost imperceptibly over several generations into gentility, gradually replenishing the ranks of the nobility. The process, however, was not simple, and expressions such as 'replenish the ranks of the nobility' scarcely approximate the slow, patient fashion in which a family insinuated itself over several generations into the upper levels of local society. Even the attainment of the legal status of nobility was unsatisfactory until a man was accepted by his peers. As the saying went, the King could make a noble, but not a gentleman. Beyond the legal frontiers of the nobility marked by the simple acquisition of a title—which any commoner could buy in eighteenth-century France if he had enough money—lay the social no-man's-land of the *anobli,* strewn with social pitfalls where a false step could delay acceptance by *honnêtes gens* for a generation or more.

[35] La Bourdonnaye, Le Charpentier, Derval, Descartes, Francheville, Le Gouvello, Kermoisan, Lantivy-Trédion, Gibon du Pargo, Le Prestre de Châteaugiron, Robien de Camezon.

[36] Meyer, *La Noblesse bretonne,* ii, 958.

[37] Vincente-Thérèse Touzée and Renée-Jeanne Le Bartz, first and second wives of F.-N. du Plessis-Grénédan; Claude-Danielle de Lourme, wife of J.-J. Bossard du Clos, Anne-Jeanne de Lourme, wife of P.-F. Dondel du Faoëdic; Rose-Edmé-Anne Jan de Bellefontaine, wife of P.-F.-V. du Plessis de Grénédan.

If we look at the *anoblis* of the Vannetais in the later eighteenth century, we can discern several who, if they were nobles, were certainly not considered *gentilshommes*. The prime example of the *parvenu* is the crafty, rich and powerful financier Laurent Bourgeois, half-Lorientais, half-Vannetais, the *régisseur* of the *octrois* and treasurer of the town of Lorient, receiver of the *fouages extraordinaires* of Vannes, *fermier* of the *devoirs* of Brittany. He owed his ennoblement to his influence at Versailles and the nobility of Brittany hated him for his wealth, his sudden rise, and his relations with the royal government.[38] Yet others had set out in the same way as Bourgeois and by the end of the eighteenth century their families had reached the havens of respectability. The Dondel family had started their ascent in the person of Yves Dondel, sieur de Pendreff, a shipowner of Hennebont in the later sixteenth century. Yves's grandson, François, a shipowner like his grandfather, became a *syndic* of the town; his brother Thomas, also a shipowner, acquired the *ferme générale* of the dioceses of Quimper and Vannes, and apparently laid the foundations of the family's prosperity under the reign of Louis XIV. His eldest son, Jean, became the chaplain of Charlotte-Élisabeth of Bavaria, the King's sister-in-law; the second son, Pierre, combined the career of musketeer with that of *sénéchal* of Vannes and *lieutenant-général* of the *Amirauté;* the third, Marc, was also a musketeer and then *trésorier-général des finances en Bretagne* and *trésorier-général de France;* the fourth, *sénéchal* of Quimper. This was the *parvenu* generation; at the *réformation* of the nobility in 1668, although they had claimed to be of old Norman noble stock, they prudently refrained from trying to prove it to the royal commissioners. In 1699 when they did try to press their claims, they were refused by the intendant, and it was only in 1707 that they managed to have their pretensions accepted. In the next generation, the *anoblis* gained respectability in the person of J.-F. Dondel, canon of Vannes in 1710, eventually bishop of Dol (1748–67) and P.-H. Dondel de Kergonano, *sénéchal* of Vannes like his father. The latter, eager to show his loyalty to his new estate, joined the marquis de Piré and the bishop of Rennes in the notorious *Réponse des États de Bretagne au mémoire du duc d'Aiguillon* in 1770, a

---

[38] Meyer, *La Noblesse bretonne,* i, 396–7; C. Cestari, 'La Ville de l'Orient et les classes sociales au xviiiᵉ siècle selon les rôles de capitation' (*Mémoire* for the Diplôme d'Études Supérieures, Faculté des Lettres, Université de Poitiers, 1967), 92.

violent defence of the privileges of Brittany (and of the nobility) against the royal government. His son, Jean-François-Ignace completed the *cursus honorum* by abandoning the minor magistrature for the army; his grandson, Jean-Jacques-Hyacinthe, achieved the apotheosis of the family's career by emigrating in 1791, escaping capture at the attempted *émigré* invasion at Quiberon Bay in 1795, and having himself shot as a royalist agent in 1796.[39]

The career of the Dondels was paralleled by that of the Boutouillic family, as was their unswerving loyalty to the interests of their new-found estate. At the *réformation* of 1699, they were forced to withdraw their pretensions to the nobility. Their family had been ennobled in 1630 by the purchase of the office of *secrétaire du Roi;* of course they claimed titles 300 years old. Subsequently they had been active in maritime commerce for several years, and the *Chambre de réformation* did not willingly grant the privilege of *noblesse dormante* except to old, established families. In 1717, the family was reinstalled in its noble status. This generation of *parvenus* was represented by G.-F. Boutouillic de la Porte de Kergonan, a *conseiller* in the Présidial of Vannes and V.-J.-L. Boutouillic de la Villegonan, a canon of the cathedral of Vannes and a fierce opponent of Jansenism. The next generation abandoned the robe: J.-H.-F. Boutouillic de la Villegonan (1732–90) joined the army. His children emigrated and some were shot after Quiberon; their uncle, P.-J. Boutouillic de la Villegonan (1734–?), another canon of Vannes, took to guerrilla warfare and headed the royalist council of the Morbihan in 1795.[40]

By the end of the eighteenth century, families such as these appear to have made their way in local society, and one can see a pattern of advancement through successive generations from riches (commerce or financial offices) through offices in lesser judicial courts, to the military career, followed perhaps by the honourable leisure of the rentier. Some members of the Third Estate in the Vannetais were caught in 1789 in a contradiction between their lifelong aspirations to noble status and the political changes which

---

[39] On the Dondel family, see Kerviler, *Bio-bibliographie bretonne*, fasc. 33, 231–7; Saulnier, *Le Parlement de Bretagne*, 305–6; Frotier de la Messelière, *Filiations bretonnes*, ii, 166–9; Meyer, *La Noblesse bretonne*, i, 216, 218; A.D. Morbihan, L 1446: District of Vannes to citizen Dufresne St-Léon, 20-10-1792.

[40] Kerviler, *Bio-bibliographie bretonne*, fasc. 14, 95–7; Saulnier, *Le Parlement de Bretagne*, 149; Meyer, *La Noblesse bretonne*, i, 143, 255 n. 3, 315 n. 5, 318. Cf. the family of Du Clos Bossard, which had a similar ascent, in Kerviler, op. cit. fasc. 10, 415–19; Meyer, op. cit. i, 354 n. 5.

threatened to wipe out the social hierarchy they had struggled so hard to ascend. The family of Guillo Dubodan, for example, an old established clan of Vannetais, had begun in the early seventeenth century as a family of barristers and notaries. One of the younger sons, *noble homme* (the title was merely honorific) Grégoire Guillo married Olive Daviers, the daughter of a prominent merchant, in 1678 and this was the origin of a series of alliances between merchants and lawyers. Grégoire's two known descendants, Jean-Baptiste and Joseph-Ange became equally prominent merchants, made a decent fortune in the grain trade, dabbled in the slave trade, and became mayors of Vannes. Joseph-Ange (1717–55) acquired the office of a *secrétaire du Roi* from the chancery of the Parlement of Toulouse and referred to himself as *écuyer*, as did his son, Jean-Vincent Guillo du Bodan (1726–?). Jean-Vincent's eldest son, Barthélémy-Ange-Xavier (1753–1842) was still calling himself *écuyer* in September 1789, but he sensed which way the wind was blowing and became a convinced, if moderate, revolutionary, in the style of the 'men of 1789'.[41] Some in this transitional state were slower to sense the change in the climate of political life. Le Gros, *sénéchal* and son of an *anobli* from Hennebont, only gradually came round to moderate support for the Revolution.[42] Others whose nobility was as recent as that of Le Gros and Dubodan could not accept the change; François-Armand Castagne, the son of François Castagne, ennobled for his exemplary military career in 1763, was denounced to the *Société des amis de la Constitution* of Vannes in February 1791 for having played mocking tunes on a violin while the local revolutionaries were organizing to repel a mass attack by the peasants.[43]

No doubt most prominent bourgeois of Vannes nourished this ultimate hope of raising themselves and their families into the nobility until the eve of the Revolution. The hope, however, was restricted to the members of about two score families who composed

[41] A.C. Vannes, BB 16: 15-4-1746; GG 46–63: St-Patern, Baptêmes, mariages, décès, 1700–90. Barthélémy's son, F.-M. Guillo du Bodan (1794–1872) became a well-known conservative jurist under the July Monarchy and the Second Republic; see Frotier de la Messelière, *Filiations bretonnes*, iii, 569–71; J.-L. Debauve, *La Justice révolutionnaire dans le Morbihan 1790–1795* (Paris, 1965), 109.

[42] Below, Chapter IV, p. 140 and Meyer, *La Noblesse bretonne*, i, 358; Frotier de la Messelière, *Filiations bretonnes*, ii, 631–3; Debauve, *Justice révolutionnaire*, 77–8.

[43] Kerviler, *Bio-bibliographie bretonne*, fasc. 20, 91; Meyer, *La Noblesse bretonne*, i, 401, 410.

the richer part of the bourgeoisie of the town, for living 'nobly' cost money, and the bourgeoisie of Vannes, with a few important exceptions, was not particularly well off. Nor was it a very permanent group. A study of the most highly taxed 25 families, or about 70 individuals, in the Breton port of St-Malo has shown that the same urban oligarchy continued to dominate the town throughout the century: 23 of the 25 most highly taxed families in 1789 were already in St-Malo in 1710, and 16 had members in the highest-taxed groups even then.[44] No doubt the prosperity of St-Malo attracted larger numbers of people than the limited opportunities of Vannes; at any rate, if we examine the highest-taxed 100 people on the *capitation* rolls of Vannes in 1704, 1733, 1760 and 1783, we find that only a little more than half of the family names represented on each were there on the previous roll, and only about a fifth were in the fortunate hundred highest-taxed on the previous roll. By 1783, only 11 people, representing eight families, (the Danet, Le Gros, Dubodan, Billy, Delourme, Brunet, Lucas de Bourgerel and Dusers clans) bore the names of the original 100 richest inhabitants. When people from the town did make their way up the ladder of wealth and prestige, their climb was probably often linked to a move elsewhere in the province, as they worked their way through the hierarchy of wealth or legal offices, just as outsiders come to make part of their careers in Vannes. *Écuyer* S.-J.-J. Borie, already bound by marriage to the Dubodan family, came to Vannes from Tréguier in 1756 to become Président of the Présidial, and picked up several other dignities in the various royal courts of the town. However, Borie was more a provincial politician than a judge, and moved on in time to Rennes, where in a new office as senechal of Rennes he could follow the affairs of the province.[45] The merchant Desruisseaux, a native of Vannes who was taxed among the wealthiest families until disasters overcame him, spent a couple of years in Nantes during the early 1730s as a clerk in the provincial *devoirs*, before returning to his native town for a long career; he planned to send one of his sons to Bayonne and then to Martinique to start his career there.[46] J.-J. Lucas de Bourgerel, though he had local ties, was born in Béganne and made his career first as a seigneurial judge

---

[44] Lespagnol, 'A propos des élites urbaines', 4–6.

[45] A.C. Vannes, GG 56: St-Patern, mariages, 4-7-1747; Kerviler, *Bio-bibliographie bretonne*, fasc. 10, 400–1.

[46] A.D. Morbihan, 11 B 47: Desruisseaux to Pitault (Martinique), 5-10-1750.

in Rochefort-en-Terre before coming to Vannes, where his success was consecrated by a tax assessment of 36 livres in 1783.[47] For families on the way up, Vannes was sometimes a way-station and sometimes a final goal.

As the years went by, however, it looks very much as if the opportunities for advancement in Vannes were diminishing. Among those whose means put them in a position to imitate the noble way of life, the royal officers and legal men were the most numerous, but their position was getting weaker. They made up 65 per cent of those paying more than four times the mean assessment at the beginning of the century, but only 53 per cent at the end. Although as a group they could hardly be said to have been poor, their professional future as office-holders was rather cloudy in the closing years of the old regime. Those who depended on the functioning of the Présidial, the Admiralty Court and the *traites* were in the most unsure position. One major problem of the Présidial was that it did not have enough cases to handle, and its members suffered both in their prestige and in their incomes as a result. Except for cases of criminal justice, which the seigneurial courts tended to hand over to the royal courts, and for civil cases arising on the territory of the King's *domaine* around Vannes, it was mainly an appeal court. Unfortunately, it received few appeal cases. According to the edict of June 1551 which set up these courts, the competence of a Présidial in the last resort was limited to civil cases involving up to 250 l. in capital or 10 l. in *rentes*, and to 500 l. in capital and 20 l. in *rentes*, subject to appeal to a higher jurisdiction. With two centuries of inflation, this sum had become inconsiderable. In criminal cases, the Présidial could hear all cases within its immediate jurisdiction and appeals from all lesser courts, royal or seigneurial, but it could not impose the penalties of death or perpetual galley service without an automatic appeal to the Parlement. As if this was not enough, it was possible in many appeal cases to circumvent the Présidial altogether. According to an edict of 1539 and later interpretations of this measure, cases could be appealed directly from courts of *régaires* (episcopal seigneurial jurisdictions) to the Parlement. Since 1732, the Parlement had reserved the right to receive appeals in criminal cases and *causes d'office* (cases involving the appointment of tutors, etc.) directly after they had been tried in first instance.

[47] Debauve, *Justice révolutionnaire*, 76.

And in cases of petty civil justice, the local seigneurial courts, whose costs were about one-third less than those of the Présidial, were the courts of first instance.[48] Something was done to raise the status of the Présidial in the eighteenth century. The Présidial of Vannes in 1763 joined its voice to a campaign which the officers of the Présidial courts waged in all parts of France for an improvement in their status, but in addition to demanding the reform or abolition of seigneurial justice and the enlargement of their competence, they also concerned themselves with what they called their loss of prestige, demanding that service in the Présidial should lead to ennoblement in the same way as it did in the Parlement.[49] If they failed to win their way on the last point, the Présidiaux did have their competence enlarged by the edict of 1774, which gave them the right to judge in the last resort all civil cases up to the value of 2,000 l. in principal or 80 l. in revenue.[50] It was doubtful whether this was very effective. The use of the price of offices to determine whether a class or group of men is 'rising' or 'falling' is fraught with difficulties, but those prices we have for the Présidial of Vannes do not show anything but stagnation, if not decline, in the value men put upon service in the local royal courts in the second half of the century.[51] In 1789, the officers were still complaining of the inroads seigneurial justice was making on their profession, a familiar complaint, but by this time it had become a revolutionary cause.[52]

---

[48] M. Marion, *Dictionnaire des institutions de la France aux xviie et xviiie siècles* (Paris, 1923), 449–51; A. Giffard, *Les Justices seigneuriales en Bretagne aux xviie et xviiie siècles (1661–1791)* (Paris, 1903), 60, 66–7; Debauve, *Justice révolutionnaire,* 17–18.

[49] *Mémoire pour les officiers de la sénéchaussée et siège présidial de Vannes* (Vannes, 1763), reproduced in A. Guyot-Jomard, 'La Ville de Vannes pendant la deuxième moitié du xviiie siècle', *BSPM* (1889), 110–17.

[50] A. Macé, 'La Réforme des présidiaux au xviiie siècle', *BSPM* (1890), 127–37. A second provision of the edict permitting the Présidiaux to judge cases worth up to 4,000 livres was revoked by an edict of August 1777.

[51] On the general problem, see P. Dawson, 'Sur le prix des offices judiciaires à la fin de l'ancien régime;, *RHES,* xlii (1964), 340–2. In Vannes it is difficult to deter-
mine any values of offices before 1750 because so many sales were made *sous signe privé* or declared in a deliberately vague form, as in A.D. Morbihan, 17 C 5193: 28-3-1727. Most of the prices declared in the general evaluation of 1665 found in B.N. 500 Colbert, MS. 259, do not appear to be strictly comparable to eighteenth-century prices; those that are suggest stability. For prices after 1730, see Le Goff, 'Vannes', 366–71, based on A.D. Morbihan B 309, 407, 1345–53; 17 C 4474, 5180–334; E^n 21, 23, 29, 51, 636, 640, 692, 1866, 3443, 3446, 3451, 3461, 4403.

[52] A.N., H^1564: Rollin de la Farge [to Necker], 6-12-1788.

A second reason for the insecurity of the legal officials was the rivalry of the booming new port of Lorient, which tried during the eighteenth century to set up judicial bodies to take over much of the important business handled by the local courts. Ever since 1732 the Présidial of Vannes and the *Sénéchaussée* of Hennebont had fought to prevent the merchants of Lorient from setting up a commercial court, which would have removed commercial litigation in that city from their control. In 1782 the merchants of Lorient finally succeeded in their campaign. Most of the officers of the Présidial held places in the Admiralty Court of Vannes and the *juridiction des traites*. Between 1783 and 1786, a new Admiralty Court for Lorient, with its own officers, was carved out of the territory of Vannes, and plans were being made in the 1780s to dismember the *juridiction des traites* in the same fashion.[53]

The situation of the legal professionals—barristers, notaries and attorneys (though not the lowly *huissiers*) was probably somewhat better. The prices of their offices, naturally, varied according to the importance of the legal practice which went with them, but they seem to have tended toward stability at the end of the century. One should not exaggerate the importance of the official complaints made by notaries and attorneys; unlike their more exalted colleagues, none of their offices was going begging.[54] This was because their income did not much depend on the proceeds of royal justice. If they had relied, for example, on their income from cases heard in the Présidial, the sixteen attorneys would have had only about 250 to 300 livres a year between them.[55] The *huissiers* who did depend on the court they served were no doubt justified in complaining of their lot and pointing out that nobody wanted to take up their offices.[56]

But for a notary and attorney or a barrister, there were other possibilities. The notaries J.-B. Rostiel, Henry Ulliac, Mathurin Goujeon, L.-M. Josse and Jean de la Noë all occupied posts of procurators-fiscal in seigneurial courts in 1768. Others like Jehanno

[53] Thomas-Lacroix, *Répertoire numérique de la série B . . . juridictions d'attribution*, 5, 9, 16; A.D. I.-V., C 1825.

[54] A.D. Morbihan, B 1350: Extrait des délibérations de la communauté des notaires royaux de la sénéchaussée de Vannes; Extrait du registre des délibérations de la communauté des procureurs du présidial de Vannes, 30-11-1771.

[55] A.D. Morbihan, B 1348: Registre tenu par Julien Nicolas Jamet, greffier de Mrs. les procureurs du présidial, 30-1-1758 to 31-12-1783.

[56] A.D. Morbihan, B 1353: Minute d'une séance du siège devant M de Limur 3-12-1750.

and Goujeon, who appear in the case reproduced in Appendix I of this book, presented cases regularly as attorneys (*procureurs*) in the jurisdictions of the Régaires and Largouet, which treated most of the lucrative litigation of the region.[57] Barristers, too, did not confine themselves to pleading before the Présidial. Lawyers such as F.-J. Clemenceau, F.-F. Regnier, J.-F. Le Maillaud de Kerharnos, J.-M. Caradec, A.-L. de Launay, P.-A. Jullien and P.-J.-J. du Lièpvre were *sénéchaux* or procurators-fiscal of seigneurial jurisdictions. Jean-Jacques Lucas, sieur de Bourgerel (1732–1806), who later won the epithet 'bon citoyen' from Prieur de la Marne, must have held some kind of record for the cumulation of offices: he was consecutively and often concurrently *lieutenant* of the *maîtrise des eaux et forêts*, barrister of the town council, deputy to the Estates of Brittany in 1772 and 1788, procurator-fiscal of the jurisdiction of Largouet and the baronies of Quintin and Lanvaux, senechal of the barony of La Roche-Bernard and the Île-d'Arz and senechal and first criminal and civil judge of the jurisdiction of the County of Rochefort.[58] Other barristers such as Jollivet, Le Monnier and Goujeon also supplemented their earnings by leasing tithes and annates, and serving as agents for absent noble landlords.[59]

During most of this time, the merchants had constituted the second largest group among the wealthiest taxpayers; they composed about a quarter of the group paying more than four times the mean *capitation* payment, but, significantly, in the period of economic stagnation in the 1780s, their numbers dwindled to 6 per cent of the top group. It is likely that some of the missing traders simply ceased to call themselves *négociants* or merchants on tax rolls until their trade picked up again; B.-A. Guillo Dubodan, for example, had retired from business by the time the tax roll of 1783 was drawn up, and appears on it as an officer of the *eaux-et-forêts*.[60] Nevertheless, there was no mistaking the collapse of the business world, a collapse

[57] A.D. Morbihan, B 1350: Registre des déclarations des procureurs fiscaux des seigneurs hauts justiciers, 27-2-1768.

[58] A.D. Morbihan, B 1346: Offices et maitrises, 1759–89; B 1350; Debauve, *Justice révolutionnaire*, 76–7; Frotier de la Messelière, *Filiations bretonnes*, iii, 569–71.

[59] A.D. Morbihan, E 1062, 1067 (fonds Jollivet): Prieuré de St-Guen, 1773–90; 77 G 6 (519).

[60] A.D. Morbihan, 190 G 12 (1044): *Mémoire pour le général* [parish assembly of St-Patern] *contre messire Le Croisier, Recteur* (1785).

directly related to the fortunes of the grain trade. The grain trade was the principal element in large-scale commerce in the Vannetais. It was not the only element; as we have seen, wine, Spanish iron, fruit and so forth made a natural return cargo for ships coming back from the grain markets of the Atlantic coast, but without it, the region would have lived in a kind of economic autarky. Vannes's role in the grain export trade was not new; it dated from at least the fifteenth and sixteenth centuries. Nevertheless, it appears to have undergone some important changes towards the end of the seventeenth century. If the testimony of several sea-captains of the region is to be believed, it appears that on the eve of the great Atlantic commercial expansion which historians now place somewhere around the 1660s, the merchants of Vannes were still specializing in a limited kind of artisanal, haphazard commerce, sailing their own ships loaded with grain or other products in demand further down the coast, or often trusting the cargo to a captain who undertook to seek out markets and sell the goods on the spot.

Within the space of two generations after the accession of Louis XIV, the port of Vannes was brought into the commercial economy of the Atlantic, drawn in the wake of the great ports of St-Malo, Nantes and Lorient. The adoption by Breton merchants of modern commercial techniques gradually permitted the entrepreneurs of even the smallest ports to follow the fluctuations of markets abroad, obtain prompt and reliable payment for merchandise, co-operate with other merchants in other ports in commission and cost-sharing arrangements, and profit from the credit and exchange facilities offered by the bill of exchange (*lettre de change*). Significantly, it was at this time that the tidal wastes around the port of Vannes were reclaimed for the new merchants' quarter, and it was also at this time that the business tribunal of Vannes was formed.[61]

The men who carried on this form of commerce were set off not simply by the degree of their wealth, but by the nature of their trade, for they were closer in mentality to the great merchants of the Atlantic ports than they were to the several score of retail merchants who served the needs of the town population. At mid-century,

[61] A.D. Morbihan, B 862: Audition d'experts . . . sur l'usement du trafic des marchandises et la forme des confiscations au pays d'Espagne, 17-10-1657. See also above, Chapter I, notes 5 and 6; A. P. Usher, *The History of the Grain Trade in France 1400–1710* (Cambridge, Mass., 1913) esp. 34–5.

important grain-merchants like Ignace Advisse Desruisseaux and the family of Guillo du Bodan were correspondents of some of the largest commercial houses in the ports of France: d'Haveloose, Grou, Danycan, Walsh and Guer of Nantes, Labat de Serene, Vignes, Treilhes and Le Chevalier of Bordeaux, Roux and Solier of Marseilles. The use of the bill of exchange to finance commercial operations put them into close contact with the Parisian banking houses, for by this time, payments, even from nearby towns such as Lorient, were almost all made with bills of exchange drawn on Paris banks.[62] The important merchants of Vannes read newspapers to find out what was happening on the markets of Europe,[63] but most of all relied on their correspondents for such news and returned the favour by giving them the latest prices and word of the appearance of the harvest in Vannes. They appear to have had the same knowledge of commercial techniques as their colleagues in the greater ports of France. Desruisseaux, for example, used a modified form of double-entry book-keeping which was primitive, perhaps, but no more so than that used by the best merchants. The practice of discounting bills of exchange, too, became quite widespread after mid-century; contrary to what has often been said, France during the eighteenth century did have a system of provincial banking, albeit an improvised one, which facilitated transfers and credits. Normally in Vannes merchants had to purchase their grain with hard cash from the suppliers, and were paid for it by their own customers in drafts on Paris, or given credit facilities in Paris banks. To obtain the specie with which they paid their suppliers, they sold these drafts for cash to the local tax-receivers or to people who held positions in the tobacco monopoly, or who for other reasons had sums available. Often these drafts were at 60, 90 or 120 days—the practice seems to have spread particularly during the Seven Years War—and then the local receivers, or *caissiers* as they were called, charged a rate of half per cent a usance (1 usance = 30 days), thereby providing the commercial credit necessary for their operations.[64]

[62] Le Goff, 'An Eighteenth-Century Grain Merchant', and Collection Debauve: J.-A. Dubodan to J.-B. Roux & Cie., Marseilles, 30-11-1734.

[63] J.-L. Debauve, 'Notes sur les chambres de lecture de Lorient et Vannes', *BSPM* (1955–6), 93–8; A.D. Morbihan, 11 B 53 (20): Desruisseaux to Captain Peter Omsen (Bergen), 26-8-1773.

[64] J. Cavignac, *Jean Pellet, commerçant de gros, 1694–1772* (Paris, 1967), 36; J. Meyer, *L'Armement nantais dans la deuxième moitié du xviiie siècle* (Paris, 1969), 119–42; R. de Roover, *L'Évolution de la lettre de change xvie–xviiie siècles* (Paris, 1953), 119–46; Le Goff, 'An Eighteenth-Century Grain Merchant', 107–10.

Other speculators in Vannes accepted bills issued on local merchants by businessmen elsewhere in France. Bellefontaine Jan, never officially styled as a merchant but a member of a family of financiers and a judge in the commercial court in Vannes, discounted commercial paper drawn on Breton businessmen during the Seven Years War by five firms in Bordeaux and two in Libourne. He took a discount of 1 per cent on bills written on Breton towns plus half per cent a usance, and paid his Bordeaux correspondents with bills on that town and on Paris. The funds for these operations came, apparently, from his stake of some 20,000 écus in the profits of a share in a cloth shipment made to Seville and Madrid by the Magon firm of St-Malo. In Bellefontaine's correspondence with David, a Bordeaux wine-shipper, it emerges that he served as the banker for a set of business friends in Vannes, including a wine-merchant, the widow Aubry, and Danet, a member of one of the biggest merchant clans in town during the later eighteenth century; he also used his profits to take a share in a shipment of wine to the Dutch West Indies, and probably had many more such dealings.[65]

Speculators like Bellefontaine, and royal and municipal receivers, had at their disposal funds which often gave them, legally or otherwise, the cash backing they needed for their operations. Nicolas Viel was styled a 'négociant' on the *capitation* roll of 1733, but he was also municipal treasurer-receiver in 1729, receiver of the royal tax-farm in the 1730s and 1740s, *conseiller trésorier receveur* des *octrois* in the 1740s, receiver-general of the tobacco monopoly for Vannes in 1748, and director of the same concern in 1753. If one did not have a financial office, a relative in the same position was the next best thing; Desruisseaux used the services of his brother-in-law, J.-N. Provost, director and receiver of the royal domain in Auray, his cousin by marriage, Penquer, director-general and controller of the domains in the diocese of Vannes in the 1720s and receiver-general of the *devoirs* in the 1730s, and the two Guérins, one his brother-in-law, the other his nephew, both *entreposeurs des tabacs;* all bought his drafts on Paris at a profit and some helped him in his dealings in grain, for a commission.[66]

Haphazard as it was, this sort of finance worked most of the time for the coastal trade in grain and other articles within France that

[65] A.D. Gironde, 7 G 1268: Bellefontaine Jan to David, Bordeaux, 4-3-1758.
[66] Le Goff, 'An Eighteenth-Century Grain Merchant', 108; A.N., G⁵ 5, dossier 8; G⁵ 31.

periods 1770–4 and 1775–9, it does not seem likely. Of these 35, the birthplaces of 23 were located; 8 of these were not even born in Vannes. Of the 20 (of 39) wives of these men, 10 were born outside Vannes, and none of the members had married into the immediate families of other members of the group. The children of four councillors did marry into the immediate families of other councillors, but their behaviour appears to have been more a form of occupational solidarity (for example, marriages between the sons and daughters of attorneys) than oligarchic unity. Nor does political activity in the town council seem to have made them into a group of political or personal friends to the extent that it might have cemented bonds between different occupational groups.

That such a group should not have been united by the bonds of friendship and kinship should be no suprise to anyone with even a slight acquaintance with the politics of small groups; they were, naturally enough, divided among themselves and did not constitute a party. Nevertheless, the bulk of them came, over the years, to act as a sort of party, perhaps because of their own lack of real power, and certainly because they were driven together by the great issues of Breton provincial politics in the later eighteenth century.

The reason for the lack of power among the dedicated politicians was that groups which dominated local society in economic and other ways were able to intervene in municipal affairs and prevent the specialists of town politics from getting on with the job. People with the social standing of the canons and nobles, to take the case most frequently cited in the polemics around the time of the Revolution, could exert influence on the council through patronage and family ties. The noble Du Pargo family, for example, prominent members of the Breton Parlement, seem to have played a role in swinging the town council behind the Parlement and Estates and against the Crown during the *affaire de Bretagne*. Intermediaries between local and higher levels of government also commanded respect and influence in town affairs: the bishop of Vannes, the town governor, the duc de Penthièvre, ministers and clerks cultivated by councilmen in Versailles—all these were important channels for patronage and pensions for individuals and the town's affairs in general.[11]

[11] M. Marion, *La Bretagne et le duc d'Aiguillon* (Paris, 1898), 51–66, 356–7; A.N., H¹ 480: (proposals for pensions put forward by the bishops of Vannes) 1771, 1773, 1775.

When a majority in the council could not be raised, it was possible for the privileged orders, or other minorities in the council for that matter, to block business by getting a large enough minority to abstain from meetings and then challenge any decisions taken, on the grounds that a quorum had not been present. At the most, in a normal year, only fifty or so members ever attended a meeting, and never all at the same time. Since the privileged made up nearly half of these votes and since some of the members of the Third Estate were always bound to be absent for their own reasons, it was not too difficult to drive the number of voting members down below the required number of twenty-four by arranging for absences and putting pressure on a few subservient clients. Thus in March 1788 the Mayor, Le Menez de Kerdelleau, complained to the intendant about

des difficultés sans nombre pour faire prendre des délibérations concernant des travaux très urgents et indispensables. J'ai assemblé au moins douze fois la communauté sans avoir pu la compléter que deux, encore fallait-il pendant la séance envoyer chercher plusieurs délibérants par les hérauts. Je puis vous assurer, Monseigneur, que c'est aujourd'hui un parti pris de ne pas délibérer en moindre nombre que vingt-quatre, non compris celui qui préside . . . [12]

This was not the first time such tactics were used, but this quarrel alluded to by the mayor, essentially between the Présidial and the inner group of the town council, represented one of the final stages in the breakdown of municipal government and the transformation of local into national issues. It was these struggles and the paralysis of local government which welded the regular local politicians into something near a coherent group. How had this come about?

The end of the period of mid-century war in 1763 and the increasing strife in the later sixties between the French Crown on the one hand and, on the other, Breton institutions and the privileged who sheltered behind them, seem to mark the turning-point. After the crisis of 1740, the life of the town council had appeared to settle into a routine which was busy but not bitter; among other tasks the council had had the perpetually ungrateful one of billeting increasing numbers of passing troops after the beginning of hostilities in 1744, to say nothing of the job of mustering the rag-tag militia for the defence of Lorient in 1746 and of organizing relief projects in the hard years of 1742 and 1752. One of the main reasons for the

[12]   A.D. I.-V., C 688: Le Menez de Kerdelleau to intendant, 4-3-1788.

political calm, beside the wars and, perhaps, the generally easier economic climate of the mid-century years, was the relatively relaxed state of relations between the French Crown and Breton provincial institutions.[13]

On the local level there had also been an important change in the office of mayor and the man who held it. In 1748, the mayor was made the effective head of the town council when he was given the right to preside over meetings, and it so happened that in the previous year, a wealthy ennobled *négociant*, Joseph-Ange Guillo Dubodan, had purchased the office. Dubodan, who had previously been elected *syndic* of the council, was a respected member of the assembly and showed his worth by using his influence in 1754 in Versailles and with the intendant of Brittany and the duc d'Aiguillon, commander-in-chief of the province, to get money to improve the port. In addition, he managed to keep the respect of the touchy Présidial: although the measure of 1748 ended the pretensions of the judges of the Présidial to chair council meetings, Dubodan was careful to make a representative of that court one of the two town delegates sent to the Breton Estates in almost all of their biennial meetings, a tradition his son Jean-Vincent kept up when he succeeded him. As a mark of respect, although it had gained the right to dispose of the mayor's office by the time Dubodan died, the council allowed his son to take it up without the slightest difficulty.[14]

Unfortunately, the Dubodans' rule did not last, and in 1761, Jean-Vincent withdrew from the mayoralty to become the intendant's *subdélégué*. The barrister to whom he sold his mayoral office, Gillot de Kerhardene, was an unhappy choice. He was not wealthy, as the Dubodans had been, and he gained a bad reputation almost immediately. He was despised by the provincial military commander, the duc d'Aiguillon, by the intendant and by Dubodan himself, as an incompetent; and Gillot's son, who succeeded him in 1768, was denounced by the intendant as a pawn of the nobility, 'incapable d'affaires, du parti de l'opposition, cherchant des occasions de

[13] A.C. Vannes, BB 16: 6-4-1742; BB 17: 1-10-1746 *et seq.*; BB 18: 21-2-1752; H. Fréville, *L'Intendance de Bretagne (1689–1790)* (Rennes, 1953), i, 390–509; Rébillon, *Les États de Bretagne*, 269–338.
[14] A.C. Vannes, BB 16: 15-4-1746: BB 17: 4-8-1747; BB 18: 12-8-1754; A.D. I.-V., C 688: intendant to Dubodan, 17-4-1776; Fréville, *L'Intendance de Bretagne*, ii, 185.

susciter des querelles . . . ivrogne.'[15] One of the most prominent officers of the town militia and a member of council wrote to the intendant in September 1768 that the elder Gillot's lack of dignity had kept 'honnêtes gens' away from meetings; what we need, he said, is 'un homme qui ne fut pas de la lie du peuple, qui eût le bien en vue, qui fut libre, afin d'y donner ses soins, qui fut dans un état d'aisance et qui eut assez de considération par lui-même pour en imposer sans avoir besoin d'annoncer qu'il est maire'.[16]

Aside from his personality and his political affiliations, Gillot was a disaster because if there was ever a time when Vannes needed a strong personality as mayor it was during the last three decades of the old regime, when the conflicts between the Breton Parlement and Estates and the Crown began to pull apart what was left of the institutions of local government. In Rennes, the meetings of the Estates grew more turbulent as the royal government requested more taxes to cover the cost of its disastrous wars, and in 1764, the Parlement of Rennes joined forces with the Estates for an onslaught on the duc d'Aiguillon's administration. This was the notorious *affaire de Bretagne*, an attack on royal authority which grew into probably the greatest crisis the Bourbon monarchy had to face before 1789. Contributing to this tension was the successful assault made by the Parlement of Rennes, in league with the other parlements of the kingdom, on another symbolic bulwark of royal power, the Jesuit order, which they forced Louis XV to expel from Brittany (and France) in 1762.[17]

These crises introduced a note of hysteria into the traditional politics of the Breton peninsula which carried over into local affairs as well. Dubodan's departure and the ascendancy of the Gillots coincided with the change in the political climate in Rennes, and the town was soon involved in the struggles of provincial politics in a way that it had not previously known. In those struggles, control of

[15] A.N., H¹ 591: État des personnes de l'ordre du Tiers qui se sont bien conduites dans plusieurs assemblées des États . . . 1778; in 1772 Gillot was the 'chef décidé du parti de l'opposition, enfant perdu de la cabale' A.N., H¹ 539, pc. 142; see also A.D. I.-V., C 688: Mémoire et lettre du duc d'Aiguillon, 9-7-1762 to intendant with copy of letter from Pontcarré de Viarmes to *subdélégués*, 8-6-1748; A.D. I.-V., C 689: Dubodan to intendant, 18-12-1766.

[16] A.D. I.-V., C 688: Billy to intendant, 17-9-1768.

[17] Fréville, *L'Intendance de Bretagne*, ii, 196–344; Rébillon, *Les États de Bretagne*, 322–69; Marion, *La Bretagne et le duc d'Aiguillon*; B. Pocquet, *Le Pouvoir absolu et l'esprit provincial. Le duc d'Aiguillon et la Chalotais* (Paris, 1890–1), 2 vols.

municipal government was both a means to an end and the end in itself. For the nobility, the Parlement and the Crown, control of town government meant control of the deputations to the Estates; for the local politicians allied to any of these parties, it also meant a share in power for themselves. The mounting excitement in local politics after 1760 was the product of the great battles of political principle being fought in Rennes and Versailles, but when those causes and principles were brought down to the local level, they found defenders and opponents in the latent and sometimes overt rivalries of local groups.

Sometimes the laconic entries in the council minutes allow us only to guess at these rivalries, but they make no secret that one of the main conflicts was a long-standing quarrel between the Présidial and the council about who should rule the town. In 1723, for example, Président Dondel had had arrested a police patrol made up of respectable citizens which the then mayor, Delastang, had sent out to maintain order in the town. It was a period of unrest in Vannes, and Dondel, claiming that the mayor had wanted to sound the tocsin and rouse the people in order to get his men released, convoked Delestang and his brother-in-law before the court. The affair was eventually brought before the Conseil du Roi, which declared that 'les contestations des parties ne proviennent que pour raison de prétendus droits et fonctions attribués à leurs offices'.[18] The political crisis of 1740 was at least partly about the same question. These disputes with the Présidial were one of the main ways in which the town council became involved in the struggle waged by the Parlement and the Estates against the King. This came about in part because of the alliance between the Parlement and its subordinate court. Although the Parlement was filled with nobles, and the Présidial, with bourgeois or ennobled men at best, officers in the two had much in common: they were all judges in the same judicial system, most had had a common legal training in Rennes, and all had an interest in guarding the quasi-legislative 'police' powers of the courts against encroachment by the King's agents. Moreover, some of the higher officers of the Présidial formed a sort of clientele for the Parlement and attached themselves to its interests. Thus in 1770, the aged ex-président Dondel became one of the most enthusiastic supporters of the Parlement in the Brittany affair; similarly Président Borie, though heavily bribed,

18 A.N., E 2051 fols. 70–4.

was considered to be in the camp of the Parlement in the crisis of the 1770s.[19]

When relations between Parlement and King worsened, so did relations between Présidial and town council as the Présidial sought to assert its right to a voice in local affairs. The immediate effect of the victory of the Parlement over the Jesuits in 1762 was that the Présidial tried to share the power of appointing the new regents of the College of Vannes with the town council. Two years later, the *procureur du roi* of the Présidial, Houet de Chênevert, put in a claim to have a member of the court chosen automatically as one of the two deputies to the Breton Estates, a reaction perhaps to the reluctance of the council to name deputies from the Présidial since Dubodan's retirement.[20] In 1769, J.-J. Lucas de Bourgerel, one of the prominent barristers of the region, was kept off the town council by the Parlement of Brittany. This happened when another barrister, Le Boulh, protested against his admission, claiming that he was senior to Lucas in the Vannes bar. The council refused the protest, but Le Boulh won on an appeal to the Parlement, on the grounds that a quorum was not present on the day the council had turned him down (as indeed was the case; none of the clergy was present—was this only a coincidence?). It was about this time that the council began to fight back: in May, the municipal attorney claimed that the mayor and other municipal officials ought to walk in public processions at the left of the officers of the Présidial. This was one of those interminable *querelles de préséances* so typical of the old regime which in themselves appear absurd but which usually are symptoms of more important struggles.[21] Finally, on Ascension Day 1779, the council competed with the Présidial in an indecent rush for seats in the newly-built cathedral stalls, an honour to which the Présidial claimed exclusive right. The council entertained dark suspicions that the Chapter was leagued with the Présidial against them and won a victory over both in 1780: at the expense of the choristers, the town council and Présidial both got places in the

---

[19]   On Dondel, see Kerviler, *Bio-bibliographie bretonne*, fasc. 33, 231–7; Saulnier, *Le Parlement de Bretagne*, 305–6; Frotier de la Messelière, *Filiations bretonnes*, ii, 166–9; Meyer, *La Noblesse bretonne*, i, 216–18; A.D. Morbihan, L 1446: District of Vannes to Dufresne St-Léon, 20-10-1792; on Borie: Rébillon, *Les États de Bretagne*, 125, 389 and A.N., H¹ 538, pc. 292–5 ff.

[20]   A.C. Vannes, BB 20: 2-7-1762, 9-8-1762, 10-8-1762, 23-8-1764, 19-9-1764.

[21]   A.C. Vannes, BB 21: 31-3-1769, 17-5-1769, 28-6-1769, 11-8-1769; BB 22: 5-9-1771.

choir stalls. But in 1787 the quarrel flared up again when the Présidial claimed that the council had infringed on its police powers by ordering some porches encroaching on the public way to be destroyed.[22]

The role of the Chapter in the dispute over the choir stalls and perhaps in the Le Boulh affair suggests a second subject of discord which increasingly preoccupied the council in the sixties and seventies. This was the rivalry between the council and the Church, which encouraged a form of institutional anticlericalism whose target was the Chapter, several religious communities and, ultimately, the most important person in Vannes, the bishop himself. The first sign of the discontent bubbled up in 1759, when the Dames de la Charité bought a small piece of land to add to their convent grounds, provoking the council's protest that two-thirds of the town and the surrounding countryside was monopolized by the property of eighteen religious communities which paid no taxes except for a nominal charge on their domestic servants.[23] Then it was the turn of the Dominicans, who in 1761 began a fourteen-year campaign of resistance to the council's attempt to expropriate their latrines for a new street: they lobbied the councillors, enlisted the bishop in their cause, mustered votes, got enough councillors to stay from meetings to prevent quorums, and ultimately even managed to extort compensation for the latrines which they themselves had destroyed in the meantime.[24] In 1761, too, some of the members of the council, led, bishop Bertin suggested, by Président Borie and Houet de Chênevert, the *procureur du roi* of the Présidial, and perhaps the *subdélégué* Dubodan, intended to block the plans of the bishop and a pious local noble, de Lenvos, to extend the men's retreat house. Since preaching retreats in Vannes was one of the most important sources of Jesuit influence there, and since Bertin was a notorious

---

[22] A.D. Morbihan, 54 G 1 (369): 22-7-1778 to 28-6-1780; A.C. Vannes, BB 24: 13-8-1778 to 5-5-1780; A.D. I.-V., C 691: Communauté de Ville to intendant, 7-9-1779; intendant to Communauté de Ville, 10-9-1779; Le Méne, *Histoire du diocèse de Vannes*, ii, 240; H. Léna, 'La Communauté de ville d'Hennebont au xviiie siècle (1689–1759) Essai sur l'organisation municipale en Bretagne' (Thèse de droit, Université de Rennes, 1964), 95–105 gives examples of similar incidents in a nearby town.

[23] A.C. Vannes, BB 19: 26-1-1759.

[24] A.C. Vannes, BB 19: 13-11-1761, 25-9-1776 and *passim*. The most active opponents of the Dominicans at the beginning of the affair were the merchants Larive, Desruisseaux, Le Croisier, Grangam, Housset, Plisson Latour and three attorneys: Launay, Le Ridant and Perret.

supporter of that order, it looks very much as if the Jansenist traditions of part of the merchant and officer classes in Vannes, the ties of Borie and Houet with the pro-Jansenist Parlement of Rennes, and Dubodan's good relations with the duc d'Aiguillon (who detested Bertin) gave a certain edge to their opposition. Nevertheless, a council meeting packed with ecclesiastics and nobles frustrated their design.[25] Small wonder then that when the local Franciscans in 1769 sent a delegation to invite the councillors to a ceremony in honour of the Holy Father and asked the council to issue them a certificate of their public utility, they received a stinging refusal, joined to a denunciation of the stranglehold of '19 communautés et maisons de main morte' on the town, adding that 'loin de pouvoir accorder le certificat demandé par les PP Cordeliers elle [the council] est d'avis de solliciter la suppression de la plus grande partie des communautés religieuses qu'elle [the town] contient'.[26]

In this way, the councillors' concern for a lighter tax burden for the town, and for space for urban development came up against the resistance of the clergy and led to questioning the clergy's right to pack assemblies with ecclesiastical dignitaries and sympathizers, or to wreck their proceedings by staying away. Viewed against this background, a second *querelle de préséance* which the council entered into against the Chapter during the seventies has some sense. It began in 1771 when at High Mass on the feast of St Vincent, the patron saint of Vannes, the archpriests and choristers rushed to kiss St Vincent's skull ahead of the council. The canons and the bishop, perhaps afraid of scandal, stopped inviting the council to ceremonies; when the councillors planned to complain about this, the Chapter and its friends stayed away from the assembly. In retaliation, the council refused in 1774 to spend money for masses to be said for the repose of Louis XV's soul, and gave it to the poor instead. When bishop Bertin died, the council took a more petty revenge, and made the canons sit on the clergy's bench when they came to council to invite them to the funeral.[27] If the town council's regular members needed concrete examples of the evils of ecclesiastical privilege, as well as the way it warps the minds of its victims, they did not have to look very far.

[25] A.D. I.-V., C 688: Bishop to intendant, 24-8-1766; A.C. Vannes, BB 21: 13-6-1766; Marion, *La Bretagne et le duc d'Aiguillon*, 71 n. 1, 188–9.
[26] A.C. Vannes, BB 22: 11-8-1769.
[27] A.D. Morbihan, C 280: Plainte de la communauté, 6-9-1771; A.C. Vannes, BB 22: 11-10-1771; BB 23: 17-6-1774 *et seq.*

The increasing interference by the Présidial and the Chapter in municipal affairs was part of a growing struggle for control of Breton political institutions. Like the clergy and the Parlement, the royal government too, began to intervene directly in town government in new ways. Royal control over municipal affairs was nothing new in Brittany, as elsewhere in France, but up to the sixties, it was principally administrative and financial tutelage intended largely to prevent the local misuse of public funds and to milk municipal treasuries of extra revenue for the Crown. Now this tutelage became political; its object, to control the choice and conduct of the deputies of the Third Estate in Rennes. In this way, Vannes, like the other Breton towns, was drawn into the great issue of political life in the 1760s: the increasingly uncompromising fight between the royal government, the intendant in Rennes and his subdelegates in each town on the one hand, and the Estates of Brittany, the Parlement in Rennes and the local judicial officers and nobles on the other. Control of the towns meant control of the Estates; as Caze de la Bove, intendant from 1774 to 1784, wrote,

Il faut considérer qu'il est très intéressant pour le gouvernement que, dans une province aussi orageuse que la Bretagne, le commissaire départi soit le seul protecteur et adminstrateur des communautés. . . . Ce n'est qu'autant qu'il aura de l'autorité dans les villes qu'il y sera considéré, qu'il pourra avoir quelqu'ascendant sur les membres de l'ordre du tiers et faciliter l'expédition des affaires dans l'assemblée des États en dirigeant leur avis et en les soutenant contre l'ordre de la noblesse dont la hauteur et la trop grande prépondérance font naître toutes les difficultés qui s'élèvent journellement dans l'assemblée.[28]

To gain the 'authority' that Caze spoke of, a series of intendants, military commanders and governors set out to create a party of supporters for the royal government inside provincial institutions.

The first step in the creation of a 'royal party' in the towns of Brittany can be dated from 1763, when the royal government began to harden its attitude to Breton privileges. An *arrêt du conseil* of 11 June 1763 placed the nomination of mayors under the direct control of the government because, as the decree stated, the mayors were *ex officio* deputies to the Estates. When the elder Gillot died in 1768, it was only by a clever manœuvre that his son managed to elude these provisions and take over his father's office. This defeat

---

[28] Fréville, *L'Intendance de Bretagne*, iii, 55.

was a source of great annoyance to the intendant, for the two Gillots were so politically unsound and so incompetent that intendant de Flesselles requested a local barrister and councillor, De Launay, to correspond with him in the elder Gillot's stead, a practice continued under his son by the barrister Lucas de Bourgerel and the attorney Le Ridant.[29] In the end, the intendant solved the problem of controling the mayor by buying Gillot's office and awarding it to Le Menez de Kerdelleau, an outsider from Quimper with a large family and reputedly modest means, who proved his usefulness to the Crown in the Estates of 1778. 'Bon sujet, plein de zèle, appliqué et laborieux, ayant de l'esprit sans avoir de grande talents, a rendu des services . . . il serait à propos de l'attacher à cette partie'; it was not long before Le Menez began petitioning the government for free lodging, pensions and ennoblement.[30]

The royal government's attempts to get the upper hand in municipal affairs were in part a reaction to the increasing power of the Estates and Parlement, which by 1784 had taken over nearly all the administrative duties of the intendant and his *subdélégués* and given it to their own provincial administrative machine, the *commission intermédiaire*. One of the crucial zones of conflict between Crown and Estates was the struggle for the control of municipal finances. This was an area where the royal government had furthered its opponents' cause by carrying on Louis XIV's shameless policy of milking the town councils through the forced sale of municipal offices. In Vannes, as in many other towns, the Crown once again made all municipal offices venal in 1733 and offered them for sale to the highest bidder. No bidders came forward. After fifteen years went by, the Crown assigned them to the council in return for a forced payment of 5,000 livres a year plus incidental costs, to be met out of town revenues. This obligation, which most Breton towns had to face in the same way, was known as the *octrois municipaux*. Eager to get its hands on a lump sum, the royal government followed its usual practice and made over the principal it hoped to gain

[29] Rébillon, *Les États de Bretagne*, 117–20; Fréville, *L'Intendance de Bretagne*, ii, 101–2, 362–3; A.D. I.-V., C 688: intendant to duc de Penthièvre, 28-11-1768, Dubodan to intendant, 20-4-1769, Launay to Raudin, 15-10-1767, intendant to Gillot, 21-10-1767; C 689: Dubodan to intendant, 18-12-1766; C 690: Bourgerel Lucas and Le Ridant to intendant, 16-5-1777.

[30] A.N., H¹ 591: État des personnes de l'ordre du tiers qui se sont bien comportés . . . [1778]; H¹ 539, pc. 147; A.D. I.-V., C 688: Le Menez to intendant, 20-8-1778 and petition; Rébillon, *les États de Bretagne*, 123 n. 78, 721 n. 61.

to a financier, Jacques Philippe Godard, who undertook to pay the King 35,871 livres. By 1759, the town had paid Godard 57,000 livres and considered its obligation might be brought to an end, but in July of 1758 the government once again leased the *octrois*, to one Joseph Varlet, for a further nine years.[31]

To meet these charges, the costs of services and the upkeep of municipal property, the council had one main source of revenue, the *octrois des villes*. These were a kind of sales tax on wine and cider brought into the town. Despite the severe strain placed on municipal finances by the Crown and by the ordinary cost of administration, the council refused to apply for an increase in the rates of *octrois*, whether out of self-interest or a genuine concern for the poor, on whom the burden of these taxes fell, and instead made up its occasional deficits with direct subsidies and loans.[32] It was hardly a brilliant financial situation, and the many public works which the council rightly judged to be necessary—the deepening of the port, the improvement and straightening of the execrably paved and winding streets, were all undertaken by half-measures, depending on subsidies capriciously meted out by the Estates and the intendant. Like the majority of its counterparts in Brittany and the rest of France, the council suffered from an excess of responsibilities and a paucity of means.

In order to improve its desperate situation, the council finally took the rash step of calling on the Breton Estates in 1778 to help them put an end to the unjust continuation of the *octrois municipaux*. The order of the nobility, only too pleased to comply, took up the question, but turned it into a general demand to supervise the finances of the town councils of the province, claiming that the *octrois* were a tax illegally levied without their consent. The deputies of the Third Estate protested vigorously against this distortion of their aims, but this did not prevent the enfeebled royal government from giving way. Over the following decade, the Estates gradually took over the supervision of municipal finances from the Crown, and, ironically, the *octrois municipaux*, which had served as the pretext for the attack on the Crown, continued to be collected, only

---

[31] A.D. I.-V., C 690: Mémoire des commissaires de la communauté de ville de Vannes, 24-3-72; C 3932: 24-10-1765.

[32] A.D. I.-V., C 694: Letter of intendant (minute), March 1789; C 3934: État des octrois . . . des différentes villes [1779], État des octrois perpétuels ou à terme [1758].

now with the Estates' consent.[33] The towns had exchanged one form of fiscal extortion for another, with the added inconvenience that the privileged orders now had an even greater influence on their affairs through the institutions of the Estates.

Throughout the 1770s and the early 1780s, then, the foundations of an alliance between the royal government and the Third Estate in the town councils of the province were built, almost in spite of the Crown's previously high-handed policy, on the basis of the convergent interest of royal and municipal government against the influence of the privileged in town affairs. Curiously, this sense of solidarity, at least in Vannes, had not grown directly out of conflicts with the nobility, for the main quarrel was with the Présidial and the Chapter; but the dispute with these two privileged institutions prepared the way for the struggle with the privileged institution *par excellence*, the Breton estates. On the level of provincial politics, the cause of the Breton Estates and the cause of the Breton Parlement merged during the Brittany Affair in the later sixties, so it came to be seen that the defence of the privileged was the *raison d'être* of Breton particularism, of the peculiar administrative system of the province, and of the Estates' resistance to the reforming action of the central government. Although it is true that the Estates did serve to keep the average Breton's revenues from being swallowed up in the insatiable maw of the Royal treasury—Necker estimated the average tax levy per head at about 44 per cent less in Brittany than in the rest of the country[34]—it is equally true that the distribution of the fiscal burden within the province was at least as iniquitous as elsewhere in France. As sincerely convinced of the importance of Breton privileges and as reluctant to provoke an open break with the nobility as they may have been, the active politicians of the Third Estate could hardly avoid noticing the inconvenience of rule by the privileged. In Vannes by 1784, mayor Le Menez and Dusers, a councillor in the Présidial, denounced in a letter 'tous les monastères dont notre ville abonde . . . le nombre immense des non-payants, savoir, les prêtres, les gentilshommes et la foule des

[33] Rébillon, *Les États de Bretagne*, 405–25; 'Les États de Bretagne', *Conférences universitaires de Bretagne (1942–45)* (Paris, 1943), 201–23; L-A. Le Moyne de la Borderie and B. Pocquet, *Histoire de Bretagne* (Rennes, 1905–14), vi, 532–56; Fréville, *L'Intendance de Bretagne*, iii, 51–91.

[34] A. Rébillon, *Histoire de Bretagne* (Paris, 1957), 145.

serviteurs et des servantes de la noblesse vannetaise'.[35]

For those who did not come to this realization themselves, agents of the royal government were there to remind them of it. In 1764 and 1766, the duc d'Aiguillon practised wholesale bribery of the deputies of the Third Estate. As a deputy to the Estates of 1764, the barrister Bernard received 500 livres, and senechal Borie, who presided over the Third Estate in 1768, 1770 and 1774, got very large payments of from 12,000 to 20,000 livres a session, partly, it is true, for redistribution to the deputies as gifts and entertainment. Mayor Le Menez, whose office had been bought for him by the government, received 300 livres for his help at the Estates of 1778 and 1780, and a further sum in 1783. At least two distressed members of the town council with exemplary attendance records, Moigno de Mezouet, lieutenant-colonel of the town militia and De la Haye, the most faithful of the noble councillors, received pensions of 400 and 500 livres respectively. [36] In 1772, in the first session of the Estates after the victory of Maupéou and Terray over the Parlements, the government, determined to reduce the nobility to silence, had de Tréverret, the senechal of Quimper, whip up the discontent of the unprivileged and distribute largesse freely, but de Tréverret was already preaching to the converted, and the Third Estate began to complain forcefully for the first time about the share of the *capitation* which they paid. The Estates of 1772 marked an important stage in the political polarization of Brittany, which Augustin Cochin mistakenly attributed solely to the events of the summer and autumn of 1788. Lucas de Bourgerel, who had been sent as deputy to the session, apparently became infected by the mood of the Tiers there and returned to Vannes armed with a copy of the geographer Ogée's new map of the province and a demand that the town council vote its support for the struggle against the nobles' *capitation* privileges. Perhaps Bourgerel made too many enemies too fast; perhaps the recent example of Le Boulh's victory over Bourgerel gave some councillors ideas; perhaps it was general unhappiness with the royal government; at any rate, members

[35] A.C. Vannes, CC 15: Le Menez and Dusers [to *commission intermédiaire*] 15-12-1784.

[36] Rébillon, *Les États de Bretagne*, 122–3; A.N., H¹ 539 pc. 147; H¹ 538, pc. 92, 292–5 ff.; H¹ 480: 'Table contenant les noms des personnes à qui le Roi a accordé des pensions depuis 1760 jusques et compris 1772' and cahiers for 1771, 1773, 1775; A.D. I.-V., C 694: Le Menez to intendant, 11-3-1783.

began to stay away in increasing numbers, behaviour acutely embarrassing for Bourgerel, who had only recently become *avocat de la communauté*. To revive enthusiasm, he brought in an *arrêt* of the intendant prescribing fines for absentees without a legitimate excuse; for the next several meetings, legitimate excuses littered the minute-book ('absent depuis quelque temps', 'en campagne', 'malade', 'incommodé'). No one was ever fined; Bourgerel, and later his successor Caradec, in 1785, tried another tack and attempted unsuccessfully to reduce the quorum to twelve.[37]

It is difficult to dissociate this craze for absention in the early seventies from the political crisis in Brittany, but equally difficult to discover exactly what was going on. Certainly the town council, inspired in the first instance by the Présidial, came out on at least four occasions to back the Parlement of Brittany in its struggle with d'Aiguillon, and celebrated its return in December 1774 with a public fête.[38] No doubt the abstentions from meetings were a sign of the unwillingness of many councillors and their patrons to have any truck with men like Bourgerel who seemed to be weakening the solid front of provincial resistance by challenging the nobles' fiscal privileges.

The same abuse of the quorum rule by a minority in the council during the 1780s drove the final wedge between the 'regulars' and the minority of obstructionists on the eve of the revolutionary events of 1788. This happened on at least two occasions. The first arose when the council tried to regroup the parish cemeteries in one location outside the town, Le Croisier, the demagogic rector of St-Patern, the bookseller and printer Galles (who bore the council a grudge because they had not satisfied his claim for damages caused to his property by road works), and a seigneurial judge, Du Liepvre, managed to hold up the removal of the burial grounds on legal technicalities; in one crucial meeting, Le Croisier slipped out of the room at the end without signing the register, thus destroying the quorum. The second occasion, and a more serious one, in which the quorum rule was abusively invoked was the fight over the new street

[37] Rébillon, *Les États de Bretagne*, 374–83, 386–91; A.C. Vannes, BB 23: 29-1-1773 *et seq.*; BB 24: 12-1-1776; BB 26: 15-12-1786; A.D. I.-V., C 3992: Ordonnance du roi, 26-11-1785.

[38] A.C. Vannes, BB 21: 26, 29-2-1768, 30-11-1768, BB 22: 13, 21-7-1769; BB 23: 16-12-1774.

which the council planned to link the town centre with the market-place. In 1785, three nobles living in the centre, Gibon du Pargo, Du Plessis de Grenédan and de Bavalan, built porches in front of their houses and otherwise impinged on the public way. The council objected and in November 1787 ordered all such construction removed. In retaliation, those who opposed the new street and had porches and awnings to defend got the Parlement of Rennes to intervene and block the council's order on the grounds that it was an encroachment on the Présidial's police powers. The council in return demanded that the nobles and Chapter name their deputies like all the other groups instead of attending council in relays, and decided once again to impose a fine for non-attendance. Regular meetings were prevented for over six months, and the plan of urban renovation remained blocked until April 1788 and then of course was postponed until the nineteenth century. The blame for the affair was put by mayor Le Menez on two or three 'mauvais sujets poussés par quelques membres de la noblesse dont ils ont pris le parti'.[39] By this time, clergy and nobles must have been lumped together, not unreasonably, by most of the regular councillors, as the enemies of progress and prosperity.

This local stalemate coincided perfectly with the increasing frustration of the deputies of the Third Estate in the Breton Estates over the privileges of the First and Second Orders. Unpleasant exchanges over the distribution of the *capitation* had taken place again at the Estates of 1778; the deputies of the Third Estate claimed to speak in the people's name, to which the nobles replied with some reason that the Third represented only a bourgeois urban oligarchy. In that year, the Third won a slight reduction in the assessment of the *capitation*, but the nobles gained their revenge by getting control for the Estates over the auditing of municipal accounts as a result of the affair of the *octrois municipaux*, and the way seemed open for the Estates to play a preponderant role in the choosing of municipal officers. This touched closely on the interests of the Third 'La noblesse deviendra prépondérante dans les communautés,' protested de Tréverret, now senechal of Rennes and president of the Third, 'elle se rendra maîtresse des élections des maires, on verra des gentilshommes siègés aux États comme députés des villes!' This

[39] A.D. I.-V., C 694: Le Menez [to *subdélégué-général*] 23-8-1788; A.C. Vannes, BB 24: 6-3-1779, 2-4-1780; BB 25: 19-8-1783; BB 26: 27, 28-5-1785, 19-10-1785; BB 27: 16-1-1787, 3-12-1787.

could not go on indefinitely, the same writer observed: 'on cherche des occasions de mortifier le tiers, je vois avec peine qu'il y est sensible, qu'il prend de l'humeur et que certainement il secouera le joug qu'on veut lui imposer depuis longtemps.'[40] In the circumstances, it was only natural for the Third Estate to turn to the only effective counterbalancing force, the royal government, and it was in this way that, in Vannes, the cause of the King was transformed into the national, 'patriot', cause and the cause of the Third. This final *prise de conscience*, long in preparation, took place during the course of what has been termed the 'pre-revolution' in Brittany.[41] This period can be said to have begun in May 1788 with the united action of all orders against the Lamoignon edicts of that month. Vannes was among the first of the Breton towns to respond to the appeal of the Parlement and the *Commission intermédiaire*, and a stream of petitions from the local attorneys, barristers, courts and the town council went to join the flood of paper descending on the King's representatives in Rennes. The meetings which the town council called to draw up protests were massively attended, and, indeed, packed by the nobility and clergy on at least one occasion, but the unanimity of the clergy, nobles and Third Estate seems to have been real. The dismay of all the orders was the result of a coincidence of principle and interest: if Lamoignon's edict threatened the liberties of the noble Parlement of Rennes, it also severely debilitated yet another of the courts in Vannes and threatened the incomes of all those who lived directly or indirectly from its revenues. For although the civil competence of the Présidial was to be raised, according to the edict's terms, to cases involving 4,000 livres, it would no longer hear appeals from the surrounding jurisdictions of Rhuys and Auray, since appeals were to go directly to a *grand bailliage* in Quimper, and in criminal cases, the Présidial would only be able to judge as a court of first instance.[42] For a town

[40] Le Moyne de la Borderie and Pocquet, *Histoire de Bretagne*, vi, 355–6.

[41] On the struggles of this period, see Cochin, *Les Sociétés de pensée;* B. Pocquet, *Les Origines de la Révolution en Bretagne* (Paris, 1885), 2 vols.; J. Egret, 'Les Origines de la Révolution en Bretagne (1788–1789)', *Revue historique*, ccxiii (1955), 189–215; H. Sée, 'Le Rôle de la bourgeoisie bretonne à la veille de la Révolution', *Annales de Bretagne*, xxxiv (1919–20), 405–33.

[42] A.C. Vannes, BB 27: 15-5-1788, 5-6-1788, 26-7-1788, 5, 18-8-1788; A. Macé, 'Les Élections du Morbihan de 1789 à 1800', *BPSM* (1890), 80–4; Cochin, *Les Sociétés de pensée*, ii, 169–70; F. A. Isambert, *Recueil général des anciennes lois françaises* (Paris, 1821–35), xxxviii, 534–50; Egret, 'Les Origines', 189–215.

which depended so heavily on the proceeds of litigation for its survival, it was a hard blow.

Unity lasted through most of the summer, during which a mass meeting of the provincial nobility was held in Vannes on 19–20 June, followed by an assembly of the members of the Parlement and 1,500 'friends' at the château du Pargo in late July. The town council responded on 21 July to a second appeal for support from the *Commission intermédiaire* of Rennes in their attempts to free twelve deputies of the Breton nobility held prisoner in Paris, and at the end of the month deputized Président Le Gros and the *négociant* Bernard to attend a meeting in Rennes along with the canons de Boutouillic and de Douhet, and two nobles, Le Gouvello and Le Sénéchal de Carcado.[43]

But even in the summer of 1788, before the Paris Parlement made its decision on 25 September that the Estates-General would have to meet as they had last met in 1614 and vote on issues by order, the patriots' enthusiasm for the cause of the province and the Parlement was only conditional, and in the town council, two separate incidents in early August opposed the mayor to the partisans of the Parlement. In one of these, Houet de Chênevert, *procureur du roi* of the Présidial, demanded, with the nobles' support, that the council refuse to attend the Assumption Day procession and that it stop the sale of seized property by the local Domain officials; this was his contribution to paralysing the Monarchy. The assembly walked out on his speech. In the other incident, Delourme, a merchant who took the side of the Parlement, challenged the mayor to a duel. It was the petty tactlessness in small matters which the Paris Parlement was soon to show in large ones, and the result was similar. Le Menez, reporting to the intendant on the visit of Botherel, the procurator-general of the Estates, who was touring the province in August to rally support, wrote that 'L'arrivée subite [of Botherel] en cette ville, où il a été accueilli comme le restaurateur de la province, a excité sans doute de plus en plus le zèle fanatique de nos parlementaires, ce qui les porte aujourd'hui à tyranniser les gens qui ne pensent pas comme eux.'[44] At the same time, subversive anti-noble propaganda, the *Mémoire Secret* of Le

    [43] Cochin, *Les Sociétés de pensée*, i, 111–36; A. Macé, 'Les Élections du Morbihan', 80–4.
    [44] A.D. I.-V., C 694: Le Menez [to subdélégué-général], 23-8-1788; Fréville, *L'Intendance de Bretagne*, iii, 255.

Deist de Botidoux, began to circulate in the region around Vannes, to the horror of the diocesan bureau of the *commission intermédiaire*.[45] To the growing political discontent was added the spectre of popular revolt. By the middle of May, 1788, as it became apparent that the next harvest would be inadequate, that the surplus grain from 1786–7 had been used up and that virtually all of the harvest from the previous autumn had been either exported or consumed in the region, the price of wheat, and then of rye, began to climb sharply. In late August grain riots broke in a series of towns, most of them in southern Brittany. In Vannes, the revolts followed a similar pattern to those of 1765: they were directed, not against the nobles, but rather against the rich merchant, Danet *aîné*. 'Les commis des fermes ont excité le peuple et les paysans à s'opposer aux chargements, eux qui devraient les protéger,' wrote Danet indignantly, protesting that he had been forced to load his grain on board ship with lighters in order to avoid the crowd's fury. Some of the grain was seized at the order of the excise officials, to render him suspect to the people, Danet claimed.[46]

Perhaps it was the fear of future rioting like this, with all its dangers to both noble and non-noble property, which caused the factions in the council to draw together on 3 October and vote a cahier for their deputies to the forthcoming Breton Estates. The cahier was drawn up before the influence of the radical correspondence committee of Nantes, soon to become the spearhead of the revolt of the Third Estate in Brittany, began to make itself felt, and it represented a compromise. On the one hand, it favoured the Third: it called for a new and unspecified form of assessment for the *capitation* of the nobility and the Third Estate, the suppression of the 8 sous per livre *franc-fief* levy, the *centième denier* and other 'illegal taxes'; it also requested scholarships in colleges and military pensions for the Third Estate. On the other hand, at least two of the articles of the cahier were favourable to the cause of the nobility, providing that the Estates alone were to have charge of the administration and enforcement of the *fouages extraordinaires*, and that

[45] A.D. I.-V., C 3899 cited in Cochin, *Les Sociétés de pensée*, i, 180–1.

[46] A.D. I.-V., C 1714: Necker to intendant, 4-10-1788, Freneau to intendant, 8-11-1788; Fréville, *L'Intendance de Bretagne*, iii, 257–9; Cochin, *Les Sociétés de pensée*, ii, 176–83.

no change was to be permitted in the form of the municipal administration in Vannes.[47] This spirit of understanding, however, began to break down during October as Vannes was drawn into the vortex of the bitter struggle waged between the Parlement and nobility on one hand, and the committees of Rennes and Nantes on the other. As in the rest of Brittany, the party of the Third Estate set up correspondence bureaux and committees to keep in contact with their brothers; at the end of October, the town council appointed the abbé de Livois, *scholastique* of the cathedral, to correspond 'avec les communautés de Bretagne, qui réclament en particulier, et réclameront réunies en corps aux prochains États de la Province contre l'injustice, le joug et la servitude où la Noblesse tient le Tiers État'.[48]

Gradually an atmosphere of fear and hatred spread throughout the town, and the patriots, bombarded with petitions and addresses from the other towns of the province, finally decided at the end of November to strike a blow for the national cause. Urged on by Caradec, the *avocat de la communauté*, an assembly of the town council decided to modify their cahier along the lines of the cahier of the Rennes commune which had been circulated by the Nantes committee. Even then, the cahier which was voted remained moderate in tone, calling only for the doubling of the third order in the *commission intermédiaire* and the Estates without the vote by head; however it did demand the exclusion from the provincial estates of *anoblis, subdélégués,* the procurators-fiscal of seigneurs, seigneurial receivers, and employees of the royal and provincial *fermes* and *régies.*[49]

From then onward, the assembly of the town council became an open battleground for *patriotes* and their opponents. On 25 November, the *patriotes* attempted to present a petition to the King calling for the doubling of the Third and the vote by the head, but the nobility and Chapter succeeded in deferring the approval of the address. On 6 December, a rump assembly of merchants, barristers and attorneys together with the mayor and two members of the

[47] B.L. 911 c. 4 (2): *Extrait des registres de délibérations de la ville et communauté de Vannes en Bretagne* (Nantes, 1788); Cochin, *Les Sociétés de pensée,* ii, 136–7.
[48] A.N., H¹ 563–182 cited in Cochin, *Les Sociétés de pensée,* ii, 137.
[49] B.L. 911 c. 4 (2): *Extrait des registres de délibérations de . . . Vannes;* B.L. 911 c. 4 (6): *Remontrances de M. Caradec, Avocat de la Communauté de Ville de Vannes . . . ;* Cochin, *Les Sociétés de pensée,* ii, 137–8; A. Macé, 'Les Elections du Morbihan', 97.

lower clergy (Livois and Le Croisier) approved without reserve the demands of the Third Estate of Rennes, calling on the deputies of the Third Estate to refuse to vote taxes in the forthcoming Estates of the province without better representation for their order, demanding the appointment of two supplementary deputies from the town to the Estates, and denouncing the *franc-fief;* two days earlier some twenty *'privilégiés'*—non-noble office holders—renounced the privileges attached to their offices.[50]

Armed with these instructions, the deputies of the Third Estate of Vannes—Bourgerel *père*, Le Menez, Bernard and Poussin—set out for the provincial estates, which began on 29 December; they were probably present in Rennes from 22 December as well for a preliminary meeting of the Third Estate of the province. This protracted absence of the leaders of the patriots gave Président Le Gros the time he needed to organize a 'non-patriot' meeting on 7 January 1789 at the town hall where, acting in the mayor's stead, he expressed his fear at the critical position of what he called 'l'Assemblée Nationale', by which he meant the Breton Estates, and the impending ruin of the provincial constitution because of the intransigence of the Third in Rennes. Le Gros succeeded in getting a motion passed by 19 votes to 10, declaring that the council did not wish to harm the franchises and liberties of the province. Nevertheless, the document was not entirely retrograde for it requested the doubling of the Third Estate in the Breton Estates and the vote by head on the assessment of taxation, nominations to all positions and offices and the internal regulation of the Estates.

But the interest of this motion lay not so much in its wording as in the vote itself, which showed that the Third Estate in Vannes was unable to muster enough support even among its own members to carry the council. Of the nineteen members of the assembly who can be clearly identified as members of the Third, nine voted for the motion and only ten against. It was clear that, with such a divided group, it would be necessary to purge the council of the nobles and clergy before a majority of patriots could be assured. This was what Le Menez tried to do in a secret session on 23 January after returning from Rennes, but he succeeded only in part, for the other orders

---

[50] A.N., H¹ 563: Le Menez to Necker, 26-11-1788, Livois to Necker, 29-11-1788; A.D. I.-V., C 688: Le Menez to intendant, 22-11-1788; A.D. Morbihan, K 1536: *Extrait des délibérations de la ville et communauté de Vannes du samedi 6 décembre 1788;* Cochin, *Les Sociétés de pensée*, ii, 128–40.

heard of his plans, attended in force, and refused to leave the chamber when asked. The meeting then split into two assemblies, each claiming to be the real town council, and town business was paralysed for the next four months.[51]

These divided assemblies of 6 December 1788 and 7 and 23 January 1789 allow us to examine the political choices of the councillors with some precision. Who then were the patriots and their enemies, and who stood on the sidelines? Given the nature of the conflict, it is not surprising to learn that most of the 23 patriots came from the Third Estate: there were 6 barristers, 6 businessmen, 6 notaries or attorneys, plus two members of the clergy, the abbés de Livois and Le Croisier. The 'antipatriot' group was more mixed; it included, naturally enough, five nobles and three members of the Présidial, three canons and one rector, but it also had two barristers, two businessmen and four attorneys. The patriots were not therefore the united front of the Third Estate that they claimed to be, and their enemies were quick to point it out, alleging that the strength of the patriot vote in January came from family connections. The weakness of support for the patriots is even more apparent if we compare their names and those of the antipatriots with the list of councillors attending from 1785 to the autumn of 1788, that is, before affairs became polarized. Thirty-two of a total of 75 members simply did not attend the crucial meetings of December and January, and of this total of 32, while 9 were nobles, 6 clergy and one from the Présidial, the rest were from the Third Estate. There were more abstainers and antipatriots among the Third Estate than there were revolutionary bourgeois.

On the whole, the patriots tended to be less wealthy than the antipatriots. Five of the seventeen patriots of the Third Estate whose *capitation* tax in 1783 is known paid more than the mean for the group, but over half the antipatriots paid more than the mean, and of course, the wealth of the clergy and nobility, who were virtually all antipatriots, is not included in these figures. There is therefore a measure of truth in a description of the revolt of the

[51] A.D. Morbihan, K 1537: *Extrait des registres des délibérations de la ville et communauté de Vannes (Vannes, 26 janvier 1789);* K 1534: *Lettre écrite de Vannes à MM. Le Menez de Kerdelleau, Poussin & Bourgerel Lucas, premier député et aggrégés de Vannes, aux États de la Province de Bretagne, & à MM. les députés du Commerce de Nantes, le 8 janvier 1789;* A.D. Morbihan, K 1535: *Extrait des délibérations . . . du 23 janvier 1789.*

patriots in Vannes as a revolution, not only of less wealthy commoners against wealthy nobles, but also of less wealthy bourgeois
against richer bourgeois.

A more significant distinction can be drawn between patriots and
antipatriots in terms of age. Of the 23 patriots whose age is known, 8
were younger than the median age for the group, while only 3 of the
20 antipatriots and 2 of the 30 absentionists can be so described.
This age difference is important, but says less about the political
disposition of the young towards a bourgeois revolution than it does
of the political astuteness of the patriots, who began to pack the
council in the crisis of 1788–9 with their sons, whom they nominated
as officers of the town militia; when we look at the relative ages of
the group of regular attenders from the period 1785–88, we find
much less difference between patriots and antipatriots, though,
interestingly, all of the abstentionists from the group of regular
attenders were older men; youth was therefore on the side of
activists in both camps, and age on that of the torpid or reserved.[52]

The real difference, however, between patriots and antipatriots
lies in the history of the town council over the previous half-century.
Of the 23 patriots of the winter of 1788–9, no less than 18 came from
the inner group of 'zealous' politicians who had attended the average numbers of meetings or more in 1785–8, but of the 20 antipatriots, only 6 were enthusiasts for municipal affairs and only 5 of
the zealous took no position at all in 1788–9. Similarly, 13 of the 17
patriots who had been on the council in 1780–4 had been zealous
attenders, compared to 6 of the 15 antipatriots on council, and the
same tendency can be observed in the councillors of 1775–9, 1770–4
and 1765–9: the men who were to become patriots had always been
more keen on municipal affairs than their future adversaries.[53]
However, in the early 1780s, the forces of those who were to
become the patriots of 1788–9 had acquired considerable reinforcement: between 1775–9 and 1780–4 the number of future patriots in
the council increased by 6 while the number of antipatriots only

[52] Political choice in 1788–9 by age group of 'inner group' 1785–8:

	Born before 1744	Born 1744 and after	Totals
Patriot	11	7	18
Antripatriot	5	1	6
Abstention	5	0	5
Totals	21	8	29

increased by 3, and the number of future patriots attending assiduously went up by 8 while that of the antipatriots increased by 2 only. The same tendency can be seen between 1780–4 and 1785–9. In general, in the last fifteen years of the old regime, there was a trend towards greater interest and participation in municipal politics, and those who were most interested tended to be those who became revolutionaries in 1788–9. Augustin Cochin's verdict on the events of 1788 was that they excluded from public life 'des "impurs"; des "malignants", c'est-à-dire presque tout le monde—du moins presque tous les politiciens compétents, formés par l'état social actuel'.[54] In Vannes, and probably elsewhere in Brittany, the opposite was the case: the privileged had manipulated the municipal constitution once too often for their own good: 1789 was the revenge of the politicians on the dilettantes.

These then were the general characteristics of an activist of the Third Estate in 1789 in Vannes: a man in his forties, not a noble or a cleric, most likely to be a lawyer, with more interest in municipal politics than the others and perhaps less wealth and years than they. But what of those who failed to conform to this pattern? Who were they and why did they act as they did?

No noble voted for the patriots, but three members or ex-members of the Présidial did: Lauzer de Larmor, Dusers and the Mayor, Le Menez de Kerdelleau. Le Menez's attitude is reasonable enough; when he became mayor he left the Présidial behind, and he got his office through the intendant's favour. His was the lot of those who had been the 'intendant's men' on the council in the old regime and continued to oppose the King's opponents even though the intendant was no longer leading the attack. The case of Dusers and Poussin, respectively councillor and lieutenant in the Présidial, is more complex. Both were officers of the Présidial, both were born about the same time in Rennes and probably went to law school

[53] Proportion of patriots, antipatriots and abstainers of 1788–9 active in politics 1765–88 and members of the inner group:

	Antipatriots	Patriots	Abstainers	Total
1765–9	5/11	5/7	5/11	15/29
1770–4	6/11	5/8	6/11	17/30
1775–9	4/12	5/11	7/12	16/35
1780–4	6/15	13/17	6/14	25/46
1785–8	6/20	18/23	5/32	29/75

[54] Cochin, Les Sociétés de pensée, ii, 216.

together.[55] The main differences between them and their antipatriot colleagues P.-T. Houet de Chênevert and Président Le Gros was that the latter two were ennobled or wanted to be. Le Gros also seems to have been something of an innocent in politics, and later came round to be a firm supporter of the Revolution.[56] Jaques-Joseph Febvrier, a councillor in the Présidial, unlike Le Gros, was an antipatriot in 1789 and stayed firm in his opinions. The mortified administrators of the Department of the Morbihan tried later to excuse their failure to prevent his election to the Five Hundred in 1797: 'nous avons toujours pensé que s'il n'avait pas été M^r le Subdélégue de l'intendance, attaché à une famille aristocrate et aussi bon catholique romain [underlined in the text] on ne l'aurait pas vu dès 1789 refuser de prendre part aux élans de la nation française.'[57] The split in the Présidial was characteristic of the attitude of the members of these courts who were forced, as one historian puts it 'to choose among their most cherished ideals . . . [and] in general, supported reform and accepted, at least by deciding not to oppose, a republican revolution.'[58] The choice was, however, not just one based on principles, but was also determined by social distinctions of a subtle kind.

No churchmen were in the group of municipal activists in 1785–8, but the attitude of the two churchmen who stood out as patriots in the municipal assembly in 1788–9 is interesting. Thus the scholastic of the cathedral, de Livois, had been humiliated in 1785–6 when the Chapter refused him the right to carry the cantor's wand in processions and to share in the perquisites, capitular assemblies and honours of the canons. He became a zealous correspondent of Necker and the provincial revolutionary committees in 1788–9. The rector Le Croisier, though he had his difficulties with the council,

[55] Debauve, La Justice révolutionnaire, 79–80; A.D. Morbihan, 42 G 22 (330): Dispenses de bans, 1779; L 1686: Société des amis de la constitution, Vannes.
   [56] A.D. Morbihan, K 1535: Extrait du registre des délibérations de la ville et Communauté de Vannes, en Bretagne, 23-1-1789; Meyer, La Noblesse bretonne, i, 358; Frotier de la Messelière, Filiations bretonnes, ii, 631–3; Debauve, Justice révolutionnaire, 77–8.
   [57] A.D. Morbihan, L 240: Administration centrale du Département to Minister of Police, 23 Germinal Year V (12-4-1797), see also Debauve, Justice révolutionnaire, 61. The 'aristocratic' family is perhaps a reference to a brother-in-law, Chautard, who held the Cross of St-Louis; see A.C. Vannes, GG 69: marriage, St-Salomon, 12-8-1777.
   [58] P. Dawson, Provincial Magistrates and Revolutionary Politics in France, 1788–1795 (Cambridge, Mass., 1972), 340.

was even less well disposed to the Chapter after several unfortunate disputes in the 1780s which had ended in his temporary reclusion at the Seminary. Throwing in his lot with the Third Estate gave him the honour of leading a delegation to Versailles and the audacity to demand a commendatory benefice from the King, but, unlike Livois, his conversion to the Revolution was temporary and he went into exile in Spain after 1791.[59] In these two cases of revolutionary clerics, quarrels with the Chapter seem to have been the deciding factor.

Of the antipatriot lawyers, Le Monnier was rather more than a mere barrister; he had a place as *procureur* in the *maîtrise des eaux et forêts*, served on the *commission intermédiaire*, and was styled *conseiller du roi*; he bought several expensive seigneuries in the 1780s and had the head of the noble Rosmadec family (whose estate agent he was) for his daughter's godparent in 1781.[60] The barrister Jollivet's only discernible motives—not unreasonable ones—for voting as an antipatriot were his father's position as procurator-fiscal of the bishop's seigneurial court and his marriage to the daughter of Le Ridant, attorney for the Chapter in 1786 and another antipatriot among the ranks of the Third Estate. The patriots thought the tie to Le Ridant decided his vote, as well as that of the book-seller J.-B.-M.-J. Galles, husband to Jollivet's sister. Galles was from one of the oldest merchant families in Vannes and made much of his living, it seems, on the sale of pious books. He had already antagonized the dynamic majority of the council in the affairs of the cemetery and the street alignments.[61] P.-J. Perret, the other anti-patriot attorney along with Le Ridant and Jollivet *père*, was married to the daughter of a recently ennobled man from Nantes, which possibly suggests aspirations towards a higher standing; his son emigrated at some time before 1794.[62] The merchant antipatriot

[59] A.D. Morbihan, 47 G 7 (376): 10-6-1785; 52 G 4 (380): Supplique de . . . J. M. de Livois, 14,15-12-1786; Cochin, *Les Sociétés de pensée*, ii, 136; A. Cariou, 'La Constitution civile du clergé dans le Departement du Morbihan', *MSHAB*, xlv (1965), 59–88; T. Le Goff, 'Les Doléances des paysans du Vannetais à la veille de la Révolution', *BPSM* (1969), 35–6.

[60] A.C. Vannes, GG 69: St-Salomon, baptism, 12-2-1781; A.D. Morbihan, 17 C 5398: 1-4-1784; 17 C 5400: 19-10-1786; on the Rosmadec family, Meyer, *La Noblesse bretonne*, ii, 713.

[61] A.C. Vannes, GG 23: St-Pierre, marriage, 16-4-1787; GG 58: St-Patern, baptism, 26-8-1763; GG 68: St-Salomon, baptism, 9-1-1769; A.D. Morbihan, K 1534: *Lettre écrite de Vannes à MM Le Menez de Kerdelleau et Poussin*, 8-1-1789.

[62] A.C. Vannes, GG 57: St-Patern, marriage, 6-11-1758; Debauve, *Justice révolutionnaire*, 225, 267 n. 34.

A.-L. Soymié, a native of Pontivy, seems to have been inclined that way from his marriage to the Le Louais family of Nantes, which made him brother-in-law of another antipatriot, the rentier Le Brun, son of a *commissaire de la marine* and brother-in-law of a local noble, J.-L. de Lantivy de Trédion; he was apparently on good terms with the *subdélégué* of Pontivy, d'Harcourt. According to the patriots, he was also related to Febvrier.[63]

What set these political eccentrics apart from their fellows who voted according to form were apparently their aspirations, interests, resentments and family connections. But if each of the lives of those who believed in the 'correct' fashion were to be examined, we might well find similar hopes and interests. The barrister Bernard, a patriot, if a lukewarm one, was a seigneurial judge; so was Lucas de Bourgerel, who was to sit with the left in the Estates-General, but who must have held the local record for accumulating seigneurial offices. Most of those who made a choice in Vannes in 1788 did so as a result of their earlier experience in politics. It is surely significant that of all these cases of 'unusual' behaviour by members of the Third Estate who sided with the antipatriots, only Le Brun, Soymié and Le Ridant were both antipatriots and members of the inner group in 1785–8: a few of the others had once been active in municipal affairs, but by 1785–8 had withdrawn. For most of the patriots, then, it it certainly arguable that their choice in 1788–9 had been long in preparation: their political education was the result of the course of provincial politics and the struggles over town affairs in the two generations before 1789. It was the way they shared in what was already a long tradition of political activity which set them apart from the apathy of the bulk of middle-class people and the suspicion and hostility of the lower orders. 'Le mouvement du tiers État breton durant les premiers mois de 1789', wrote Jean Egret, 'reste un soulèvement de bourgeois.'[64] In Vannes—and very likely elsewhere—it was a movement of only a minority of bourgeois.

For a threatened minority, they made remarkably few attempts to recruit popular support in town and country. Although some attempt was made to rouse the nearby countryside in November 1788 when some artisans and peasants from the rural part of the parish of St-Patern were encouraged by their rector, Le Croisier, to

---

[63] A.C. Vannes, GG 23: St-Pierre, marriage, 6-2-1786; GG 62: St-Patern, baptism, 20-3-1784; A.D. Morbihan, K 1534: *Lettre écrite de Vannes . . .* 8-1-1789.

[64] Egret, 'Les Origines', 209.

present a motion of support for the cahier which the town council adopted in November, the revolutionaries continued to speak only of essentially urban, middle-class demands for political and administrative reform in all the cahiers they presented down to the end of the year, even though some peasant opinion certainly must have existed by that time.[65] It was equally this group which remained in control of the elections to the Estates General in April and which directed the preparation of the cahiers for the Estates which were drawn up in April.

In Brittany, only two or, more correctly, one and one-half of the traditional three orders of the realm met to elect deputies to the Third Estate, for at a joint meeting held at St-Brieuc on 16 April the nobility and upper clergy of the province decided not to nominate representatives in protest against the refusal of the Crown to allow the election of all deputies by the Breton Estates. However, both the Third Estate and the lower clergy did elect representatives and prepare *cahiers de doléances* in the same manner as in the rest of France. In the diocese of Vannes, the electoral assemblies of the Third Estate took place in three stages, and the revolutionaries of Vannes managed to dominate all the proceedings in which they were involved.

In the first stage of the elections, the towns and parish assemblies in the *sénéchaussées* of Vannes and Auray and the *juridiction royale* of Rhuys were to elect deputies and prepare cahiers for an electoral assembly in each of their jurisdictions. In Vannes on 5 April ten deputies were chosen: Le Menez, Lauzer de Larmor, Poussin, Dusers, De la Chasse, Caradec, Hervieu, Brulon, De Bray and Rollin. All of these with the exception of De Bray, an apothecary, and Rollin, an outsider, had proved their patriotism in the town council during the autumn and winter; in addition to these, some members of the group such as Lucas de Bourgerel and Bachelot had managed to have themselves elected in neighbouring parishes as deputies to the *sénéchaussée* assembly. Held at Vannes and attended by 119 deputies, this assembly chose twelve electors. Of the twelve, eight came from Vannes; of the eight, seven were 'zealous' members of the council in 1785–8, and all of those were legal men, either members of the Présidial or barristers. When they met with the representatives of the *sénéchaussées* of Auray and Rhuys, they

[65] Le Goff, 'Les Doléances', 31–50.

picked as deputies to the Estates-General those tried warriors of town politics, Lucas de Bourgerel and Dusers.[66]

It seems likely that, as everyone expected, it was the barristers of Vannes who drafted the cahier of Vannes for the Estates-General and the final general cahier of the *sénéchaussée* as well.[67] Like most of the general cahiers of the Third Estate throughout France, that of the *sénéchaussée* of Vannes deals mainly with wider questions of constitutional and administrative reform: it requested the establishment of a constitutional monarchy with its appropriate mechanisms, complete legal equality for the Third Estate, the doubling of its representatives and the vote by head in all legislative bodies and commissions, and a certain number of liberal reforms of the administrative and legal system. No doubt many of the general proposals for reform were made with local grievances in mind: thus article 40, which called for town councils to have exclusive control of police within their boundaries was probably a slap to the Présidial and to seigneurial justices; article 130, which asked that municipalities have sole right to decide whether to engage in lawsuits without referring to the intendant and grant public works contracts without entertaining open bidding was a protest against the intendant's tutelage; and article 99, which demanded an end to Lorient's status as a free port, was part of a long-standing local rivalry. Articles 104 to 119 proposed that the provincial Estates should be extended to all the kingdom, but the forms they prescribed for the provincial constitutions and administration of taxes were a total denial of everything that the Breton Estates had stood for.

Not a great deal was said about concerns other than these, although some space was given to commercial reforms, on which the merchants of Vannes had drawn up a lengthy separate cahier. There is only one mention of a programme drawn up by a guild, the shoemakers, who directed their deputy to request only 'l'égalisation de droits royaux. Le soutien des droits qui concernent l'état des cordonniers suivant l'ancienne coutume. L'exécution de la marque des cuirs . . .'—apparently without success, for the cahier of the

---

[66] A.N., B^A 26 (Vannes), pc. 1, 4; B III 37, 851–95; Cochin, *Les Sociétés de pensée*, ii, 141–2; A. Brette, *Les Constituants* (Paris, 1897), 174. In the diocese of Vannes, the lower clergy met, but dispersed without drawing up a cahier because of the need to return to their parishes for Easter.

[67] A.D. I.-V., C 1807: Le Gros to intendant, 2-4-1789. There was apparently no single cahier drawn up by the meeting of the three *sénéchaussées*.

sénéchaussée called for the 'suppression des maîtrises et jurandes qui étouffent l'émulation en enchaînant les talents', carefully exempting the middle-class guilds of surgeons, apothecaries and goldsmiths from this provision (arts. 78–9). Day-labourers without property were to be let off taxes (art. 75), a well-meaning if inexpensive concession, since this class in Vannes paid only about 1 per cent of the total *capitation* of the town. A gesture was made towards the country districts, probably at the insistence of Le Quinio, mayor of Sarzeau, in suggesting reforms of the local system of land tenure, the *domaine congéable,* but here, as in the clauses requesting the abolition of seigneurial justice with compensation to the seigneurs and judges, the authors of the cahier called only for reforms, not the abolition of the system: leases of eighteen instead of nine years' length, the possibility, perhaps, for the tenant to carry out improvements on his own initiative and share in the proceeds of the sale of chestnut-trees, letting the price of the edifices reflect market value instead of being fixed at 6 livres a *journal* (an odd request, since the value of edifices did change; but then in general the cahier appears misinformed on the subject of the *domaine congéable*). Seigneurial dues were to be made redeemable and various minor accessories of the seigneurial regime to be abolished, usually with compensation (arts. 134–44) and the tithe was to be collected at a uniform and moderate rate (art. 132). Except for the ineffective articles on the *domaine congéable*, this was the small change of the *cahiers de doléances* drawn up at the *sénéchaussée* level throughout France, if not irrelevant to local conditions.[68]

Up to this point, then, the revolutionary history of Vannes was one of a quarrel among factions within the dominant classes. Contrary to what happened in some of the other Breton towns—Auray, for example—the initial stages of the Revolution retained this character in Vannes. It was during the month of July, rather than April, when the first real challenge to the oligarchy occurred. The three months following the opening of the Estates-General were marked by the breakdown of municipal authority and manifestations of popular discontent. In Vannes itself, the presence of the *régiment de Rouergue* appears to have assured the maintenance of civil order, but serious grain riots, coinciding with sharp upward

[68] A.D. Morbihan, E 1041: Communauté des maîtres cordonniers de la ville de Vannes, registre des délibérations. The texts of the cahier of the *sénéchaussée* and the merchants of Vannes is printed in *Archives parlementaires*, vi, 107–17.

swings in the price of grain and directed against merchants and seigneurial officials, broke out at Auray in April and Arzon in May.

As the time of the harvest approached, as the stocks left over from 1788 diminished, and as the merchants laid up supplies of grain to be exported at the moment of greatest demand, prices rose according to the usual pattern. However, this year, the high prices were caused not only by hoarding and speculation but also by the prospect of a late and indifferent harvest, made worse by the absence of a surplus from previous years and the unwillingness of the country districts to part with their grain.[69]

Caught between the unrest of the populace and the unappeased hostility of the nobility and upper clergy, the revolutionaries in the town council at first lay low and then, when the news of the taking of the Bastille arrived on 21 July, began, in the midst of the momentary euphoria, to establish themselves. Assuring themselves first of all of the loyalty of the Rouergue regiment, the town council set up on 28 July a corps of National Militia and seized available arms and powder. Then, on the 29th, 50 members of the 'revolutionary youth' were sent to investigate the report of a noble plot at the chateau du Grégo—where they discovered two nobles and thirteen hunting guns. The following day however there came more serious news of the precipitate flight from the town of several nobles, suspicious of the intentions of the towns, and the council protested in what amounted to a veiled threat, to the doyen of the local nobility. All these actions of the council took place in meetings open to the public, and it is not surprising that the latter now took it upon themselves to make certain that the town officials secured them a food supply in the crisis that was upon them; on 29 July, the assembly forced Le Gros, despite his protests, to decree the seizure of a ship in the channel which had been charged by the Government with 55 tons of grain for Rouen, and, at the same time appointed a commission of ten men, to take charge of the provisions of the town.

This, however, marked the extreme limit of the municipal revolution. On 31 July, expressing its concern with the multitude of persons appearing at its sessions, the assembly decreed for itself a

⁶⁹ A.D. I.-V., C 1654, 1655: État des récoltes, Febvrier to intendant, 15-12-1789; comparison des récoltes de 1788 et 1789, 15-12-1789 (Febvrier) and letter of Danet aîne 17-9-1789 to intendant; C 1714: Necker to intendant, 4-10-1788, Freneau to intendant, 8-11-1788; Fréville, *L'Intendance de Bretagne*, iii, 257–9 and Cochin, *Les Sociétés de pensée*, ii, 176–83.

new constitution. The new 'municipality' would be composed of 37 members, and the list of participants reads like a roll-call of the previous municipal administrations, minus the nobles and canons. To this were added 63 representatives of the 'communes', many of them people of modest condition. But power, it shortly became apparent, lay with the old rather than with the new group; on 3 August, a kind of steering committee composed of Kerdelleau, Le Gros, Rollin, Malherbe, Quelleneau, de Bray and Bachelot was appointed, with power to review and reject all notions presented to the assembly; sessions, moreover, were to be held in secret. During the following fortnight, the estranged Chapter and nobility acquiesced grudgingly in the new order. But the assembly, realizing that it now had the upper hand, played on the nobles' fear of a popular rising and of being implicated in the 'Brest plot' in order to force the nobles and Chapter to adhere without reservations to the decrees of the National Assembly, to swear fidelity to the King and the Nation, and to repudiate the oaths they had taken at St-Brieuc and Rennes. After considerable hesitation, at first the Chapter and then the nobility followed the lead of bishop Amelot and adhered formally on 8 August.[70]

By the final week of August, the victory of the revolutionaries seemed consolidated against the dangers from above and below, and they could afford the luxuries of public ceremonies and a magnanimous attitude. The occasion was the oath-taking of the Milice Nationale and local revolutionary youth. The troops, ranged along the promenade next to the port, in the presence of the *municipalité*, wearing their robes of office, took the oath amid universal acclaim; and then, the civil ceremony done, the entire assembly proceeded up the hill to the cathedral to chant the *Te Deum* and the *Salve fac Regem* and receive the bishop's blessing. It was a memorable occasion: 'Fut-il jamais de plus beaux jours pour la France que ceux nous voyons maintenant se succéder!' apostrophized Bachelot, the new *avocat-sindic* of the municipality,

Fut-il jamais présage plus heureux pour elle! Tous les Ordres de l'État travaillent à l'envi à asseoir irrevocablement sa gloire et son bonheur. Ce feu patriotique qui embrase tous les cœurs fait dans un instant ce qu'une longue suite de siècles n'a pu opérer; c'est lui qui, dans un jour, vient de détruire ces

---

[70] A.D. Morbihan, K 1544: *Procès-verbal des séances tenues par l'assemblée de la municipalité et des communes de la ville de Vannes*, [1789].

monstreux préjugés qui nous tenaient dans un anéantissement moral; les Ordres qu'on eut cru intéressés à les perpétuer sont plus que convaincus qu'ils ne pourraient leur procurer qu'une félicité apparente. . . .[71]

It was more a pious wish than an exact observation. Within little more than a year both the clergy and nobility had broken irrevocably with the Revolution, and the inhabitants of the surrounding countryside had risen up in the first of a long series of revolts against a new order which apparently had in it no place for them.

[71] Loc. cit.

PART II

CHAPTER V

OWNERSHIP OF LAND AND
CONDITIONS OF TENURE

Once outside the walls and the faubourgs of Vannes, one passed
quickly and almost immediately into the countryside. In all directions lay the *bocage*, concealing behind its hedgerows and wastelands a densely-settled rural population; farther to the south were
patches of openfield land on the peninsula of Rhuys and near Séné.
Under what economic conditions did these people live, and what
was the distribution of wealth among them? How did they view each
other and the world outside their settlements? The answers to these
questions depend in the first instance on a knowledge of their basic
resource, the land.

The countryside of the Vannetais was predominantly an area of
small holdings. A rough indication of the nature of landholding
appears in the *recensement des grains* of the Year II (1793–4), a
survey whose purpose was to discover the surplus of marketable
grain on each holding and the amount of land under the plough.
When these facts are set out in a series of histograms illustrating the
relative preponderance of the different sizes of arable land on each
holding, the predominance of small and middle-sized property immediately becomes apparent.[1] Even those few properties which
stand out as 'large' holdings in a parish or commune seldom contained more than ten hectares of arable land.

Within this region of small holdings, there were two contrasting
areas. On the coast were the areas of openfield farming, covering
most of the peninsula of Rhuys, low gently rolling open country that
was described by one observer as a 'Beauce armoricaine'.[2] This was
a region characterized by extreme fragmentation of peasant holdings,
communal usages of a sort, biennial crop rotation, and the persistence of wine-growing, even though the area was well north of the

[1] See Graph 1.
[2] Ogée, *Dictionnaire*, ii, 884.

Graph I

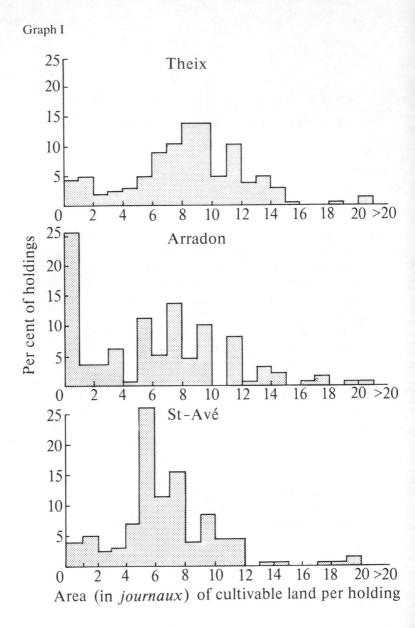

Area (in *journaux*) of cultivable land per holding

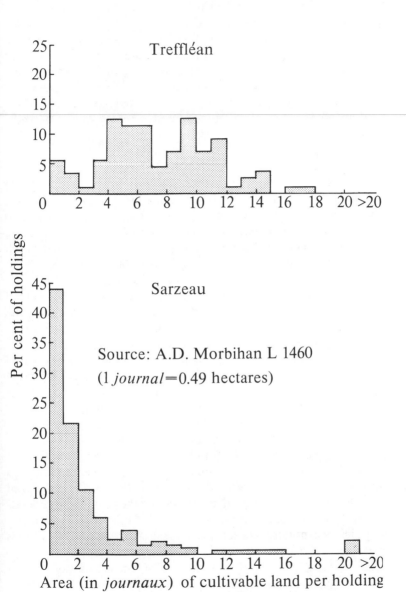

Loire. About a quarter of the rural population of the region lived in this area. The rest lived in the more typically 'Breton' interior where, as the histograms show, holdings of the middling sort, with 2.5 to 6 hectares of arable land each predominated. This was *bocage* country, made up of small fields enclosed by hedgerows of trees and bushes, each set of fields radiating outwards from a hamlet at whose limits were large tracts of unenclosed wasteland (*landes*). Each holding, worked by a single set of tenants or proprietors, enjoyed a degree of independence from its neighbours. It is with this area that the greater part of this chapter is concerned.

Who owned these plots of land? The question is not easy to answer as it might appear. According to estimates based on the *vingtième*, drawn up in mid-century in the three parishes of Surzur, Theix and Grand-Champ, the nobility owned outright around 70 per cent of all holdings, not including commons (and in Brittany, commons also belonged in principle to the seigneurs). The Church and the bourgeoisie were very much the junior partners of the nobility. In Theix and Surzur, the Church possessed less than 5 per cent of holdings, and even in Grand-Champ, where there existed one of the highest concentrations of ecclesiastical holdings in the region, it held only 13 per cent of the total. The bourgeoisie, principally inhabitants of Vannes rather than of the parishes themselves, held only about 5 per cent of the holdings in Theix and Surzur and 10 per cent in Grand-Champ. The peasants' share was small; although they owned 17 per cent of the holdings and 7 per cent of the total area in Theix, and 32 per cent of holdings (but less than 4 per cent of the area) in Surzur, the average size of peasant tenures—2.3 hectares in Theix and 0.8 hectares in Surzur—was not great. In Grand-Champ, they held an even smaller proportion of the total number of holdings. Finally, about 2 per cent of holdings consisted of land donated to the local parishes for the upkeep of chapels, missions and special devotions and the payment of stipends to priests who performed extra services.[3] This pattern of ownership, in which the nobility owned the largest share of rural land, was characteristic of most of Lower Brittany.

However, to consider the distribution of land in this way only is a little inadequate; it is necessary also to look at the way in which the owners disposed of their holdings. Most peasant owners worked their own holdings (called *héritages*) themselves, though as we have

[3] See Table V-1.

Table V-1: Distribution of land and land use

(1) Distribution of land in the parish of Theix c. 1750

Number of tenures	% Total	Proprietors	Area (ha)	% Total	Av. (ha)
286	73.0	Nobles	} 1997	86.1	6.6
17 +	4.3	Clergy (instit.)			
20	5.1	Bourgeois	125	5.4	6.3
65	16.6	Peasants	148	6.4	2.3
4	1.0	Chapel and parish endowments	49	2.1	12.3
392 +	100.0	Total	2319 +	100.0	5.9

(2) Land use in the parish of Theix c. 1750

Number of tenures	% Total	Proprietors (forms of rental or holding)	Area (ha)	% Total	Av. (ha)
		Domaine congéable:			
204	52.0	Worked by tenants	1205	52.7	5.9
85	21.7	Sublet by tenants	497	21.7	5.8
56	14.3	Fermes & *métairies*	384	16.8	6.9
8	2.0	Noble, occupied	112	4.9	14.0
39	9.9	Peasant prop.	90	3.9	2.3
392 +	99.9	Total	2288	100.0	5.8

(3) Distribution of land in the parish of Grand-Champ c. 1750

Number of tenures	% Total	Proprietors
411	70.1	Nobles
		Clergy:
2 }	13.1	(a) Individuals
75 }		(b) Orders, Chapter
57	9.7	Bourgeois
35	6.0	Peasants
6	1.0	Chapel and parish endowments
586	99.9	Total

Table V-1: Distribution of land and land use (*continued*)

(4) Land use in the parish of Grand-Champ c. 1750

Number of tenures	% Total	Proprietors
		Domaine congéable:
279	57.5	Worked by tenants
93	19.2	Sublet
		Fermes & métairies
92	19.0	Occupied by noble proprietors, or not let
8	1.6	Worked by peasant proprietors
13	2.7	
485	100.0	Total

(5) Distribution of land in the parish of Surzur

Number of tenures	% Total	Proprietors	Area (ha)
		Nobles	
14	4.7	(1) *Métairies, fermes & pourpris*	n.a.
166	56.1	(2) *Domaines congéables*	1713.9
		Clergy (*domaine cong.*)	
2	0.7	(1) Institutions	
2	0.7	(2) Individuals	
13 +	4.4	Bourgeois (*d.c.*)	
97	32.8	Peasants (*héritages*)	68.8
2	0.7	Chapel and parish endowments	n.a.
296	100.1	Total	

(6) Land use in the parish of Surzur

Number of tenures	% Total	Proprietors (form of rental or holding)	Area in ha Arable	Mead.	Past.	Gardn.	Waste	Vine	Total	Av.
		Domaine congéable								
172	54.1	(1) Worked by tenants	916.3	206.9	56.8	18.2	486.4	29.1	1,713.3	9.9
35 (+ 4)	11.0	(2) Sublet by tenants	167.4	39.5	10.6	2.6	127.3	2.2	349.6	10.0
207	65.0	Totals	1083.7	246.4	67.4	20.8	613.7	31.3	2062.9	10.0

Table V-1: Distribution of land and land use (*continued*)

Fermes & métairies, pourpis									
(1) Occupied by noble proprietors	2	0.6	—	—	—	—	—	1.6	0.8
(2) Leased ,, ,,	12	3.8	—	—	—	—	—	0.0	0.4
Totals	14	4.4	—	—	—	—	—	1.6	1.2
Peasant property									
(1) Occupied	79	24.8	27.7	3.0	3.2	16.4	8.8	60.7	
(2) Leased	18	5.7	4.1	0.1	1.4	2.3	0.1	8.0	
Totals	97	30.5	31.8	3.1	4.6	18.7	8.9	68.7	
	318 (+4)	100.0						2131.6	6.7

Sources:

(1), (2): P. Thomas-Lacroix, 'La Condition des terres', 347. Church property: A.D. Morbihan, Q 185, 205–7, 226 (Ventes de biens nationaux). The 17 *tenues* listed in Table VI-1(1) were all held by the monastère de Nazareth in Vannes. In addition, there were some 7 small tenures held by the bishopric of Vannes for which the area is not known.

(3), (4): A.D. Morbihan, C Subdélégation de Vannes: Paroisse de Grand-Champ, Vingtièmes, 1751–53. Because the rolls are incomplete—many declarations do not give the surface of land under cultivation—it was impossible to give totals of areas under cultivation. Note the discrepancy between the totals of tenure given in (3) and (4) (586 and 485 respectively). The figures in (4) were obtained from peasant declarations; those in (3) from the declarations of proprietors. Some noble proprietors did not furnish declarations (e.g. the prince de Rohan-Chabot), but errors appear to come for the most part from peasants' tendency to declare fractions of tenures as complete tenures. Church property: A.D. Morbihan, Q 184–5, 208, 210, 212–13, 215–17, 226–7 and E 2620 (Seigneurie de Largouet).

(5), (6): A.D. Morbihan, C Subdélégation de Vannes: Paroisse de Surzur: Vingtièmes, 1751–3; Church property A.D. Morbihan Q 186, 209, 219, 225. Note again the slight discrepancy in the total number of holdings in comparison with Table 6. (Cf. above, (3) and (4).) The total of arable land per holding under *domaine congéable* is somewhat higher than in Theix: this is explained by the practice of biennial fallow peculiar to this parish. Cf. A.D. Morbihan, L 1460: Recensement des grains, which gives the equivalent of 1135 ha arable land, 287.0 ha meadow.

seen, this sort of holding was rare. The rest were nearly all leased out to peasants by absentee landlords. Some were let as *fermes* or *métaires* (the two terms were interchangeable). In the seventeenth century, such land had been leased under the *bail à détroit*, in which the tenant paid the landlord a third of the grain harvested plus a fixed payment in money or kind. By the middle of the eighteenth century, if not earlier, this kind of lease had fallen out of favour and been replaced by a simple rent in money or kind stipulated in a seven or nine year lease. A little less than one-fifth of the total area was let in this way.[4]

Most holdings, however, were occupied by tenants under the system of tenure known as the *domaine congéable*. This shared the characteristics of both the *héritage* and the simple tenant farming typified by the *fermes* and *métairies*. The basic principle of the *domaine congéable* was a legal fiction according to which the owner-ship of the land (the *fonds*) belonged to one proprietor, called the *seigneur foncier*, while that of the *édifices*—buildings, crops and fruit trees—belonged to another, usually a peasant, known vari-ously as a *colon, tenuyer*, or *domanier*. The tenant, proprietor of the edifices, rented the land on which they were situated from the *seigneur foncier*.

This system predominated in Brittany in the area stretching west of a line running from the bay of St-Brieuc, in the north, to the harbour of Penerf, on the River Vilaine in the south, a line which coincided roughly with the linguistic frontier dividing Upper and Lower Brittany.[5] There were four main regional usages or *usements* governing the forms of this system in Brittany: the *usements* of Tréguier (or Tréguier and Goello), Cornouaille, Rohan and Brouerec. The *usement* of Brouerec covered most of the area in the Vannetais, and this is the form which will be described here.

The *domaine congéable* can be considered in part as a leasehold, for if the peasant owned the edifices, he only leased the *fonds*, and

<hr/>

[4] A.D. Morbihan, C: Subdélégation de Vannes: Parishes of Surzur and Grand-Champ: *vingtième* declarations, 1751–6; P. Thomas-Lacroix, 'La Condition des terres et les modalités du domaine congéable dans le pays de Vannes, au xviiie siècle', *Commission de recherche et de publication des documents relatifs à la vie économique de la Révolution. Assemblée générale . . . 1939*, i (Besançon, 1942), 346–58. The *métayer* was himself obliged to furnish cattle and equipment, unlike his counterpart in Poitou described by L. Merle, '*La Métairie et l'évolution agraire de la Gâtine poitevine de la fin du Moyen Âge à la Révolution* (Paris, 1958), 146–85.

[5] Dubreuil, *Les Vicissitudes*, i, carte hors texte; Meyer, *La Noblesse bretonne*, ii, 720–3.

the lease, whether tacit or written, determined the conditions of his occupancy. The written leases, which by the eighteenth century had become more the rule than the exception, specified the length of the tenancy (nine years), the date of entry and the date for the annual payment of rent, inevitably the feast of St Giles, 1 September. Then came the 'ritual clauses'; the tenant agreed to work his tenure as a 'bon père de famille' or a 'bon ménager'. He undertook not to destroy or change the form of the edifices or build new ones, nor cut trees (other than fruit trees), which were the property of the *seigneur foncier;* he was to be allowed only the cuttings from trimming and pruning trees and clearing wasteland (*landes*) in the proper season. He was forbidden to sublet his holding or designate anyone else to take up his lease without the express written permission of his landlord.

After this his services and obligations were listed. The tenant was required to grind his grain at the seigneur's mill. He had in theory to attend his court. But this was a requirement without substance; according to the *usement* of Brouerec, land held under *domaine congéable* was considered to be part of the seigneur's demesne; since it was thus the seigneur's own land, it was reasoned, tenants on it had to be subject to the court of the seigneur's own overlord.[6] The tenant was expected to acquit all taxes due on the land as well as any 'feudal rents' (*rentes féodales*) due to the seigneur's overlord on the tenure. In addition, although this is not mentioned in the leases, he had to pay the tithe in full.[7] He was expected to perform all the *corvées* required by the *usement*, which meant six ordinary *corvées*, three to reap, harvest and thresh the landlord's grain and cut his hay, and three with his cart and horse. However, in the course of the eighteenth century, landlords in the Vannetais were tending to replace the obligation both to use their mills and to perform *corvées* with a simple cash payment. The tenant had to furnish, in theory, a declaration to each new *seigneur foncier* of the surface, area and contents of his tenure, but it is doubtful whether this was done regularly.[8]

    [6] M. Sauvageau, *Coutumes de Bretagne* (Rennes, 1737), ii, 25–30 [Excerpts from the commentary of Gatechair]; A. Giffard, *Les Justices seigneuriales en Bretagne aux xviie et xviiie siècles (1661–1791)* (Paris, 1903), 28–31.
    [7] A.D. Morbihan, C: Subdélégation de Vannes: *vingtième* declarations, *passim.*
    [8] Sauvageau, *Coutumes de Bretagne*, i, 25–30. Included among the *corvées* were the transport of rents in kind to the landlord's granary or whatever other destination within three leagues that he choose; see also M. Baudouin de Maisonblanche, [*p. 160 for n. 8 cont.*]

Finally, the amount of his rents was stipulated; these were principally in kind, in wheat, rye, oats or a combination of two or more of these, but there were also certain dues of a 'feudal' nature (capons, chickens, sometimes butter or sugar, and a small payment in cash). However, here again, these tended in the eighteenth century to be converted into cash payments. To these was usually added a lump sum, paid at the beginning of the lease or within the first year, called the *nouveautés*, or *commission*. If the person to whom the lease had been granted had been given permission by the landlord to expel the current occupier of the land, this was also stated in the lease.

The most significant characteristic of the *domaine congéable* as a system of leasehold is its ambiguity; because it gave the tenant an important stake in the land he worked, its practical effect was to make the Vannetais, and indeed most of Lower Brittany, a country more of peasant proprietors than of tenant farmers. If a landlord wished to expel his tenant at the end of the lease, he had to arrange to reimburse the value of the edifices. If the lease was not renewed, and the landlord took no steps to expel him, the tenant remained undisturbed on the land, paying the same annual rent, and still could not be expelled without reimbursement. In the rest of Lower Brittany it remained theoretically possible for the landlord to expel him during the term of his lease, even though it was awkward to do so; in the region covered by the *usement* of Brouerec, the tenant was in an even stronger position, for the lease guaranteed him undisturbed use of the land.[9] It was thus very difficult to get rid of a tenant.

The anomalous character of the *domaine congéable*, disquieting to the minds of eighteenth-century jurists, is understandable if we

Institutions convenantières ou traité raisonné des domaines congéables en général & spécialement à l'usement de Tréguier et Goëlo (St-Brieuc, 1776), 148–62. In addition, the seigneur could demand 'extraordinary' *corvées*, for the repair of his house, for example. But these could not have been demanded often, especially as most landlords were absentees. Baudouin (i, 163–70) is emphatic on the necessity of a notarized declaration for each new seigneur, but his remarks on i, 172–5 suggest that the lease or the *prisage* (survey) made at the expulsion of a tenant may have often filled this role.

[9] Under the *usement* of Cornouaille (art. 3) the seigneur could only expel during the lease if he wished to take up residence in the tenure; under that of Tréguier and Goello (art. 26), all leases were assumed to be in perpetuity, but the tenant could be expelled at will, provided that he was reimbursed, while under that of Rohan (art. 8 and 10), the tenant could be expelled during the term of the lease only if the commission or *nouveautés* were repaid. Dubreuil, *Les Vicissitudes*, i, 91–119; Baudouin de Maisonblanche, *Institutions convenantières*, i, 110–31.

remember that, as elsewhere in France, the legal categories of a system of land tenure meant different things at different times, and were interpreted according to shifts in the respective economic situation of landlord and tenant. The first recorded act which mentions the *domaine congéable* dates from 1380, and land appears to have been conceded under this system in the fourteenth and fifteenth centuries to attract settlers and retain them on depopulated or unsettled land by giving them a large share in its ownership.[10] At this point, the advantages appear to have been all on the side of the tenant. By the end of the sixteenth century, with the rise in population in the peninsula, the advantage was shifting towards the landlord, and this was the period in which the local usages were collected and codified by jurists such as Gatechair. Yet even at this point, the use of the formal lease as spoken of in Gatechair's commentary on the usement of Brouerec, was exceptional and long but informal tenancies were the norm.[11] By the end of the seventeenth century, however, landlords appear to have tried to collect arrears, expel tenants on a larger scale, and to raise rents. The Chapter of Vannes, for example, made a conscious effort to tighten up its management of its holdings at the end of the seventeenth century.[12] In return for higher rents, the seigneurs granted written leases which gave tenants greater legal protection at a time when competition for land among peasants became more serious as the pressure of population continued. From being an informal arrangement made by a seigneur looking for tenants, the *domaine congéable* appears to have become, by the beginning of the eighteenth century, a formalized system of land tenure in which the advantages and disadvantages were balanced equally between landlords and tenants looking with increasing unease over their shoulders at possible competitors for their holdings. And, as we shall see, the *domaine congéable* did not stop evolving through the eighteenth and, indeed, the nineteenth century.

[10] P. Lesage, *Étude historique et critique du bail à domaine congéable dans le département du Morbihan* (Rennes, 1932), 25–45.

[11] 'Le seigneur foncier peut congéer le domanier ou détenteur lorsqu'il lui plaît, en payant préalablement des édifices & superfices, appelez autrement droits convenanciers ou réparatoires, & le laissant jouir de ses stucs & engrais.

'Si ce n'est qu'il y ait bail fait par le seigneur au domanier à certain temps non encore expiré, auquel cas le congément ne peut estre fait avant l'expirement du terme porté par le bail.' 'Usages locales de Brouerec', art. 2 in Sauvageau, *Coutumes de Bretagne*, i, 25–6.

[12] A.D. Morbihan, 65 G 6 (491).

Given the balance of advantages and obligations which both the
landlords and tenants found in the *domaine congéable* during the
eighteenth century it is not surprising that there should have been a
real confusion in the minds of both proprietors and tenants about
the nature of the property in which they each had a share, a
confusion which, to be sure, both proprietors and tenants were
capable of exploiting consciously according to the needs of the
moment. Thus, when the *vingtième* was introduced in the 1750s, the
tenants under *domaine congéable* denied that they should be taxed,
since, by their own account, they were only simple tenant-farmers
who happened to have a peculiar form of lease; on printed forms
made up for their declarations of revenue by, one suspects, the
eighteenth-century equivalents of tax consultants, tenants protested
that their declarations had been made

uniquement pour obéir au Roy & aux ordonnances de Monseigneur
l'Intendant. Car il [the tenant] croit aux termes de l'édit, ne devoir point
être compris dans l'imposition du vingtième. 1º Il n'est ni propriétaire ni
usufruitier, il n'est que simple laboureur, qui gagne sa vie au dépens de ses
sueurs & de ses travaux & qui peut être mis hors de la tenue à la fin de sa
ferme 2º Les édifices qu'il possède consistent en maisons non affermées &
qu'il occupe, dont les fonds appartiennent toujours à son seigneur, & dans
quelques fossés dont il ne retire que quelques émondes pour son usage,
encore si l'arbre n'excède pas dix pieds, auquel cas il appartient au seigneur.
Les dits édifices ne paroissent pas aussi devoir être sujets à l'imposition de
vingtième.[13]

This self-denying attitude, needless to say, did not prevent tenants
and those who took up their cause forty years later from insisting
that the real proprietorship belonged to the man who owned the
edifices. When it was to the advantage of the tenants to claim that
the *domaine congéable* was a feudal form of tenure and should be
abolished or declared redeemable along with all other feudal rents
which went on the night of 4 August 1789, they did so without any
hesitation:

Le seigneur a le fonds, a la tenue des fonds dont on doit des rentes; mais le
domanier est le propriétaire des édifices et superfices; et il est le cultivateur
et conservateur. C'est lui qui doit avoir le produit de la terre. . . .[14]

[13] A.D. Morbihan, C: Subdélégation de Vannes: Paroisse de Grand-Champ:
declaration of Julien Corsmat, 17-7-1751.
[14] *Extraits du procès-verbal de l'assemblée de la Bretagne et de l'Anjou tenue à
Pontivy, les 15 et autres jours de fevrier 1790, no VI: Mémoire des députés de
Languidic*, cited in Dubreuil, *Les Vicissitudes*, i, 190.

Le domaine congéable en Bretagne tient essentiellement du regime féodal. Donc il se trouve supprimé par les décrets du mois d'août . . . La rente sur la tenue à domaine congéable a le caractère de rente foncière. Donc elle est rachetable comme toutes les autres suivant les mêmes décrets.

La tenue à domaine congéable dans la main du vassal est un véritable immeuble. Donc elle ne peut être comparée à la ferme.[15]

If, as the authors of the last quotation would have us believe, the *domaine congéable* is considered as essentially a peasant holding, the countryside takes on the appearance of a region dominated by small peasant proprietors: 74 per cent of holdings and 75 per cent of the area of the parish of Theix were held in this way by peasants and only 14 per cent of holdings (17 per cent of the area) were leased from landlords by *métayage* and *fermage*. Similar proportions characterized the parishes of Grand-Champ and Surzur and, according to the studies of other areas, still rather fragmentary, the mass of Lower Brittany.[16] Although the *tenuyer* undoubtedly did not feel the same sense of full proprietorship as the peasant who held his land outright and paid only feudal dues on it to a distant landlord, there was nevertheless both subjectively, in the mind of the peasant, and objectively, from a purely economic point of view, a strong element of peasant proprietorship in the *domaine congéable;* there was a sense of ownership which was, as we shall see, encouraged by a certain permanence on the land.

Some idea of the structure of these individual holdings under *domaine congéable* can be had by examining a summary of the *aveu* of the seigneurie of Keral and Couëtergraff in Grand-Champ, rendered by the Chapter of Vannes, its seigneur, to their overlord, the seigneur of Largouet in 1679.[17] All the tenures under *domaine congéable* contained, besides their built-up properties and kitchen gardens, four main elements: arable land, pasture, meadows and wasteland (*landes*). Except for the *landes*, the most considerable

---

[15] *Pétition du corps électoral du Morbihan à l'Assemblée Nationale* [June 1790], cited in Dubreuil, *Les Vicissitudes*, i, 207; on this confusion see also the pertinent remarks of Meyer, *La Noblesse bretonne*, ii, 726–34.

[16] Table V-1; cf. P. Goubert, 'Recherches d'histoire rurale dans la France de l'Ouest (xviie–xviiie siècles)', *Bulletin de la Société d'Histoire moderne*, 13e série, no. 2, 64e année (1965), 2–9; V. Le Floc'h, 'Le Régime foncier et son application pratique dans le cadre de la paroisse de Plonivel (Finistère) au xviiie siècle', *Bulletin de la Société archéologique du Finistère*, xcii (1966), 126–37.

[17] Table V-2. This seigneurie is cited not as an isolated example but as a typical case.

Table V-2: Seigneurie of Keral et Couëtergraff—Chapter of Vannes (1679)

(1) Surface	Arable land	Pasture	Meadow	Gardens, etc.	Wasteld.	Built-up property	Other	Total
					Area of holdings (ha)			
Seigneurie de Couëtergraff								
Moulin d'en haut, Bodéan	—	—	—	—	—	0.6	—	0.6
Moulin d'en Bas, Bodéan	—	—	—	—	—	1.3	—	1.3
Ruined mill	—	—	—	—	—	0.1	—	0.1
Tenures:								
Séb. Le Goueff	4.1	0.2	1.0	0.2	2.4	0.3	—	8.2
Fr. Losevis	3.7	1.0	0.4	0.2	0.5	—	1.1	6.9
Alexis Losevis	4.3	1.1	1.8	0.1	2.6	0.2	—	10.1
Louis Anezo (vill. Le Grisso)	4.1	0.5	1.3	0.5	6.8	0.3	—	13.5
Fr. Larguère								
Jul. Eveno (Le Porzo)								
Guill. Le Barch (Lesolvan)	2.1	1.1	0.5	0.3	2.9	0.1	1.2	8.2
Guill. Le Barch (Lesolvan)	4.1	0.5	0.6	0.3	1.6	0.1	1.1	8.3
Mᵉ M. Le Thieis (bourg)	—	—	—	—	—	0.01	—	0.01
Total	22.4	4.4	5.6	1.6	16.8	3.0	3.4	57.2
Seigneurie de Keral								
Maison noble de Penprat	4.5	0.2	2.1	—	0.2	0.4	—	7.4
Bois taillis de Keral	—	—	—	—	—	—	2.3	2.3
Moulin à eau	—	—	—	—	—	0.5	—	0.5
Tenures:								
Guill. Nicolazo (Moustoir)	6.0	1.2	0.8	0.2	18.3	0.2	—	26.7
Guyon Riguidel (Moustoir)	5.7	0.9	0.8	—	9.3	0.6	—	17.3
. . . (le bourg)	3.9	0.3	0.2	0.3	5.8	0.1	—	11.4
Total	20.1	2.6	3.9	0.5	33.6	1.8	2.3	65.6

Table V-2: Seigneurie of Keral et Couëtergraff—Chapter of Vannes (1679) (*continued*)

(2) Rents and dues (in perrées and decimal livres)

	Wheat	Rye	Oats	Cash	Poultry	Corvées	Other
Seigneurie de Couëtergraff							
Moulin d'en haut, Bodéan	—	48 p.	—	18.00	—	—	Rente féodale to Largouët: 18 p. rye
Moulin d'en bas, Bodéan	—	—	—	—	—	—	—
Ruined mill	—	—	—	—	—	—	—
Tenures:							
Séb. Le Goueff	1 p.	11 p.	1 p.	3.60	4 ch. 1 pl	cor.*	—
Fr. Losevis	1 p.	1 p.	1 p.	3.60	4 ch.	cor.	—
Alexis Losevis	1 p.	1 p.	3 p.	3.60	4 ch.	cor.	—
Louis Anezo	1 p.	1 p.	1 p.	3.60	4 ch.	cor.	—
Fr. Larguère							
Jul. Eveno							
Guill. Le Barch	1 p.	1 p.	1 p.	3.60	8 ch.	cor.	—
Guill. Le Barch	1 p.	1 p.	1 p.	3.60	8 ch.	cor.	—
Mᵉ M. Le Thieis				0.90	7 poulets		+ Honorific rights in the church of Grand-Champ.
Seigneurie de Keral							
Maison noble de Penprat	—	—	—	—	—	—	—
Bois taillis de Keral	—	18 p.	—	—	—	—	—
Moulin à eau	—	—	—	—	—	—	—
Tenures:							
Guill Nicolazo	2 p.	2 p.	2 p.	7.85	8 ch.	cor.	Rente féodale to Largouët 1 p. oats, 1 hen
Guyon Riguidel	—	—	—	10.80	8 ch.	cor.	Rente féodale to Largouët 1 p. oats, 1 hen
. . . (le bourg)	½ p.	1½ p.	1 p.	4.80	4 ch.	cor.	1.5 l., chef-rente
2 tenures at Coullac	—	—	—	—	—	—	1 p. oats, 1 hen to Largouët, each.
2 tenures, Rescourlais	—	—	—	—	—	—	1 p. oats, 1 hen to Largouët, and La Chenaie.
1 tenure, Rescourlais	—	—	—	—	—	—	

Source: A.D. Morbihan, 65 G 1–6 (491).   * ch. = chapons, pl = poules, cor. = corvée.

portion of each tenure was given over to cultivation—about eight *journaux* (four hectares) in each case. Another hectare consisted of pasture and meadow, and the rest, except for a few garden plots, was wasteland. The surface under wasteland varied widely from one tenure to another, but as each tenure also carried with it rights to common fields, also under *landes*, this was probably not important.

The people working these tenures lived in those small dispersed settlements characteristic of *bocage* country called, rather misleadingly, 'villages' but which are really hamlets, or even isolated settlements. Each village contained from one to a dozen families; some of the larger ones were even provided with a chapel of their own. One such settlement was Lopabu, shown in Map III; in it can be seen most of the characteristics of settlements in the region. In the middle of the eighteenth century, there were eight separate households in the village: four were *tenuyers*, three were *métayers*, who in fact leased their land from other peasants, and there was one artisan, a blacksmith.

Around the village were arrayed the various parts of the tenures worked by the inhabitants, like the pieces of a puzzle which interlock but remain distinct from one another. Nearest to the farm buildings were kitchen gardens, occasionally small patches devoted to hemp-growing, small farmyards and the 'aire à battre', where grain was threshed. On the edges of the settlement itself were ranged the best pieces of land, given over to cereal and pasture, and occasionally lying fallow, all divided up into tiny plots of less than half a hectare each. Farther out on the approaches to the village were the permanently uncultivated *landes*, called *landes frostes* to distinguish them from arable land lying fallow temporarily; the latter was referred to as being 'sous lande' ('un clos sous lande', 'un parc sous lande', etc.). The cultivable parcels were generally set apart by hedgerows, but occasionally a whole group of plots would be surrounded with a hedgerow and divided one from another by boundary markers only, even though each field in the enclosure belonged to different proprietors. In all cases, however, the various parcels were worked only by their tenants and were not subject to the rigorous communal practices often followed in openfield country to regulate crop rotation (*assolement*) and the pasturing of cattle (*vaine pâture*). Only on the 'commons', on the periphery of the village, was there any sort of communal use of land for grazing purposes (*parcours*), and then only between adjoining villages,

T = terre
L = lande
P = pré
Pᵗ = pâture
C = courtil

Hedgerow _____   Scale 1:16 000

Map III: Villages of Lopabu, Kerhouarn and Bremenic (Commune of Grand-Champ) from Cadaster 1856

never between whole parishes.[18]

Agricultural production on these holdings rested upon intensive cultivation of cereal crops on the best land. The other elements in the holding were subordinated to this end. Witnesses in the eighteenth century described the region as an area dominated by a triennial system with one-third of the land in fallow and two-thirds under crops. In reality, the rotation of crops was much more anarchic, although in the end probably more productive than a strict triennial system. Land was allowed to lie fallow as infrequently as possible, but then for relatively long periods. In such cases it was returned to *lande*, while a different plot previously lying fallow was put under cultivation.[19]

This kind of intensive cultivation was made possible by two practices. The first was the way in which crops were rotated. On his three to four hectares of arable land, the peasant cultivated half in wheat and rye and the rest in smaller grains. 'Wheat after wheat is worthless', ran the proverb,[20] and the peasant tried to arrange his sowings so as to avoid as much as possible repeating the same crop in two succesive years on the same ground. There was generally an interval in which land lay fallow during the winter months between harvest and sowing times: a year of heavy winter grain (rye or wheat) or oats, sown from November to December and harvested in late July and August, was usually followed by one or more years of

---

[18] Cayot-Délandre, 'Usages et règlements locaux du Département du Morbihan', *Annuaire du Morbihan* (1857), 224–5. There were of course practices of cultivation more or less common to a given parish (see note 29 below), but as long as a peasant's habits of cultivation did not interfere with those of his neighbours, he was free to sow what he wanted, when he wanted. The only occasions for lawsuits over the use of private fields occured when an expelled tenant under *domaine congéable* did not leave enough fertilizer on his land or had sown the whole of his tenure in heavy grains, leaving the soil exhausted; on such disputes see A.D. Morbihan, B: Largouet, minutes, 1-10-1773, 28-10-1775, 1-12-1780, 13-9-1783, 24-3-1786, 31-3-1786; mesurage et prisage 14 to 18-3-1786, etc.

[19] A.D. Morbihan, M 1242: Draft memorandum, probably for the *Statistique agricole* of 1819, which speaks of regular rotation of crops with fallow or cover as being 'encore inconnu. . . . Les terres en labeur servent sans intermission à la culture des céréales.' Cf. also Cayot-Délandre, *Annuaire du Morbihan, passim*, on this point; only in parishes far in the interior (Bieuzy, Melrand, etc.) was there anything like a regular period of fallow employed in the early nineteenth century. According to Kuntz, *Monographie agricole du Morbihan*, 58, wasteland still occupied three-fifths of the surface in the coastal regions in 1929, and even then few farms used regular crop-rotation.

[20] P. Le Goff, *Proverbes bretons du Haut-Vannetais (Vannes, Auray, Baud, Pontivy)* (Vannes, 1912), 16.

spring grains, sown in March (spring wheat) or May (barley, millet and buckwheat) and harvested in September, so that a harvest was followed immediately by sowing only once in two years at the most, and never by the same crop.[21] 'Voilà l'ordre profitable', said a tenuyer, Mathurin Bocher, in a lawsuit in 1775, 'établi afin de pouvoir labourer tous les ans les terres en culture sans les laisser comme ailleurs, plusieurs années à délaisser et incultes.'[22]

The second practice which made this intensive use of arable land possible was heavy and continual fertilization. The local saying hardly exaggerated when it claimed that 'no land is bad when it is well fertilized',[23] but it might have added that the most barren land was more use as a source of fertilizer than as arable soil. Here, the *landes* played a crucial role. Arthur Young described his shock at seeing how in the Vannetais, piles of grass and scrub vegetation

are formed in the spring . . . Here they consist of three-fourths or seven-eighths of turf, pared off from every hole and corner from commons and bad fields, and carried to the good ones; and if this execrable practice is of any antiquity it will account for the barren and wretched state of the country. Every poor field is made good for nothing, and the good one cropped, in consequence, till it is almost as bad. These heaps continue about Vannes in amazing quantities.[24]

What Young was describing in this passage was a form of archaic but intensive agriculture which he did not understand. The clumps of turf were mixed with animal manure and spread over the land used for the winter cereals, although on land closer to the seacoast, the mixture was replaced to a certain extent by seaweed (*goëmon*). The presence of extensive tracts of *landes* was doubly essential to this peculiar form of cultivation; the wasteland provided the bulk of the fertilizer and also most of the pasture land for the cattle, whose manure was essential to the preparation of this mixture. The farther away from the seacoast one moved, the worse was the quality of the soil, and the more difficult it was to obtain seaweed; the ratio of

[21] Le Goff, 'Vannes', 400, summarizes the regime for each parish given in Cayot-Délandre, *Annuaire du Morbihan, passim;* A.D. Morbihan, B: Largouet, minutes: payements, 28-10-1775, 1-12-1780. On harvest and sowing times, see A.D. Morbihan, M 1242: Tableau comparatif des récoltes de 15 années, 1807 à 1821 (Arrondissement de Ploërmel). Details on the variations in this regime in each parish are given in Cayot-Délandre, *Annuaire du Morbihan, passim.*
[22] A.D. Morbihan, B: Largouet, minutes: payement, 28-10-1775.
[23] Le Goff, *Proverbes bretons*, 16.
[24] Young, *Travels . . .*, ii, 136–7.

landes to arable land increased correspondingly, attaining quite remarkable proportions in the interior of the region, to the north of the Vannetais. Everywhere, however, the system remained the same in principle.[25] Young and other contemporary agronomists such as Huët de Coëtsilan saw its deficiencies, but not its inner logic; for much of the wasteland that they constantly deplored (*'landes, landes, landes'* lamented Young) was ill-suited, even today, to much more than occasional use.[26] Besides which, they did not recognize that to remove one of the elements of this intensive system by promoting the enclosure or division of commons and waste was to risk a radical change of the whole rural economy and, inevitably, of the complex of relations, economic and cultural, which were based on it.

The rigidity of this system was significantly reinforced by the prevalence of the *domaine congéable*. To be sure, it alone cannot explain the backwardness of agricultural techniques in the area: the inadequacy of the little plough used in the Vannetais, drawn on a two-wheeled carriage by a pair of oxen, led sometimes by a pony— or by the peasant's wife—with a ploughshare too small to bite properly into the soil; the absence of cover crops of any kind; the reluctance of the peasants until the middle of the nineteenth century to take up the cultivation of the potato; all these were complaints which in varying degree could be made about other sections of Brittany which were not subject to the same form of tenure.[27]

The principal defect of the *domaine congéable* was that it tended to reinforce the permanence of the rural landscape and limit innovation and expansion, even when peasants had the resources to

[25] A.D. Morbihan, L 72[1]: *Procès-verbal de la troisième réunion du conseil général du Département du Morbihan* (Vannes, 1792), 174; L 1463: État de la population du district de Vannes, 1790; A.D. I.-V., C 1944: petition of Guillaume Roland, Joseph Le Becque . . . capitaines de navire de la paroisse d'Ambon; *Description abrégée du Département du Morbihan* (Paris, 18 floréal, An VII), 1–4; Cayot-Délandre, *Annuaire du Morbihan* (1840), 163; (1834), 67; J.-B.-C.-R. Huët de Coëtsilan, *Recherches statistiques sur le Département de la Loire-Inférieure pour l'An XI* (Nantes, An XI), 63–7; Choveaux, 'L'Influence des engrais marins', 417–25.

[26] See the remarks of W. Abel, *Crises agraires en Europe (xiiie–xxe siècle)* (Paris, 1973), 155–6. Young's obsession with the need to cultivate even the poorest land led him to suggest the clearing of Epping Forest and the cultivation of Dartmoor; see J. G. Gazely, *The Life of Arthur Young* (Philadelphia, 1973), 354, 474–5.

[27] A.D. Morbihan, M 1242: Draft memorandum [1819]; Cayot-Délandre, *Annuaire du Morbihan* (1833), 49; *Statistique générale de la France. Statistique de la France. Agriculture* (Paris, 1842), *passim;* ibid., *2e série, Résultats généraux de l'enquête décennale de 1862* (Strasbourg, 1870), *passim;* Young, *Travels*, ii, 127.

carry it out. This it did in two ways. First of all, it prevented peasants from improving their edifices, for they could not claim reimbursement for the value of the additions if they were expelled by their landlords. Secondly, it tended to preserve the structure of the individual holding. Land held under *domaine congéable* was indivisible in principle, and in this way the system of tenure prevented the fragmentation of rural property which took place, for example, in the peninsula of Rhuys and in certain parishes of Upper Brittany.[28] If, as we shall see, it did not prevent the impoverishment of the smaller peasant, it did prevent the subdivision of the land. But at the same time, it closed the door to whatever agricultural progress might have been achieved in the long run by enterprising landlords or their farmers through the harsh, but perhaps necessary, pauperization of a section of the peasants living on the land. In the Vannetais, although peasants might become poorer and eventually leave the land, the shape of agriculture remained the same.

Not suprisingly, productivity under such a system was fairly low and to all appearances stationary through the eighteenth century. Crop yields necessarily varied from year to year and from one tract of land to another, but the statistics and estimates of the eighteenth and early nineteenth centuries are generally in agreement that the yield of heavy grain on ordinary land did not much surpass 5:1, although farther up the coast on better soil it may have gone as high as 8:1.[29]

Using these figures it is possible to make a very rough estimate of the importance of rents and profits under the system of the *domaine congéable* in the region. Take for example Sébastien Le Goueff and his successors, who cultivated one of the tenures of the Chapter of Vannes in the parish of Grand-Champ.[30] The amount of cultivable land he worked, 8 *journaux* (4 hectares), was a normal-sized holding for the area. In an ordinary year, he could grow perhaps as much as the equivalent of 11 or 12 hectolitres of rye for each hectare, giving

---

[28]   See below, p. 203, 234–7.
[29]   Le Goff, 'Vannes', 397–8 summarizes the data from Ministère de l'Agriculture et du Commerce—Direction de l'agriculture. Bureau des subsistances, *Récoltes des céréales et des pommes de terre de 1815 à 1876* (Paris, 1878); Ministère des Travaux publics de l'Agriculture et du Commerce, *Archives statistiques* (Paris, 1837); A.D. Morbihan, C: Subdélégation de Vannes: Grand-Champ: déclarations de vingtièmes, 1751 and H. Sée, *Les Classes rurales en Bretagne du xviᵉ siècle à la Révolution* (Paris, 1906), 386. These figures should all be treated as minimum estimates.
[30]   Table V-2.

him a gross yield of about 45 hl. Out of this he had to pay an
ecclesiastical tithe at the rate of one sheaf in thirty-three (1.4 hl) and
his rent, which consisted of one *perrée* (1.7 hl) of each of rye, wheat,
and oats, a token cash payment, plus four capons and a hen,
evaluated together at 6 livres 12 sous. Taken all together, his annual
rent amounted to the equivalent of 4 hl of rye, or 9 per cent of his
harvest. The amount of seed he required for the following year
came to something between 2.4 and 3.2 hl per hectare, say 2.8 hl, for
a total of 11.2 hl, or 25 per cent of his harvest. With what remained,
he would have to pay about 12 livres in *capitation* at the most, and
another 6 or 7 in *vingtièmes, fouages* and related taxes, say 20 livres,
the equivalent of 2.5 *perrées* (4.2 hl) of rye, or another 9 per cent of
the harvest. This left him with a net profit after fixed costs, of about
24 hl, or 53 per cent of his original yield. By way of contrast, an
haricotier, the typical middling peasant proprietor of the Beauvais
region had, according to one estimate, only about 39 per cent of his
original harvest of 36 hl of wheat after his fixed costs were removed.[31]
This suggests that the margin of survival enjoyed by the *tenuyer* of
the Vannetais was rather larger than what is commonly assumed as
typical of an ordinary eighteenth-century peasant.

Of course, a peasant had to live as well as pay his fixed costs.
Whoever worked the Le Goueff holding would need about 25 hl of
grain annually, or another 58 per cent of his harvest, to nourish a
family of five or six if they consumed only rye. Few peasants in the
Vannetais did, however; the staple diet was made up of buckwheat
gruel, made with milk or water, and *crêpes;* by using buckwheat or
millet, with a much higher yield, he could reduce his expenses on
food to the equivalent of 10 hl rye, or 21 per cent of his harvest. This
left him with about a quarter of his original yield which he could
market for a profit. In a bad year he might just break even, but his
chances of going under, except in a very bad year indeed, were not

---

[31] Goubert, *Beauvais et le Beauvaisis*, 165. Rye-equivalents have been chosen
because rye was the predominant cereal crop of the region. On the basis of the
production estimates used in the calculation of the *vingtième* 1751–6, 1 unit of rye
equals 0.60 units of spring wheat (*petit froment*) or 1.60 units of oats (*gros avoine*).
On the basis of average prices for 1726–39, the equivalents are roughly the same:
winter wheat 0.62, spring wheat 0.60, oats 1.43. I have therefore used the equivalents
based on the production figures from the *vingtième*. In calculating rye-equivalents of
dues and taxes in cash, I have used the same rye-equivalents and the price averages of
1726–39; if dues remained stable, their real value would have dropped as prices rose
later in the century.

very great.[32]

This estimate is based on revenues from cereal crops alone. It has been claimed that one of the most important factors distinguishing the *bocage* country characteristic of western France from the open-fields of the north and north-east is the importance of cattle and other livestock in the rural economy of the *bocage*.[33] Yet it is difficult to say that, in the Vannetais at least, cattle-raising contributed greatly to agricultural revenues. The basic livestock required for an independent holding like Le Goueff's was a team of oxen; with these, a *tenuyer* usually had a horse, most often a mare, to pull his cart, and three or four cows, perhaps as many heifers and calves, a pig, sometimes a small bull and less than a dozen fowl. The market value of a heifer was about twelve livres in the second half of the eighteenth century; that of a calf, six livres.[34] In Le Goueff's case, this would have meant that the sale of a calf and a heifer would have brought him about 4 per cent of his annual gross income from grain; a useful sum, no doubt, but not a fortune. The principal use of cattle seems to have been rather in providing milk, dairy products and occasional meat used to supplement a cereal diet: 'The meadow feeds the cattle and the cattle feed men', ran the proverb.[35] Certainly, in comparison to the cattle raised by the *métayers* of Poitou, or even to the stock held by the peasants of the Mauges in Anjou, the little domestic herds of the *tenuyers* of the Vannetais are modest, and only constituted a subsidiary source of income.[36] Grain remained, then, the essential product in the rural economy of the region.

This kind of estimate of agricultural production, like those indulged in by most of the eighteenth-century agronomists, always has a certain air of unreality.[37] Land is of course never uniformly

[32] A.N., F[20] 229: Essai statistique sur le Morbihan, An IX; Meyer, *La Noblesse bretonne*, i, 445–74. This estimate of cereal consumption is taken from F[20] 229; cf. Goubert, *Beauvais et le Beauvaisis* i, 182 (20 hl for a family of six).

[33] F. Braudel and E. Labrousse, *Histoire économique et sociale de la France* (Paris, 1970), ii, 108–9.

[34] A.D. Morbihan, B: Largouet, minutes, 1765, 1775, 1780.

[35] Le Goff, *Proverbes bretons*, 16.

[36] R. H. Andrews, *Les Paysans des Mauges* (Tours, 1935), 124–35; C. Tilly, *The Vendée* (London, 1964), 114–15; Merle, *La Métairie*, 108 ff. Merle speaks of an average herd for an average *métayer* as including about 21 large cattle and 59 to 83 ovines.

[37] Cf. Huët de Coëtsilan, *Recherches statistiques*, 66–7 and A.N., F[20] 229. The declarations for the *vingtième* are themselves a fine example of this genre.

fertile, and production varies from year to year. This estimate does not take account of the amount spent on tools, casual labour, upkeep and clothing, but neither does it include income from the sale of cattle, honey, eggs and so forth. What is important to realize is that, under normal conditions the amount of arable land in this example, typical enough for tenures in the area, was adequate of itself to ensure the running of a holding. If the *tenuyer* managed to acquire another holding, of course, his profits would increase, since the same household could as easily manage eight hectares as four.

Fortunately, however, there is more convincing proof of the existence of a certain profit margin for the *tenuyer* than these admittedly abstract calculations. In fact, we know that at least one-fifth of such tenures in the area were sublet by their peasant proprietors to other peasants at rates far in excess of the original rents. Sometimes these tenures were let under *métayage*: one-third of the product, plus a supplementary commission, often with only a verbal agreement.[38] More often they were simply leased in return for a fixed payment in money or, most frequently, money and kind, in addition to which the subletting tenant undertook to pay the original rent under *domaine congéable*, plus all other charges due on the land, including personal services. The conditions of such second leases were invariably harsher than those of the original leases granted under *domaine congéable*, reflecting a real competition for land and proving the possibilty of a profit for the peasant who held his land directly from the landlord. In the parishes of Theix and Grand-Champ, such sub-tenants paid on the average three times as much as did the tenants from whom they sublet their lands.[39] It is therefore certain that the *domaine congéable* allowed a certain profit margin to the tenant, provided—and this, as we shall see, is an important condition—that he had a clear title to a normal-sized holding.

The peninsula of Rhuys presented a somewhat different pattern of land use and landholding. It was marked, as the histogram in Graph 1 suggests, by greater extremes between a few large and

---

[38] See Table V-1; further examples in A.D. Morbihan, C: Subdélégation de Vannes: Paroisses de Surzur et Grand-Champ; and Thomas-Lacroix, 'La Condition des terres', 354–7; Cf. A.D. Morbihan, C: Vannes: Commission intermédiaire: Observations du Sieur Caradec, [c. 1759]; Thomas-Lacroix, 'La Condition des terres', 354–7; H. Sée, 'L'Administration de deux seigneuries' de Basse-Bretagne au xviiiᵉ siècle: Toulgouët et Le Treff', *Annales de Bretagne,* xix (1903–4), 285–320.

[39] Le Goff, 'Vannes', 401 and Thomas-Lacroix, 'La Condition des terres', 354–7.

middling-sized holdings and a proliferation of small holdings. The *domaine congéable* did not exist on the peninsula; owners had title to their own land, except for the payment of a *rente féodale* to the Crown, and when land was let, it apparently was let on a kind of sharecropping system: in return for one-half or one-third of the produce, the proprietor—peasant, noble or bourgeois—contributed half or one-third of the seed.[40]

The existence of such wide gaps between *tenuyers* (or, on the peninsula of Rhuys, the occasional properous peasant-proprietor) and peasants subletting lands or living from the sale of their labour, would seem to imply that rural was sharply divided into rich and poor, all under the tutelage of a class of absentee landlords. This diversity of conditions, and its implications for people living in the countryside form the subject of the succeeding chapters.

---

[40] A.D. Morbihan, B: Rhuys, minutes, 1763.

CHAPTER VI

WEALTH AND POVERTY
IN THE COUNTRYSIDE

The forms of land tenure discussed in the previous chapter imposed economic burdens on the landholder which varied considerably; land held under *domaine congéable* cost much less in rent than land sublet from a *tenuyer*, or held under *métayage* or *fermage*, while land owned outright as a *héritage* involved the least onerous of burdens, though it was hard to come by. But land is one thing; the wealth of people living on it and the distribution of that wealth is another. What shape did the pyramid of wealth take in the rural Vannetais? Did that pyramid correspond to the hierarchy implied by these different forms of landholding? To what real conditions of existence did the different relative levels of wealth correspond?

A first approach to the distribution of wealth in the countryside is to examine the rolls of the poll tax (*capitation*); the same source that was used in the analysis of the town of Vannes in Chapters II and III. In Brittany, the portion of this tax which fell on rural parishes was a lump sum varying little from year to year. This sum was divided among the nine dioceses of the province and shared out among the parishes of each diocese roughly in proportion to the population and resources of each. In each parish it was assessed by committees of assessors (*égailleurs*) made up of local inhabitants and assisted by representatives of the diocesan permanent commission of the Breton Estates.[1]

The *capitation* was supposed to be assessed proportionately to a person's wealth. The correspondence of the permanent commission makes it plain that the main criterion of rural wealth used was the land a person worked and the conditions under which he held it, but

---

[1] Rébillon, *Les États de Bretagne*, 536–59. Before 1734, the *capitation* was imposed and collected by the intendant and his *subdélégués;* afterwards, by the Estates and their *commission intermédiaire*. Under both regimes, the estimates made on the spot were those of the parish *égailleurs*.

parish assessors also attempted to estimate the amount of money a taxpayer had invested outside the parish. They looked as well at the number of his livestock which, they found, tended to correspond to the rental value of his land if he was a *tenuyer* or a *fermier*, but when it did not, they adjusted the tax downwards. Artisans and day-labourers were generally assessed at a low rate; a standard amount was imposed on a master for each servant or domestic he employed. It appears that the commission levied a higher tax on a man who could depend on his family for help around his tenure than on one who was forced to rely on domestics. The records of those disputes which did arise over assessments show that the assessors were capable of forming a fairly shrewd notion of these forms of wealth, as indeed they ought to have been.[2]

In most of Brittany, the records of the *capitation* can be relied on to give a pyramid of wealth, but, like most other sources for the study of rural society, they remain remarkably mute on the status of the taxpayers. When they do refer to rural people, they most often use the generic term *laboureur*, which in western France means simply someone who tills the soil, or, more often, give no description of the person's state in life at all.[3] However, around Vannes, *capitation* rolls dating from before 1760, and even some dating from after this period, do make these distinctions, as well as listing with some precision the occupations of rural artisans. With several such rolls from a half-dozen parishes in the region, it is possible to obtain an overall view of the distribution of wealth among rural people around the middle of the eighteenth century.

Even a superficial glance at the tables based on these tax rolls is sufficient to distinguish a fairly marked hierarchy of wealth among, in descending order, the *tenuyers, métayers* and *fermiers*, and artisans.[4] A clearer notion of these distinctions can be obtained by comparing the distribution of wealth among each of the classes of inhabitants to its distribution among the total population of the parish. Thus, in the parish of Grand-Champ, which has one of the most complete of these tax rolls, the highest-taxed quarter of the

[2] A.D. Morbihan, C: Commission intermédiaire de Vannes: Observations du sieur Caradec avocat chargé . . . de la confection du rôle de la capitation des paroisses de Grandchamp, Ambon, Naizin, Remungol et Moustoir Remungol, [1759], Brénugat de Kerveno, Sarzeau to the commission, 9-7-1759; A.D. I.-V., C 4364: Petition of Joseph Le Texier, Plaudren, 25-5-1780, etc.

[3] Sée, *Les Classes rurales*, 60–76.

[4] Table VI-1.

population paid over 9 l. 10 s. in 1767. Forty-one per cent of the *tenuyers* were included in their group, but only 0.4 per cent of the *métayers* and *fermiers*. Another 25 per cent of the taxpayers paid between 5 l. 12 s. (the median assessment) and 9 l. 10 s. and again in this group the proportion of *tenuyers* (29 per cent) exceeded that of the total community while only 4 per cent of the *métayers* paid this amount. It is only in the next group, the quarter of the population paying taxes between 3 l. 8 s. and 5 l. 12 s. that we can begin to find a sizeable proportion of *métayers* and *fermiers* (34 per cent), although it is true that there was also a residual of 21 per cent of the *tenuyers* in this group as well. But it is in the lowest quarter of the population, paying less than 3 l. 8 s. that the bulk of *métayers* and *fermiers* were to be found; no less than 66 per cent of *métayers* and *fermiers*, but only 9 per cent of *tenuyers*, paid taxes in this category.

The situation of rural artisans and shopkeepers appears slightly more complex. Some of them were also *tenuyers;* thus a certain number of men were listed in the *capitation* roll as *menuisiers et tenuyers, marchands et tenuyers*, and so forth; but there were not many of these, and very few—in Grand-Champ, only two—paid more than 6 l. Whether the artisan-*tenuyers* are grouped with the rest or not, they appear to occupy roughly the same condition as the bulk of the *fermiers* and *métayers*, with only 1 per cent of their numbers above the upper quartile (paying over 9 l. 10 s.), 19 per cent above the median assessment (5 l. 12 s.), but with 23 per cent below the median and above the lowest quarter of assessments, and the bulk of their numbers, 58 per cent, in the lowest-taxed quarter of the population, where 66 per cent of the *métayers* were also grouped.

The overall impression which emerges from this analysis is confirmed by studying the distribution of domestic servants in this and other parishes.[5] Only the *tenuyers* employed domestics, used mainly for farm labour, in anything like sizeable proportions. In Grand-Champ, 296 *tenuyers* employed between them 124 servants in 1747, while the *métayers* kept a total of only 13 domestics.

As for the servants themselves, their taxes were assumed by their masters, who paid them an annual wage, and fed and clothed them. They were normally the unmarried young of each parish for whom labour on a neighbour's tenure provided a temporary employment until the day when the young man or woman was provided with a

[5] Table VI-2.

Table VI-1: Wealth levels and social groups

(1) Arradon (1779)
Classification   *Capitation assessment* (livres)

	< 1	1–1.9	2–5.9	6–9.9	10–19.9	20–29.9	≥ 30	Totals
Tenuyer	—	—	2	3	9	1	1	16
Métayer	1	1	5	3	5	—	—	15
Fermier	—	—	1	1	1	—	—	3
Jardinier	1	—	—	—	—	—	—	1
Meunier	—	—	—	—	1	—	—	1
Journalier	3	5	—	—	—	—	—	8
Artisan & Boutiquier	5	8	8	1	5	—	—	27
Matelot	—	9	2	—	—	—	—	11
Total, professions known	10	23	18	8	21	1	1	82
Widow & minor	2	2	5	1	8	—	—	18
Unkown	3	18	20	6	23	8	1	79
Totals	15	43	43	15	52	9	2	179

Notes:
Artisans &   10–19.9   l.: Maréchal 2, boulanger 1, poissonnier 1, forgeron 1.
Boutiquiers   6–9.9   l.: Poissonnier 1.
             2–5.9   l.: Charpentier 1, maçon 1, cabaretier 1, tisserand 2, tailleur 3
                          (1 in *bourg*).
             1–5.9   l.: Cabaretier 1, menuisier 2, tailleur 1. tisserand 2 (2 in *bourg*).
                          poissonnier 2.
               < 1   l.: Tailleur 2 (1 in *bourg*), poissonnier 1. cordonnier 1 (1 in *bourg*).
                          coch[r] (cochonnier?) 1.
Excluded   Four domestics with separate impositions.

(2) Grand-Champ
(a) Including Brandivy and Locmaria, 1747:
Classification   *Capitation assessment* (livres)

	< 1	1–1.9	2–5.9	6–9.9	10–19.9	20–29.9	≥ 30	Totals
Tenuyer	—	3	110	114	109	25	7	368
Métayer, fermier	3	65	170	25	3	—	—	266
Journalier, valet	7	9	1	—	—	—	—	17
Meunier	—	—	7	3	1	—	—	11
Artisan, boutiquier	8	25	21	—	—	—	—	54
Widows, minors, unknown	—	10	16	5	1	—	—	32
'Bourgeois'	—	—	—	2	2	1	—	5
Totals	18	112	325	149	116	26	7	753

Notes:
Tenuyers   20–29.9   l.: Incl. 1 fermier et tenuyer.
             6–9.9   l.: Incl. 2 menuisiers-tenuyers, 1 cabaretier-tenuyer, 1 métayer-
                          tenuyer.
             2–5.9   l.: Incl. 3 tailleurs-tenuyers, 1 maréchal-grossier-tenuyer,
                          2 menuisiers-tenuyers, 1 tisserand-tenuyer, 1 maréchal-tenuyer.
Métayers   10–19.9   l.: Incl. 2 fermiers.
             6–9.9   l.: Incl. 2 fermiers, 1 fermier-métayer.
             2–5.9   l.: Incl. 4 fermiers.

Table VI-1: Wealth levels and social groups (*continued*)

Artisans & *Boutiquiers*	2–5.9 l.:	1 Boucher, 5 cabaretiers, 2 cordiers, 1 fournier, 1 maçon, 4 maréchaux-grossiers, 2 menuisiers, 1 fossoyeur, 4 tailleurs, 1 tailleur d'habits, 1 tisserand.
	1–1.9 l.:	1 Barbier, 2 boulangers, 2 carbaretiers, 1 fossoyeur, 1 fournier, 2 maréchaux-grossiers, 1 marchand, 2 menuisiers, 2 moulayeurs, 6 tailleurs, 5 tisserands.
	< 1 l.:	2 Boulangers, 1 crieur (?) 1 maçon, 1 tailleur, 3 tisserands.
'Bourgeois'	20–29.9 l.:	Sr. Le Thieis de Keraudrain.
	10–19.9 l.:	1 Notaire.
	6–9.9 l.:	2 Notaires.

(b) Main parish only, 1778:

Classification   *Capitation assessment* (livres)

	< 1	1–1.9	2–5.9	6–9.9	10–19.9	20–29.9	≥ 30	Totals
Tenuyer	—	1	14	41	51	16	3	126
Fermier	11	34	43	4	1	—	—	93
Métayer	—	—	2	—	1	—	—	3
Laboureur	1	—	—	1	—	—	—	2
Meunier	—	2	4	1	2	—	—	9
Artisan	10	11	10	1	1	—	—	33
Journalier	—	1	—	—	—	—	—	1
'Bourgeois'	1	—	2	1	—	—	—	4
Total, known	23	49	75	49	56	16	3	271
Widows & minors	3	13	21	17	15	2	4	75
Unknown	10	41	47	26	17	2	2	145
Totals	36	103	143	92	88	20	9	491

Notes:
Artisans	10–19.9 l.:	1 Forestier.
	6–9.9 l.:	1 Maréchal.
	0–6 l.:	3 Texiers (1 in *bourg*), 2 tisserands (1 in *bourg*), 8 tailleurs (1 in *bourg*), 1 cordonnier (*in bourg*), 1 sabotier, 5 maréchaux (1 in *bourg*), 1 fournier (in *bourg*), 5 menuisiers (2 in *bourg*), 2 moulayeurs (2 in *bourg*), 1 cordier, 2 cabaretiers (in *bourg*), 1 aubergiste (in *bourg*), 1 courvreur (in *bourg*).

Total: 33: in *bourg*, 18.

Not included: 150 *pauvres mendiants* in entire parish.

(3) Ploeren–1770

Classification   *Capitation assessment*

	< 1	1–1.9	2–5.9	6–9.9	10–19.9	20–29.9	≥ 30	Totals
Tenuyer	—	1	11	7	18	3	—	40
Fermier	—	—	1	1	2	—	—	4
Métayer	—	4	9	6	5	—	—	24
Jardinier	—	1	—	—	—	—	—	1
Meunier	—	2	1	—	—	—	—	3
Journalier	—	1	—	—	—	—	—	1
Artisan, boutique	4	3	9	1	—	—	—	17
Total, known	4	12	31	15	25	3	—	92
Widows & minors	—	1	3	3	3	—	—	17
Unknown	14	8	18	8	9	1	—	58
Totals	18	21	52	26	37	4	—	158

Notes:
Artisans &	6–9.9	l.: 1 Cabaretier (in *bourg*).
Boutiquiers	2–5.9	l.: 2 Tailleurs (in *bourg*), 2 tisserands (in *bourg*), 2 cabaretiers (1 in *bourg*), 3 boulangers (1 in *bourg*).
	1–1.9	l.: 1 Cabaretier, 1 tailleur, 1 maréchal (in *bourg*).
	< 1	l.: 1 Maçon, 2 tisserands, 1 blanchisseuse (all in *bourg*).

Total: 17 (in *bourg*: 12).

(4) St-Ave–1774:

Classification	Capitation assessment							
	< 1	1–1.9	2–5.9	6–9.9	10–19.9	20–29.9	≥ 30	Totals
Tenuyer	—	—	1	6	21	3	2	33
Métayer	—	7	13	7	1	—	—	28
Fermier	—	—	1	2	1	—	—	4
Jardinier	—	—	1	—	—	—	—	1
Meunier	—	—	3	1	2	—	—	6
Journalier	—	2	—	—	—	—	—	2
Artisan, boutiquier	1	9	7	—	3	—	—	20
Total, known	1	18	26	16	28	3	2	94
Widows & minors	1	2	7	4	7	1	2	24
Unknown	2	7	31	14	17	5	1	7
Totals	4	27	64	34	52	9	5	195

Notes:
Artisans &	10–19.9	l.: 1 Maçon, 1 tailleur, 1 cabaretier.
Boutiquers	2–5.9	l.: 1 Grossier, 1 cabaretier, 2 tailleurs, 1 tisserand, 2 maçons.
	1–1.9	l.: 1 Débitant de tabac, 2 cordonniers, 1 maçon, 4 boulangers, 1 tailleur.
	< 1	l.: 1 Boulanger.

(5) St-Nolf–1774:

Classification	Capitation assessment							
	< 1	1–1.9	2–5.9	6–9.9	10–19.9	20–29.9	≥ 30	Totals
Tenuyer	—	—	6	14	27	11	3	61
Métayer	—	8	27	3	5	—	—	43
Fermier	—	—	1	—	—	—	—	1
Tenancier	—	—	4	—	—	—	—	4
Journalier	2	4	—	—	—	—	—	6
Meunier	—	—	2	1	1	—	—	4
Artisan	2	6	8	—	1	—	—	17
Total, known	4	18	48	18	34	11	3	136
Widows & minors	—	1	3	1	2	—	—	7
Unknown	—	5	10	7	6	1	1	30
Totals	4	24	61	26	42	12	4	173

Notes:
Artisans &	10–19.9	l.: 1 Cordier.
Boutiquiers	2–5.9	l.: 2 Forgerons, 2 cabaretiers, 2 couturiers.
	1–1.9	l.: 1 Tailleur, 1 maréchal, 1 forgeron, 1 couturier, 1 cabaretier, 1 menuisier.
	< 1	l.: 1 Tisserand, 1 couturier.

piece of land or a dowry and a marriage partner. They formed about 3 per cent of the total population of Grand-Champ in mid-century, a proportion which, according to the census of 1807, was about representative for the region.[6] The widespread practice of hiring domestics in this way no doubt kept down the number of day-labourers *(journaliers)* and migrant labourers, who only played a significant role in the rural economy at harvest and mowing times, but some of the artisans, *métayers* and *tenuyers* in need of extra income must have supplemented their revenues by selling their labour.

Thus, to summarize, rather less than half of the taxpayers in the five parishes studied in this way paid over 6 livres in poll tax, and this half was mostly composed of *tenuyers*, along with a very few of the richer *métayers*, perhaps a miller or two, and one or two of the rare 'rural bourgeois' who were not peasants. Although some *tenuyers* did pay poll tax assessments comparable to those of most of the *métayers* and *fermiers* and did not keep domestics, the *tenuyers* nevertheless appear from this analysis to be the most prosperous single group in the countryside. No doubt the poverty of a few *tenuyers* helped blur distinctions between rich and poor, but on the whole, 'tenuyer' and 'better-off peasant' seem to be synonymous.

It is relatively easy to describe the economic hierarchy of *tenuyers*, *métayers* and *fermiers*, artisans and domestics from fiscal sources, because all of these people were more or less permanent residents and were considered sufficiently affluent to bear taxation. But from time to time there appear disquieting references which suggest that beside these inhabitants lived marginal members of the rural community, too poor or too mobile to be taxed. On the *capitation* roll of Grand-Champ in 1776, for example, appears a cryptic mention of 'pauvres, 150'.[7] Then, from time to time, in criminal records, the historian catches a fleeting glimpse of figures living camped in huts on the edge of woods or wasteland, men like Jean Le Goff, 'prétendu médecin', whose irregular existence in the parish of Elven, where he lived apart from his wife with a girl, only became known briefly around 1759 when half of his wife's bisected body was found in a well. When the crime came to light, Le Goff had vanished, never to be found again.[8]

Some of these marginal residents, unlike Le Goff, lived perma-

[6] A.D. Morbihan, M 1657, reproduced in Le Goff, 'Vannes', 414–15.

[7] A.D. Morbihan, C: Commission intermédiaire de Vannes: Grand-Champ, capitation, 1770.

[8] A.D. Morbihan, B 5804: Présidial de Vannes, minutes, 1759.

Table VI-2: Vingtième assessments, by social category. Sarzeau, 1754

	< 10	10–29	30–49	50–99	100–199	200–499	500–999	1000–4999	≥ 5000	Total
Laboureur	16	43	57	102	63	27	—	—	—	308
Journalier, domestique	14	30	6	12	2	—	—	—	—	64
Saulnier, paludier, salant	12	44	31	26	4	1	—	—	—	118
Mᵉ de barque, seamen	20	29	26	36	13	6	—	—	—	130
Artisan, boutiquier	24	40	14	32	10	1	—	—	—	121
Bourgeois	1	—	—	1	4	1	1	2	—	10
Clergy (individuals)	1	4	—	6	2	2	1	2	—	18
Nobles*	—	—	—	1	6	4	8	7	3	29
Non-resident	—	—	6	11	9	10	—	1	—	42
Unknown	127	172	97	127	45	32	5	2	—	607
Totals	216	366	237	354	158	84	15	14	3	1447

* Non-resident: 50–99:1; 100–199:6; 200–499:4; 500–999:2; 1000–4999:5; ≥ 5000:1.
Source: A.D. Morbihan, C: Subdélégation de Rhuys, Vingtièmes, 1754.

Table VI-3: Distribution of domestic servants by tax assessment level and social category in the parish of Grand-Champ, 1747 (main parish only)

(1) Tenuyers

Number of servants	Capitation assessment (livres)							Total tenuyers	Total servants
	< 1	1–1.9	2–5.9	6–9.9	10–19.9	20–29.9	≥ 30		
1	—	—	1	6	13	4	—	24	24
2	—	—	—	3	7	2	—	12	24
3	—	—	—	—	1	1	2	4	12
4	—	—	—	—	1	—	—	1	4
Total, *tenuyers* with servants	—	—	1	9	22	7	2	41	64
Total, *tenuyers* with and without servants	3	16	79	74	79	45	0	296	

(2) Métayers

Number of servants	Capitation assessment (livres)							Total métayers	Total servants
	< 1	1–1.9	2–5.9	6–9.9	10–19.9	20–29.9	≥ 30		
1	—	—	7	3	—	—	—	10	10
2	—	—	2	1	—	—	—	3	6

Table VI-3: (*continued*)

				Capitation assessment (livres)				Total 'bourgeois'	Total servants
	< 1	1–1.9	2–5.9	6–9.9	10–19.9	20–29.9	≥ 30		
3	—	—	—	—	—	—	—	—	—
4	—	—	—	—	—	—	—	—	—
Total, *métayers* with servants	—	—	9	4	—	—	—	13	16
Total, *métayers* with and without servants	4	—	114	13	—	—	—	131	—

(3) 'Bourgeois'

Number of servants	< 1	1–1.9	2–5.9	6–9.9	10–19.9	20–29.9	≥ 30	Total 'bourgeois'	Total servants
1	—	—	—	1	—	—	—	1	1
2	—	—	—	—	—	1	—	1	3
3	—	—	—	—	—	1	—	—	—
4	—	—	—	—	—	—	—	—	—
Total, *'bourgeois'* with servants	—	—	—	1	—	1	—	2	4
Total, *'bourgeois'* with and without servants	—	—	3	1	3	1	1	9	—

(In addition, one *fermier* paying an assessment of 6 livres employed one servant, one artisan paying 2 livres employed one servant, and one *meunier* paying 6 livres employed one servant.)
Source: Same as Table VI-1.

nently in their parishes. How many? Parish registers of baptisms, marriages and burials scarcely hint at their existence. The somewhat slapdash census of 1807, carried out in confusion and after a generation of disorder, made an attempt to list the inhabitants of the countryside according to their professions and activities, and there are some remnants of an inquiry of 1794 into the number of indigents resident in each parish. These sources agree in showing that the proportion of beggars and indigents residing in the communes who were not exercising a profession or who were incapable of working for their living was relatively small: not greater than 6 per cent in 1807 and less in 1794.[9] The counts which have been made of professions in parish registers seem to support this conclusion in showing a comparable proportion of professions to those indicated by the *capitation*. It therefore appears safe enough to say that these rolls reflect the professional composition of the rural population.[10]

But in addition to the resident poor, the countryside was inhabited by more or less itinerant, more or less professional beggars, whose numbers varied from year to year, depending on economic conditions in the area and elsewhere in the province. Nearly half of the people arrested as beggars in the area around Vannes by the mounted police in the years 1768–70 came from regions outside the diocese of Vannes, mostly from the northern part of Brittany. However, except for this brief period, there are few traces left in the records of the itinerant poor. Taken as a group, they may have been a considerable number of people, certainly more than the two score collected by *maréchaussée* in what was supposed to be a draconian repression during these two years.[11] Their numbers must have increased as they did elsewhere in the depression of 1770–89,[12] and their psychological impact was no doubt immense, but they cannot have been significant economic burdens on the parishes through which they wandered.

[9] A.D. Morbihan, M 1657: Population, 1807–1831; L 1465, État général du nombre des indigents . . . [3ᵉ sansculottide, An II or after]; both tables are resumed in Le Goff, 'Vannes', 414–16.

[10] A.D. Morbihan, Eᶜ: Baptémes, mariages, sépultures, Arzon (1778–80) Elven (1785–7), St-Gildas-de-Rhuys (1781–5), Sarzeau (1781–3), Surzur (1777–9), resumed in Le Goff, 'Vannes', 409–13.

[11] A.D. Morbihan, B 1279–1280: interrogatoires de mendiants, 1768–9; E. Guéguen, 'La Mendicité au pays de Vannes dès la 2ᵉ moitié du xviiiᵉ siècle', *BSPM* (1970), 105–34.

[12] There was a wave of arrests of beggars and prostitutes in 1789–90. A.D. Morbihan, B 3431, Lz 1699: Registre d'écrou.

To say as much does not in any way imply that poverty and insecurity were not the lot of many more than 6 per cent of the rural population in the Vannetais. It is abundantly clear that there was a very large group of artisans and poor tenants who formed the base of the economic pyramid, and to this number must be added the domestic servants, whose fate was bound up with that of their masters. Rural poverty was intense, but for the most part it was the poverty not of drifting vagabonds nor of temporary marginal inhabitants, but rather of many of the people who lived on the land. What, then, did the different levels of existence indicated by poll tax assessments mean when translated into the basic elements of rural wealth: land and personal property?

Some notion of the hierarchy of landholding can be obtained by comparing the declarations for the *vingtième*, the tax on rural land revenue, for 1753–6 and the *capitation* of 1747 in the parish of Grand-Champ, and by combining this information with what we already know about the distribution of land in the other parishes of the region. Such a comparison shows that within the group of *tenuyers*, although there existed a whole scale of gradations, the majority possessed sufficient arable land to permit them in an average or even less than average year to subsist independently. Some of course did much more than this; at the very top of the hierarchy in the parish of Grand-Champ stood men such as Guillaume Cougoulic, one of the seven *tenuyers* in the parish to pay *capitation* assessments of over 30 l. Around 1750, Cougoulic owned the edifices of no less than five separate tenures in the parish, one of which he worked with help of three servants while leasing the other four holdings to other peasants. By the time he died in 1779, he possessed no less than thirteen such tenures, two of which were outside the parish, estimated at a total worth of 29,352 l; in addition, he had a total of 2,970 l. in *constituts* (guaranteed debts).[13] Still in the same class were those who paid assessments over 20 l. and cultivated around ten to twelve hectares. These two constituted the most prosperous and the least numerous class of peasant. Beneath them, in the group of tenuyers paying from 6 to 20 l. in *capitation*, were the bulk of the *tenuyers*, who enjoyed a certain security and independence though rather less than opulence, with usually something between 4 to 6 hectares of land under cultivation. Almost half of the group paying over 10 l. in *capitation* could afford one or more

[13]   A.D. Morbihan, 17 C 5318: 18-9-1779.

servants to aid them, but in the group paying from 6 to 10 l. they became distinctly rarer.

These two groups accounted for a little over two-thirds of *tenuyers* and over a third of the total number of taxpayers. The remaining third, paying between 2 l. and 6 l., appear in a much less secure position; most possessed less than two hectares, worked their tenures with co-heirs, or were tailors, blacksmiths, joiners, spinners, supplementing their meagre income by cultivating a little land. Only one single *tenuyer* in this group maintained a servant.

It is difficult to make the same kind of direct comparison between *capitation* assessments and surface under cultivation for the third of the peasant population who sublet tenures under *domaine congéable*, or leased property directly in return for simple land rents. The bulk of this group of *fermiers* and *métayers* rented from other peasants and in so far as we can judge from the figures presented in the previous chapter, there was no difference in size between tenures sublet and those which were worked directly under *domaine congéable* by the *tenuyers*.[14] The size of *métairies*, on the other hand, tended to be a little larger than tenures held under *domaine congéable*. Basically, though, the condition of *métayers* and *fermiers* who let or sublet was the same, and in both cases the proportion of rent to revenue was about three times as high as it was under *domaine congéable*. Consquently, their taxes were usually lower than those of the *tenuyer*.

The results of a study of 297 post-mortem inventories of personal property (*inventaires après décès*) from 1732 to 1780 in the large seigneurial jurisdiction of Largouet-sous-Vannes, to the north of the town, suggest a similar, perhaps even less equitable distribution of wealth. The inventories evaluated the movable property of the deceased person's household; they included cash on hand in their total evaluations, but not landed property or debts, although they did usually indicate the existence of debts and gave a catalogue of the leases, receipts, deeds and so forth kept in the household. Of these households, the most wealthy 25 per cent amassed from 52 to

---

[14] Of the 170 *métayers* and *fermiers* paying between 2 l. and 6 l. on the *capitation* roll of 1747 in Grand-Champ, it was possible to trace 67 on the *vingtième* of 1751–6 for the same parish. Of these, 40 were renting tenures under *domaine congéable* from *tenuyers*; 26 were leasing *métairies* and *pourpris* from nobles and bourgeois, and one owned a *métairie* outright. The terms *métayer* and *fermier* are used interchangeably in the documents.

65 per cent of total wealth invested in goods and chattels. Around half of the deceased persons had not owned the draught oxen necessary to work a holding, and virtually all of these were in the quarter of the group whose property was assessed at the lowest values. Many of those poorer folk were artisans or retired people living in *bourgs,* but there were also men called *laboureurs* (no doubt *fermiers* and *métayers* in the main) in this category as well.

The results of this examination of inventories are set out in Table XI-6; a few examples of what these people owned and what they paid in *capitation* tax may serve to give some substance to these abstract percentages. Julien Thomazo, a *tenuyer* in Brandivy, belonged to that relatively prosperous group of *tenuyers* who paid *capitation* taxes over 10 l., (his assessment was 13 l. in the year before his death, 1780). Yet his possessions were not extensive: two oxen, three cows, one heifer, one bull, a calf, a goat and three chickens made up the total of his livestock, plus just enough grain for himself and his family (10 hl rye, 2.5 hl millet) and a little hemp seed. The value of his possessions came to 638 l.[15] His neighbour, Yves Ribouchon, also a *tenuyer*, who died in that year, paid less in *capitation* (9 l. 8 s.) but had somewhat more extensive possessions: two oxen, a mare, four cows, two heifers, a bull, three goats and a kid, a couple of score sheep. He also had a sizeable surplus of grain, though the inventory was made late in the year, in May: 8.5 hl millet, 2.1 hl buckwheat, and nearly 30 hl rye.[16]

These two examples come from the group of peasants occupying the middle range of wealth. More typical of the few peasants at the top of the hierarchy was Yves Seveno, *tenuyer* at Poulfang in Grand-Champ. Besides a fairly ample collection of clothing and furniture, he possessed a pair of oxen, a horse, six cows, four heifers, three bulls, a goat and two pigs. In his granary was a good supply of grain, for the inventory was made in November, after the harvest was in, but also after all dues had been paid and his sowing, presumably, finished: 36 hl of rye, 6.8 hl each of wheat, millet and oats, and 10 hl of buckwheat, worth a total of 485 l. alone, plus a little hemp seed and some hemp in various stages of preparation. Seveno also had on hand 300 l. in cash, a fairly rare phenomenon for peasants in the area. The total value of his possessions was 1968 l.[17]

[15] A.D. Morbihan, B: Largouet, minutes: 18-4-1780.
[16] Ibid., 1-5-1780.
[17] Ibid., 28, 29-11-1780.

At the other extreme, Jacques Le Maligorne, *tenuyer* at Kergal, near Brandivy, in the parish of Grand-Champ, possessed a harrow, a plough, two oxen, one mare, four cows, two heifers, two bulls, two calves and a pig, in addition to his modest furnishings, and he was burdened with a debt of 300 l. he had contracted five years earlier, in the difficulties which followed his purchase of the tenure. In his granary was barely enough millet and buckwheat to last until the harvest; although the inventory was taken in March, there remained only 3.8 hl of rye and 6.8 hl of millet. The total value of his possessions, less the debt, was 521 l. 15 s. Le Maligorne paid 4 l. 6 s. *capitation* in the year before his death, 1779, which placed him in the group of *tenuyers* on the fringes of penury.[18]

Compared with the more impoverished *tenuyers* such as Le Maligorne, certain *métayers* appear rather more prosperous. Julien Le Boulaise, of La Granville in Brandivy, had more cattle than Le Maligorne, but he paid only 5 l. 2 s. *capitation* in 1779. In addition to the normal pair of oxen and a mare, he owned two pigs, eight cows, six heifers, a goat, a rooster and ten chickens, which together with his modest furnishings, was valued at 1490 l. 3 s. Rather than reflecting real prosperity, however, these extensive possessions were probably necessary to work and make a profit on his large *métairie*.[19] More typical of the state of the *métayer* appear to have been cases such as that of Jean Le Nouail, of Kerblay in Elven, who leased a *métairie* from a relative, and whose total possessions were valued at only 388 l. 19 s.,[20] or François Ruaux, who rented a *métairie* at Trussac, near Vannes, on which he kept two oxen, a horse, a mare and five cows, and who was burdened with debts of 224 l. and his annual rent of an equal amount, still due in November, when the inventory was taken.[21]

If this kind of insecurity was the case for peasants possessing enough land, or nearly enough, to maintain themselves, it was all the more so for those who depended on their own labour for a living. To be sure the extreme case of Jean Garel, wheelwright in the *bourg* of Trédion was seldom approached; his total possessions at death consisted of one old and lidless trunk, worth 3 sols—

[18] Ibid., 9-3-1780.
[19] Ibid., 30, 31-10-1780.
[20] Ibid., 24-2-1775.
[21] A.D. Morbihan, B: Régaires, minutes: 20-11-1775.

c'est l'unique meuble qui est resté après le décès dudit Jean Garel, ses habillements étaient si mauvais qu'on les jeta sur un buisson proche sa maison où ils sont encore actuellement tout pourris.[22]

In addition to his household furnishings, an artisan or day-labourer living in the countryside might have a few domestic animals; Jean Brien, a weaver living at Loperhet in Grand-Champ, kept a cow and six beehives in addition to his clothing and looms,[23] but these were the exceptions. Pierre Boterel, who owned about a hectare of cultivable land in the wastelands of the parish of Plaudren, kept a cow and a heifer; obviously neither his land nor his livestock were enough of themselves to permit him to live, and he must have survived by selling his labour.[24]

It would be possible to multiply such examples to infinity, but the common characteristics of all these lists of possessions should be apparent already. If a man had enough land, his essential equipment was simple and his livestock few; the latter might provide him with a couple of heifers to sell each year, bringing in enough to make up the deficiences in rents or taxes in bad years, or enough to reimburse a loan from a wealthier neighbour in a better one. Most such peasants had on hand a certain amount of hemp which their wives, daughters or servants spun, and which then was put out to local artisans; not enough to market on a large scale, it none the less provided them with a little extra money and the material for their clothing.

Furniture was modest: a few benches, the closed beds peculiar to Brittany, or a simple couch, some chests or cupboards. A rich *laboureur* might show his wealth by the number of shirts he owned, but otherwise his dress remained sober. In general, the standard of housing was low; peasants lived together, shut off from one another only by the provisional privacy of the *lit clos*, when they had one, under the same roof, if not in the same room, as their livestock, all permeated with what one witness called the 'mephitic odours' of the stable.[25]

---

[22] A.D. Morbihan, B: Largouet, minutes: 18-4-1775.
[23] Ibid., 3-4-1781.
[24] Ibid., 11-4-1780.
[25] A.D. Morbihan, M 1242: Draft memorandum for the *Statistique agricole* of 1819, cf. also Young, *Travels*, ii, 450: '*Aury* [sic] *to Vannes*—Pass many cabins almost as bad as the worst Irish, a hole at the corner, by way of chimney and no windows.'

Cattle formed the bulk of all peoples' wealth, at least if they were wealthy enough to have the basic necessity, a team of oxen to plough with; between 40 and 60 per cent of the value of movable property was made up of cattle; herds which gave an additional bit of revenue but which were by no means large: people in the wealthiest quarter of the population had only four or five cows on the average, a heifer or two, a couple of calves, a horse (usually a mare), a pig or (rarely) two, and a handful of barnyard fowl and, very rarely, a little herd of a couple of dozen sheep. These proportions did not vary much across the century.[26]

If it is relatively easy to know the physical surroundings and possessions of the people of the Vannetais in the eighteenth century through the examination of these inventories, it is less simple to determine the amounts of cash each had on hand. Of the nearly 300 inventories examined in the period from 1732 to 1780 just referred to, only seven list any cash on hand at all, a number so small that one must come to the same conclusion as does a study of inventories from the Beauvaisis in the eighteenth century, that 'cette discretion . . . doit être mise au compte d'un prudent usage paysan'.[27] The documents themselves confirm that at least a part of the cash left by the deceased was used to meet day-to-day expenses of the holding, to pay the servants the wages due them by their late master, or to cover the costs of the funeral and settle outstanding debts, before the formal inventory was drawn up. No doubt the heirs in many cases simply shared out the money before the bailiff arrived. For the major transactions of the peasant's life and for the payment of rents in cash (particularly by *métayers* and *fermiers*), to be sure, the peasant had to use legal tender, so that there was usually a certain amount of cash circulating in the countryside. Nevertheless, the impression which remains from the inventories is of a society in which debts were settled at infrequent intervals by mutual arrangement.

This impression is confirmed by a study of peasant indebtedness from the inventories in the period 1732–80. Here again, the same practice of paying debts before the inventory was prepared reduces the number of documents available; only 25 inventories contain indications of the debts incurred by the deceased persons. However, where they do exist, such lists seem to be complete. To judge

[26] Tables XI-6, XII-7.
[27] Goubert, *Beauvais*, 145–6.

from these, admittedly a small sample, indebtedness in the rural Vannetais does not seem to have approached anything like the proportions reached in the Beauvaisis of the seventeenth century.[28] In only five of the cases studied did the amount of the deceased person's debts exceed half of his total assets (not including real property), and in one of these cases this was due to the fact that the year's rent had not yet been paid. Another five had debts between a quarter and a half of the value of their non-real assets, and again all but one of these were as high as they were only because the year's rent was due. The majority of the debts of peasants and artisans were of three kinds: wages due to domestic servants, which were a normal part of the year's expenses, small payments owed to artisans and debts of a few livres between peasants, and finally the occasional large loan, between 100 and 500 livres.

A different form of debt, which does not appear in these inventories, took the form of the sale of land with an option to repurchase within a fixed term (*vente à réméré*), an operation which could in practice conceal a loan. The number of such sales, however, was quite small; even in large parishes such as Grand-Champ or Plaudren it came to only about four a year. Still another form, which again is hard to find in the *inventaires après décès*, were the mortgages taken out by peasants who borrowed in order to reimburse tenants under *domaine congéable* whose lands they had taken over. The proportion of expulsions in which such mortgages were employed was quite high, but surprisingly, very few of these turn up in inventories as being still due; one may presume—and there are good reasons for doing so, as will be seen—that these mortgages were usually paid up within a short time.

In all these cases, it is not really possible to speak of these debts being concentrated in the hands of a bourgeoisie—that is, in the hands of a non-agricultural class who did not work with their hands for a living—either in Vannes or in the countryside. To be sure, each bourgeois who lived in the countryside had his share of *constituts* which had been made over to him by peasants in need of money, but then so did any *laboureur* who had had money on hand to lend at one time or another, so that in such a society in which the bourgeoisie formed a very small element, their economic impact was necessarily limited. There may have been—there undoubtedly was—a concentration of creditors at the top of the scale of wealth and a cluster of

---

[28] Ibid., 183–9.

debtors at the bottom, but the use of credit for all sorts of trans-actions, long and short-term, spread debt around in the rural com-munity, making it difficult to distinguish anything with the specific appearance of a creditor class.

To say as much is not to claim that a bourgeoisie of this kind did not exist in the countryside. Those examples of it who can be found turn out to be among the wealthiest—in a relative sense—of the people living outside towns. Most of these who lived permanently in the countryside appear to have been notaries, men like Mᶜ Charles-Pierre Caris, notary of the seigneurial jurisdiction of La Chenaye in Grand-Champ. Before his death in 1786, Caris lived in the chateau of Coetcandec, apparently lent to him by its noble owner, the *seigneur* of his jurisdiction; he owned some land and three houses in the *bourg* of Grand-Champ, and part or all of the edifices of three tenures in the parish, one which he had resold by the time of his death. His furnishings were fairly opulent, including an ornamented bed with curtains, five dozen china plates, four dozen shirts, 128 table napkins, 2,474 livres in cash . . . ; the total value of his personal property came to 5,146 livres, one of the biggest fortunes of this kind in all the inventories examined.[29] A similar person was the sieur Yves Pouliguen, who lived in a modest manor in Grand-Champ; included in the common property which he held with his deceased wife in 1765 was no less than 1,000 livres' worth of spun hemp and 289 livres' worth of grain.[30] But men of this stamp were hard to find. If we look at all the land transfers carried out in the period from 1772 until the Revolution, there are only a handful of non-peasant rural purchasers: a half-dozen notaries and lawyers and one or two rural merchants and artisans.[31]

If one wants to find a rural bourgeoisie in the Vannetais, one has to look to the peasantry itself for it. And indeed, among the *tenuyers* were sufficient examples of wealthy men to whom the epithet, in the sense of a peasant of means who participates in a market economy, could apply: the peasants in the group of people paying more than 10 l., even those who paid more than 6 l. in *capitation*. These were the people who had a tenure or even several, had no debts, leased a tithe or two,[32] sold their surplus grain on the market in Vannes, and sent their sons to the college in Vannes.

[29] A.D. Morbihan, B: Largouet, minutes: 3, 15-6-1780.
[30] Ibid., 25, 26-2-1765.
[31] See below, p. 306–14.
[32] e.g. A.D. Morbihan, 31 G 35 (100): Dîmes de Surzur.

However, if they were a 'rural bourgeoisie', they were one which bore the unmistakable stamp of western France: there were more of them than in most other parts of the northern half of France, and on the whole, their condition was probably more homogeneous and modest. One is accustomed to taking as a model of the more prosperous peasant the *grand fermier* or the wealthy *laboureur* described by George Lefebvre and Pierre Goubert in their studies of the Nord and the region of Beauvais in the old regime: a handful of dominating, profit-minded men atop a hierarchy of wealth with a tiny apex of wealthy people and a huge base of poverty, their status in the rural community symbolized by their solid dwellings set apart in the countryside from the wretched huts of the *haricotiers, journaliers* and artisans of the villages.[33] In the typical Beauvaisis parish of Cuigy-en-Bray, according to the roll of the *taille* in 1690, only 12 to 15 per cent of taxpayers paid more than 50 per cent of the total assessment of the parish, so concentrated was wealth in the hands of a few.[34] In the region around Vannes, through the eighteenth century, the same proportion of the *capitation*, based on the same criteria of wealth, was paid by the heaviest-taxed 20 per cent or more of the rural population. In Walloon Flanders, less than 14 per cent of the population occupied enough land to live on.[35] Wealth, generally speaking, was less concentrated in the Vannetais then than on the plains of the North of France. The same appears when we contrast the people of the Vannetais with the scrubby exploited peasantry of Northern Burgundy, though it is less easy to make a direct comparison of this sort.[36] The rich are always with us, but there appear to have been many more 'middling' peasants in the Vannetais than in the parts of France from which historians customarily take their models of rural social structure in the old regime.

This persistence of large numbers of better-off peasants in the land seems typical of Lower Brittany, wherever the *domaine co-*

[33] G. Lefebvre, *Les Paysans du Nord pendant la Révolution français* (Paris–Lille, 1924), i, 10–60, 307 ff.; Goubert, *Beauvais*, i, 158–82.

[34] Calculated from Goubert's table in *Beauvais*, i, 153.

[35] Lefebvre, *Paysans du Nord*, 10–60. This was not true of northern Flanders, which had a more intensive agriculture and where 18 to 39 per cent of the population was 'independent'.

[36] P. de Saint-Jacob, *Les Paysans de la Bourgogne du Nord au dernier siècle de l'ancien régime* (Paris, 1960), 158–9. Compare, for example, the inventories of personal property of peasants in the Vannetais with the meagre possessions of the *laboureurs'* inventories given in Saint-Jacob's work.

ngéable existed. Studies of other regions in the interior of the Morbihan and elsewhere in Lower Brittany demonstrate, or leave us to conclude, that this was the case.[37] It also seems to have been true of the region farther east, in Upper Brittany and northern Anjou. Thus, in the parishes of Balazé and Argentré in Upper Brittany, the highest-taxed 22 to 23 per cent of the people assessed on the *capitation* paid 50 per cent of the levy on the parish; in the typical northern Anjou rural community of Mouliherne, 50 per cent of the parish *taille* assessment was acquitted by the highest-taxed 23 per cent.[38] Still in *bocage* country, but farther east and to the south of the Loire, these patterns appear to fade. In the Sarthe, the figures are less precise, but of the three types of rural taxpayer in the region at the end of the old regime, the more prosperous *laboureurs* made up about 20 per cent; the *bordagers,* close to subsistence level or beneath it, 60 per cent; and day-labourers, 20 per cent.[39] In the Vendée, in the *subdélégation* of Cholet in 1764, of 560 peasants holding leases, 360, or 64 per cent, had tenures which were so small that they barely sufficed for the subsistence of the tenant and his family. The remainder—36 per cent—were above the survival level. However, all these leaseholders, taken together, formed less than half of rural society: below their level were large numbers of rural artisans and day-labourers who made up about 53 per cent of the rural population of the area of the Mauges. So when this is taken into account, the number of independent leaseholds falls to less than a fifth, and there were virtually no independent peasants who were full proprietors.[40] In the neighbouring region of the Gâtine poitevine, the *métayers* who worked the sharecropper holdings typical of that region constituted 'un véritable prolétariat'. Apparently rich in cattle and land, the *métayers* of the Gâtine in reality were reduced to managing the cattle and property of noble and bourgeois land-

[37] F. Le Lay, *Le Paysan et sa terre sous la seigneurie de Coetanfao, paroisse de Séglien au xviiie siècle* (Vannes, 1911); Sée, 'L'Administration de deux seigneuries'; Le Floc'h, 'Le Régime foncier et son application', 117–205; P. Goubert, 'Dans le sillage de Henri Sée. L'histoire économique et sociale des Pays de l'Ouest (Bretagne, Maine, Anjou) du xvie au xviiie siécle', *Annales de Bretagne,* lxxi (1961), 315–28; 'Recherches d'histoire rurale dans la France de l'Ouest', 2–9.

[38] R. Plessix, 'Une Paroisse angevine au xviiie siècle, Mouliherne', *Revue du Bas-Poitou* (1969), 52–68; the figures for Upper Brittany were kindly supplied to me by Dr D. M. G. Sutherland.

[39] P. Bois, *Paysans de l'Ouest; des structures économiques et sociales aux options politiques depuis l'époque révolutionnaire dans la Sarthe* (Le Mans, 1960), 436–48.

[40] Andrews, *Les Paysans des Mauges,* 25–38, 227 ff.

lords under the pitiless eye of the entrepreneur who leased the right to collect whatever rents he could extract from them.[41] Compared with the Vendée and the Gâtine, perhaps, too, with the Sarthe, Lower Brittany, if it may have had as many poor, also had more men of relative ease in the countryside. The generally low rate of the lease under *domaine congéable*—less than 20 per cent of the gross produce, so low that it was possible to extort sub-leases from wretched sub-tenants at three or more times the value of the original payment, a varied system of agriculture and the generally low level of taxation in Brittany helped maintain the middling sort of peasant on the land.

Thus, the more we examine the distribution of wealth in the Vannetais, the more we are obliged to admit that it formed part of a political, economic and social complex peculiar to Brittany in the old regime, depending in many ways on the nobility; on their dominance in the Breton Estates which kept down royal taxes, and their reluctance to force up the rents under *domaine congéable* to a point where a restructuring of rural property and a reduction of the number of tenants would have been necessary. The moderation of the tax burden and the psychological obstacle to rack-renting created by the semi-'feudal' character of the *domaine congéable* meant that within the framework of this system of tenure was nurtured a kind of 'yeoman' class.

The rigidity of the *domaine congéable* also helped perpetuate this pattern by making it difficult to remove tenants. As a result, families tended to hold on to their lands for very long periods. This is a feature of the system which has not been perceived by most writers who, looking at the letter of the law rather than its application, have considered that there was a rapid turnover in tenants, since the *usements* gave the landlord the right to expel his tenant at will after the conclusion of the nine-year lease, making (so it was thought) the peasant's life a nightmarish succession of migrations from one tenure to the next. But this was not so.

To begin with, very few landlords themselves expelled their tenants under provisions of the leases and the *usement*. A *congément* was a long and expensive legal procedure, the costs of which fell on the person carrying out the expulsion. The case had to be taken through several separate hearings in the courts: first came the judgement, then the appointment of surveyors, followed by their swearing-in, then the actual survey of the tenure in question, and finally the formal reimbursement of the value of the edifices. Added to the court fees was the cost of recording the act of payment (*enregistrement*) in the registers of the *centième denier* and the *contrôle des actes*, all of which brought the price of the operation to around 125 livres, about the equivalent of a year's rent by the end of the century, and 5–6 per cent of the value of the edifices.[42] Even more important, the cost of the edifices of a normal-sized tenure ran between 2,000 and 3,000 livres, a sum which was often prohibitive. Out of all the cases of expulsions pleaded between 1740 and 1784 in the jurisdiction of Largouet, which covered almost the entire region to the north of Vannes, only three were both initiated and terminated by a proprietor himself.[43] This does not imply, of course, that the peasant was free from the threat of expulsion, but it does mean that the main threat to his security of tenure did not come from the landlord himself.

In fact, virtually all expulsions carried through in the region around Vannes were made on the initiative of other peasants, who obtained the landlord's permission to expel the existing tenant by signing a new lease, sometimes for a higher rent, and then carried out the *congément* at their own expense. It is possible to measure the effects of this competition on security of tenure in two ways; first, by looking at the proportion of leases in a large sample which contain provision for *congéments* and then by studying the real number of *congéments* in the area.

An analysis of two sets of leases signed between 1781 and 1790 in the records of two notaries, Josse, in Theix, who had mainly a clientele of absentee landlords, and Le Ridant of Vannes, who dealt principally with local nobles residing in Vannes, shows similar results: every fourth or fifth lease signed included provision for expulsion. If a calculation were to be based solely on these figures, the average length of tenure at the end of the eighteenth century would be in the neighbourhood of 36 to 45 years, assuming that every lease was renewed promptly upon expiry.[44]

[41] Merle, *La Métairie*, 203 and *passim*.
[42] See the example in Appendix I.
[43] A.D. Morbihan, B: Largouet, minutes, 1740–89.
[44] A.D. Morbihan, E[n] 3459–68: minutes Le Ridant, 1781–90; E[n] 33–6: minutes Josse, 1781–90. Forty-nine of 183 leases handled by Josse and 87 of 395 drawn up by Le Ridant had expulsion clauses.

An estimate made in this way, however, exaggerates the speed of turnover of tenures by expulsion. The annual number of *congéments* we know was higher during the period in which these leases were signed than it had been earlier in the century.[45] Moreover, leases were not necessarily renewed every nine years; landlords often allowed leases to lapse for several years before renewing them. And the fact that permission was included in the lease to expel the current tenant did not mean that such an act was always carried out; sometimes such provisions were merely options granted to one tenant to expel a co-tenant, and not acted on.

A study of the number of expulsions recorded in the *centième denier* from 1726 to 1789 in the rural parishes surrounding Vannes shows that these calculations do in fact underestimate the length of tenure under *domaine congéable*. The *centième denier* was a tax imposed in 1703 on all transfers of real property except direct successions. Within the jurisdiction of the bureau of Vannes, it was fairly strictly enforced, especially after a tightening of controls by the inspectors in the early 1730s. All expulsions of tenants under *domaine congéable* had to be recorded, since they were considered to be transfers of real property (the edifices).[46] According to these figures, the average length of uninterrupted tenure in the parishes of Grand-Champ and Theix, where we know the total number of holdings, would be around 57 years in the one and 90 in the other.[47]

Both these sets of calculations may appear abstract, but both are based on solid sources, and they both underestimate if anything the length of tenure. And they confirm the impression, purely subjective, obtained after working with large numbers of leases and seigneurial papers in the region: tenures are often named after the family holding them, and it is not rare to see several generations

[45] See below, pp. 318–19.

[46] Marginal notations by the inspector of the *domaine* in A.D. Morbihan, 17 C 5172, 5202, 5396: 1714, 1732, 1781; P. Thomas-Lacroix, *Répertoire numérique de la série C: 17 C—domaines et droits joints* (Vannes, 1932), 1–2; P. de Saint-Jacob, 'La Propriété au xviii° siècle, une source méconnue: le contrôle des actes et le centième denier', *Annales: E.S.C.*, i (1946), 162–6; M. Vovelle, 'Problèmes méthodologiques posés par l'utilisation des sources de l'enregistrement dans une étude de structure sociale', *Comité des travaux historiques et scientifiques. Section d'histoire moderne et contemporaine. Bulletin*, fasc. 3 (1961), 49–104.

[47] The breakdown by parishes is given in Le Goff, 'Vannes', 487. There were 372 tenures in Grand-Champ and 289 in Theix in mid-century, and a total of 416 expulsions in the former and 205 in the latter over a period of 64 years, or a yearly average of 6.5 in Grand-Champ and 3.2 in Theix.

succeed one another on the same piece of land. In short, all the evidence tends to prove that the tenant under *domaine congéable* in the Vannetais both felt himself to be the near-proprietor of the land on which he lived and behaved as if he were.[48]

The third feature of the *domaine congéable* which was responsible for the pattern of wealth and poverty among the peasants of the Vannetais was indivisibilty of land held under this system. In theory, Breton customary law provided for the widest possible distribution of the possessions and land of a deceased non-noble person; in fact, the edifices of land held under *domaine congéable* were not supposed to be subject to physical division, not even under the *usement* of Brouerec, considered to be the least onerous of the *usements*. This provision was intended to keep ultimate control over the *fonds* in the hands of the *seigneur foncier* and ensure the regular payment of rents by making one man responsible for them. The way in which peasants dealt with this provision will be discussed in a later chapter; here, it is sufficient to note that tenures were kept intact and, whatever method of compensation the heir who kept the tenure provided for his co-heirs, he was considered to hold a distinct advantage over them. The most acute of the critics of the system, J.-M. Le Quinio de Kerblay, who knew the peasants of the Vannetais, found this fact embarrassing, because it seemed to imply that the system had advantages for agriculture:

quelque remboursement même [he wrote in 1790] que le détenteur donne à ses cohéritiers, il conserve toujours avec eux dans une inégalité immense de mesure . . .

Il est inévitable que le domanier . . . soit à l'aise, mais autour de lui circule l'indigence.[49]

Here, Le Quinio put his finger on one of the most perplexing problems of this rural society, for coexisting with the middling and prosperous group of *tenuyers* was a large mass of poor. On this point, testimony is unanimous. Freneau, the *subdélégué* of the indendant of Brittany in Vannes, took it as a rule of thumb in calculating the amount of poor relief necessary in the hardship of

[48] This confirms the impressions of A. du Chatellier, *L'Agriculture et les classes agricoles de la Bretagne* (Paris, 1863), 23, 221, note 1.

[49] J.-M. Le Quinio, *Élixir du régime féodal autrement dit domaine congéable en Bretagne* (Paris, 1790), 57–60. Le Quinio solved the dilemma for himself by asserting that even if the *domaine congéable* prevented the fragmentation of holdings, it was contrary to the principles of equality, liberty and property.

1785–6 that a third of each rural parish would be 'très indigent'.[50] Le Quinio, admittedly not always a trustworthy witness, exaggerates a little, but his description of Ploeren in 1790 has a ring of truth:

Depuis quatre ans je vis . . . dans la paroisse de Ploeren . . . j'y vis familièrement avec les laboureurs mes frères et j'affirme à tout l'univers que j'y connais une grande et générale détresse, quelques domaniers moins misérables, un très petit nombre plus à l'aise, et pas un homme riche.[51]

The physician Aubry, the correspondent in Vannes of the Académie Royale de Médecine, described the population of Surzur in similar language: 'Ce sont en grande partie de pauvres laboureurs que le plus petit dérangement imprévu dans les saisons réduit bientôt à la disette.'[52] Not all parishes were as poor as Surzur, which had perhaps a larger share of artisans than most and a hazardous system of biennial crop rotation. But it is possible to trace on a map a series of 'black' areas in the region which in 1788 had a population smaller than what it had been a generation earlier.[53] To the observer of the time, the poverty of the poorest was widespread enough to mask the relative prosperity of the *sanior pars* of the rural community. It is as if the rural socio-economic structures which we are accustomed to regarding as typical of old regime France, and which Goubert characterized vividly as a pyramid with a small apex of rich and a large base of poor, had been replaced by a sort of two- or three-tiered economic hierarchy with larger numbers of 'middling' sorts of peasants, with less flagrant examples of real rich, but the same numbers of poor, if not more, than elsewhere.

This is in fact the paradox of Breton rural social structure which has plagued all observers of the peninsula in Le Quinio's time and since; the existence of wretchedness and poverty on a large scale, side by side with certain signs which we take for prosperity. Wealth or poverty? Both, in all probability: heartbreaking poverty, which seems to have been at its worst in the interior of the province, and a group of small farmers enjoying a modest well-being.

What, finally, were the proportions of rich and poor in the Vannetais? Probably the best answer to this in the final analysis is

[50] A.D. I.-V., C 1747: distribution de secours aux pauvres, 1786.
[51] *Élixir du régime féodal*, 62.
[52] J. Meyer, 'Une Enquête de l'Académie de Médecine sur les épidémies (1774–1794)', *Annales: E. S. C.*, xxi (1966), 729–49.
[53] e.g. the parishes of Elven, Meucon, Plaudren, Theix, Surzur and Sulniac. Sarzeau would almost certainly be in this list if the figures were not lacking. A.D. Morbihan, E^c: Baptêmes, mariages, sépultures, 1770–88.

provided by the *inventaires après décès*. These show fairly conclusively the existence of a large number—which increased through the century—of people in conditions of poverty. About half had the oxen necessary to their land, and these were the more-or-less independent, but not all people living on the land had oxen, and such depended on their labour for a living, either as artisans or as labourers. Perhaps a safe estimate would be that a third of rural society was beyond the reach of all but the most serious economic disasters, a third lived in poverty, and another third enjoyed a certain security which was, however, precarious.

Thus, what gave the Vannetais, and the rest of Lower Brittany, its peculiar form of rural civilization and attenuated the very real poverty of the mass of people was the persistence of the sizeable group of *tenuyers* who gave the rural community stability, at least where the number of poor was not too great, employment for the young and a certain degree of charity. 'Il y a toujours du pain dans la cabane du plus humble paysan pour le mendiant qui ne fait que passer', wrote a prefect in 1822, 'et chez lui la portion du pauvre est toujours mise en réserve dans les fêtes importantes.'[54] A rural municipal official in the commune of Treffléan put it less romantically in 1790:

Dans notre paroisse il n'est personne qui ne donne annuellement à la porte ce sur quoi on pourrait l'imposer pour aider à l'entretien d'une maison des pauvres . . . Quand on serait assuré que la loi aurait pourvu au sort de tous on n'aurait plus à craindre des menaces de gens sans aveu qui quand ils sont refusés en imposent à nos timides, mais bons habitants de campagne.[55]

To the extent that there was such a stable element in the countryside, the *domaine congéable* can be held responsible. What happened without it, but in the same overall conditions, could be seen in the peninsula of Rhuys and at Séné, where the immediate seigneur of the greater part of both parishes was the King of France, as the immediate successor of the dukes of Brittany. According to the story used in litigation in the eighteenth century and after 1789, Henry II abolished the *domaine congéable* on lands under his direct domain in 1556, in order to be able to levy *lods et ventes* on property transactions under his overlordship. The provisions of this royal

[54]   A.N., F¹ Cᵛ Morbihan 2: Rapport du Préfet, 1826.
[55]   A.D. Morbihan, L 1463: commune of Treffléan to District of Vannes, 29-10-1790.

decree were, however, not put into effect until the middle of the seventeenth century, when incommutable rights to the property were given to the inhabitants in return for an increased *rente féodale.*[56] Whether this actually happened or not, it is true that in the eighteenth century the *domaine congéable* was practically non-existent in the peninsula of Rhuys. The result was that the equal division of non-noble land, prescribed by Breton customary law but held in check by the peculiar provisions of the *domaine congéable* elsewhere in the Vannetais, had permitted the fragmentation of peasant holdings to almost unbelievable extent. Of the 1340 *vingtième* assessments made in mid-century in the parish of Sarzeau, 80 per cent listed annual revenues of less than 100 livres, corresponding usually to less than two hectares of arable land, plus a few pieces of vineyard. Only half of the cultivable land, moreover, was put under cultivation each year, the rest lying fallow.[57] 'L'on y compte . . . des milliers de petits propriétaires qui ont des sillons ici et là,' wrote a contemporary

mais tellement dispersés que, pour avoir un journal de terre possédé par une famille, il faut faire souvent une lieue de chemin. Sans la navigation à laquelle se livrent les hommes, laissant aux femmes le soin de semer et de récolter, ce serait le pays le plus misérable de la France, et il y a longtemps qu'il n'y existerait pas un seul cultivateur.[58]

The result, as this quotation suggests, had been that the population had been driven to take up other professions as seamen, salt-marsh tenders, day-labourers and smugglers. *Laboureurs*—and a good number of these had to earn their living by working for others— accounted for only 47 per cent of the population in the 1780s.[59]

They were also nearly all very poor, except for the few *laboureurs* who owned enough land or rented large *métairies,* and their situation

---

[56] A.D. Morbihan, 8 A 1: petition to the princesse de Conti, 1730; Dubreuil, *Les Vicissitudes*, i, 296–7; Le Quinio, *Elixir du régime féodal*, 63, 93–6.

[57] Table VI-2; Cayot-Délandre, *Annuaire du Morbihan* (1838), 78–140; L. Le Cam, 'Le Problème de l'openfield sur les rives du golfe du Morbihan', *Chronique géographique des pays celtes. Annales de Bretagne*, lviii (1951), 164–70; A. Meynier, 'Pseudo-pratiques communautaires en Bretagne méridionale', ibid., lii (1945), 92–6.

[58] 'Réflexions sur les pétitions des colons à domaine congéable', *Bibliographie de Jurisprudence bretonne,* ed. Corbière, no. 11 cited in Dubreuil, *Les Vicissitudes*, i, 246.

[59] From the professions of parents of newborn children in A.D. Morbihan, E^c: Arzon (1778–80), St-Gildas-de-Rhuys (1781–5), Sarzeau (1781–3) summarized in Le Goff, 'Vannes', 409–13.

was precarious; according to the *subdélégué* Jouchet de la Villaloys

Le paysan qui en a trop [de grains] le va vendre aux marchés à Vannes, mais ce n'est pas le plus grand nombre, y ayant beaucoup plus de journaliers qui n'ont que leurs ʰras pour les faire vivre et faire subsister leurs familles, même parmi les laboureurs il y en a nombre qui après avoir ensemencé leurs terres en ont très peu de reste pour leur subsistence et qui actuellement se trouvent sans grains.

The writer of this went on to add that at the time of writing, the harsh winter of 1772, several inhabitants, mostly *journaliers,* had gone for two to three days without bread: 'le tiers ou la moitié de tout le peuple pour ne pas dire davantage est dans la misère.'[60]

Thus, whether we look at the distribution of wealth, land or personal property, the same conclusions emerge. The rural Vannetais was a country with a social structure typical in large measure of western France, which, if it had large numbers of poor, also managed to find a place for a considerable group of middling peasants, mostly *tenuyers,* who were safe from all but the worst agricultural crises. Indeed, there seem to be grounds for believing that life in the Vannetais was probably easier for more people than in many other parts of·western France. But even so, the lot of the poor and the economically insecure was not pleasant. With the exception of the peninsula of Rhuys, where a much larger proportion of the rural population lived on the fringes of poverty, the rural Vannetais was a society in which one-third lived in relative security and one-half to two-thirds in a state of hardship and even of indigence.

---

[60] A.D. I.-V., C 1772: Jouchet de la Villaloys to intendant, 4-3-1772.

CHAPTER VII

RURAL SOCIETY FROM WITHIN: (1) INSIDERS AND OUTSIDERS

To unravel and describe the complex ties which unite a community and the fine distinctions which separate its members from one another is not an easy task, but a proper study of rural social structure would be incomplete without it. Purely circumstantial evidence of patterns of settlement or distribution of wealth can never on their own tell us what is going on inside peoples' heads. A rural community scattered across a map in clumps of isolated dwellings may, contrary to expectation and sociological speculation, be one in which intense social and community life exists. A parish marked by extremes of wealth and poverty can nevertheless be a place where such differences are masked or attenuated by the image of society that its members create for themselves, or inherit from their predecessors. A society to all appearances rigid and hierarchical may nevertheless conceal a large measure of social and geographical mobility. Somehow, the attempt has to be made to understand rural society with the eyes of the insider.

The inside view is difficult to obtain at the best of times, even in contemporary society. Breton rural society has always seemed to pose more of an enigma than most to outside observers, even to Bretons of birth or adoption, who have turned an inquiring eye inward on it. Some have spoken of it as an 'individualistic' society and laid emphasis on the influence of habitat: the isolation of country people in hamlets, the exiguity of the rural *bourg* are supposed to have developed a suspicious, individualistic and even asocial outlook. Others have drawn attention to the spirit of co-operation and self-help supposed to exist among rural people.[1] If, as

---

[1] Sée, *Les Classes rurales*, 493; P. Goubert, *L'Ancien Régime* (Paris, 1969–73), i, 80; P. Thomas-Lacroix, 'La Condition des terres', 367–8.

the preceding chapters have attempted to establish, there was an apparently large contrast between rich and poor in the rural Vannetais in the eighteenth century, a contrast reinforced by the system of landholding, how did these differences carry over into everyday conduct and affect people's sense of basic solidarities?

Unfortunately, historians, unlike sociologists, have no means of sending questionnaires to their subjects, and in a very large measure, the mental world of the peasant of the eighteenth century is a 'world we have lost' beyond recall. Yet a fleeting glimpse of it can be got from the testimony of contemporary observers of the eighteenth and early nineteenth centuries, especially when they were people who were born in or knew the region and its customs well. Another, often richer, source, consists of the records of civil and, especially, criminal cases tried in the courts. French criminal records of the old regime have two advantages over most comparable records elsewhere: they are very full, and they relate a mass of circumstantial and hearsay evidence collected by the examining magistrate, often completely irrelevant to the case being tried, but in which people sometimes speak directly and describe their world and their values, or fragments of them. Sources like these have their limitations—one of them being a barrier of language, for testimony in nearly all rural cases in the region was given in Breton, translated for the court by an interpreter and set down in French—but such cases are the closest things we have to a real conversation with people of the time. Used obliquely, not for the purpose of establishing guilt, as the courts meant them to, but as testimony about behaviour patterns and beliefs, they can provide glimpses of the attitudes and loyalties of rural people.

One of the most frequent crimes tried in the courts of the Vannetais in the eighteenth century, and one of the most revealing for the study of mentalities, were prosecutions for defamation and insult, which always began in the courts as criminal, not civil, proceedings. The content of these insults helps us define, *a contrario*, the basic values and solidarities of the countryside. The more of these cases one reads, the more it becomes apparent that they nearly all refer back in one way or another to the basic unit of loyalty, the family. This is almost invariably the case where women are insulted; they are referred to as 'garce', 'putain', 'bougresse', 'reste de soldat et d'armées', 'reste de moines et de prêtres', and other less complimentary epithets, and sometimes accused of having killed their offspring or relatives. Men were judged by a somewhat more extensive standard: by their supposed violations of the sexual code or their weakness in defending their honour ('bougre', 'bougre de chien', 'cornard', 'jan foutre'), but also by their honesty ('fils de maltotier et voleur', 'fripon', etc.).[2] In general, such insults were taken much less literally by men than women—though on one occasion an old woman who kept a tavern drove an old sailor to desperation by calling him by the name of a man, Patary, who some thrity years previously had murdered a wife and illegitimate child and threatened a mistress with the same fate.[3] If people went on in this fashion, it was because insults were not the faded abuse they are today; women, especially, found it wise to take their antagonists to court when insults had been made in situations where their honour could be easily damaged. Thus the wife of a sailor took another sailor to court for casting doubt on her respectability with an insult because, she explained, she was especially vulnerable in her husband's absence as a prisoner in England.[4] In a world where people had few material belongings, honour was an important if intangible possession.

Honour, however, was not only private property; it belonged to a family. A grandmother who in 1761 got rid of her married daughter's illegitimate child by exposing it on a church porch in Vannes explained that they had decided to take this desperate step 'pour éviter la honte qui en résulterait à sa famille'.[5] Insults and injuries done were a collective blow to a whole lineage, extending backwards in time and outwards through relations, friends and allies. The way to intensify an insult was to make it, and then repeat it with a wider application. Hence the exchange between a cloth merchant and a butcher in Sarzeau: 'capon'—'capon à toi bougre'—'fils de bourgre'; or a ploughman to a serving-girl: 'putain bougresse', and then, as an afterthought: 'ton père était un voleur et un fripon de châtaignes'; or between two sea-captains: 'fils de maltotier et voleur'—'ton père l'était avant moi'—'cornard'—'tu est plus cornard que

[2] A.D. Morbihan, B: Sénéchaussée de Rhuys, minutes: 1730 (trials of Anne Le Besque, G. Pichon), 1731 (S. Le Cabellec, V. Le Moyec, J. Josso), 1732 (S. Le Cabellec, P. Le Coquen, J. Payen, M. Jobe), 1760 (F. Le Divillec), 1762 (G. Corchuan), 1763 (J. Cailloche, M.-A. Delhomme, P. Le Mitouart, J. Oillic), 1789–90 (T. Cottier, J.-P. Le Biboul); B: Régaires de Vannes, minutes: 1764 (J. Le Port).

[3] A.D. Morbihan, B: Rhuys, minutes: 1730 (Patary), 1763 (J. Cailloche).

[4] A.D. Morbihan, B: Rhuys, minutes: 1762 (G. Corchuan).

[5] A.D. Morbihan, B 1267: Présidial, minutes: 1761 (J.-M. Le Barre et al.).

moi parce que j'ai couché avec ta femme'. Another method was to accuse someone of having killed his cousin, uncle, or children, or simply to show total disdain for the lot, as a quarrelsome timber-merchant from Elven told an equally quarrelsome ploughman, Joseph Le Rohellec dit Cougan, after they had downed a bottle of cider, 'il se foutait de tous les Cougan'.[6]

To be sure, nobody could deceive themselves that family disputes did not take place: husbands mistreated their wives or their step-children, grandchildren quarrelled over the possession of their aged relation's cupboard, and children fought over the possession of inherited land, brothers-in-law came close to murder over unpaid debts. Such conduct, however, was not approved: 'Vous êtes tous deux cousins, pourquoi voulez-vous vous battre?' said a woman tavern-keeper to two cousins, one of whom eventually killed the other in a drunken brawl.[7] In 1730, a woman upbraided her brother-in-law who was chasing his wife through the village, throwing stones after her—'Que pensez-vous mon beau-frère en exerçant tant de cruautés à l'égard de ma sœur, avez-vous déjà oublié que nous ne faisons que de finir la Pâque, ce sont cela les progrès que vous avez faits des instructions de notre prédicateur?' (upon which, he began, perhaps understandably, to throw stones at his sister-in-law).[8]

Women were of course the members of rural society most directly responsible for carrying on the family and avoiding stains on family honour and on the institution of marriage itself. This no doubt explains the vindictiveness with which they appear as the main accusers of the unmarried mother; taunting her beforehand with remarks about her widening girth, and pursuing her with their accusations after the clandestine delivery and the disappearance of her baby. In 1794, all the witnesses in a case of infanticide in Arradon were women.[9] In 1764, the women of the village of Kerelec in Ambon heard from some ploughmen that an unmarried woman had previously been forced out of another parish by the rector after a long period of scandalous conduct culminating in a fourth illegit-

[6] A.D. Morbihan, B: Rhuys, minutes: 1732 (S. Le Cabellec, G. Banal), 1764 (A. Eudo), 1789 (J.-P. Le Biboul); B: Régaires, minutes: 1762–3 (G. Guillodo); A.D. I.-V., 1B^n 2215: 1762–3 (indirect discourse changed to direct in all citations).
[7] A.D. Morbihan, B: Rhuys, minutes: 1730 (M. Le Digabel et al.), 1732 (J. Payen, P. Le Coquen): A.D. I.-V., 1B^n 1801; 1B^g 274; T. J. A. Le Goff and D. M. G. Sutherland, 'The Revolution and the Rural Community in Eighteenth-Century Brittany', Past & Present, lxii (1974), 102–3.
[8] A.D. Morbihan, B: Rhuys, minutes: 1730 (P. Le Vaillant).
[9] A.D. Morbihan, Lz 282: Year II (M. Hulcoq).

imate pregnancy, whose results were about to appear. They began to pursue her with questions, and suggested that the rector of Ambon drive her out of the parish. When her child's corpse was discovered in a nearby marsh, 'tout aussitôt presque toutes les femmes de Kerelec et des environs affluèrent auprès de la porte(. . .) et accusèrent unanimement ladite Boulhouach en face d'être la mère et l'auteur de la mort de cet enfant'.[10] Not surprisingly, when the curé of Brandivy preached against the Civil Constitution of the Clergy in 1791, one of the accusations which stuck most in his congregation's minds was 'que désormais les mariages ne seraient plus que des marchés, qu'on se prendrait et qu'on se quitterait quand on voudrait', just as the constitutional priest and ex-monk Le Quinio in Sarzeau shocked country people by proclaiming (with perhaps a certain relish) that priests and nuns would soon marry and that the Church would be the better for it—a statement which helped push the parishioners into making an official protest to the National Assembly against the disorders of the times.[11]

The family, then, was a unit whose honour and integrity had to be protected. And if insults and imputed misdeeds might do ill to a family's reputation, the guilt or ill-fortune of one of its members could, it was thought, harm it materially. A.-F. Rio recounted how, when he was a boy in the college of Vannes in the uneasy atmosphere of the Empire, the students, mostly country boys brought up in admiration for the grisly exploits of the *chouans,* delighted in drawing political lessons from the Old Testament

Avec quelle aprêté [he wrote] ils propageaient toutes ces légendes qu'on aurait pû appeler vengeances, et qui, comme les Euménides du paganisme, s'attachaient à tel personnage ou à telle famille reputée maudite! Et avec quelle dureté ils interpretaient certains passages de la Bible sur les châtiments solidaires!

They retailed with glee, he records, popular rumours that two girls who worked constantly in the window of their room in the town were under a curse: because their father had committed a crime, they could never leave the home, for when they tried, their shoes filled with blood.[12] Similarly, according to the nephew of Georges Cadoudal, the *chouan* leader, a family legend often repeated to him had it that when Cadoudal was a baby, a wandering beggar came up

---

[10] A.D. I.-V., 1B^n 2935, 1B^g 330: 1779–80.
[11] A.D. Morbihan, Lz 272^7, 278^{11} (A. Loget), 281 (J. Jaunes).
[12] Rio, *La Petite Chouannerie,* 8–10.

to his mother as she held little Georges in her arms on the doorstep, laid his hands on the child's head, and prophesied: 'Celui-là sera cause que de grands malheurs viendront frapper sa famille'.[13] Whether collective curses or misfortunes really struck these individuals or not, they certainly carried conviction.

And because collective guilt was an article of faith, real misfortune did fall on entire families. The case of the 'arsonists of Theix' who sowed terror for five years or more in a *bourg* near Vannes illustrates this point well. Around Christmas of the year 1778, the family of a draper, Louis Fleury, who served as an occasional messenger to the bishop's seigneurial court in Vannes, had tried to clear some land and dig ditches around his hut in the commons. The inhabitants of the *bourg* destroyed them on the spot, and Fleury uttered vague threats. In January, at least four fires were set in the *bourg*; while the courts began their ponderous investigations, more fires were set. Suspicion fell, needless to say, on Fleury; not just on him, but on his wife, his sister-in-law, his niece, and also on his brother and his adult children who were working in Vannes as drapers and spinners. 'Ils ont la famille longue', 'ils n'ont pas bonne réputation dans le canton', it was said, vaguely (for no previous misdeeds could be brought up), but with feeling, for the Fleurys were probably considered as pawns in the longstanding struggle of the parish with the bishop of Vannes over control of the commons. Fleury was released after questioning, fire broke out again, and after his second arrest, a third time, and then a fourth— set, it was assumed, by his family. Most of the Fleurys were given severe sentences on the basis apparently of very flimsy evidence, for they seem subsequently to have been released on appeal, although too late for Fleury, who died soon after.[14]

In the meantime, fires had broken out again, and continued to blaze up a score or so times over a space of three years, from 1779 to 1782, all in the *bourg*. Suspicion this time fell on a different family group, three middle-aged sisters, Jeanne, Bertranne and Marie Olligo, married to a baker, a tailor and a day-labourer respectively (there was also some rumour that the remnants of the Fleury family had been responsible, but this was not pursued). Louis Fleury's widow saw the hand of God in the events, and was reported as having said while in prison and at the retreat-house in Vannes, 'si

[13] G. de Cadoudal, *Georges Cadoudal et la Chouannerie* (Paris, 1887), 3.
[14] A.D. I.-V., 1B^n 2916, 1B^g 329: 1778–9.

elle et Louis Fleury son mari avaient tant souffert . . . c'était les trois filles Olligo qui en étaient cause mais que dans peu Dieu permettrait que cela se découvrirait.' In fact, the Olligos appear to have been the cause of a series of incendiary outbreaks dating back to 1761; once the Fleurys had been eliminated as suspects, public opinion put the blame on the sisters, and this time it was probably right. The fires were no doubt an unconscious way of wreaking revenge for their wretched state—one of them seems to have come down in the world, since she had once employed a servant, and in general the late 1770s and 1780s were a bad time for artisans and the poor. In any event, the Olligo sisters delighted visibly in threatening their intended victims beforehand: as far as they were concerned, it was a series of revenges for real or imagined wrongs done them or their families. Far from stopping their activities, the more the net of suspicion closed in on them, the more they took a desperate pleasure in setting fire to the property of the people who denounced them.[15]

A family suffered together, but a family could avenge itself. An aged *laboureur,* Gervais Corfmat, had the same end in view as the Olligos after a rival family, the Palluds, outbid him in the 1770s for the lease on a tenure at the village of Loperhet in the parish of Grand-Champ. According to some testimony, he had threatened that when his second son returned, vengeance would be theirs: that he had enough money to help him escape after killing off the Palluds. Once, when drunk on an empty stomach, he was alleged to have said 'qu'il avait une bonne maison qui le protégeait, qu'il . . . ferait embarquer [son fils] et puis d'ailleurs après cela que pourrait lui faire la justice.' The long feud between the two families, in which the sons had ambushed each other after fairs, upset each other's carts, and wreaked a series of petty revenges, culminated in a pitched battle.[16]

It could be claimed that the emphasis on the integrity of a family, its collective honour and its group responsibility, and the disapproval of behaviour, particularly sexual behaviour, which did not fit into this pattern, was the result of a repressive pattern of sexual morality, the result of the reinforcement and stiffening of Christian doctrine and practice in the seventeenth and eighteenth centuries. Certainly the illegitimacy rates in the eighteenth century in the region remained low. In nearby Allaire, it was less than 1 per cent

[15] A.D. I.-V., 1B^n 3433: 1781–4.
[16] A.D. I.-V., 1B^n 3615: 1785–6.

for the period 1693–1790, in Arzon, 1.2 per cent in 1778–80, in Elven and St-Gildas-de-Rhuys, 1.8 per cent or less in the 1780s; and 1.1 per cent in Surzur in 1771–9. Rigorism, if not Jansenism, appears to have been strong in the Vannetais, reinforcing and reinforced by family traditions and fitting in well with what we know of the 'second evangelization' of Brittany in the seventeenth century.[17]

This is more than a plausible contention, but it is not unreasonable to suggest that there was also an economic reason for behaviour which placed such importance on the family in belief and conduct. The family was an economic unit; this generalization, true to some extent of most of France, was certainly true of the Vannetais, at least as a standard. Those who held land under the *domaine congéable* had a responsibility for keeping it in one piece and retaining it within the family; it was not for nothing that holdings took the name of the family living on them. Sacrifices of various sorts therefore had to be made: the usual one was a deferral of marriage, until both men and women had the means to maintain a family. The way to do this was by going off in service as a servant or even by hiring oneself to one's own family. The rival families of the Palluds and the Corfmats alluded to above are a good case in point. The Corfmats were five on their tenure in the village of Loperhet in Grand-Champ. There was the father, Gervais, sixty-eight years of age, and too old to work his land, his wife, and their five sons, ranging in age from eleven to thirty. The eldest son, Yves, had left home for a year when he was in his teens, in order to go into service; at the age of twenty-two he returned and stayed with his family for the next eight years. On Shrove Tuesday 1785 he went into the service of the widow Perel, who had begged the father 'comme pour l'amour de Dieu' to lend her his son, because her servants had just gone off to be married. The second son, Jean, had also been away for ten years in service, that is, from the age of fourteen; two of these years he had spent at sea with, no doubt, another relation, a Corfmat in Baden, but his parents had forced him to leave the sea, and eventually, when his father grew too old, to return to the land. Thus, during the years when they might have been considered for marriage if they had had land, the two eldest sons had been kept single, and because they had employment elsewhere, had avoided putting a burden on the household. Gervais, during their early

[17] Le Goff, 'Vannes', 409–13; cf. H. Mitchell, 'Resistance to the Revolution in Western France', *Past and Present,* lxiii (1974), 126–30.

manhood, must have managed his land alone, along with his third and fourth sons. Now, no doubt, Yves or Jean would have taken over the land. Meanwhile, the two younger sons, aged fourteen and eleven, were occupied tending the cattle and were called 'laboureurs' by their father; in time they would go out and work until some land came their way. Already the eleven-year-old André lived apart from the family in the sheep pen.

Their adversaries, the Palluds, were a contrast to the Corfmats. Their father had died in 1783, and the eldest son, Jean, had been married on Shrove Tuesday 1785 to Marie Le Priol. They lived together at the village of Kerdual Loperhet on a *métairie* with Pallud's unmarried sister, thirty-one years of age, and a boy, Guillaume Bertic, who kept the cattle, and perhaps with a cousin, called Jean, who at least lived in the same village. It appears that, unlike the Corfmats, the Palluds had less potential difficulties with large numbers of heirs.[18]

Deferral of marriage was thus the means of keeping land in the family, and in cases like this one, where the family possessed an economic base to begin with, one can speak of a kind of family economy which functioned, paradoxically, in the opposite way to Chayanov's celebrated model of the 'peasant economy': instead of being a source of labour and therefore a benefit to the holding, in the Vannetais, surplus children were a liability and better put out temporarily to make their own way elsewhere. Significantly, the average age of the mothers of illegitimate children in the region at the end of the eighteenth century was about the same as that of women marrying for the first time. These unwed mothers, largely domestic servants, clearly had accepted the basic premise of waiting their turn to be married, and only abandoned their standards when honest alternatives no longer seemed open to them. Their personal downfall was thus a reflection of the breakdown of their family economies, and the rise in illegitimacy and celibacy in Brittany at the end of the eighteenth century reflects the attempts and partial failure of the family economy to deal with the malaise of the general economy.[19]

[18] A.D. I.-V., 1B^n 3615: 1785–6.
[19] A.D. Morbihan, B: Largouet-sous-Vannes: déclarations de naissances illégitimes, 1782–90; Guyot, 'Allaire'; Blayo and Henri, 'Données démographiques sur la Bretagne', 111–14; A. V. Chayanov, *The Theory of Peasant Economy* (Homewood, Ill., 1960), 53–69.

A family economy, then—but perhaps less of an economy of generous mutual assistance than some have suggested. Labour, on or off the holding, had its price. The labour of servants, even if they were relations, was defined by a price and so were other benefits granted out of the common fund of labour and land. Servants were hired annually at the feast of St Barnabas or St John: 'quand la Saint-Jean est venue chacun est bien libre de gager ses domestiques'. Good servants were an object of competitive bidding—apparently Jeanne Olligo's first attempt at arson was in revenge for losing her servant to another *laboureur* in 1762. But the relationship was contractual, and, though we have unfortunately testimony only from the nineteenth century to sustain the statement, even members of the family received apparently a payment of some kind for labour, even the youngest children.[20]

Similarly, compensation paid to the aged parent for a tenure they had abandoned to their heirs before their death was settled at least some of the time by contract. A fine text from that acute but, alas, nineteenth-century observer, Du Chatellier, writing in 1863, explains why: when Breton children arrive at the age of maturity, he said

leurs intérêts se séparent de ceux de leurs pères, si bien que les fils et les filles de la maison deviennent les salariés de leurs parents ou s'en éloignent quelquefois si les conditions faites aux enfants ne leur paraissent pas suffisants.

The respect due to age, he added, was less marked in Brittany than elsewhere:

si les parents vieillissent et viennent à jouir longtemps de leur prélévation [allowance] il manque rarement de se trouver dans la famille de mauvais esprits pour faire remarquer combien ces bouches improductives nuisent aux profits réels du travail des plus jeunes . . .[21]

Perhaps this is an exaggeration, and perhaps the commercialization of the rural economy was accentuated in the course of the nineteenth century, exacerbating this form of elementary greed, but the elements of it seem to be well in place already in eighteenth-century Brittany. Families were considered to be the basic units of society, then, but they were microsocieties in which affection and loyalty to

[20] A.D. I.-V., 1B^n 3433: testimony of Julien Gain, 2-3-1781: see also 1B^n 3615 and Du Chatellier, *L'Agriculture et les classes agricoles,* 199.

[21] Du Chatellier, *L'Agriculture et les classes agricoles,* 186; Thomas-Lacroix, 'La Condition des terres', 354.

one's relations were tempered by at least some material considerations.

Not all families, however, had resources to fight over. The Fleury family in Theix, for example, appears to have been linked only by a common occupation—all the men were drapers or spinners of wool—but they lived apart and had few resources to speak of: merely a series of points of contact which bound them together, to their disadvantage, in times of trouble and perhaps (if the courts were right) spurred them on to vengeance. Likewise the Olligo family was linked only by the three sisters and their fantasies of vengeance, but little else. Yet they hung together, united only perhaps in their common misery.

Were there many real extended families under the same roof in the region? Even a full-scale effort at family reconstitution from parish registers would not answer the question and perhaps, after all, when we reflect on the personal and collective tragedies of the Corfmats, the Palluds, the Olligos and the Fleurys, the mere physical presence of a common roof has little importance in the creation of such bonds. At any rate, if we look at a looser criterion of association, habitation in the same hamlet, very few people appear to have had adult relatives living in their immediate vicinity, let alone under the same roof. When children were left orphans, the adult members of their families, starting with the brothers and sisters, and then the other nearest collateral relations, were obliged by law to meet and appoint a guardian. The 53 rural families who appointed tutors between February and October 1783 and January and May 1775 in the jurisdiction of the *régaires* of Vannes assembled a total of 130 uncles or uncles by marriage; only 14 of these lived in the same village or *bourg* as their orphaned nephews or nieces. Only 6 of the 53 families had surviving grandparents. Thus J.-M. Le Quinio's claim that it was common to find adult sisters and brothers working as domestics on the same holding as the principal heir of a family has to be taken with a certain scepticism. The extended family, in the sense of a group living under the same roof, seems rare in the Vannetais. But then perhaps this definition of an extended family is a misleading one; in any event, the sense of the family as a unit remained important.[22]

[22] A.D. Morbihan, B 650: *Édit du roi portant réglement pour les tutelles en Bretagne, donné à Versailles au mois de décembre 1732*; B: Régaires, minutes, 1775, 1783. [*p. 216 for n. 22 cont.*]

These results lead us to ask about the importance of larger groupings in rural society. Beyond the individual holding and the group associated with it, whether present or not, were the 'villages', that is, the hamlets in which rural dwellings were usually grouped. The village played the role of a real social nucleus, with its own rules and loyalties. A peasant put upon by the excisemen or the court bailiffs could appeal to the village for support; thus, to cite only one example among many, J.-P. Cadio, a *laboureur* of Lesulit in St-Avé, when given a summons in 1763 to appear in court, kicked the court bailiff's dog and told the man that he would bring out the village against him. This actually happened many times, when the village-dwellers defended the local tavern-keeper from the excise-men.[23] In 1731, the most crushing insult a certain Vincent Le Mitouart could find when he tried to pick a quarrel with a cloth merchant of Surzur was that 'tous ceux de son village étaient des gueux et des fripons, de la canaille et des gardiens de chemins et que le suppliant [the cloth merchant] en étoit un des premiers'.[24] A modern folklorist with a fine sense of the realities of the Breton countryside, J.-L. Guilcher, wrote that the village was

une unité réelle de vie sociale. Les rapports entre familles sont beaucoup plus que de simple voisinage. D'habitude immémoriale chacun a accès à la vie de tous. Tenir sa porte fermée passe pour une marque de défiance injurieuse . . . tout lie les individus, l'enfance passé en commun, les données du milieu, la mentalité identique, les exigences d'un travail qui met constamment les uns dans la dépendance des autres. Prêter attelage, des outils, donner au voisin son temps et ses forces, sont des secours ordinaires et qui vont de soi.[25]

Perhaps a little idyllic if applied to the eighteenth century—but at least Guilcher laid proper emphasis on the impossibility of escaping from one's neighbours, and the necessary constraints life in close quarters imposed. And occasions for dancing, for meeting in com-

Three of the grandparents lived in the same locality as their orphaned grandchildren. Some of these relations lived in the same *bourg* rather than the same village, which means that the real proportion of uncles living under the same roof or close together must have been even smaller. However, unmarried adult aunts are not listed by the courts. Cf. Le Quinio, *Élixir du régime féodal*, 61.

[23] A.D. Morbihan, B: Largouet, minutes: 1764 (trial of J.-P. Cadio); B 1177: 1762 (G. Derff *et al.*); B 1273: 1764 (G. Lorcy *et al.*); B: Rhuys, minutes: 1731 (C. Le Boulicaut *et al.*); Le Goff and Sutherland, 'The Revolution and the Rural Community', 100–1.

[24] A.D. Morbihan, B: Régaires, minutes: 1731 (V. Le Mitouart).

[25] J.-L. Guilcher, *La Tradition populaire de danse en Basse-Bretagne* (Paris–The Hague, 1963), 16.

mon in *veillées* and celebrations had the village it seems, rather than the *bourg* for their locale: the threshing ground to be beaten down, the buckwheat to be trampled; the bride and groom to be welcomed back from the church by a child holding a little bush surrounded by a ring of dancers, or by a ceremonial breaking of bread and drink of cider, symbolizing welcome and fertility for the new couple, their fields and the village.[26]

Beyond the level of the village, there was a certain social life, incumbent. But as often as not, the *frairie* was no more than a to a chapel and the cult of its saint,[27] though this must have been intermittent, variable from one area to another, and limited to the saint's feast day and, sometimes, Sunday mass, if the chapel had an incumbent. But as often as not, the *frairie,* was no more than a convenient geographical division for the purposes of tax-collectors. The parish, on the other hand, had a real presence in the countryside, if only because church and state working together for centuries had made it so. The *bourg* was the normal place to go for Sunday mass, even if people sometimes went to the *bourg* of a neighbouring parish, or a chapel, or, in very large parishes, to one of the *trèves*— lesser *bourgs* in the same parish, with a church and a resident vicar. The *bourg* was the seat of municipal government of a kind, too, albeit intermittent: the *général de la paroisse,* composed, not as the name implies, of all the inhabitants, but rather of fourteen of the principal citizens: twelve ex-treasurers of the parish and the two occupying the office currently, plus the rector and, if they were about, the judges of the local seigneurial jurisdiction. On occasions of great importance, an *assemblée générale* of the 'habitants notables possédant biens dans la paroisse' was also called. The solider citizens, then, could be called together in this way from time to time to vote on issues of common concern: the mending of a church tower, a request for help to the intendant, or a protest against an unfair tax levy.[28] The *général* levied taxes jointly with the *commissaires des états,* who sometimes had an unofficial 'correspondent' in the parish. They left few records and probably kept few, contenting themselves

[26] Ibid., 18–35; De Morval, 'Lettres morbihannaises', *Lycée armoricain*, x (1827), 437; A.D. Morbihan, B: Largouet, minutes: 1789 (trial of J. Lorho *fils, et al.*).

[27] E. Sageret, *Le Morbihan et la Chouannerie morbihannaise sous le Consulat* (Paris, 1911–18), i, 46; Du Chatellier, *Les Classes agricoles,* 63–4.

[28] Potier de la Germondaye, *Introduction au gouvernement des paroisses suivant la jurisprudence du Parlement de Bretagne* (St-Malo–Rennes, 1777), 155–9 and *passim*: Luco, *Pouillé historique,* 87–92.

with drawing up their documents as the need arose, and having them notarized if necessary. They defended the interests of the *sanior pars,* sometimes of the whole parish. Thus in 1780–1, the parish assembly of Treffléan protested against a rich *laboureur* from Plaudren who had expelled two local men from their tenure but paid no *capitation* tax in the parish (as was his right, as a non-resident, but this increased the burden on all the inhabitants of Treffléan).[29]

The parish had a real identity *vis-à-vis* outsiders, and a certain sense of community. In 1762 in Arzon, when the ciborium containing the consecrated hosts was stolen during Holy Week (probably by some passing soldiers as a prank), the local sailors were reported as saying hopefully that 'le Bon Dieu n'était point hors de la paroisse parce que le temps était trop calme, et que quand celui qui avait fait un pareil vol aurait voulu passer la mer il vient une tempête.'[30] In the food crisis of May 1789 in the same parish, an elderly widow of a schooner captain, Jeanne Le Scouharnec, firmly told the receiver of the royal domain, when he tried to export some wheat, 'ce grain est provenu de la paroisse, et nous n'entendons pas qu'il en sorte.'[31] But such loyalties were too flexible to be tightly tied down to the boundaries of a parish. Styles of dress, for example, seem to have been common to groups of parishes rather than individual ones; thus there was the style of Baden, of Plougoumelen;[32] prefiguring, unconsciously, the later administrative grouping of parishes which the documents in French referred to already as 'cantons'.[33] The game of *soule,* a primitive form of football, accordingly, seems to have been played between groups of parishes.[34]

Sometimes this sense of identity went farther, to include all those who could speak the local dialect of Breton which covered the western part of the diocese. Thus, around 1782, a day-labourer from Loudéac working for the rector of Theix was made fun of by the inhabitants of the *bourg* because, he thought, 'il était étranger';[35]

[29] A.D. I.-V., C 4364: supplique de Joseph le Texier, 27-5-1780; reply of the assembly, 18-3-1781.
[30] A.D. Morbihan, B: Rhuys, minutes: testimony of G.-M. Le Rousseau, chevalier de St-Ridan, 1762.
[31] A.D. Morbihan, B 1342: 1789.
[32] A.D. I.-V., 1B^n 1799, 1B^g 274: 1741-2.
[33] e.g. A.D. Morbihan, B: Largouet, minutes: payement par Mathurin Bocher contre la veuve Gautier, 28-10-1775.
[34] Rio, *La Petite Chouannerie,* 47–8.
[35] A.D. I.-V., 1B^n 3433: interrogation of L. Jartel, 27-3-1783.

and in 1789, one of the Benedictine monks of Rhuys, apparently Breton-speaking, but from Tréguier, had to use the monastery porter as an interpreter when dealing with the local people.[36] Only in documents which come from the élite, including people of rural origins but who had passed through the college of Vannes or other secondary schools can one find much of a sense of Breton nationalism, as, for example, in the writing of Le Croisier, rector of St-Patern and the son of a woman of apparently prosperous means from near Sarzeau, married to a merchant of Vannes.[37] The 'nationalism' of the Breton nobility so evident in the quarrels between the provincial Estates and the Crown does not seem to have raised much enthusiasm or interest in the countryside. In the case of the maritime parishes, if there was patriotism, it seems to have been rather a kind of attachment to the King as a military leader. The hymn of the sailors of Arzon, an authentic piece of popular devotion dating from their participation in the battle of Schooneveldt (1673) managed to describe the fleet as being 'under the King's command'.[38] Those who had something to do with the recruiting administration had no doubts about where power was in the state; when asked who his master was, the *syndic* of the sailors of Arzon promptly replied 'le Roi et son ministre'.[39]

Few extended their vision even this far. Family, village and parish were the basic cells of existence to which people referred. It is difficult to find examples of conscious representations of the community in which all members appear; the only one which appeared in this inquiry was a story told in the early nineteenth century about a man on the Île d'Arz who, passing the church on his drunken way homeward late at night, noticed the door open and the interior ablaze with light; when he looked inside, his hair stood on end as he saw the nave full of people, and a preacher in the pulpit. This constant theme of Breton folklore, half pagan, half Christian, of the community of the dead and the living within the Church was per-

---

[36] A.D. Morbihan, B 1342: testimony of J. Rolland, domestic of the Recollets of Bernon, 1789.
[37] Le Goff, 'Le Doléances des paysans du Vannetais', 39–41. Le Croisier, however, rejected the political pretensions of the Breton Estates.
[38] A. Cariou, 'Les Arzonnais et Sainte Anne. La bataille de Schooneveldt (7 Juin 1673)', *BSPM*, cii (1975), 61.
[39] A.D. Morbihan, Lz 273³: trial of Y. Fardel, 1791.

haps the only collective vision of society imaginable for most people.[40] If these were the limits of consciously expressed loyalties, is it possible to see a negative solidarity of country folk against the towns? Probably, but the distinction between town and country is a much more subtle one than might be thought. It is, of course, possible to give an impressive list of reasons for conflict of town and country: economic reasons—the nobles, the *rentiers du sol* and their agents lived in the town as parasites on the rural economy, and in turn supported the town's parasitic inhabitants; political—the forms of repression which collected or backed up royal taxes, seigneurial revenue, ecclesiastical tithes, were based there; cultural —the town was French-speaking, at least in its centre, while the countryside spoke Breton, and the way of life in the town was different.

But at the same time the countryside was permanently present inside the town in a hundred different ways. There was the recently arrived rural immigrant population of the suburbs. There were the endless town–gown conflicts between the students of the college, mostly of rural origins, and the younger clerks and agents of the *fermes*, transposing the antagonism of bourgeois and peasants within the walls. Moreover, town and country were in many ways complementary. Produce and supplies were bought and sold in Vannes. It was a place of recreation and a religious centre for all. If, under the Revolution, conflicts arose between the urban revolutionary bourgeoisie and the countryside, solidarities also existed between the *petites gens*, especially of the peripheral suburb of St-Patern, and their rural cousins. As the revolutionary commissioner of the tribunal of Vannes noted in 1797, fifteen-sixteenths of the town population were opposed to the politics of the Revolution, and they were as one with the country people 'par intérêt et par besoin'.[41] 'Town' and 'country' were symbols then, as now, for differences in economic functions and ways of life between a certain number of people thought of as being typical townsmen and a certain number of people thought of as being countrymen. It did not prevent the town from being open to the influence of the countryside, nor the

[40]J. Mahé, *Essai sur les antiquités du département du Morbihan* (Vannes, 1825), 114–16.
[41] A.N., BB[18] 551: Situation politique de l'arrondissement du tribunal correctionel de Vannes (Kerviche *aîné*), 7 Thermidor Year IV (25-7-1797).

countryside from being penetrated by the economic and cultural activity of the town.

Within these patterns of regional and local loyalties, people were born, and died, but as we have seen, the rural society in which they lived was homogeneous neither in wealth nor in occupation. What were the ways in which people associated within their communities, what were the rivalries and social cleavages which cut across them? For the sake of analysis, sociable activities in the region can be divided into sport, dancing and convivial occasions, though these various activities, naturally enough, tended to overlap. The games played in the Vannetais which I have been able to trace in documents, and of which later observers spoke, are few: there was *soule*, which has been described above, played between men from different parishes or groups of parishes; bowls, played by children or adults; in the one case found, between the inhabitants of the *trève*, including a priest, and the members of the principal part of the parish—an affair which ended in the priest being shot, perhaps because he was on the winning side.[42]

Dancing appears on two occasions: at a rural fair and on a July night in 1789, when young people from a few villages in Arradon met to beat down the threshing ground of a *laboureur*.[43] Both of these were semi-spontaneous events, and no doubt in the eighteenth century dancing played the same part in the great occasions of life—births and marriages, if not deaths—that nineteenth-century folklorists have described, and this despite the disapproval of the Church and the repression of the Parlement.[44] There was also a certain amount of theatre: mystery plays, nearly always on a sacred theme, which the Church approved when they were under its control, and disapproved when they became more spontaneous.[45]

It is difficult to speak of sports, or indeed of any other form of activity, as being the property of any one age group. J.-L. Guilcher, in his exhaustive study of popular dancing concluded that one of the distinctive features of the Breton dance was that it excluded no age groups and that it was not reserved exclusively to the young nor to

[42] A.D. Morbihan, Lz 281: trial of R. Poirer, 1792.

[43] A.D. Morbihan, B: Largouet, minutes: 1773 (F. Cadoret v. F. Seveno); 1789 (J. Lorho *fils et al.*).

[44] Even Canon Mahé's Jansenism won out over his love of local customs ('je regarde cet exercice comme tres-dangereux'), *Essai sur les antiquités*, 374–5.

[45] C. Langlois, *Le Diocèse de Vannes au xixe siécle. 1800–1830* (Paris, 1974), 544–6; A.D. Morbihan, B: Régaires, minutes: 1783.

the unmarried; indeed, it appears to have been considered desirable to encourage everybody, including the old, to join in dances, which had a communal and recreative, rather than an erotic, function. These judgements are of course based on observations from the nineteenth and twentieth centuries, but in all probability can be extended backwards to the eighteenth. *Soule* was of its nature a male sport, and if, according to Rio, admitting a boy into the company of the *souleurs* constituted a sort of *rite de passage* into manhood, it was also one of the last pleasures older men abandoned.[46]

Unlike games and dancing, meetings and convivial occasions appear more frequently in the documents. This conclusion is not one which fits the traditional view historians have taken of the west of France, its inhabitants cut off from human contact six days of the week in their isolated farms, and coming together only on Sunday under the watchful eye of the parish priest. For those who make this assumption, it is only a short step to making the connection between scattered dwellings, clericalism, and political backwardness, in the manner of Michelet, describing the Vendean *bocage*: 'Si la Vendée est une révolution, c'est celle de l'insociabilité, celle de l'esprit d'isolation. Les Vendéens haissent le centre, mais se haissent euxmêmes'; an extreme statement of a common theme extended without much discrimination to the whole of the west of France. It is difficult to accept this view, at least as far as the Vannetais is concerned; here the *bocage* seems just as sociable a place as the rest of France. The Church was not the only focal point of social life. To be sure, after Sunday High Mass, the local court officials read their notices of land for sale and leases available; in the pulpit the priests read the proclamations of the royal government, and sometimes of the seigneurs, or on occasion the *monitoires* of the bishop demanding, at the request of the courts and under pain of grave sin, information relating to the rare serious crimes which occurred. After mass, the parish political assembly took place, if it was necessary to hold one.

But people appear rather less tied to the parish church than one

---

[46] Rio, *La Petite Chouannerie*, 47–8; Guilcher, *La Tradition populaire de danse*, 48–50. Mahé also mentions two games: *aiguillaneuf* (collecting forfeits on New Year's Day) and the *jeu de Quasimodo* (played by passing old pots rapidly from hand to hand in a circle), both the property of the young, *Essai sur les antiquités*, 335–52.

[47] J. Michelet, *La Révolution française*, ed. G. Walter (Tours, 1952), ii, 264; cf. also Bois, *Paysans de l'Ouest*, 306.

might think. They wandered about on Sundays, and occasionally went to mass outside their parishes.[48] More important, there were other centres of association which were to some extent the Church's rivals. One might classify these as 'public' and 'personal' centres. The chief public ones were of two sorts: the tavern (*cabaret*) and the fair; the one a more or less permanent establishment, the other of necessity temporary. Alcoholic sociability was widespread in the Vannetais in the eighteenth century, and probably became more marked as the century went on. Its centre was usually the tavern, operating either legally under licence from the *devoirs* (excise) of Brittany—in which case the publican bought his drink from the tax-farmers' monopoly—or else illegally, when he sold his own wine or cider or bought it in wholesale quantities from local producers or merchants. The clandestine operator, naturally, occurs most frequently in court records. Prosecutions by the excisemen show an interesting pattern of drinking. On the whole, Sarzeau and its region appear as the most notorious areas for imbibing and its corollary, fraud. In 1764, the solicitor acting for the *devoirs* complained that 'on a vu souvent dans l'île de Rhuys la fraude et ses suppots mettre en usage contre le fermier et ses commis des ressorts capable de faire rougir de honte l'humanité'[49]—a happy sort of collusion which led to a united class front in Sarzeau against the excisemen during the early 1730s: the local noble Boisruffiez de Francheville imported wine from Piriac across the Vilaine, and sold it to local tavern-keepers; the surgeon Du Bertaud, the *procureur* of the *sénéchaussée* Rollando, and the court bailiff Cozette were accused of selling Rhuys and Bordeaux wine illegally themselves or of supplying it to tavern-keepers below the monopoly's price. Du Bertaud, in the *bourg* of Sarzeau, had a convenient arrangement: he slipped the wine out of the rear entry to his cellar and into the back entry of an adjoining cabaret. Local officials were so unreliable that cognizance of these cases was temporarily taken out of the hands of the *sénéchaussée* of Rhuys by an edict of 29 November 1732 because the court's impartiality was highly suspect.[50]

If Rhuys appears as the dominant area of wine consumption in the 1730s, by the 1760s cases of fraud on the rural part of the

---

[48] A.D. Morbihan, B: Largouet, minutes: 1761 (trial of P. Le Glehuer).
[49] A.D. Morbihan, B: Rhuys, minutes: 1764 (trial of F. Magré and V. Le Floch).
[50] A.D. Morbihan, B: Rhuys, minutes: 1730–1 (trials of J. Olliver *et al.*, M. Jégat, R. Le Boulicaud, L. Cozette, F. Le Bloc, J. Rollando).

mainland had become far more common, so perhaps there was a gradual extension of social drinking in the eighteenth century. At any rate, the rural tavern, legal or clandestine, was a permanent feature, not only of the *bourg,* but also of the hamlets and cross-roads (where, needless to say, it was easier to escape the eye of the excisemen). Although in the interior parishes of Elven and Plaudren, there were also mentions of fraudulent sale of cider, the tavern-keepers principally sold wine. There is only one mention of eau-de-vie, later to become the scourge of western France. On the peninsula of Rhuys the local wine, the repulsive *vin breton,* was drunk because it was so cheap that people could not afford not to, but almost everywhere else they drank white wine—*vin nantes,* it was called, probably a kind of *gros plant,* from the Loire.[51] The drinkers were mostly men; women seem to have met in each other's houses, not in the taverns. Men drank after the harvests, after their work, on journeys, returning from fairs, and, very frequently, to conclude a business deal: the *vin du marché,* consumed after payment for labour or goods.[52] They drank during the High Mass on Sundays, and indeed went to mass tipsy. Alcoholism has always been a problem in Brittany in modern times; perhaps this is the period from which its beginnings can be dated. In any event, a strong odour of *vin nantes* and cider permeates most of the criminal cases pleaded in the region, and the *cabaret* was a place for men to exchange news and insults, and to fight, a place which appeared faintly sinful, disreputable and noisy.[53]

If the tavern was a permanent centre of sociability, the fair was an intermittent, but much larger collective gathering, combining business such as cattle-trading with pleasures like dancing and drinking,

---

[51] Fraud cases in the 'district' of Vannes:

	Vannes (town)	Rhuys	Other, rural
1730–2	35	10	4
1760–4	50	9	41

A.D. Morbihan, B 1137–41, 1172–9, 1267–73: 1730–2, 1760–4; B: Rhuys, minutes: 1730–2, 1760–4.

[52] A.D. Morbihan, B 1140: 1732 (trial of R. Dromart and F. Langlo); B: Rhuys, minutes: 1730 (M. Delhomme), 1731 (S. Lapartient); B: Largouet, minutes: 1773 (F. Cadoret v. F. Seveno).

[53] A.D. Morbihan, B: Largouet, minutes, 1760 (trial of Y. Rio); B: Rhuys, minutes, 1730 (O. Le Molgat and wife); Lz 278³: 1791 (Y. Nio, *dit* Guerec).

either in taverns or from stands set up in open fields. These were annual events, sometimes linked to the feasts of patron saints (*jours d'assemblée*) or spaced through the year: the fair of Mériadec in Grand-Champ, of Liziec in St-Patern (1–2 October), of Sarzeau, St-Patern (22 May), Bondon (1 August), and St-Symphorien (22 August) in Vannes. No doubt the twice-weekly markets in Vannes played the same role, and of course so did the annual Shrove Tuesday carnival. By combining such feasts scattered through the year with visits to the taverns, either on the same day or in succession, one could have a fairly gregarious existence, and it is possible to follow, in some criminal cases, the trajectory of rural people passing on little drinking tours from one crossroads tavern to another, in a steadily thickening alcoholic haze.[54]

Finally, there was what might be called 'domestic' sociability, dinners or gatherings held by families to honour a special event or simply for friendship: feast day and fair day dinners for family and friends, weddings, the death of a child, or when the peasant slaughtered his pig: 'lorsqu'on tue un cochon c'est l'usage d'inviter les parents, amis et même leurs voisins à la fête du boudin' said a defendant in a case of fraud.[55] Thus in Arradon, a miller brought in wine to 'régaler ses amis et domestiques le jour de St-Pierre assemblée de la paroisse';[56] on Assumption Day, 15 August, a tailor, Pierre Kersuzan, had his neighbour, a *laboureur,* Jan Hémon, to dinner, and in return, Hémon invited Kersuzan to his house to taste his wine.[57] A court case from 1764 described a feast day in the countryside. A *laboureur,* Pierre Le Chatellier, brought a young miller's hand and a relation to dine at the millhand's father's home after mass: 'il était déjà tard lorsque finit la messe, on fut quelque temps sans commencer le dîner, après le dîner on s'arrêta à discourir de chose et d'autres en buvant quelques coups, comme c'est assez l'ordinaire des jours d'assemblée et il était plus de trois heures lorsque [François le Quinio, the millhand] sortit'—after which, he wandered homeward, stopping on the way for an illegal drink of

[54]   A.D. Morbihan, B: 1174: 1761 (trial of Tual Le Bourvellec); B 1177: 1764 (J. Boulicaud *et al.*); B: Rhuys, minutes, 1732 (V. Pecar, G. Tascon père, G. Tascon fils); B: Largouet, minutes, 1760–3 (P. Le Glehuer, J. Le Rohellec *dit* Cougan, J.-P. Cadio; Lz 273⁴: 1791 (Jean Roussin).

[55]   A.D. Morbihan, B: 1178: 1763 (trial of Y. Trionaire and A. Le Meur); B: Regaires, minutes, 1762 (Ollivier and Julien Le Bras).

[56]   A.D. Morbihan, B 1138: 1731 (B. Arz).

[57]   A.D. Morbihan, B: 1177: 1762 (P. Kersuzan and J. Hemon).

wine at a temporary cabaret, an uprighted barrel in a field.[58] There were of course the marriage feasts, attended by large numbers of guests, if the bride and groom were prosperous enough, and by the poor, with special tables set up for them at the end of the field.[59] Finally, there were the everyday occasions of sociability: the *veillée*, a way of keeping warm and passing long winter evenings.[60]

From all these cases, there emerges a kind of geography of sociability and enmity: the scenes and occasions at which long-simmering resentment came out and inhibitions were cast off: the rural fair, or the great fairs in Vannes, rich in drunken brawls and illegitimate children; the cabaret in the *bourg* or at the lonely crossroads in the *bocage*; the *veillée* into which the intruder stumbles, mumbling imprecations and vague accusations of wrongs done in the past, the church in the *bourg*, where local news was exchanged after mass, the road back from the markets and fairs where country people stayed to drink and returned in over-excited little groups of a half-score to their parishes. When the Corfmats of Grand-Champ were accused of proffering threats against their neighbours, it was said that they did it at the fairs, the *fileries* (*veillées*) and the tavern—a catalogue of rural sociability to which should be added, but only as one occasion among many, Sunday mass.[61]

These, then, are what we can discern of patterns of solidarity and sociability, of the ways of the 'insider'. A group, however, can also be defined, and very often defines itself, in contrast to outsiders. Who were the excluded in this society?

To some extent, women and of course children fell into this category, but only in a limited way. Breton customary law gave women a better share in inheritances than elsewhere in France, but it is true that they remained social 'minors', as all students of the old regime agree. If women took their own quarrels seriously, men paid less attention to them. In 1762, two women in Plaudren engaged in a fierce tussle, rolling about and clawing at each other in the dust over an obscure wrong: their husbands stood by amused, and one shouted

[58] A.D. Morbihan, B: 1177: 1764 (F. Le Quinio, J. Boulicaud *et al.*).
[59] Grand Moulin, 'Mœurs et usages des Bretons du departement du Morbihan', *Mémoires de la Société royale des sciences, arts, belles-lettres et agriculture de la ville de Saint-Quentin,* iii (1841), 113–23; Le Goff and Sutherland, 'The Revolution and the Rural Community', 105.
[60] A.D. Morbihan, B: Largouet, minutes, 1764 (trail of G. Le Faucheux, M. Tregaro and family); Mahé, *Essai sur les antiquités,* 481–3.
[61] A.D. I.-V., 1B^n 3615: 1785.

'Courage, courage, étrillez-vous bien',[62] but if a man insulted a woman, as one plaintiff in a suit pointed out, it was a much more serious business: 'un homme qui adresse à une femme pareilles injures ['coquine', 'friponne'] persuade beaucoup et expose cette femme non seulement à la risée mais même aux insultes.'[63] In general, women stayed clear of *cabarets,* although they kept them.[64]

But women and children were too much a part of this society to be considered, as a group, 'outsiders'; the real outsiders were the newly arrived, the semi-transient domestic or tailor or peddler, the people who lived encamped, like the notorious Jean Le Goff[65] or the wretched salt thieves of Sarzeau, geographically as well as sociologically on the edges of the parish. Certain classes of domestic servant as well, seemed to be temporarily, if not permanently beyond the rules of conventional morality.[66] One can point to individual examples, but just where the boundaries were placed was difficult to say.

Nowhere is the blurred distinction between insider and outsider more evident than in the treatment of the domiciled and the itinerant poor. The poor were objects of fear and dislike in the Vannetais: they were always thought to take their revenge for their condition by setting fire to the houses of the inconsiderate and the parsimonious.[67] They were among the first to be accused of crimes; thus in the Fleury affair, the wife of a *laboureur* told a beggar 'que les pauvres mettaient le feu à Theix'; 'qu'on ne devait point donner la charité à des gens comme lui'.[68] Sometimes, when the poor were not local folk, or not feared, or sufficiently disliked, they were denounced and handed over to the *maréchaussée*; yet at least the resident ones were recognized to be the responsibility of the parish and the peasants were apt to resist ill-considered efforts of townsmen to take them away. They had a place at the wedding-feast, but their place was at special tables set up at the end of the field, and they

[62] A.D. Morbihan, B: Largouet, minutes: 1764 (trial of M. Conan).

[63] A.D. I.-V., 1B^n 2085, 1B^g 304: 1755 (trial of M. Moussart).

[64] But see A.D. I.-V., 1B^n 3433: 1784 (trial of Marie Olligo *et al.*), where Marie Olligo protested that she bought only half-pints and never bottles from the tavern. Admittedly, Marie was already a marginal personality in Theix by then.

[65] See above, p. 182.

[66] A.D. I.-V., 1B^n 2424, 1B^g 321: 1771 (trial of F. Le Pronec, M. Lapartien *et al.*).

[67] A.D. I.-V., 1B^n 2069, 1B^g 303: 1744; A.D. Morbihan, L 1463: Commune of Trefféan to District of Vannes, 29-10-1790; Lz 273²: 1791 (trial of P. Morvan, J. Texier *et al.*).

[68] A.D. I.-V., 1B^n 2916, 1B^g 329: 1779 (trial of L. Fleury *et al.*).

were not allowed to take food out of turn, or become disorderly. Their presence at the wedding feast was both an act of Christian charity, and also a way of buying their goodwill, of making sure that the more desperate did not burn your hay-rick.[69] The poor were the community's property, they, too, belonged, as long as they stayed in their place.

[69] Sée *Les Classes rurales*, 486–7; Grand Moulin, 'Mœurs et usages des Bretons', 120–1; Guilcher, *La Tradition de danse populaire*, 31–5; Le Goff and Sutherland, 'The Revolution and the Rural Community', 104–5.

CHAPTER VIII

RURAL SOCIETY FROM WITHIN:
(2) WEALTH AND SOLIDARITY

The wedding feast, with the ambiguous position that the poor occupied within it, poses the delicate and almost insoluble problem of the way in which rural people in the Vannetais were conscious in their daily lives of differences in wealth and the importance of these differences in shaping their lives. Traditional popular wisdom, in the form of songs and proverbs collected in the nineteenth century, suggests a rather realistic view of affairs. If one proverb proclaimed righteously that 'no trade is ignoble, for all trades come from God',[1] this was countered by the traditional contempt in which certain vocations were held, often for the poverty or the ill-gained wealth which was thought to accompany them. Cordwainers, once a trade reserved for lepers, still carried their unpleasant medieval epithet of 'caquins'; millers kept the reputation which Chaucer recorded; tailors were considered, by men at least, as drifters, smooth-tongued weaklings who might all too easily win the favour of a woman while her husband was working in the fields.[2]

More generally, popular wisdom held that society was stable, that advancement by talent or marriage was difficult, if not impossible, and probably unnatural. 'Each to his own, peasants among peasants', 'money makes money', 'if you will but marry someone of your own condition, you may marry at will'. This was not perhaps a pleasant state of affairs, no doubt, for 'poverty is no sin, but gives no joy' and the daughter of a rich *laboureur* who chose to marry a *sabotier* lamented her foolishness in a song: 'I could have married a rich man, an only son . . . In my father's house . . . I was happy . . . All that I had to do was make gruel and soup, and care for the milk and

---

[1] Le Goff, *Proverbes bretons*, 122.

[2] A.D. Morbihan, B: Régaires, minutes: trial of the wife of Botherel, slate roofer, 1762; Le Goff, *Proverbes bretons*, 125, 127; Y. Brekilien, *La Vie quotidienne des paysans en Bretagne au xixe siècle* (Paris, 1966), 136–40, 335–42.

the butter . . . But now I work all day and far into the night . . .
Hollowing out *sabots* and blacking them . . . For the girls who walk
on the cobblestones of Vannes'.[3]

The *sabotier's* wife represents a case of downward mobility,
beyond a doubt; but perhaps for the *sabotier* she was a means of
getting a part of her father's property. How rare were marriages
between people of different rank? It is not easy to tell. The vague-
ness or total absence of descriptions of social standing in rural
marriage acts makes it almost impossible to determine who is
marrying whom. A simple count of marriages and professions recorded in marriage acts, no matter on how large a scale, would lead
to no other conclusion than that most people in the countryside
married other rural folk.

In principle, the study of marriage contracts ought to compensate
for the silence of the parish registers. Each contract, passed before a
notary, gave an estimate of the value of the dowries and sometimes
of the landed wealth of the partners. But in Brittany, far more
marriages took place than were sealed by a notarized marriage
contract. In the parish of Pluvigner, close to the region around
Vannes, only 41 marriage contracts were registered in the bureau of
the *contrôle des actes* over the twenty-seven years from 1764 to
1781, or a little more than two contracts a year in a parish of some
3,000 inhabitants. Even in the city of Nantes, the most advanced
area of Brittany, only one-half to one-third of all marriages were
concluded with a contract. The normal practice was to take advantage of article 424 of the customary law of Brittany, which provided
that if there was no contract, all the goods of the husband and wife
were to be put in common. As a result, the poor are bound to be
heavily underrepresented in studies based on this extremely scarce
source. Even when large numbers of contracts can be found, they
are not very revealing; the table of marriage contracts from which
the figures for Pluvigner were drawn shows only that rural girls
tended to marry rural men with identical dowries, almost all of
whom were called 'laboureurs'. To some extent this could be said to
indicate rigid social stratification, but it may also mean simply that
custom dictated dowries should be equal.[4]

[3] Le Goff, *Proverbes bretons,* 51, 53, 55, 66, 122; Y. Kerh'en, 'Moez er botou
koed', *Revue de Bretagne, de Vendée et d'Anjou,* xxii (1899), 223–7.
[4] A.D. Morbihan, 17 C3808–24: Contrôle des actes, bureau de Pluvigner; 17 C
3866: Tableau des actes de mariage, 1764–1822. The correlation coefficient for the
cases in which the dowries of both partners are known is $r = 0.99$. On this source, see

One way around this problem though an extremely laborious one, is to compare the *capitation* paid by parents of marriage partners. A comparison of the payments made by parents of newly-weds in the parish of Grand-Champ for the years 1779–81 yielded 43 marriages (of a total of 118) for which information could be found. The results can make little claim to satisfy the rigorous demands of social scientists, but they do nevertheless refer to real events: 43 marriages which did take place. At first glance, the results seem to show some degree of upward and downward mobility: a little less than a quarter of the marriages occurred between children of parents who paid more than the mean tax assessment in 1776, and those who paid less. Most of this upward mobility was male: 7 of 26 'richer' women married 'poor', but only 3 of 22 'richer' men married 'poor', a pathetic but normal enough pattern for the old regime, corresponding to the situation described by the *sabotier's* wife. But a closer look at the figures suggests that even this apparent mobility was really an illusion, for there is a quite high correlation between the levels of wealth of the families allied by marriage.[5] The mobility which did exist took place only because there were so few rich people: there were simply not enough well-endowed partners to go around. The 'rich', that is, those paying more than the mean in *capitation,* formed only about 25 per cent of the population of Grand-Champ, while the number of marriages in which both partners were children of 'rich' parents accounted for almost half ($^{19}/_{43}$) of the marriages. This marriage pattern seems to suggest a trend towards increasing inequality and a rigid social statification along lines of wealth. This is especially likely when we make allowance for the fragility of the sources, the chance that some of the upwardly mobile 'poor' in this example may have had expectations of inheritances, and the 'rich' the knowledge that their patrimony would be subdivided. Perhaps, as is often the case, the examples of a few brilliant marriages by a few poor people helped maintain the illusion of mobility for the many.

P. de Saint-Jacob, 'Une Source de l'histoire sociale au xviiie siècle: là table des contrats de mariage dans le fonds du contrôle des actes', *Actes du quatre-vingt-quatrième congrès national des sociétés savantes, Dijon, 1959 Section d'histoire moderne et contemporaine* (Paris, 1960), 415–18; cf. also Meyer, *La Noblesse bretonne* (Paris, 1967), ii, 635.
    [5] The correlation coefficient is r = 0.56, with a Z-score, of 3.63, indicating that correlations of this order would occur less than once in 100 times by chance alone.

The existence of a large number of maintained domestic servants in the countryside probably helped contribute to the blurring of lines between rich and poor. In an excess of enthusiasm Armand Du Chatellier, writing in the 1860s, praised this aspect of rural society as a means of social mobility: each peasant proprietor begins, he says, as a *valet de ferme,* either on his parents' holdings or elsewhere. Some young men take over their parents' land, some earn enough to rent, and then buy, a tenure and marry.[6] As in most myths of social mobility, there was a grain of truth in Du Chatellier's story, but no more than that, at least as far as the eighteenth century was concerned (indeed, even his own description of the permanence of tenure under *domaine congéable* seems to suggest the contrary). In the parish of Grand-Champ, there were some 80 servants, male and female, in 1747; if the people in the age group from 15 to 25, the right age for servants, formed about 15 per cent of the population, or about 600 young men and women, then in any given year only around one in seven young people was actually employed away from home in the parish, although over a series of years a larger proportion of young may well have undergone the same experience. But the fact that large numbers of young men and women lived as servants in their youth, whether at home or on other people's holdings, probably did blunt the antagonism which comes from an acute sense of material deprivation, even if deprivation there most certainly was.

The system of land tenure and inheritance also helped make rural society appear more uniform than it really was. As we have just seen in Chapters V and VI above, the same legal conditions of landholding, and especially the *domaine congéable,* embraced categories of both rich and poor peasants. Even if most *tenuyers* were in the better-off class of peasant, as much as a third of this group lived a marginal existence similar to that of the *métayers, fermiers* and artisans, and yet had the same economic interests as the richer peasants. The same is true, though to a lesser extent, of the *métayers* and *fermiers,* for a small fringe of this group lived on a level comparable to that of the more prosperous *tenuyers.*

One of the signs of this deprivation was the way in which the combined effects of death, striking down the poor man before his richer neighbour, and the tendency of poorer people to be moving on, combined to make the less wealthy countryman less likely to

---

[6] Du Chatellier, *L'Agriculture et les classes agricoles,* 199–204.

leave a trace in the collective memory of his parish. In the parish of Sulniac, after two years, 83 per cent of men were still present, a rate of persistence considerably higher than was observed in the town of Vannes, but just as in Vannes, the poor did vanish from the scene faster than the wealthy: 88 per cent of men paying more than twice the mean *capitation* payment were still present after two years, while of those paying less than one-quarter, only 79 per cent were still there. However, the difference, while real, was less marked and probably less visible at the time than it was in the town, especially as most of these disappearances must have been by death rather than migration.[7]

Different economic conditions among the bulk of peasants holding land under *domaine congéable* were not merely the result of the extent and quality of land under cultivation and pasture, but also of the legal provisions and customary usages regulating the inheritance, sale and transfer of land. One of the most interesting of these is the use by peasants of mortgages to finance the operation of expelling each other from lands under *domaine congéable*. The cost of the edifices of a normal tenure ran as high as 2,000 to 3,000 livres; a peasant might borrow the whole or part of this amount from a prosperous neighbour, a widow, a notary, or a group of his relatives and friends as guaranteed loan (*constitut*) at 5 per cent, offering security on the value of the edifices. Take for example Joseph Renaud, who in 1786 expelled Joseph Le Martelot and his wife from their tenure in their parish of Plaudren. The total value of the edifices came to 2,250 livres; Renaud borrowed 2,160 livres from three peasants to carry out the operation. For the lenders, it was a safe enough investment. According to Breton jurisprudence, they had the first claim on the reimbursed value of the edifices in the unlikely event of the new tenant being expelled, and a sort of mortgage as security in the meantime. The yearly payments on this mortgage, however, reduced Renaud's income for the time being to little more than what a peasant subletting the same tenure would have obtained. He paid an annual rent to the *seigneur foncier* of 4 l. 4s., two pairs of capons, and 5 *perrées* (8.5 hl) of rye, worth in all about 80 l. at the time of his lease, but the payment of 5 per cent annual interest (or 108 l.), to say nothing of the costs of amortizing

---

[7] A.D. Morbihan, C: Commission intermédiaire de Vannes: Sulniac, capitation, 1786–8. Of a total of 248 men in 1786, there remained only 217 in 1788.

his principal, more than doubled his effective rent.[8] Mortgages thus acted as a levelling agent, reducing some apparently well-off *tenuyers* to the economic level of the *fermier*.

This does not mean that indebtedness completely flattened the economic differences between rural people, or that they never managed to rid themselves of these debts. Not all had them, in any case; some families managed to pass on their lands intact and unencumbered for many generations without recourse to loans. Of the 936 expulsions carried out between 1749 and 1789 in the court of Largouet-sous-Vannes, the biggest seigneurial jurisdiction in the area, 380, or 41 per cent, were financed in whole or part by mortgages, for about 26 per cent of the total property value exchanged. This was a large proportion of tenants, but clearly not all new tenants started their careers under this handicap. Of those who did begin by taking over another holding by an expulsion financed with a mortgage, a large proportion appear to have paid the principal at some stage. In only 8 of the 936 expulsions in Largouet is there record of previous mortgage-holders putting in a claim for their principal. Nevertheless, it is not difficult to understand why it was possible for a *tenuyer* to free himself from debt. On Joseph Renaud's tenure it was possible to earn a gross income three times the value of the rent, or to sublet for that amount.[9] If Renaud or his successors applied their profits to amortizing their principal and interest, they could obtain a clear title to their land within twenty-five years. This is only a hypothetical example, but it does show how such peasants, slowly working their way toward full proprietorship, contributed to masking the distinction between those who possessed the tenures under *domaine congéable*, and those who did not.

Breton succession law had the same effect as these practices, and was probably just as effective in helping redistribute some wealth in each generation, since it provided for the widest possible sharing of the possessions and land of a deceased non-noble person. In direct successions, the widow acquired at least a third of her husband's land and assets, or all of the land, if she preferred to waive her rights to the other assets. In addition she had a claim to one-half of the marriage 'community', that is, of the land and assets which the

---

[8] See Appendix I and Baudouin de Maisonblanche, *Institutions convenantières*, ii, 156–8.

[9] A.D. Morbihan, B: Largouet, minutes: 1741–90. Usually leases stipulated that the *tenuyer* had to have the landlord's permission to sublet, but it is doubtful whether this provision was regularly enforced.

couple had put in common at the beginning of their marriage. The remainder of the property was divided equally between all the children, the men having first choice in order of age, followed by the women.[10]

However, the edifices of land held under *domaine congéable*, which constituted the bulk of peasant property in Lower Brittany, were not in principle subject to physical division: this provision was intended to keep ultimate control over the *fonds* in the hands of the *seigneur foncier* and ensure the regular payment of rents by making one man responsible for them. On the death of a *tenuyer*, it was up to the children and surviving marriage-partner to arrange between themselves the management of the land as a block of property while giving each heir a share in its value. Traditionally the eldest son took control. If he had enough money and his co-heirs were willing, he could buy their shares and round out his inheritance. In 1784 on the death of the *tenuyer* Jean Allano in Grand-Champ, his property had to be shared between his widow, Anne Celibert, his eldest surviving child, Louise Allano, and her husband Jean Cassac, and the widow and children of a younger son of the deceased, François, who had gone to the grave before his father. After dividing up a set of mortgages the heirs dealt with the Allano tenure. A quarter had no doubt been inherited by Allano: in any event it formed part of his personal property (*propres*), distinct from the marriage community, and went to his widow, Anne. The remaining three-quarters had been bought with funds belonging to the marriage community in 1753 and had to be divided equally between the widow and her children. In this case, Louise's husband, Cassac (there were no sons left) bought out his mother-in-law's share of the remaining three-quarters, ostensibly in the name of all the heirs, but in fact with his own money. This left the widow with one-quarter of the holding and Cassac with one-half of the three-quarters of the remainder which he had purchased, plus the part of the tenure which fell due to his wife, that is, one-half of the half of the three-quarters. There remained the widow's quarter, which would fall into the hands of the heirs when she died, and the three-

---

[10] Sauvageau, *Coutumes de Bretagne*, i, articles 424, 455–6, 586. According to Sauvageau's commentary on art. 424, if it was not stipulated that a part of the land and assets of either partner was to be kept outside the marriage community, it was assumed to be in common. This provision applied to land under *domaine congéable* under the *usement* of Brouerec as well; see E. Chenon, 'L'Ancien Droit dans le Morbihan', *Revue morbihannaise*, iii (1893), 70.

sixteenths remaining to the children of his brother-in-law François, who could not be bought out until they came of age.[11] In the meantime, no doubt, the heirs worked out some means of sharing the revenues from the land, or else sublet it.

If no one heir had sufficient funds, if one or more of the heirs were unwilling to sell their shares, or if some of the heirs were minors, it was possible for all of them to sublet the tenure to one of themselves, or to an outsider. In 1783, the eight heirs and widow from the three marriages of a particularly prolific *tenuyer*, Jean Jouanguy of Guernevé in Monterblanc, divided their tenure into nine shares: a quarter for the surviving widow, and eight shares of one thirty-second apiece for each of the children of all the marriages, plus a quarter to each of the children of the second marriage, during which the tenure had been acquired. But since several of the heirs were still minors, the beneficiaries decided to let out the tenure, and divide up the revenues proportionally in the meantime. Similar arrangements were also made between aged parents and sons or sons-in-law.[12]

It does not take a great deal of imagination to realize that arrangements of this kind, multiplied each time a peasant with land died, acquired land, or married, contributed in no small measure to blurring the otherwise sharp lines of the economic hierarchy in the countryside. In fact, to a much greater extent than even the *vingtième* roles would suggest, the peasant must have been bound to his neighbours, poor and well-off, tenants and properietors, in complex relationships of debtor, creditor, farmer, proprietor, 'shareholder' and subtenant.

To say this much is not to deny the existence of very real antagonisms, even among members of the same family; a relative could

---

[11] A.D. Morbihan, E^n 3467: minutes le Ridant: partage et accord, 1-5-1784. Article 483 of the customary law forbade the alienation of a minor's rights until his majority. On the practice followed for dividing inheritances, see 'Extrait des mémoires du sieur Gatechair', in Sauvageau, *Coutumes de Bretagne*, i, 28: 'Les droits réparatoires [edifices] au respect du domanier détenteur, sont reputés immeubles et susceptibles d'hypothèques, de retrait lignager, mais non de division ou partage'. Cf. Chenon, 'L'Ancien Droit dans le Morbihan', 70; d'Espinay, 'L'Ancien Droit successoral en Basse-Bretagne', *Nouvelle revue historique de droit francais et étranger*, xvii (1895), 153 and Baudouin de Maisonblanche, *Institutions convenantières*, ii, 174 n. (b). An informal system of primogeniture with compensation for the other heirs was implied in Article 577 of the *Coutume*; cf. A.D. Morbihan B: Largouet, minutes: tutelle de la famille Le Roel, 17-5-1775.

[12] A.D. Morbihan, E^n 66 (Gougeon): traité, 13-3-1783; Thomas-Lacroix, 'La Condition des terres', 354.

be just as harsh a creditor or landlord as a stranger. In 1780, a minor, Jan Le Ray of St-Patern, brought a lawsuit against his uncle and former guardian, Jan Dano, who had farmed out Le Ray's land to himself for a pittance. The guardian tried to defend his action in court by drawing a distinction between a *'ferme des étrangers'* and a *'ferme accordée aux parents'*, but, retorted his ward's lawyer: 'on dit qu'elle [the lease] a été donnée par plusieurs parents, mais quand [even if] elle eût été consentie en justice au plus haut donnant, le tuteur ne pourrait pas l'avoir.'[13] Arrangements of this sort between heirs could lead to court cases, even to blows. In 1786, a certain Guillaume Jouhannic bought out the shares of his brother-in-law Louis Le Garnec and of Le Garnec's sister Marie and her husband in a tenure when the couple fell into debt, and then forced the other heirs to divide up the personal possessions of their late mother, Marie Nicolas. Louis, who was the eldest surviving son and who had lived on the tenure while his mother was alive, felt cheated by his brother-in-law, tried to ruin the crops Jouhannic had sown, and began a campaign of terror against the intruder and his wife, firing warning shots about his ears and menacing him with his knife.[14]

Another source of such quarrels arose out of the expulsion of *tenuyers*. In the eighteenth century, competition for good cultivable land by peasants in the Vannetais grew, and an expelled tenant, even though reimbursed by his successor, could hardly have viewed the process with equanimity. In fact several cases reached the courts in which incoming tenants complained that they had been cheated by resentful occupants whom they had evicted: the previous tenants, knowing that they were going to be expelled, would overwork the land, or carry away fertilizer.[15] Sometimes the antagonisms between the partners went beyond litigation. In 1786, Louis Le Clainche, a *laboureur* in Elven, obtained a new lease from a local landlord, M. de Penhouet, on a tenure at Logodec in Elven, and prepared to expel the current occupant, Joseph Le Derf *fils*. The lease, Le Clainche's lawyer complained to the court in the criminal case which ensued, was the cause of implacable hatred between the new and old tenants. In March 1786, Le Derf and his brother threatened Le Clainche's life if he were expelled. At the end of April, he attacked Le Clainche, throttling him and threatening that

[13] A.D. Morbihan, B: Régaires, minutes: Jan Le Ray v. Jan Dano, 1780.
[14] A.D. Morbihan, B: Largouet, minutes: 1786.
[15] See above p. 169.

's'il ne rendait pas la prise [lease] au seigneur, il l'eût étranglé'. After further menaces, in March 1787, Le Derf and a drunken beggar, Pierre Courtois, called on the intruder, informing him 'qu'il ne serait jamais entré dans la tenue . . . et qu'ils l'auraient tué avant un an, et qu'on prendrait le soleil avec la main avant qu'il n'entretait dans la tenue'; they then beat him with their cudgels and attempted to strangle him.[16]

Such cases between relative strangers were bad enough, but a large number of *congéments* took place between heirs to tenures, all members of the same family. No doubt many of these were amicable arrangements. Baudouin de Maisonblanche asserts that occasionally expulsions were carried out by prearrangement to remove mortgages.[17] Customary law, in addition, forbade the division of the minor's heritage, but left a loophole whereby part of the family might carry out a *congément* against the minor, reimbursing him with cash which could be invested in *constituts* until his maturity. Yet so many expulsions of minors took place that some serious conflicts were unavoidable. Thus in 1775 Julien Caudal, the guardian and uncle of Marguerite Caudal, renewed in his own name the lease on a tenure of which his wife had inherited three-quarters and Marguerite one-quarter, and subsequently served notice of expulsion on his niece and ward. When the case was brought before the court, Marguerite's lawyer, citing Domat's *Lois Civils,* tried to prove that a guardian cannot buy property from his ward; if all guardians could do this, he protested, minors would be dispossessed of their property wholesale. Caudal's lawyer replied by emphasizing the non-real quality of the edifices under *domaine congéable* and the indisputable right of the seigneur to grant a lease to whomever he wished. He pointed out that according to Gatechair's commentary on the *usement* of Brouerec, a sixteenth-century gloss which had acquired something like the force of law, the edifices were not subject to division; the guardian had the right to initiate the division of goods in which ¹; ; ward had a part, but because of the special provisions of the *usement,* this sharing-out could not take place by physical division, only by expulsion.[18]

---

[16] A.D. Morbihan, B: Largouet, minutes 1787: Louis Le Clainche v. Joseph Le Derf and Pierre Courtois; see also Le Goff and Sutherland, 'The Revolution and the Rural Community', 105–6.

[17] Baudouin de Maisonblanche, *Institutions convenantières,* ii, 154–5, 158.

[18] A.D. Morbihan, B: Largouet, minutes: 1775.

Thus, if it was a potential source of conflict, the system of land-holding also helped to maintain a fairly cohesive sort of community, or at least diffuse grievances and hatreds which in other forms of rural society tended to concentrate against the rich, or the seigneurs, or the Church. But other economic factors as well contributed to this end. One was the nature of rural settlement. The *bourg*, the centre of the parish, was, in Lower Brittany, only a small settlement in relation to the whole territory of the parish, a large hamlet among many. With small groups of people of different economic conditions and occupations living side by side in isolated settlements, and not divided between artisans and the *bourg* and peasants in the country-side, it was possible for solidarities between economic groups within the rural community to be subordinated to feuds and quarrels in which everyone in each hamlet took a part.[19]

One of the forms in which one might expect tensions between rich and poor to be translated into everyday life is through criminal activity. Admittedly, criminal phenomena are sometimes dubious guides to the nature of the society which engenders them. Criminals are almost by definition abnormal and deductions from their behaviour about the attitudes of ordinary people, it might be argued, are bound to be false. Thus the social significance of crimes such as organized theft, certain kinds of murder, and the crimes of psychopaths is difficult to determine. But this is not true of crimes which can be seen to be the outgrowth or prolongation of quarrels and strife within a community. In particular, this has been found to be true of crimes against persons in the old regime: the appearance of these cases in court is usually the ultimate stage in a quarrel which has already been going on for some time.

The overwhelming weight of these crimes against persons—assault, slander, insults and the occasional murder or accidental homicide—is the outstanding characteristic which emerges from intensive study of crimes reported in all courts in the region around Vannes in 1730–2, 1760–4, 1789–92, and all the cases appealed to the Parlement of Brittany from the area between 1700 and 1789.[20]

[19] For example, while the *bourg* of Grand-Champ in 1778 had a larger proportion of artisans (16 out of 41) than the proportion of its population to the rest of the parish (10 per cent), nevertheless, the total number of artisans scattered about the parish was high enough to avoid a marked *bourg*–country distinction.

[20] Two approaches were taken to the study of crime: one was to examine all the cases brought in appeal before the Chamber of the Tournelle in the Parlement of [*p. 240 for n. 20 cont.*]

Such matters represented the bulk of rural crime in the region throughout the eighteenth century. These quarrels might appear to us as petty and very often irrational. When they do not begin in open violence without apparent explanation, they usually consist of a kind of escalation of verbal violence. One could also point to the role of drink in arousing the passions and the audacity of the combatants, and indeed some of the incidents which came before the courts seem to have been no more than drunken brawls over a chance word or a joke which turned sour: thus around 1759, Charles Le Falher began a quarrel which reportedly cost him his life when, after a round of drinks in a country tavern, he was unable to pay for his pint of wine and his companions passed around his hat to take up donations.[21] It would be easy to dismiss these disputes and their consequences as a sign of the persistence of a 'primitive' mentality or as a characteristic of 'backwardness' or an archaic social structure.

In most cases, however, it is possible to discern material issues of one kind or another, often only by chance asides in the testimony. Eighteenth-century examining magistrates were seldom interested in motives if they did not cast light on the fact of a crime, so these have to be looked for carefully, but behind most of these quarrels was a tangible wrong, done or imagined. Few or no cases exist of attacks on noble landlords, but there are plenty of cases of people threatened, injured, even killed, by other rural folk for damaging fields, and ponds and water-courses by letting the cattle graze and drink in them, or by putting linen to ret in them.[22] Quarrels between landlords and tenants were comparatively rare, but rural people made up for this by fighting each other for having taken over leases on land held under *domaine congéable:* the system of landholding thus helped divert antagonism inward within rural society. Reading large numbers of these assault and slander cases leaves one with the strong impression that this was a rough sort of society in which people fought each other fiercely over small, sometimes tiny sources of wealth, and that only a small proportion of these struggles ever reached the courts.

Rennes throughout the eighteenth century; the other was to take all the crimes reported in *all* the courts in the region, both seigneurial and royal, for certain limited periods (1730–2, 1760–4, 1789–92).

[21] A.D. Morbihan, B: Largouet, minutes: trial of Pierre Le Glehuer, 1761.

[22] Examples in Le Goff and Sutherland, 'The Revolution and the Rural Community', *passim.*

Would it be too far-fetched to suggest that there was a certain difference between the inhabitants of the mainland, on the one hand, and those of the peninsula of Rhuys, on the other, and that this difference had something to do with the economic divergencies of the two regions? Contemporaries and near-contemporaries were aware of a difference, but they put it down to 'character'. The inhabitants of the mainland, thought the intendant Des Gallois de la Tour, writing in 1731, were 'durs pour eux-mêmes, comme pour les autres, fort laborieux', but those of Rhuys were 'd'un génie grossier, brutaux, et peu laborieux'.[23] A half-century later, in the 1780s, Ogée in his *Dictionnaire* observed, rather less harshly, that 'le peuple de Sarzeau est bon et doux, contre l'ordinaire des peuples situés sur la mer; mais s'il n'a pas le défaut de ces derniers, il n'en a point aussi les qualités estimables et utiles: il manque d'industrie dans la situation la plus avantageuse pour le commerce, soit intérieur, soit extérieur, il vit dans l'indigence et le repos.'[24]

The peninsula of Rhuys contained, as we have seen, a population which was on the whole much poorer than that of the mainland, and which lacked that sizable minority of substantial peasants which gave stability. Certain areas, such as that near and in the village of La Tour du Parc, inhabited in the main by salt-marsh tenders and salt-merchants, were especially reputed for their lawlessness and disorder, continually suspected as the haunt of thieves, constantly at war—literally—with the inhabitants of the neighbouring village of Penerf, who refused to allow them the right to collect the seaweed so necessary for the cultivation of their land. Rhuys was also an area in which winegrowing constituted a marginal activity for the peasants, and the agents of the *devoirs*, all strangers to the region, whose duty it was to assess tax on wine sold retail for consumption, were disliked by the small winegrower who wanted to sell a few bottles to his neighbours. The archives of the *sénéchaussée* of Rhuys are full to overflowing with cases of seizure of contraband wine, perquisitions in the houses of peasants suspected of operating clandestine wine shops, and, the inevitable consequence, attacks on excisemen. This was a difficulty throughout the region but nowhere was it more widespread than the peninsula. The usual method of avoiding prosecution, if the excisemen got wind of the illegal operations, was decribed in an official complaint of 1730: 'lorsqu'ils

---

[23] B.N., fonds français 8753, fols. 87^v–88, 95^v.
[24] Ogée, *Dictionnaire*, ii, 882–8.

veulent faire leurs emplois tout le peuple se soulève contre eux, fait des rébellions les assommant à coups de bâton, de pierres et avec des armes à feu, les empêche de faire leur visite et exercice et les force même de s'enfuir pour mettre leur vie à couvert'.[25]

Then, too, the coastline of Rhuys offered several ideal locations for fraudulent landing of tobacco; in 1775, for example, some 300 peasants and professional smugglers known as the Bande Angevine, their faces blacked, took over the *bourg* of St-Gildas-de-Rhuys, and terrorized the employees of the *ferme* in order to cover a landing of tobacco from Jersey. In 1761, the inhabitants of Ambon arose up *en masse* to defend a soldier arrested for tobacco smuggling.[26] Tobacco smuggling and avoiding the tax on wine were a part of local culture in which all levels of society shared, and directed their hostility against the 'outside'; in this case, the excisemen.

Subsidiary occupations like smuggling were merely one of the ways, some legitimate and some not, by which peasants with insufficient land got by. Because both peasants and those who followed other occupations in Sarzeau were nearly all poor, they formed a relatively unstructured rural society in constrast to the people of the mainland. In 1837, an observer remarked that on the peninsula 'chaque famille n'embrasse point, comme à Locmariaquer, une profession fixe, soit celle de marin, soit celle de laboureur; le plus grand nombre, au contraire, compte un ou plusieurs de ses membres dans la marine.'[27] To judge from the background of all the seamen of Rhuys registered in the *Bureau des Classes* of the Royal Navy in 1786, this statement was just as true of the old regime as it was of the July Monarchy; almost half of the seamen were the sons of *laboureurs*, and a third were sons of artisans or shopkeepers.[28]

When we take into account the distribution of poorer taxpayers in the region, and the fact that Sarzeau had by far the highest proportion of these, it becomes more and more apparent that the peninsula was an extreme case, an area in which the wealthier peasants and sailors were by far outnumbered by the horde of poor, trying to sell their labour or to wring a living from tiny holdings. True to a lesser extent of some of the nearby mainland parishes like

---

[25] A.D. Morbihan, B: Rhuys, minutes: requête du Me Jan Pleine, fermier des grands et petits devoirs, 22-11-1730.

[26] Le Goff and Sutherland, 'The Revolution and the Rural Community', 100.

[27] Cayot-Délandre, *Annuaire du Morbihan* (1837), 102–3.

[28] A.N. Marine, C⁴ 208.

Surzur and Theix, this observation does not hold at all for parishes like Grand-Champ, which also appear more peaceful, less racked by petty thievery and popular disturbances.

But one must not exaggerate such contrasts; if Sarzeau was an extreme case, it remained true that throughout the region, marked contrasts of rich and poor, secure and insecure, existed, but it was difficult to speak of 'classes' and conflicts along consistently-drawn economic lines. Too many factors prevented such cleavages from presenting themselves clearly or continually to people's minds: the importance of the family, the patterns of sociability, the dispersed pattern of settlement, the absence of a concentration of poor and artisans in the *bourgs,* the operation of Breton customary law, and the peculiar provisions of the *domaine congéable.* Conflicts about the possession and division of property were real, and occasionally bloody, but they had the appearance of group and clan feuds, even if it is possible to see in some of them, as in the case of the arsonists of Theix, a kind of unconscious war between the better-off and the poor, with the poor avenging themselves in the desperate enjoyment of a fleeting moment of power. But the illusion, or perhaps the reality, of the unity of rural society was too powerful to make their behaviour systematic and continuous. If the rich in the countryside—the occasional prosperous *laboureur* or rural *bourgeois*—were resented, they were not wealthy enough to command respect or fear in the way that, for example, the handful of wealthy *fermiers* of a village in Artois could. As for the landlords, there were usually too many screens between them and the people from whose misery they indirectly profited. When the Revolution came, the peasants made it against the *bourgeois* of the towns and those few members of the rural élite who were foolish enough to join hands with the men who hoped to bring about a newer and better political order without a social revolution in the countryside.

CHAPTER IX

THE CHURCH AND
THE COUNTRYSIDE

For most people living in the Vannetais, the Church was the parish clergy, and the clergy was a predominantly rural clergy. The parish clergy served the local needs of parishioners and were associated with the Church buildings, shrines, chapels, holy wells and the other settings in which the Church's ceremonies took place; they were the men who ministered at the religious rituals solemnizing the stages of life—baptism, marriage, death and burial—and at the regular acts of devotion which gave a rhythm to the seasons and the year: mass, communion, confession, the annual mission and the visit of the bishop or his representative.

At the head of each parish was a rector (*recteur*, or *personn* in Breton), the priest called the *curé* in most other parts of France. Strictly speaking, the title of 'rector' applied only to parish priests who held their livings in their own right from either the bishop or the Court of Rome; the rest were 'perpetual vicars' (*vicaires perpetuels*), named by independent lay or religious persons or organizations who usually paid the vicar a *portion congrue* or allowance, while reserving the revenues of the living to themselves. About a tenth of the 101 livings in the Breton-speaking section of the Diocese of Vannes were held by perpetual vicars; about a quarter of the 64 livings in the French part were similarly endowed. To parishioners, this made little difference, and they called both rectors and perpetual vicars by the same title of 'rector'. The rector was usually aided by one or two assistant priests, called *curés* (known as vicars outside Brittany). A large parish like Plaudren might have as many as fifteen priests attached to it, but most of those around Vannes had only four or so. Besides these, there were often other priests who were more or less free, who subsisted by saying occasional masses, fulfilling the duties attached to a chapel endowment, serving as chaplains to convents or chateaux, or living on their own incomes.[1]

[*p. 245 for n. 1.*]

In the middle of the seventeenth century, there had been more than 1,200 secular priests in the diocese. There were no proper censuses of the clergy in the later eighteenth century, but it is possible to make a rough calculation of their numbers for that period. At the end of the old regime, about eight or so livings were open for replacement each year; some of these went to outsiders, but not many, by this date. About thirty men were ordained in the diocese in a given year. In other words for each living there were nearly four candidates available; for the livings in the diocese, there were therefore likely to be about 900 secular priests, and probably more earlier in the century. If the total population of the diocese was about 350,000 this gave very roughly a ratio of one priest to every 390 inhabitants, or about one in 90 adult males. The secular priest was therefore a fairly common figure, even though only about half of these 900 priests occupied the position of rectors and assistants.[2]

A clerical presence of this size might suggest that the faith was as solidly rooted in the diocese in the eighteenth century as tradition would have it, and there is considerable evidence to back this claim. Possibly more important than the sheer number of clergy present—not that extraordinary for an eighteenth-century diocese—was the spirit in which the clergy worked and in which they were heard by their faithful. Here, all writers agree that the diocese of Vannes had followed and sometimes led the remarkable religious renaissance which had swept across western France in the seventeenth century. This movement had had a profound effect on all classes of society in town and country. Popular devotion had received considerable encouragement after 1624 from the cult of Saint Anne at Sainte-Anne-d'Auray, where the mother of the Virgin was believed to have appeared to a humble *laboureur,* Nicolazic, asking that a shrine be built on the spot where to this day come vast crowds of

[1] Luco, *Pouillé,* 20–6 and *passim;* Archives de l'Évêché de Vannes [unclassified]: Paroisses, prêtres et fondations du diocèse de Vannes, 1784; A.N., D xix 17 (260) Département du Morbihan: Traitement du clergé régulier et séculier [1791].

[2] J. Mahuas, 'Le Jansénisme dans le diocèse de Vannes au xviiᵉ siècle' (Faculté des Lettres, Rennes, thesis for the *doctorat de troisième cycle,* 1966), 2. Calculations, here and later in this chapter, of the number of rectors and their death, tenure of living and replacement are based on Luco, *Pouillé, passim;* those of ordinations come from A.D. Morbihan, 40 G2–8 (301–7): 1633–1793; I have used the figures in C. Estienne, *Inventaire sommaire des archives départementales antérieures à 1790 . . . Série G (Clergé séculier: Évêché de Vannes)* (Vannes, 1901), 131–6 for the period before 1680; cf. Langlois, *Le Diocèse de Vannes,* 296.

pilgrims from all over Brittany. Under the direction of the great missionary Father Rigoleuc, the institution of the annual parish mission became widespread in the countryside, a practice complemented by the introduction of closed retreats for men in 1662 and for women ten years later. These retreats were held in Vannes, and attended by large numbers of rural as well as city folk. It was also during this period that the devotion of the Perpetual Adoration of the Blessed Sacrament became widespread in the diocese.

In the seventeenth century, too, facilities for the instruction and continuing education of the parish clergy were set up; the College of Vannes, which served as a junior seminary as well as a college for the laity, was taken over by the Jesuits in 1629, and a major seminary was established in the 1680s for the spiritual perfection of candidates for the priesthood. Under the direction of the vicar-general Kerlivio, theological conferences for the parish clergy began to be held regularly. At the origin of these institutional changes was the rise of a sturdy current of religious thought, indeed of mysticism, among the religious orders in Vannes, especially the Carmelites, Jesuits and Ursulines. The seventeenth-century reformers were not content to keep their piety for an élite however, and embarked on a vast pastoral programme which through the retreat houses in Vannes and through parish missions brought the piety and mysticism of the seventeenth century to the countryside and the humble folk of the towns.

Whether the flame of this remarkable religious revival burned less brightly in the eighteenth century than at its beginning, is not easy to say. The impression given by the numerous articles written by local historians and by Claude Langlois's synthesis of the religious activity of the eighteenth century is that some of the initial enthusiasm diminished, and that the mystical impulse from the lay and clerical élite was checked temporarily during the episcopates of two crypto-Jansenist bishops, Caumartin (1717–20) and, especially, Fagon (1720–42). However, according to Father Marsille, Jansenism and the reaction against Quietism at the end of the seventeenth century had no lasting impact on devotional practices which had already struck deep roots.[3]

---

[3] On all the foregoing, see J. Buléon and E. Le Garrec, *Sainte-Anne-d'Auray, histoire d'un village* (Vannes, 1924), i, 310–11 and *passim*, iii, i–xii; Le Mené, *Histoire du diocèse de Vannes*, ii, 56–176; J. Allanic, 'Histoire du Collège de Vannes',

To be sure, certain types of devotion seem to have declined. Thus endowments for masses or pious works became less frequent in the eighteenth century; from ten to twenty in each decade at the beginning of the century in the future 'district' of Vannes, by the twenties, they had fallen to a half-dozen a decade, apparently ceased altogether in the later forties and only made a timid comeback in the later seventies. Less people wrote religious testaments in which they made pious requests and arrangements for masses to be said for their souls after death.[4] But much of this decline can be put down to changing economic conditions and to new fashions in devotion. Against it must be set what is almost certainly a strong revival of the institution of the Dominican Third Order at the end of the old regime, after a long period of inactivity. The Third Order was made up of laywomen who took the vows of chastity; it was centred in Vannes and drew its members almost exclusively from Vannes and the Breton parishes of Plaudren, Grand-Champ, Baden, Arzon, and Locmariaquer. Similarly, the second half of the eighteenth century saw the first flourishing of published works of devotion and Church doctrine in Breton, translated and in some cases written by the rectors Cillart de Kerampoul, Pourchasse and Morice.[5] These

59–105; C. Langlois, 'Jésuites de la province de France, Jésuites de Bretagne vers 1750', _Dix-huitième siècle,_ viii (1976), 77–92 and _Le Diocèse de Vannes,_ 72–94; H. Marsille, 'Note sur les origines de l'école spirituelle vannetaise au xviiᵉ siècle', _MSHAB,_ xxxv (1955), 31–7; 'Vannes', in _Les Établissements des Jésuites,_ ed. Delattre; 'Prêtres vannetais du xviiᵉ siècle', _BSPM_ (1964), 31–45; 'La Retraite de Vennes', _BSPM_ (1951–2), 127–51; G. Le Bras, 'La Vitalité religieuse de la Bretagne depuis les origines chrétiennes jusqu'à nos jours', in _Études de sociologie religieuse_ (Paris, 1955), i, 76–7; Mahuas, 'Le Jansénisme dans le diocèse de Vannes', 11–73, 245–50, 274–85.

[4] A.D. Morbihan, 42 G 3–25 (311–33), 43 G 1–3 (342–3) analysed in Estienne, _Inventaire sommaire . . . Série G,_ 166–526.

The figures for testaments are as follows:

	Vannes	Countryside
1695–9	8	2
1700–9	8	9
1710–19	5	3
1720–9	3	3
1730–9	4	3
1740–9	4	3
1750–9	1	0
1760–9	0	0
1770–9	2	0
1780–9	2	2

[5] C. Langlois and P. Wagret, _Structures religieuses et célibat féminin au xixᵉ siècle_ (Lyons, 1971), 14–24, 103; Langlois, _Le Diocèse de Vannes,_ 86–95, 427–32.

characteristics of revival and ruralization at the end of the eighteenth century appear as well in the pattern of recruitment to the priesthood.

The largest number of ordinations to the secular priesthood occurred in the seventeenth century, during the time of the great religious revival in Brittany: an average of 30 priests a year from the diocese of Vannes were ordained in 1645–63 and again in 1693–1706. There are gaps in the records down to 1729, but the number of candidates who produced the *titre clérical*—the proof of independent income required of candidates for the order of subdeacon, the first of the three major orders—remained high. In the 1730s, something of a decline in ordinations began; there was a fall in the number of ordinands which became apparently quite serious between 1740 and 1744. Numbers of candidates increased again in the early 1750s, though not to pre-1740 levels, and then fell in the later fifties to a record low of 20 a year. After this point, however, the number of ordinations rose steadily to an average of 30 or so in the eighties, almost what it had been in the 'Golden Age' of the seventeenth century.

It would be unwise to put too much weight on these figures. They no doubt reflected many factors, several of which had little to do with the intensity of religious feeling. Thus, in the diocese of Vannes, there appears to be a relation in some years between the fluctuations in the number of livings vacant by resignation or death, and the number of candidates presenting a *titre clérical;* perhaps young men anticipated the forthcoming departure or death of older clerics, or were encouraged by their masters at the college to go forward to the priesthood when it appeared that more places were about to open. Nevertheless, when we can compare the number of livings vacant in each year with ordinations to the secular priesthood, it is clear that the availability of livings had only a limited effect on recruitment; ordinations varied much more than the availability of places, since there were so many more prospective candidates for livings than there were rectors.[6] The general movement of the population may also have played an important role in the slowing of recruitment after 1739, and especially 1753; economic crises such as those of 1741 and 1785–6 clearly had a short-term effect, too, and

---

[6] The figures for ordinations, deaths and resignations are as in note 2; those for *titres cléricaux* and tonsures have been calculated from A.D. Morbihan, 42 G 3–25 [*p. 248 for n. 6 cont.*]

no doubt the improvement of conditions in the 1760s and early 1770s help explain the Indian summer of recruitment to the priesthood in the 1780s. Looked at in a wider setting, the recruitment of clergy in the diocese of Vannes seems to be part of a pattern common to much of France.[7] In any event, the long and steady recovery at the end of the old regime, almost without a break from 1760 to 1786, is unmistakable.

The social background of this clergy changed only a little during the century. From at least 1710 onwards (with a brief exception in

transcribed by Estienne, *Inventaire sommaire* . . . *Série G*, 137–526; the following are averages:

	Tonsures	Titres cléricaux	Ordinations (secular clergy)	Vacancies of livings
1645–9	74.2 —	—	—	—
1650–4	83.4	—	—	—
1655–9	59.8	—	—	—
1660–4	—	—	—	—
1680–4	70.6	—	60.2	—
1685–9	—	—	—	7.0
1690–4	—	—	—	6.0
1695–9	43.6	12.8	34.4	6.6
1700–4	38.0	9.0	35.0	10.0
1705–9	56.8	12.2	27.6	10.4
1710–14	50.4	35.4	—	7.2
1715–19	56.4	30.2	27.4	9.4
1720–4	—	35.4	—	10.2
1725–9	—	38.2	—	8.4
1730–4	52.8	31.4	36.2	9.2
1735–9	66.8	29.6	34.8	7.8
1740–4	50.4	26.6	29.4	11.2
1745–9	46.0	21.2	25.0	7.4
1750–4	56.4	26.8	29.2	6.6
1755–9	41.4	21.2	21.8	10.0
1760–4	35.4	19.0	24.0	8.8
1765–9	40.2	21.4	23.4	8.2
1770–4	45.6	17.0	25.8	9.2
1775–9	51.6	22.8	28.4	8.0
1780–4	47.6	21.2	30.4	7.8
1785–9	35.2	14.4	27.6	9.4

On the regulations for the *titre clérical*, see *Ordonnances de Monseigneur François d'Arouges evêque de Vannes* (Vannes, 1693), 357–9; on the significance of quantitative studies of vocations in the old regime, see L. Pérouas, 'Le Nombre des vocations sacerdotales est-il un critère valable en sociologie religieuse historique aux xvii⁰ et xviii⁰ siècles?', *Actes du quatre-vingt-septième congrès des Sociétés savantes, Poitiers, 1962. Section d'histoire moderne et contemporaine* (Paris, 1963), 35–41.

[7] T. Tackett, 'L'Histoire sociale du clergé diocésain dans la France du xviii⁰ siècle', *RHMC*, xxvii (1979), 198–234; *Priest and Parish in Eighteenth-Century France* (Princeton, 1977), 43–5.

the twenties), about half of the candidates for the subdiaconate who registered their *titres cléricaux* with the bishop's chancery and mentioned the estate of their parents, said that they were sons of *laboureurs, ménagers* or *gens de labeur,* and another 10 to 17 per cent were from families of rural artisans or shopkeepers and merchants. In reality, the proportion of rural candidates must have been higher still, since most of these who did not give their qualities were probably sons of *laboureurs.* Only 20 to 26 per cent were of bourgeois origin, many of these being bourgeois who lived in a predominantly rural milieu, mostly notaries, seigneurial judges and the like. Three to 7 per cent normally came from families of urban artisans and shopkeepers. There appear to have been rather fewer noble candidates at the end of the century than at the beginning: they formed from 6 to 12 per cent of the candidates down to the thirties, but less than 2 per cent in the forties and thereafter. The proportion of urban artisans also declined drastically: after rising slowly to a high of 11 per cent in the forties, it declined to less than 2 per cent in the seventies. Seamen of all sorts also sent fewer of their sons to the seminary after mid-century. Probably economic fluctuations explain most of these minor shifts, with the exception of the nobility, among whom an increasing indifference to clerical careers is certainly possible.[8]

[8] *Titres cléricaux* taken out by sponsors in each social group:

	1710–14	1720–4	1730–4	1740–5	1776–80	1785–8
'Laboureurs', etc.	49.3%	30.1%	50.0%	54.4%	50.7%	54.3%
Rural artisan & shopkeeper	14.5	24.7	10.5	8.9	14.5	17.1
Seamen	5.8	4.3	3.5	7.8	5.8	2.9
'Bourgeois'	23.2	22.6	23.3	15.6	26.1	22.9
Urban artisan, shopkeeper	1.4	6.5	7.0	11.1	1.4	0.9
Nobles	5.8	11.8	5.8	2.2	1.4	2.9
	100.0	100.0	100.1	100.0	99.9	100.1
Number of titles	69	93	86	90	68	35
Plus: sponsored by:						
Priests	5	3	1	2	1	—
Others	103	81	70	41	28	25
Total titles	177	177	157	133	97	60

The figures for 1710–45 were calculated from Estienne's transcription in *Inventaire sommaire . . . Série G,* 166–412; those for 1776–88 were taken from A.D. Morbihan, 42 G 21–25 (329–33).

Thus, the majority of candidates for the priesthood, probably much larger than these figures suggest, were rural people. Although it is difficult to make exact comparisons with other areas of France, it seems that this higher proportion of peasant recruitment was peculiar to the north-western corner of the country, or at least to those dioceses which did not include major urban centres. It is comparable to the proportion of sons of *laboureurs* recruited in the Norman diocese of Coutances—a phenomenal 75 per cent—and far exceeds the proportions of peasant recruits found further east in the dioceses of Lisieux (22 per cent), Reims (19 per cent), and south in the diocese of Luçon (9 per cent).[9] It is virtually impossible to tell from the sources used here what section of the peasantry these rural priests came from. The revenue of 80 livres did not require a large amount of land, to be sure. Yet the fact that so few sons of urban artisans succeeded in entering the priesthood suggests that their rural counterparts, and persons living on a similar economic level in the countryside, were not found frequently among the students of the college and seminary of Vannes. This is what the biographer of Georges Cadoudal, the *chouan* leader and an ex-student of the college in 1789 claimed, at any rate: 'Fils de cultivateurs ou de marins, ils appartenaient presque tous à la classe des domaniers et des cultivateurs propriétaires ou à des familles parvenues à l'aisance par le cabotage ou le long cours, c'est-à-dire à l'aristocratie des campagnes et des grèves bretonnes.'[10] And there, unless some better source is found, the question must rest. Probably it does not matter much in a rural community in which distinctions of wealth, though real, were blurred as they were in the Vannetais.

Although the locally recruited secular clergy remained predominantly rural throughout the century, there were significant changes in the relative importance which men of rural background had in the organization of the Church. Of course not all the priests who served in the diocese were ordained locally, and not all who were ordained locally were natives of the area. But as time went by, the diocesan

---

[9] Y. Nèdelec, 'Aperçus de sociologie religieuse du xviiie siècle, d'après les titres cléricaux. L'exemple coutançais', *Revue historique de droit français et étranger*, 4e série, xl (1962), 500; C. Berthelot du Chesnay, 'Le Clergé diocésain français au xviiie siècle et les registres des insinuations ecclésiastiques', *RHMC*, x (1963), 241–96; D. Julia, 'Le Clergé paroissial dans le diocèse de Reims à la fin du xviiie siècle', *RHMC*, xiii (1966), 201; J. Dehergne, *Le Bas-Poitou à la veille de la Révolution* (Paris, 1963), 106 n. 32; cf. also Tackett, *Priest and Parish*, 56–8.

[10] Cadoudal, *Georges Cadoudal*, 10–11.

clergy as a whole came to reflect the patterns of local recruitment as fewer and fewer outsiders were ordained in the diocese. Bit by bit, with this absence of outsiders and the beginning of fairer procedures of nomination to livings, countrymen came to occupy more of the higher posts in the secular clergy. At the same time as clergymen became more local and rural, they also improved in quality and became more closely tied to the parishes in which they served.

Fewer and fewer priests, then, came from outside the diocese. In the seventeenth century, the proportion of outsiders ordained had been extremely high—51 per cent of ordinands to the secular clergy in 1633–44 and 32 per cent in 1645–63. No doubt this was partly the result of a shortage of adequate colleges elsewhere in France, and the relative ease with which young men could come from other Breton dioceses to the college of Vannes. However, the proportion of outsiders ordained to the secular clergy declined steadily from the beginning of the seventeenth century. In the first half of the eighteenth century, between 1707 and 1758, outsiders accounted for only 11 per cent of ordinands, a proportion which fell to 7 per cent in 1759–80 and 4 per cent in 1781–9, so that at the end of the old regime, virtually all the graduates of the seminary of Vannes were local men.[11]

At the same time, the number of livings in the diocese held by outsiders steadily declined, and in general the rectors appeared to have become more attached to their parishes. A comparison between the corps of 165 rectors in office in 1740 and their successors in 1789 is much to the advantage of the latter. In 1740, many of the rectors in the diocese of Vannes came from other dioceses: 21 per cent of all rectors in the Breton-speaking part of the diocese, 25 per cent in the rural French-speaking section. Besides this, only 55 per cent of rectors in office had succeeded to men who had died in office. The rest had taken over from rectors who had often given up their posts (in return for a pension) to successors whom they had themselves designated, either by the device known as the *resignatio in favorem* or else by abusing the procedure of ordinary resignation. The most flagrant example of such practices were two cases of triple successions of relatives: Pierre Le Tallec (1660–1705), Jean Le Tallec (1705–28) and Joseph Le Tallec (1728–38), each in turn

---

[11] A.D. Morbihan 40 G 2–8 (301–7) summarized in C. Estienne, *Inventaire sommaire . . . Série G*, 130–47, and set out in tabular form in Le Goff, 'Vannes', 421–2.

rectors of Plumergat, and three individuals, each named Pierre Guillemot, who succeeded one another in the cure of Camors (1680–1712, 1712–36, 1736–7). In addition, the prescription that rectors in Breton-speaking parishes had to be fluent in the language of their parishioners does not appear to have been rigorously applied to the outsiders, to judge from the number of rectors from non-Breton dioceses occupying these posts. Finally, of those priests who were recruited locally, a rather high proportion were of urban origin: 28 per cent in French rural parishes.[12]

This picture changed progressively during the course of the century. Before 1740, a considerable number of the outsiders occupying rectories obtained their position through competitive examinations. Over 80 per cent of the rectors in the diocese were nominated alternately by the bishop or by the Pope, depending on the month of the year in which their livings had been vacated. Before 1740, each time it was the Pope's turn to nominate, a competition was arranged in Rome itself, open to any and all candidates. In 1740, this practice ended, and papal nominations were then made on the basis of an examination held under the supervision of the bishop and a commission appointed by his diocesan bureau. This examination was open only to natives of the diocese, and one of the requirements, which was strictly enforced, was that candidates should have a knowledge of the language used in their parishes.

There were other factors which contributed to reducing the numbers of the non-native clergy. One was the death in 1742 of the controversial Bishop Fagon, the son of Louis XIV's physician. A Jansenist sympathizer, Fagon bears much of the blame for appointing so many outsiders dependant on him during his long episcopate (1720–42). After Fagon's death, the Jansenists, never very numerous but occupying key positions, were purged or eliminated by death or retirement. The fall in outside recruitment after 1740 may also be due in part to a decline in priestly vocations in the neighbouring dioceses of St-Pol-de-Léon and Nantes.[13]

[12] Tables IX-1; and Le Goff, 'Vannes', 429–30; Luco, *Pouillé*, 209, 593; Le Mené, *Histoire du diocèse de Vannes*, ii, 109. There were three priests from the diocese of St-Malo holding livings in 1740, and one each from the dioceses of Paris, Meaux, Avranches and Rennes holding livings in Breton-speaking parishes in 1740. However, some of these men may have been born in Breton-speaking regions and , of course, some may have learned enough of the language to carry out their duties.

[13] Le Mené, *Histoire du diocèse de Vannes,* ii, 194–206; Meyer, *La Noblesse bretonne*, ii, 1151–2. Fagon had packed his diocesan bureau with Quesnellists or at [p. 254 for n. 13 cont.]

The rectors of the diocese in the last decade of the old regime present a remarkable contrast to their predecessors of 1740. The proportion of locally-recruited rectors had grown from 58 per cent in 1730 to 81 per cent in 1770 and 89 per cent in 1789. At the same time, the proportion of these locally-recruited rectors who came from rural parishes also was on the increase: 51 per cent in 1730, 63 per cent in 1770, and 71 per cent in 1789. These two tendencies towards rural and local recruitment were even more pronounced in the Breton-speaking region of the diocese than these overall figures show. At least 57 per cent of the Breton rectors came from the diocese in 1730; by 1740, 71 per cent were locally recruited; by 1770, 89 per cent; and in 1789, the proportion had risen to 92 per cent. Of those priests serving as rectors in Breton parishes who had been recruited in the diocese, 53 per cent came from rural parishes in 1730, 66 per cent in 1770 and 75 per cent by 1789. Given the strongly non-bourgeois character of recruitment from the rural parishes, it seems likely that a large proportion of the rural clergy was of peasant origin, even if it came from the upper levels of rural society.

Some other changes confirm the impression that the rural clergy of 1789 was closer to the countryside than it had been at the beginning of the century. Rectors tended to remain longer in their posts, or at least, a higher proportion of them died in office at the end of the century. In 1730, the proportion of rectors in the whole diocese whose predecessors had died in office was 55 per cent. By 1770, it had risen to 69 per cent, and by 1789, to 74 per cent. Along with this change went a marked decline in the proportion of rectors who had succeeded to their posts by the quasi-simoniacal procedure of the *resignatio in favorem,* which declined from 18 per cent in 1730 to 10 per cent in 1789. Probably the decline was somewhat larger than this, since among the priests who resigned unconditionally were some who had in fact made arrangements to pass on their livings to successors of their choice,[14] and the number of these simple resignations declined from 30 per cent in 1730 to 17 per cent in 1789 (diocesan totals).

Up to this point, we have been looking at diocesan figures, since the careers and activities of the clergy extended across the whole

least men who were his creatures; of the nine rectors in this body, Faron, Maurice and David were outsiders; cf. J. Mahuas, 'Le Concours pour l'obtention des cures dans le diocèse de Vannes au xviiiᵉ siècle', *MSHAB*, xlv (1965), 41–58; 'Le Jansénisme dans le diocèse de Vannes', 167–212.

[14] Luco, *Pouillé*, 593.

Table IX-1: Rectors in the diocese of Vannes, by diocese of origin, 1730–1789

	1730 number	%	1740 number	%	1750 number	%	1770 number	%	1789 number	%
Breton-speaking region (rural)										
From dio. Vannes	58	57.4	72	71.3	79	78.2	90	89.1	93	92.1
From other dioceses	26	25.7	21	20.8	12	11.9	7	6.9	3	3.0
Unknown origin	17	16.8	8	7.9	10	9.9	4	4.0	6	5.9
Total	101		101		101		101		101	
French-speaking region (rural)										
From dio. Vannes	31	60.7	30	58.8	30	58.8	36	70.5	44	86.2
From other dioceses	12	23.5	13	25.5	15	29.4	8	15.7	5	9.8
Unknown origin	8	15.7	8	15.7	6	11.8	7	13.7	2	3.9
Total	51		51		51		51		51	
French-speaking region (all parishes)										
From dio. Vannes	37	57.8	36	56.3	39	60.9	44	68.8	54	84.4
From other dioceses	17	26.5	18	28.1	17	26.5	11	17.1	7	10.9
Unknown origin	10	15.6	10	15.6	8	12.5	9	14.1	3	4.7
Total	64		64		64		64		64	
Total, diocese of Vannes										
From dio. Vannes	95	57.6	108	65.5	118	71.5	134	81.2	146	88.5
From other dioceses	42	25.3	39	23.6	29	17.6	18	10.9	10	6.1
Unknown origin	28	16.8	18	10.9	18	10.9	13	7.9	9	5.5
Total	165		165		165		165		165	

Source: Luco, *Pouillé historique, passim.*

Table IX-2: Rectors originating in the diocese of Vannes, by parish of origin

	1730 number	%	1740 number	%	1750 number	%	1770 number	%	1789 number	%
Breton-speaking region (rural)										
Rural parishes	31	53.4	40	55.5	48	60.8	60	65.8	69	75.0
Urban parishes	10	17.2	15	20.8	25	31.6	21	23.1	17	18.5
Unknown	17	29.3	17	23.6	6	7.6	10	11.0	6	6.5
Total	58		72		79		91		92	
French-speaking region (rural)										
Rural parishes	14	45.2	12	41.4	19	63.3	22	62.8	30	66.7
Urban parishes	6	19.4	8	27.6	8	26.7	10	28.6	11	24.2
Unknown	11	35.5	9	31.0	3	10.0	3	8.6	4	8.9
Total	31		29		30		35		45	
French-speaking region (all parishes)										
Rural parishes	17	45.9	16	44.4	23	58.2	25	58.1	35	64.6
Urban parishes	3	24.3	11	30.6	12	30.8	14	32.6	15	27.6
Unknown	11	29.7	9	25.0	4	10.3	4	9.3	4	7.4
Total	37		36		39		43		54	
Total, diocese of Vannes										
Rural parishes	48	50.5	56	51.9	71	60.2	85	63.4	104	71.2
Urban parishes	19	20.0	26	24.1	37	31.4	35	26.2	32	21.9
Unknown	28	29.4	26	24.1	10	8.5	14	10.4	10	6.8
Total	95		108		118		134		146	

Source: As in Table IX-1.

Table IX-3: Accession to livings in the diocese of Vannes

	1730 number	%	1740 number	%	1750 number	%	1770 number	%	1789 number	%
Breton-speaking region (rural)										
Death of predecessor	53	52.4	53	52.4	58	57.4	67	66.3	72	71.3
Simple resignation, etc.	30	29.7	32	31.7	31	30.7	25	24.8	19	18.8
Resignation *in favorem*	18	17.8	16	15.8	12	11.9	9	8.9	10	9.9
Total	101		101		101		101		101	
French-speaking region (rural)										
Death of predecessor	32	62.7	30	58.8	32	62.7	39	76.4	39	76.4
Simple resignation, etc.	15	29.4	19	37.3	11	21.6	9	17.6	7	13.7
Resignation *in favorem*	4	7.8	2	3.9	8	15.7	3	5.8	5	9.8
Totals	51		51		51		51		51	
French-speaking region (all parishes)										
Death of predecessor	38	59.4	36	56.3	40	62.5	46	71.9	50	78.1
Simple resignation, etc.	19	29.7	24	37.5	15	23.4	13	20.3	8	12.5
Resignation *in favorem*	7	10.9	4	6.3	9	14.1	5	7.8	6	9.4
Total	64		64		64		64		64	
Total, diocese of Vannes										
Death of predecessor	91	55.2	89	53.9	98	59.3	113	68.5	122	73.9
Simple resignation, etc.	49	29.6	56	33.9	46	27.8	38	23.0	27	16.5
Resignation *in favorem*	25	15.2	20	12.1	21	12.7	14	8.5	16	9.6
Total	165		165		165		165		165	

Source: As in Table IX-1.

diocese, and priests could move about from one part of the diocese to another when vacancies opened. Did these patterns also hold in the immediate region around Vannes? In this area there were twenty-five parishes, of which sixteen were held by *décimateurs*, priests who received all or part of the tithe, and nine by *congruistes*. The parish clergy in all probability numbered over a hundred. The revenues of this group were highly unequal, with a handful of rich *décimateurs* and a larger number of rather poorly paid rectors, to say nothing of the rest of the parish clergy. The highest net tithe revenues collected in the 1780s were, by a conservative estimate, the 2,500–2,600 l. received by the rectors of St-Patern, Sarzeau and Grand-Champ; but the median tithe revenue for a *décimateur* was only about 800 l., not very much more than the meagre 500 l. or less which all but two of the *congruistes* received.

If we consider the men who skimmed the cream of clerical revenues in 1740, the 8 of the 16 *décimateurs* who collected 75 per cent of the net tithe revenues of the region between them, we find that this group was largely made up of outsiders or sons of local notables. It was also heavily tainted by Jansenism, for Bishop Fagon rewarded his rather small band of supporters with places close enough to Vannes to allow them to play a predominant role in his episcopal administration. There was one priest from the diocese of Quimper, Yves Menguy, rector of Surzur. His neighbour at Sarzeau, J.-B.-P. Faron, was a Jansenist from the diocese of Meaux whom Fagon had made one of his vicars-general in 1732. G.-J.-B. Maurice, a benefice-hunter from Paris, had defeated one of the leaders of the local opposition to Fagon in a legal battle for the office of capitular treasurer and then abandoned his choir stall for a generous living as rector of Elven; he subsequently exchanged Elven for the parish of Fontenay-aux-Roses, near his native city. Louis Bonnard, rector of St-Patern, was the son of a local *négociant* and a notorious Jansenist. A fifth cleric, Guichard, had been born in Vannes, and presumably had some substance, for he had been rector of Ste-Croix in Nantes before taking up the parish of Baden. The origins of one other priest in this group are untraceable; two others were of minor robe families: Le Tenours de Kersimon of Ambon and Cillart de Kerampoul at Grand-Champ. Cillart, a rigorist but not a Jansenist, was the only really outstanding member of the group, a scholar and the author of an early French–Breton dictionary and works of piety written in the Breton language.

The nine *congruistes* were at the other end of the scale from these comfortable churchmen. The six whose origins can be discovered were nearly all local men, born in or around the region, all of them from rural areas. Among these and also among the less well-endowed of the *décimateurs* one can find an élite whose importance did not correspond to the paucity of their livings: the rector of the cathedral, Joseph Touzée, son of a prominent bourgeois family of Vannes who held his doctorate of theology from the Faculty of Bourges; Jean Dufeuil, sometime archpriest of the diocese who had taken the small urban parish of St-Salomon; Pierre Rhodes, the director of the diocesan seminary who was rector *ex officio* of the smallest urban parish, Le Mené; François-Guillaume Le Viquel, rector of the little parish of Plescop, where the bishop had his country residence, and an ardent Jansenist, whom Fagon set to examine the doctrinal soundness of candidates for the priesthood.

Most rectors were men of ripe years; their median age was 53; their average 51, and only one was in his thirties, but four of them had become rectors at a relatively tender age, in their late twenties. The group who replaced them in 1789 were a little older (median age, 53; average, 57); none had become a rector before his thirty-second year. This seems to reflect the tendency just noted in the diocese as a whole towards a rather older, more stable clergy, appointed in a less haphazard fashion.

There were other changes too. If we look as before at the eight richest livings we find that they were all but one in the hands of local men. At least one of these rectors was the son of a *laboureur;* all save the one outsider and Le Croisier, rector of St-Patern, came from non-urban parishes; at least one, Fardel, had the reputation of being not only learned—he occupied a chair at Salamanca in the Revolution—but also a saint. The one outsider, P.-B. de Keroignant de Trezel, from Guingamp, looks very much as if he owed his living to merit alone; he took first place at the examination for the position held in 1785, at which there were over seventy competitors. Only Keroignant and Le Croisier, the son of a minor *négociant,* stood out by their birth. Among the less well-provided rectors, Fagon's Jansenist clique had of course long since disappeared. There were still some outsiders, C.-F.-M. de La Villeloays (St-Salomon) and J.-M. Froger (St-Avé), but these came from Breton dioceses, not from afar; of the remainder, two were from Vannes, of whom one, Jallay, rector of Séné, was the son of a humble *huissier* and the

other, Le Sant, rector of Trefflèan, was of unknown origin. In so far
as learning is represented by university degrees, there was one
licentiate in civil and canon law (La Villeloays) and one Doctor of
Theology, Le Duin, an ex-professor from the Eudist seminary at
Rennes. Thus the changes which had taken place in the diocese as a
whole were mirrored in the region about Vannes: a more 'Breton'
clergy, recruited from the élite of rural society, fewer priests from
the bourgeoisie and officer classes than before; probably a group of
men better trained than the very mixed band of clerics at the head of
the parishes in the region a half-century before.[15]

Whatever their social origins, the rectors could not avoid being
marked by the milieu in which they lived and worked. There was
little in their personal fortunes to distinguish them as men of wealth.
Their personal property was generally limited to a couple of *fonds*
or edifices on holdings under *domaine congéable,* a meadow which
they could farm out or work themselves; no more than the better-off
peasants in their parishes, usually less.[16] Nor was the revenue which
went with the living normally a burden to their parishioners. Fourteen of the 165 rectors in the diocese had estimated tithe revenues in
the 1780s of more than 2,000 l.; of these, one had more than
3,000 l., but these relatively high revenues came from large parishes, and they had heavy responsibilities—the rector of Grand-
Champ had one of the biggest tithe revenues, 2,600 l., but had also
three vicars to feed and charity to distribute. None of the tithes
levied for the rectors in the diocese surpassed the rate of one sheaf
in thirty-three or 3 per cent of the crop. In some parishes, particularly in the northern and eastern parts of the diocese, a higher tithe
was levied, sometimes as high as one sheaf in nine (11 per cent), but
in those cases, the surplus always went to an outside body: the
Chapter of Vannes, a priory, or to a seigneur who had at some time
taken over the tithe or imposed his own rate. In 29 of the 165
parishes of the diocese, the rector did not levy a tithe at all; instead it
was collected by bodies such as the Chapter, priories or the bishopric itself, which had presentation of the living and paid its holder the

[15] Archives de l'Évêché de Vannes: Paroisses, prêtres et fondations . . . 1784;
Luco, *Pouillé, passim;* Estienne, *Inventaire sommaire . . . Série G, passim;* Mahuas,
'Le Jansénisme dans le diocèse de Vannes', 179, 183, 205, 256.
[16] e.g. A.D. Morbihan, 17 C 5386–93: 23-7-1768, 18-10-1768, 8-7-1769, 30-12-
1769, 10-2-1773, 11-2-1775, 27-9-1775, 19-8-1778.

inappropriately-termed *portion congrue*.[17] In short, while various orders or bodies in the Church might own large tracts of land, or cream off the bulk of a heavy tithe, its immediate representative, the rector, appeared more a member of the rural community than one of its exploiters.

This position was of course, reinforced by the role of the Church in the rural community in *bocage* country with which historians and sociologists have made us familiar. The parish church itself was both the symbol of the universal Church and an important social centre for the community, a function especially vital in an area of semi-dispersed habitat. Before it, young couples pledged their engagement before marriage; from its steps were read notices of sales, leases and expulsions; from its pulpit and altar, and in its confessional, the rector and his assistants preached sacred doctrine, delivered the pronouncements of the royal Government, married, advised, absolved and buried their parishioners. The curious use in some of the parish records of the phrase 'la sainte mère l'Église,' usually applied to the Church as a spiritual organization, to describe the physical building is highly evocative of this blending in the popular mind of the concrete, immediate and social role of the Church with its supernatural functions.

The rector himself was supposed to be counsellor and defender of the rural community. The case of the rector of Surzur, who brought a lawsuit along with his parishioners against the usurpation of common lands in the parish, is described in the next chapter.[18] The rector's revenues were supposed to be as much the property of the poor as his own, and although none were tempted as far as we can tell to reduce themselves to the level of the indigent, the rectors did give of their own in charity. In the terrible winter of 1785–6, for example, Gauthier, the rector of Theix, provided bread for the poor of his parish, but believing that simple charity was insufficient, he tried, not just to 'donner à la paresse qui aime mieux la pure & gratuite charité & au sentiment qui ne prend que ce qu'il gagne, mais de retirer du travail des pauvres quelqu'effet sensiblement utile à la paroisse.' Out of his own funds, and despite a recalcitrant vestry council, he paid the poor of his parish, at the rate of eight sols

---

[17] Archives de l'Évêché de Vannes: Paroisses, prêtres et fondations . . . 1784; Luco, *Pouillé*, 29–30 and *passim; J.-M.* le Mené, *Histoire archéologique, féodale et religieuse des paroisses du diocèse de Vannes* (Vannes, 1891–4), *passim.*

[18] Below, p. 276.

a day for men and six sols for women, to build two bridges. He asked the intendant to subsidize a third bridge and to provide him with flax to be spun by the most needy women of his parish, pointing out that he could have paid for this too, if he did not have to share his tithe with the bishop of Vannes and several lay seigneurs.[19] Other rectors took it upon themselves to write to the intendant or the *Contrôle-Général* to plead for more parish relief. In general, the *subdélégué* Freneau reported, the rectors did all that was in their power to alleviate hunger.[20]

The religious revival of the seventeenth century, the trend toward increasingly local and rural recruitment of the rectors, and the social predominance of the parish clergy combined to give the secular priests undoubted authority over their parishioners, based both on familiarity and respect. After 1789, the revolutionary authorities certainly believed that this was the case, for they clearly thought that as a friend, the rector could keep the countryside favourable to the Revolution, but that as an enemy, his word could turn the parish against the strangers from the towns: 'Si les ecclésiastiques prêtent le serment [of the Civil Constitution of the Clergy]', Le Maillaud, one of the administrators of the Department, was reported as saying in 1791, 'nous serons bien, mais s'ils le refusent, nous sommes perdus et tout est fichu.'[21]

Nevertheless, the rector's sway was not unlimited, and there were certain matters in which the clergy had little power. The popular tradition of dancing, of which the Church has always been suspicious, was forbidden by at least one rector, in Grand-Champ in the 1780s, but as one dour and slightly tipsy spectator at a rural fair remarked before aiming his cudgel at a dancer who had jostled him, 'Monsieur le Recteur défend de danser cela n'empêche pas de le faire.'[22] Similarly, the rector of Meucon, Mathieu, could not summon up enough authority or presence to persuade six peasants from the neighbouring parish of Plaudren not to present a 'farce' called 'La vie des trois roys', in the Christmas season of 1764; on the contrary,

---

[19] A.D. I.-V., C 1747: Gauthier, rector of Theix, to intendant, 15-12-1785, 22-4-1786.

[20] A.D. I.-V., C 1747: Distribution de secours en argent aux pauvres, vieillards . . . 1786: 'Les autres paroisses de mon département souffrent beaucoup mais les recteurs et quelques seigneurs donnent des secours'.

[21] A.D. Morbihan, Lz 274: Anonymous circular [by Le Monnier], February 1791.

[22] A.D. Morbihan, B: Largouet, minutes; François Cadoret v. François Seveno, 1773.

Lucas le Lohé, who played the role of Herod, drew his sabre on the priest, 'et le menaça en jurant de lui couper le col'—a threat which drove the rector to reinforce his moral authority by beating the unfortunate Le Lohé about the shoulders with the butt of a gun he was using to intimidate the revellers. The incident culminated in an attack on the presbytery by the band of players.[23] Finally, one might mention the simple refusal, without precedent in the living memory of the parish, of several of the inhabitants of St-Avé to pay the rector the first fruits due on the tithes of 1770.[24] Such incidents are only straws in the wind, but they do serve to warn against assuming that the population of the Vannetais were nothing but the submissive subjects of an all-powerful local clergy. The rural priest, like the other members of society, had his place in the community but it was a place which, if it commanded considerable respect, nevertheless had limits.

Would it be safe to go one step further and suggest that there was something in the very training the priests of the diocese received in the College of Vannes at the end of the eighteenth century which made them particularly close to the ways of the people, which even included the elements of Breton nationalism? The biographer of Georges Cadoudal stated that after the expulsion of the Jesuits, when the College of Vannes was handed over to a local board of governors:

Le collège passa sous la conduite des prêtres du diocèse, instruits à leur école [by the Jesuits] qui poursuivirent l'œuvre de la Compagnie avec les mêmes principes et les mêmes méthodes, mais en y joignant un cachet particulier au caractère et à l'esprit bretons. Pendant près de trente années de 1762 à 1791, la jeunesse du diocèse de Vannes fut dirigée par des maîtres de son sang, dont le premier souci fut de former leurs élèves dans l'esprit des traditions locales et de leur apprendre à aimer et à respecter tout ce qu'avaient aimé à respecter leurs pères.[25]

Perhaps. Certain traces of an inflated local pride and the remains of the 'nationalism' of the Estates and Parlement of Brittany, though used to a different end, can be found in the writing of M.-G.-A. Le Crosier, rector of St-Patern and a prominent *patriote* agitator in

---

[23] A.D. Morbihan, B: Régaires, minutes: 1783.

[24] A.D. Morbihan, C: Commission intermédiaire de Vannes: Paroisse de St-Avé: État des personnes qui ont refusé de payer les prémices aux fermiers des dîmes de la dite paroisse de St-Avé pour l'année 1771.

[25] Cadoudal, *Georges Cadoudal*, 6–7.

1788–9.[26] There was a good chance that many of the locally re-cruited rectors—and, *a fortiori*, the mass of the lower clergy—had passed through the college within the generation described by the younger Cadoudal; the median length of time in office of rectors in 1789 was eleven years in both the French and Breton-speaking sectors of the diocese; in the region around Vannes, a little less than half of the rectors ($^{11}/_{25}$) had received their *titre clerical* after 1761.[27] But Cadoudal's nephew, royalist that he was, may well have tended to read his own attitudes to the Revolution back into a past which he had not known directly. After all, if Chouan leaders such as Georges and Rohu went to the college, so did many of the partisans of the Revolution.[28] More important in the attitude of the rural popu-lation towards its priests and of the priests towards their superior, the bishop, was the simple fact that the priests shared the reactions of the people from whom they had come and whose language they spoke. They returned to the countryside after undergoing a training in the college and seminary under the close supervision of two zealous bishops, Bertin and Amelot, both men who resided in their bishoprics and were active, able administrators. This makes it easier to understand the conduct of the rectors during the Revolution when, with a uniformity unparalleled anywhere else in Brittany, they followed Amelot's orders and rejected the Civil Constitution of the Clergy[29]. By the end of the old regime, the Church in the diocese of Vannes, as far as the lower clergy was concerned, was a local affair.

If this was the situation of the secular clergy, it is appropriate to ask the same questions of the regular clergy. Evident religious fervour, common utility or at least local connections would no doubt have helped anchor the religious orders in local society. How did the monastic ideal fare in the age of Enlightenment?

Evidence on the intensity of religious life in the regular orders in the diocese is, to say the least, not very abundant. The rector of Rieux kept a record of what he considered to be the unmistakable fall into perdition of his neighbours, the Trinitaires, a tiny religious establishment which had three members in 1790:

[26] Le Goff, 'Les Doléances des paysans du Vannetais'.
[27] Calculated from Luco, *Pouillé, passim*.
[28] Debauve, *Justice révolutionnaire*, 67, 73, 80, 530–1.
[29] A.N., D xix 17 (260): État des religieux et religieuses en communauté au premier décembre 1790; Archives de l'Évêché de Vannes: Paroisses, prêtres et fondations, 1784; J.-M. Le Mené, *BSPM* (1897–1907), *passim*.

L'an 1725, les moines de Rieux cessèrent de manger au réfectoire, et de faire la lecture pendant le repas. Jusqu'en l'an 1735, les moines de Rieux n'avaient jamais porté d'aumusse; ils la portèrent cette année pour le première fois, se firent appeler Messieurs, et défendirent de les appeler Pères. L'an 1742, les moines de Rieux abbatirent leur cloître, qui étaient situé entre leur église et le bâtiment où sont leurs cellules.

Unfortunately, the rector did not continue his laconic chronicle beyond this date.[30] In 1780, a visitor to the abbey of Prières noticed that at High Mass the organist managed to slip tunes from light operas into his offertory improvisation, but the same visitor was also astonished to find the monks abstained from meat every day.[31]

Examples like these, alas, serve only to demonstrate the futility of anecdotal history. At least there is more abundant record of the public role of the religious orders. Here, one fact is immediately apparent: with a few exceptions, most of the convents and monasteries in the diocese were urban phenomena, and their locations somewhat restricted the possibilities of contact between rural people and religious. Only about a fifth of the twenty-five men's orders in the diocese, and virtually none of the twenty-seven orders for women were in the country. Even when an abbey or monastery was located in the countryside, physical barriers and differences in culture, origins and language separated the orders from the people who lived around the monastic buildings. Such contact as did take place between rural monasteries and their neighbours was more likely to be in the form of conflict between landlords and tenants or seigneurs and *censitaires*.

This side of their activity can hardly have helped the reputation of the religious orders and the Chapter of Vannes in the countryside. There is no reason to suppose that distant ecclesiastical bodies such as the Chapter of Vannes, whose management of its direct domain was among the harshest in the region, or the monasteries and convents which emulated them, were loved or greatly respected. In the summer of 1790, just to the north of the diocese, the monks of the priory of Notre-Dame-de-Langonnet were threatened by the inhabitants of nearby La Trinité when they tried to collect arrears, like many another landlord at the time.[32] Probably many tenants of

[30] J.-M. Le Mené, 'Communautés situées hors Vannes', *BSPM* (1905), 14–20.
[31] Desjobert, 'Notes d'un voyage en Bretagne', 150–1.
[32] J.-M. Le Mené, 'Abbaye de Langonnet', *BSPM* (1904), 28–9; A.D. Morbihan, L 134: Directory, District of Vannes to Administrators of Department, 27-7-1790.

ecclesiastical landlords in the diocese felt the same way. In 1790, the family of the great Chouan leader, Georges Cadoudal, showed no hesitation in buying up Church land.[33]

To be sure, there were some ties of dependence and advantage between religious communities and their neighbours. A rural abbey could give alms and provide people in remote corners of large parishes with a more convenient place than the parish church for Sunday mass. Thus in 1768, when the abolition of the diminutive Abbey of Lanvaux was proposed (it had only six members at the time), its occupants protested that it served the five surrounding parishes, that people heard mass and received sacraments and alms there. But it was above all in the towns, or in semi-urban settings like Sarzeau where the religious and social uses of some religious orders was more evident. This was especially true of the women's orders. Congregations such as the Carmelites of Ste-Anne-d'Auray and the Dames de la Retraite, who managed the retreat house in Vannes, or the Dominican nuns in Vannes who organized the Third Order for women; charitable and teaching orders like the Filles de la Charité, who looked after the poor in the parish of Sarzeau and on Belle-Île; the nursing order of St Augustine, who tended the sick in Vannes; the Dames de la Charité, who tried to save wayward women, or the Ursulines and, until their expulsion, the Jesuits, who taught the young in towns like Vannes and Hennebont—all these did have an influence which was felt first of all in the towns, but also to some degree in the countryside. Nevertheless, set beside the influence of the parish priest beyond the town walls, it seems unlikely that it was very great.[34]

It is somewhat easier to assess the influence of the religious orders by measuring their power to attract new members. On the whole, the record of the diocese in local recruitment, especially to the men's orders, was rather uneven. The number of priests ordained as religious in the diocese was never very high, and showed a slight decline in the 1780s. Many of the orders for men such as the Capucins of Hennebont, the order of St Bernard, who occupied the abbey of Prières at Muzillac, and the Benedictines of Lanvaux were

[33] J. Moisan, *La Propriété ecclésiastique dans le Morbihan pendant la période révolutionnaire* (Vannes, 1911), 31.

[34] J.-M. le Mené, 'Abbaye de Lanvaux', *BSPM* (1902), 203–55; Buléon and Le Garrec, *Sainte-Anne-d'Auray, passim*; J.-M. Le Mené, 'Carmes de Sainte-Anne', *BSPM*, (1906), 13–38; Archives de l'Évêché de Vannes: Paroisses, prêtres et fondations . . . 1784.

filled almost entirely with men who came from well outside the region. Of the fourteen monks in the abbey of Prières in 1790, only one came from the region, and he was from the town of Vannes; five others were Bretons, but from other dioceses. The remainder, except for one man whose origins are unknown, came from Angers, Reims, Clermont, Bordeaux, Valenciennes, Cambrai and the province of Lorraine. Other orders such as the Recollets at Île-Sainte-Catherine, Port-Louis, Pontivy and Sarzeau, had more members from the immediate region and may have recruited more extensively from the popular classes. These difficulties of recruitment showed in the sparse monastic populations recorded by the revolutionaries whose job it was to liquidate the religious houses in 1790–1: in the district of Vannes, only one of the ten monasteries had more than eight members, and there were only 57 monks in all.

Religious orders for women were much better filled than those for men. In the District of Vannes, the six convents and institutions for women had a total of 212 members with anywhere from twenty to fifty nuns in each. In the diocese as a whole, women's orders appear to have enjoyed the same relative popularity and had a wider basis of recruitment than most men's orders. There were, of course, convents such as the aristocratic abbey of La Joie at Hennebont, peopled almost entirely by the daughters of the nobility and the wealthy, but houses such as the priory of Monte-Cassino at Josselin had a high proportion of members from the rural parishes of the region. Reading over the lists of members of religious houses drawn up in 1790–1 by the revolutionary authorities, one has the impression that the women's orders, especially through the institution of the lay sisters, had a much closer tie to the region through local recruitment than did the men. Certainly they were better filled and more constantly replenished with new members than the men's houses.[35]

When we look at the changes in the recruitment to religious orders for men and women, it is difficult to avoid the impression that the region conformed to the general eighteenth-century pattern of decline. Nevertheless, there are some signs that this decline was

---

[35] Tables in Le Goff, 'Vannes', 431; J.-M. Le Mené, 'Abbaye de Prières', *BSPM* (1903), 75; 'Capucins', *BSPM* (1906), 199–209; 'Abbaye de Lanvaux', 228, 'Mineurs de l'observance', *BSPM* (1906), 170–81, 182–9, 192–8; 'Abbaye de la Joie', *BSPM* (1903), 174; 'Prieurés du Diocèse', *BSPM* (1904), 41–92; A.N., D xix 17 (260) Département du Morbihan: Traitement du clergé séculier et régulier [1791].

partly reversed in the generation preceding the Revolution. To be sure, such information as we have suggests that vocations to the regular orders for men were falling. In 1766, it was reported that the number of priests and lay brothers at the abbey of Prières had declined from fifty to twenty within a generation, and this was blamed on the financial difficulties of the establishment. At the abbey of Lanvaux, membership decreased from six in 1773 to three in 1790 and, if we are to believe the Abbé Le Mené, similar falls in membership had taken place in other religious orders for men in the region.[36]

Orders for women also lost members during the course of the century but unlike the men's orders most were clearly on the way to recovery by the end of the old regime. If the aristocratic abbey of La Joie saw its population fall by one-third, from 34 to 23 between 1719 and 1790, other orders appeared to have increased the number of their vocations. The Cordelières of Auray had a total of eight professions in the period 1730–9, only four in 1740–9, five in 1750–9 and six in 1760–9, but in the last two decades of the old regime, the number of women professed rose to ten and twelve respectively. The same pattern appears in professions made at the convent of the Ursulines in Muzillac: six in 1730–9, four in 1740–9, only one in 1750–9 but twelve in 1760–9, twelve in 1770–9 and ten in 1780–9. The experience of the Ursulines of Josselin was similar: five professions between 1736 and 1739, thirteen in 1740–9, nine in 1750–9, fifteen in 1760–9, ten in 1770–9 and six in 1780–9.[37] In all these examples, the real drop in vocations came in mid-century, not at the end, and these figures are a strong argument for the continued vitality of the women's orders. Significantly, the rise in women's vocations took place in orders which appear to have drawn at least some of their members from the bourgeoisie and the countryside.

A further contrast between men's and women's orders appears in the comparative ages of men and women in orders.[38] In the District of Vannes, the median age for women was rather lower than for men: forty-three as against forty-five, but the reality was more

---

[36] Table of ordinations in Le Goff, 'Vannes', 421; but this includes outsiders; a better, though fragmentary, source are the records of professions described in Le Mené, 'Abbaye de Prières', 75; 'Abbaye de Lanvaux', 228.

[37] Le Mené, 'Abbaye de la Joie', 174; 'Cordelières d'Auray', BSPM (1907), 12–20; 'Ursulines de Muzillac', BSPM (1907), 178–97; 'Ursulines de Josselin', BSPM (1907), 21–30.

[38] All of the following is derived from A.N., D xix 17 (260).

dramatic than this difference suggests, for the majority of men's orders appear to have been suffering from a real crisis of recruitment at the end of the old regime. While roughly a fifth to a third of all nuns were aged thirty-five or less, six of the ten houses for men in the District in 1790–1 had no members in this age group at all, even though the normal age when men joined their orders was around twenty-two. The record for men's orders was held by the Carmelites of Bondon, a religious house of four men, all beyond their fiftieth year. On the other hand, among the other four orders in the District, a healthy proportion, 31 per cent, were 'young', that is, aged thirty-five or less. Why did these four orders, the Decalcinated Carmelites, the Franciscans, the Trinitaires of Sarzeau and the Recollets of Bernon have this greater appeal? It was not their resistance, or susceptibility, to Jansenism: among these religious, only the Decalcinated Carmelites of Vannes had sympathized in the 1730s with the teaching of Port-Royal.[39] Perhaps these orders retained their attraction because of habits of drawing new members from rural and non-noble families; this appears to have been the case with the Recollets, whose recruitment pattern was rather like that of the women's orders, with a brief drop in mid-century followed by a return to earlier levels.[40] At least the continued popularity of these four men's houses does serve to remind us of the danger of drawing too abrupt a contrast between men's and women's orders, the one in decay, the other in rebirth.

It would be altogether too neat if we found that, in the Revolution, it was the women's orders and the less decayed male orders whose members refused to abandon the monastic life. No such clear pattern emerged, however. To be sure, all the nuns in the District of Vannes remained completely faithful to the religious life in 1790–1, but among the men the only ones who decided unanimously to stay were the aged Carmelites of Bondon and the Benedictines of Lanvaux; the other houses split or were still undecided by 1790–1. The orders in 'renewal' were all divided, and not divided on age lines either. As one historian has noted, the decision to accept or reject the drastic reforms of the religious life proposed by the Constituent Assembly was a complex choice in which age, principles, present and future prospects of a devout life and comfortable

[39] Mahuas, 'Le Jansénisme dans le diocèse de Vannes', 213–308.
[40] Le Mené, 'Mineurs de l'observance', 192–8.

existence all weighed.[41] Attempts to analyse statistically the choice of the religious in the District of Vannes only lead to the conclusion that age, age at the time of profession and the time spent in orders had little importance in the outcome; but there was a measurable difference between houses in this matter. Just as with regiments' behaviour on the battlefield, it may in the end have been largely a question of leadership and morale. Although the behaviour of the men's orders as a group was in marked contrast to that of the women, here again, this difference should not be exaggerated. Both had been alike in having had difficulties in the middle of the eighteenth century, some of them shared in a promising but tragically shortened pre-revolutionary revival; most rejected the ill-conceived reforms the Revolutionary authorities thrust upon them, and nearly all played largely minor roles in the religious and wordly life of the faithful.

---

[41] A.N. D xix 17 (260); B. Plongeron, *La Vie quotidienne du clergé français au xviiie siècle* (Paris, 1974), 167–9; *Les Réguliers de Paris devant le serment constitutionnel (1789–1801)* (Paris, 1964); J. McManners, *The French Revolution and the Church* (London, 1969), 32–7.

CHAPTER X

THE LANDLORDS AND
THE COUNTRYSIDE

If it were possible to forget for a moment what we know of the social structure of the Vannetais countryside and the way in which peasants dominated the land; if we were to concentrate instead on the letter of the law and the physical appearance of the region, we might well be led to think that it was dominated by the nobility. They owned, after all, the largest portion of the land, as we have seen. 'Bocage aristocratique, openfield roturier'; Roger Dion's formula seems to fit the *bocage* of the Vannetais so well.[1] Legally, the seigneurial regime was in full force; article 328 of the customary law proclaimed that 'Nul ne peut tenir terre en Bretagne sans seigneur, parce qu'il n'y a aucun franc alleu en iceluy pays'; all land was held from a seigneur, most seigneurs were nobles, and these seigneurs in turn had their own seigneurs, all the way up to the duke of Brittany (who happened to be the King of France), faithfully reproducing the hierarchy of *fief* and *arrière-fief* with its multiple and fantastically complicated hierarchies of subordination familiar to students of medieval society. At the top of this creaky feudal edifice were two of the eight *baillies* of the duke of Brittany, the territories of Brouerec and Ploërmel, which covered the territory of the diocese of Vannes, but these jurisdictions seem to have had no functions whatsoever in the eighteenth century.

It is below the level of the *baillie* that the remains of the feudal system in Brittany had some direct relation to property ownership. Each of the *baillies* was subdivided into secondary fiefs, some of which had been retained in the hands of the Duchy and later the Crown, while others had their own seigneurs. Around Vannes, the major fiefs of this kind were the seigneurie of Largouet, the *régaires* of Vannes and the royal jurisdictions of Rhuys, Auray and Vannes.

---

[1] M. Bloch, *Les Caractères originaux de l'histoire rurale française*, (Paris, 1952), ii, 65.

Largouet had been bought by Fouquet under Louis XIV's reign; during most of the eighteenth century it was owned by the *président* of the Parlement of Brittany, Toussiant de Cornulier and his heirs. The *régaires* of Vannes were the fief of the bishop, while the jurisdictions of Rhuys, Vannes and Auray were held by the Crown.

In relation to their size, these fiefs had very little land remaining to them as part of their domains; most of their territory was enfeoffed (*afféagé*) as noble or *roturier* fiefs. On these lesser fiefs, the superior lord had two rights; the collection of small feudal dues and the exercise of justice over that part of the inferior fief reserved by its lord and worked either by himself or by his tenants.[2] The direct impact of these greater fiefs on the life of the rural community was slight except, as will be seen, for the administration of justice.

Those parts of the great pyramid left from feudal society which were most apparent to country folk were the lesser fiefs which extended over the land they worked and lived on. Their visible symbols were the sixteenth- and seventeenth-century manors and the occasional neoclassical country house which dotted the region and around which peasant holdings were at least legally and often physically grouped, evoking even today the deceptive impression of a paternal rural society under the aegis of a resident gentry. Consider, for example, a fairly typical *arrière-fief*, the seigneurie of Coëtcandec and La Chenaye, in the parish of Grand-Champ, made up of two fiefs which had been united and which, when their boundaries are traced on a cadastral survey of the mid-nineteenth century, can be seen to have suffered considerable fragmentation before 1789.[3] There was, first of all, a chateau, attached to the seigneurie of Coetcandec. Beyond the chateau and the woods which stood by it extended the demesne. This land was not worked directly by the seigneur, but farmed out. Around the chateau were two or three *métairies,* which were leased for a simple rent in money and grain, but the greatest part of the demesne was leased under the system of *domaine congéable.* Finally, beyond the limits of the demesne the seigneur claimed certain *rentes féodales* on property which had been alienated from his demesne and which was now held mostly by other seigneurs, who in turn leased out their own demesne to peasant farmers.

---

[2] L.-A. Le Moyne de la Borderie, *Essai sur la géographie féodale de la Bretagne avec la carte des fiefs et seigneuries de cette province* (Rennes, 1889), 105–61; Giffard, *Les Justices seigneuriales,* 44–8.

[3] Appendix 3.

Although this seigneurie does contain most of the elements of the lower fiefs of the region, it is not typical in all respects. It was, to begin with, the largest seigneurie in the parish, and as its seigneur resided for part of the year, the chateau was kept in a state of repair. Only one or two nobles did reside on their lands in each parish; most farmed out the manor house, the manorial enclosure (*pourpris*), forests and gardens to peasants, or even bourgeois on occasion, in return for simple land rents. In the parish of Theix, there were ten seigneuries, one of which belonged to the convent of Nazareth in Vannes; in Grand-Champ there were twelve seigneuries, plus two ecclesiastical seigneuries. But although most lands were held within the framework of the seigneurie, there were nevertheless a large number of detached plots owned by nobles and bourgeois which did not form part of their seigneuries. At least thirty nobles and twenty-five bourgeois, for example, held such plots in Grand-Champ, composed of one or more tenures without the dignity of fiefs, which they leased out in turn as *métairies, fermes* or *domaines congéables* to peasants who tilled the soil.

Thus the countryside of the Vannetais was, apparently under the domination of the seigneurs who were usually nobles, apparently masters of the soil. What were the conditions of their rule? The first question to ask is a simple but important one: where were they? A short answer would be that they were not as present as the abundance of their little chateaux and manors might suggest. In the fifteenth and the sixteenth century the nobility—no doubt a combination of declining petty feudal nobles and new 'gentry'—really do appear to have dominated the countryside, like so many Squire Westerns. But, in contrast, during the seventeenth and eighteenth centuries, the rural landlord was more likely to be absent than resident. Nothing is more revealing than to compare the lists of nobles who appeared for the *montres* and *réformations* of the fifteenth and sixteenth centuries[4] with the decimated ranks of the nobility mustered in 1694 at the last *arrière-ban* of the old regime,[5] or with the *capitation* rolls of 1710 or the 1780s.[6]

It is also highly suggestive to compare the distribution of the nobility in the countryside of the Vannetais and the Breton-speaking

[4] De Laigue, *La Noblesse bretonne.*
[5] Guyot-Jomard, 'La Ville de Vannes et ses murs', 68–85.
[6] Meyer, *La Noblesse bretonne* i, 10–27; ii, carte hors texte; A.D. Morbihan, C: Commission intermédiaire de Vannes: 4 paroisses de Vannes: Capitation de Messieurs de la Noblesse, 1781.

part of the diocese in these three later documents with that in the French-speaking part of the diocese, since a poor and numerous petty nobility is often thought of as being characteristic of Lower Brittany. An analysis of the residences of the nobles in all these documents shows a clear pattern. At the *ban* of 1694, there appeared from the rural Breton-speaking part of the diocese—with a population more than twice as great as that of the French-speaking region—only half as many nobles (46) as in the French-speaking section (86). The *capitation* of 1710 reveals a similar pattern, and so does the *capitation* roll of 1781, seventy years later. A more detailed analysis based on this last document shows that there were a total of 85 noble households in the 52 rural parishes of the French-speaking part of the bishopric, but only 80 families for the 97 rural parishes of the *bretonnant* section. Using the population figures given by Ogée for the number of adults in each parish, the contrast between the two regions, French and Breton-speaking, becomes all the more apparent, with an average of only 4 noble households for each 10,000 people in the Breton region as against 10 for 10,000 in the French-speaking area. The region around Vannes, with which we are more directly concerned, reflects this division, with only 6 noble families for 10,000 of rural population (a figure which would be even lower, were it not for the anomalous situation of Sarzeau, which will be discussed later).[7]

This method of determining residence by fiscal domicile does present some difficulties, since it does not take account of double residence, the return of the noble to his country property during the summer months while remaining registered for tax purposes at his town residence. It is impossible to assess exactly how frequently this occurred, but all the contemporary sources seem to indicate that if anything the *capitation* rolls overestimate the presence of the nobility in the countryside. Unlike the bourgeois, nobles gained no fiscal advantages from being taxed in the country rather than in town, since the *capitation* was levied upon them as an order, without taking account of their place of residence. In these circumstances fiscal domicile ought to have corresponded to real domicile, and yet it did not seem to by the end of the eighteenth century. In 1786, for example, two noble families, Du Grégo and Le Sénéchal de Kerguisé, paid their taxes in the parish of Surzur, but, the *subdélégué* Brenugat de Kerveno reported in the same year,

[7] Population figures taken from Ogée, *Dictionnaire.*

les maisons de campagne autrefois peuplées sont aujourd'huy désertes, exceptée celle de M. le Marquis du Grégo, mais encore ne l'est-elle que par intervalles et depuis plusieurs mois il n'y est pas [mais] on y est revenu depuis quelques jours.[8]

In St-Jean-Brévelay, it was reported that the parish, 'quoique grande n'a aucun seigneur qui y réside';[9] in Séné the parish council complained in the 1760s that 'les Messieurs de la Noblesse ont tous abandonné un si triste séjour; pas une seule maison noble en Séné n'est habitée.'[10] Many of the nobles resident in Vannes on an apparently permanent basis were still being taxed in their country residences.[11] It seems likely then, that official records exaggerate, rather than underestimate, the proportion of nobles residing on their lands.

When nobles were present, they could make their influence felt in the community, and they do occasionally appear as the paternal protectors of 'their' peasants. The comte de Châteaugiron, *président* of the Parlement of Brittany who owned a seigneurie situated in the parishes of Grand-Champ, St-Avé, Plumergat, St-Jean-Brévelay, Bignan, Meucon and Plaudren, and who resided in his chateau of La Chenaye in the parish of Grand-Champ during part of the year, was particularly distinguished for this kind of activity. During the hard winter of 1785–6 he gave generously to the inhabitants of St-Avé in their difficulties.[12] His wife founded a school in Elven in 1767 which provided free education to all children of the parish.[13]

Similarly, when in the 1740s a company of entrepreneurs sought to drain some marshlands belonging to the royal *domaine* near the village of Bilion in the parish of Ambon and the local seamen protested that these activities would block the channel to the harbour, the inhabitants were seconded by Madame de Bavalan, a local seigneur with a rival claim to ownership of the marshland, who went so far as to employ a straw man to outbid the entrepreneurs for the land and then declare himself insolvent.[14] About the same time

---

[8] A.D. I.-V., C 1747: Brénugat de Kerveno to intendant, 1786.
[9] Ibid., Freneau to intendant, 18-5-1786.
[10] A.D. Morbihan, C: Commission intermédiaire de Vannes: Domaine [1763].
[11] Above, pp. 61–3.
[12] A.D. I.-V., C 1747: Distribution de secours en argent aux pauvres, vieillards . . . 3-1-1786.
[13] P. Thomas-Lacroix, 'Mémoire inédit sur l'instruction populaire avant la Révolution', *BSPM* (1936), 93.
[14] A.D. I.-V., C 1944: 1741, 1772.

an enterprising canon in the Chapter of Vannes, Le Mercier, tried to obtain from the royal *domaine* several tracts of coastline near Carnac on which he planned to construct saltmarshes. Not surprisingly, his request met with the united opposition of the inhabitants of Carnac and the villages nearby, who complained that they would lose their access to the scrub vegetation of the beaches which they fed to their cattle, and to the seaweed they needed for fertilizer. The local *laboureurs* found a champion in another seigneur, Le Gouvello de Kerantré, whose prosperity depended on that of his tenants, and who vigorously supported their claims, informing the intendant that 'les nouveaux salinaires sont ennemis de l'état et de la province en ce que l'état n'est fort et puissant que par l'aisance des peuples'.[15]

A similar case occurred in Surzur, where the local nobles united with the rector of the parish and the peasants in resisting the encroachments of a bourgeois from Vannes, Kermasson de Riniac, on their common lands. In 1731, the bishop of Vannes, Fagon, seigneur of four villages in Surzur, had sold the rights over the commons of these villages to Kermasson in return for a feudal *cens* payment of 10 livres annually, on condition that the purchaser would divide up the lands with the inhabitants according to the procedure of *triage*. This would have given Kermasson one-third of the commons and the inhabitants the remainder. The peasants refused to proceed, so Kermasson began on his own to plant trees and dig ditches along the side of the road bordering the commons, ostensibly to protect the road. The inhabitants then took to destroying by night what had been built by day. In 1739, and again in 1740 and 1743, Kermasson met with the same resistance. Outraged, he started proceedings against seventy-two individuals, but was countered by the rector of the parish (whose presbytery bordered on the common land which he had been accustomed to use for his own purposes), by three nobles who owned land in the parish and nine other individuals. By 1771, one of these nobles, Le Sénéchal de Kerguisé, was still fighting the same battles against Kermasson's heir; like the other nobles, his own tenants' income would have been diminished and his own income from the rents they paid put in jeopardy if they could not use the common pastures.[16]

[15] A.D. I.-V., C 1994: Le Gouvello to intendant, 23-1-1740 etc.
[16] A.D. Morbihan, 31 G 36 (101): Surzur: affaires diverses.

Nobles seem to have played a similar role in the parish of Sarzeau, which, as has been seen, possessed a different system of land tenure and an economic and social structure different from the mainland. But Sarzeau contained many more nobles and bourgeois in residence than any other rural parish in the region, and with few exceptions, the propertyholders in Sarzeau were on the same footing, since all, noble, peasant, or bourgeois held their land directly from the King as the successor of the dukes of Brittany. The main exception was a local noble, Le Gouvello de Keriaval, who besides being one of the largest single landowners, also leased the local Crown lands and levied a feudal rent on all the other inhabitants. In 1781, Le Gouvello attempted to force all the inhabitants of Rhuys to carry out *corvées* or pay compensation, an innovation which neither his father, nor even his financier predecessor, Le Vacher de Lohéac, had ever attempted. In order to forestall resistance by making an example, Le Gouvello tried to force Kermasson, a local notable, and some of the priests of the parish to carry out *corvées*. It proved an unwise move, for Kermasson, together with the local bourgeois and the popular governor of the peninsula, the comte de Serent, regarded as a sort of local benefactor, led a united front of propertyholders against the encroachments of Keriaval, and took measures to put an end to the exactions of his millers.[17]

Sarzeau, in fact, presents a rather anomalous picture of a rural community in which few economic interests divided large and small proprietors though both probably combined to keep down the propertyless. The main cause of antagonism, the right of the *fermier* of the *domaine* to collect a feudal rent, served rather to unite all ranks of rural society. Certain of the local nobles, as well, living on the land, maintained a close 'paternal' relation with the multitudes of poor peasants and tenants who surrounded their properties. The older Le Gouvello himself, it was claimed, had behaved in this way; when he died, there flocked to his funeral

tous les notables . . . et très grande affluence d'habitants et de gens de campagne de toutes les frairies de la paroisse, surtout des pauvres fondant en larmes sur la perte de leur père et bienfaiteur généralement regretté de tout le pays.[18]

Similarly, the family of Francheville, which had contributed one

[17] A.D. Morbihan, B: Sénéchaussée de Rhuys, minutes: extrait du registre des délibérations de la ville et communauté de Rhuys, 22-5-1781.
[18] A.D. Morbihan, E^c: Sarzeau, décès, 18-9-1780.

mystic and one bishop to the Church, maintained at its own expense a hospital for the shelter of the poor in Sarzeau.[19] The eccentric and not untalented comte de Serent gave patriotic *fêtes* in the 1780s which combined aspects of the religious *pardon*—the feasts were held on saints' days—with tinges of philosophy and the atmosphere of a country fair. Serent was regarded half in fear, half in awe by the members of the *communauté de ville* and the parish at large as a power at court and the protector of the community.[20]

In these and similar cases the noble—or any other propertied person—who resided on his lands could play the role of a paternal notable in his parish. However, outside of the anomalous *pays* of Rhuys, such cases were the exception, and most often the landlord of the Vannetais, noble or otherwise, was an absentee. In these circumstances, he had little of the feudal or patriarchal about him. There is little evidence to prove that the landowning notable in the Vannetais dominated the peasants and other rural folk in any special way by virtue of his prestige, munificence and the role he played in the rural community. This was not to say that he could not do so to some extent when he was present, but with a few exceptions, the peasant was largely left to himself.

There is, however, another kind of control and another way in which landlords could make their influence felt and possibly earn the antagonism of the rural community, no matter how distinct they were from it. This was by economic pressure, and more particularly through the seigneurial system. It will be as well to look, then, at how the various aspects of the seigneurie, closely tied up with the position of the nobility and the bourgeoisie in the countryside, impinged on the world of the peasant.

The day-to-day administration of the seigneurie in the lord's absence was such that it did not intrude greatly in the social life of the peasants. The *domaine congéable,* the chief form of landholding on seigneuries in Lower Brittany was a system admirably designed

---

[19] A.D. Morbihan, C: Subdélégation de Rhuys, Paroisse de Sarzeau, vingtième, 1754; J.-M. Le Mené, 'Communautés situées hors Vannes', 27; *Histoire de diocèse de Vannes*, ii, 105–7, 129–30, 143–4, 155; A. Guillemot, 'Fondation de l'hôpital de Sarzeau par Marie-Pierre de Francheville', *BSPM* (1967), 13–20.

[20] e.g. A.D. Morbihan, B: Sénéchaussée de Rhuys, minutes: Guillaume Rufflet, marchand chaudronnier contre François Bosquet, 1777. On the *Société patriotique,* see P. Kerviler, *Armorique et Bretagne* (Paris, 1892–3), ii, 283–340; A. de La Borderie, 'Le Baron de Kerker et son château', *Revue de Bretagne et de Vendée*, nouvelle série, ii (1887), 337–54; S. Faye, 'La Société patriotique bretonne 1780–1790', *BSPM* (1942), 92–108.

for the absentee landlord, requiring only a check at the end of the lease, if then, to make sure that the tenant had not improved or damaged his holding. The provision, traditional in all leases of tenures under *domaine congéable,* that tenants were to transport their rents in kind to any place within three leagues designated by the landlord or his representative meant the close supervision of the harvest and collection of the rents on the spot was unnecessary. Six *corvées* a year were due to the seigneur, but in his absence, they were rendered to whoever farmed the manorial *pourpris,* if indeed they had not been converted to cash payments.[21]

Seigneurial justice was rarely meted out by the landlord because, under the *usement* of Brouerec, land held under *domaine congéable* was considered to form part of the landlord-seigneur's demesne and so was subject to the next highest seigneurial jurisdiction. In most cases in the Vannetais the higher jurisdiction was either the *régaires* of the bishop of Vannes or the seigneurie of Largouet, owned by the absentee Toussaint de Cornulier and his descendants. Both of these courts held their sessions in Vannes, and functioned as impersonally as the district and local courts which succeeded them after 1789.[22]

Thus the power of judging civil and criminal cases in first instance, which seigneurs elsewhere in France could sometimes wield against peasants was largely non-existent. True, as local notables, the seigneurs could use the machinery of royal justice or of superior feudal jurisdictions to enforce their predominance, if they lived in the area. One of the examples used to illustrate this kind of control is the general 'disarming' of the peasants undertaken in Brittany by the royal government after 1769 on the request of the nobles, who were concerned to prevent poaching; legally no peasant was supposed to usurp the hunting rights of the landlords. At Ouis in Surzur in 1771, two nobles used the proclamations of the commander-in-chief of Brittany, the duc de Duras, to disarm several individuals.[23] But it may be doubted how effective was royal justice as an extension of the power of the seigneurs unless the lord actually lived in

---

[21] For example, A.D. Morbihan, E^n 33–34: Minutes Josse: Ferme par écuyer A.-J.-F.-L. Henry, capitaine garde-côte . . . du pourpris du lieu noble de Kerdu en Plescop, 4-7-82; ferme des pourpris, maison des Farrières en Sulniac donnée par les héritiers Rosmadec à la ve Lozevis & enfants, 15-9-1781: Thomas-Lacroix, 'La Condition des terres', 360.

[22] Giffard, *Les Justices seigneuriales,* 28–31, 99.

[23] Sée, *Les Classes rurales en Bretagne,* 149–54.

the parish and was able to keep a check on the activity of 'his' peasants. Even after the proclamation of the duc de Duras, guns were still listed in the *inventaires après décès* of peasants.[24] Then, too, royal justice had its limitations, limitations imposed above all by the pitifully small numbers of police available in the *maréchaussée;* in the face of a silent community, defending itself against the 'outside', royal justice was practically powerless.[25]

In the absence of most of the landlords, the day-to-day control of estates was not very thorough. One means of administering the seigneurie was to leave the affair in the hands of a notary or businessman, sometimes from the immediate area, more often from Vannes. In the 1780s, demoiselle Yvonne Thimony, widow of Augustin Symon, served as receiver and agent for nobles such as Malo de Query, seigneur of Larré, while Le Monnier, in Theix, acted for the heirs of the Rosmadec family in Paris, who possessed large holdings to the southwest of Vannes, in Theix and Surzur.[26] Yves Curière of Vannes signed leases for the abbé du Pargo, who lived in Rennes, and for M. de la Sentière, resident in Morlaix; P.-J. Perret, a notary in Vannes, acted as the agent for demoiselle Jeanne-Marie Le Mintier Le Hellec, who was a *pensionnaire* at the convent of the Sisters of Charity in Vannes.[27] Sometimes rents could be paid to a prosperous peasant acting as the landlord's agent; although not many instances of this are to be found.[28] A large number of leases were signed by the nobles who lived in the region themselves.[29]

The practice of the *ferme générale,* the letting out of the whole seigneurie at once to a single person who then ran the operation as best he could for his own profit, seems to have been rarely employed; at least in the several hundred examples of inventories of papers after death examined for the last generation of the old

---

[24] e.g. A.D. Morbihan B: Largouet, minutes: *Inventaires après décès* of Marie le Quil, veuve Mathurin Conan (Plaudren), Julien Anno (St-Nolf), François Nouail (Elven), 1775. In addition, members of the *milice gardes-côtes,* the coastal militia, to which several of the parishes were subject, were armed; C. Durand, *Les Milices garde-côtes de Bretagne de 1716 à 1792* (Rennes, 1927), 31–2, 70–2.

[25] Le Goff and Sutherland, 'The Revolution and the Rural Community', 96–107.

[26] A.D. Morbihan, E^n 33: Minutes Josse, 1780.

[27] A.D. Morbihan, E^n 3459–68: Minutes Le Ridant.

[28] Two of the few are in A.D. Morbihan B: Largouet, minutes: inventaire chez Pierre le Chenay, 11-5-1775: 17 C 5325–6: 25-6-1783, 5-4-1785.

[29] Cf. Meyer, *La Noblesse bretonne,* ii, 813.

regime it has been impossible to find more than one example of a lease granted by a *fermier-général*.[30] There were a few other rich peasants, businessmen, or relatives of clerics who undertook such leases,[31] particularly for the holdings of court nobility such as the family of Rohan-Chabot;[32] but on the whole one is forced to the conclusion that the practice was not widespread in the Vannetais. The reason is not difficult to guess: the seigneurial regime, as practised in Lower Brittany, required little direct management of the demesne, and it was scarcely worth giving a *fermier-général* a sizeable share of the profits for managing an enterprise which a landlord's notary could handle just as easily for a fixed fee.

It has been claimed that the peculiar nature of the *domaine congéable* gave the proprietor of the *fonds,* absent or resident, immense power over the *tenuyer.* According to the rector of St-Patern in 1789, claiming to speak for the peasants, the *tenuyers* were 'sujet au caprice du seigneur qui les expulse à volonté'[33] while the *cahiers de doléances* of the region claimed that

La crainte des congés rend les colons vraiment esclaves; à la fin des baux, on leur dit; 'Vous payerez en augmentation, tant pour rente annuelle et tant pour commission ou pot de vin, autrement, je vous congédie.' L'homme attaché aux lieux qui l'ont vu naître, où il a des habitudes, subit la loi rigoureuse et s'épuise.[34]

or again

La faculté qu'ont les seigneurs de congédier tous les neuf ans le colon, leur donne les moyens d'augmenter et d'étendre les rentes et le prix du renouvellement des baux.[35]

Nothing is of course harder to establish than this kind of vague but potentially very great coercive power which a landlord can wield over his tenants. Part of these claims can be said to be false, in that

---

[30] Pierre, Jacob and Louis Le Marouille, *fermiers-généraux* of the seigneurie of Tremantec in A.D. Morbihan, B: Largouet, minutes: inventaire chez Bertrand Guillerme, St-Avé, 26, 27-9-1785.

[31] A.D. Morbihan, E[n] 3460: Ferme de Kergonan dans Plouharnel par M. l'abbé de Boutouillic de Villegonan, Vannes, 23-3-1782. The annual rent of 1,220 l. over nine years gave the right to dispose of the principal house, garden, *pourpris*, and an income of 47¾ *perrées* of wheat from dependent tenures.

[32] Meyer, *La Noblesse bretonne,* ii, 813.

[33] Le Goff, 'Les Doléances des paysans du Vannetais', 43.

[34] P. Thomas-Lacroix, 'Les Cahiers de doléances de la sénéchaussée d'Hennebont', *MSHAB,* xxxv (1965), 51 art. 181.

[35] 'Cahier des plaintes, doléances et demandes du tiers-état de la sénéchaussée de Vannes en Bretagne', *Archives parlementaires,* vi, 111 art. 145.

the landlords did not carry out expulsions themselves. The *seigneur foncier* was, however, certainly able to profit from the demand for land to raise rents, allowing peasants to exercise the landlord's right to expel their neighbours in return for a higher rent. But this did not give the landlord unlimited power, for he too was a victim of the fluctuations of the economy. As we have seen, it was not the landlord who raised the cash necessary to reimburse the outgoing tenant; it would have been foolish for the seigneur to take the trouble of raising cash to reimburse the value of the edifices in an area where specie was often in short supply and when his own means were as likely as not rather limited themselves; if Jacques wished to expel Pierre and take over his holding, Jacques could raise the capital himself. Unfortunately for the landlord, however, the ability of peasants, land-hungry as they were, to expel their neighbours varied widely from year to year, depending on the amount of cash they could raise, which in turn depended on the vagaries of harvests and grain prices.

Similarly, the seigneur could in theory refuse the peasant the right of subletting his land, but it may be wondered how effective such a right was when the landlord and his agent saw the occupant of the tenure only once a year. In any case, the tenant, if he wanted to, could simply sell the edifices of the tenure to another peasant, and leave it to him to conclude a new lease with the landlord; for this operation no preliminary agreement was necessary and the landlord, faced with a new tenant on his *fonds,* had the choice of accepting the *fait accompli* or looking for yet another tenant—and possibly sacrificing a year's revenue in the meantime.[36]

In general, the too-obvious wielding of a landlord's or seigneur's powers was likely to provoke costly reprisals. The Parlement of Brittany, acting as the landlords' defender, had proclaimed in judgements in 1724 and 1736, and reiterated in later pronouncements, that the seigneurs had the absolute property of all wastelands, but when local landlords like the bishop of Vannes, the Chapter or nobles like the Du Grégo family tried to exercise those rights and concede waste generally regarded as common land to chosen tenants, they provoked enduring and costly wars of attrition with the rest of the peasants, for the commons were an important source of fodder, temporary crops and *marnis,* a kind of marl used for ferti-

---

[36] Baudouin de Maisonblanche, *Institutions convenantières,* ii, 174–6.

lizing.[37] The Du Grégo family, like some others, did try to assert these and other seigneurial rights in the course of the eighteenth century, attempting, for example to make their tenants holding land under *domaine congéable* present *aveux* outstanding for many years. Such conduct is part of what historians have long considered the 'seigneurial reaction', to which the intendant of Brittany, Bertrand de Moleville, alluded in 1788 in speaking of 'un régime féodal de plus en plus rigoreux'.[38] What is less often noted, but equally significant, is that the behaviour of the seigneurs suggests that laxity, not rigour, was a frequent vice of seigneurial administration. Or perhaps it was mere prudence; one of the reasons for Du Grégo's near bankruptcy at the end of the old regime seems to have been the large numbers of lawsuits in which his harsh treatment of his tenants involved him.[39]

A heavy hand did not make seigneurs or landlords liked either, as Bertrand de Moleville went on to note. How many peasants must have felt as Jean Dréan, the *métayer* of a certain Sieur de Kermorin who, expelled by his landlord in 1780, refused to leave, cutting firewood and scouring what he could from the land until forced out. Upbraided by Kermorin's wife for this churlish behaviour, he retorted by calling her 'putain, bourgresse, charogne' and threatened to skewer her with his pitchfork.[40] It was a far cry from the patriarchal society.

If it is true that, notwithstanding, the landlord under *domaine congéable* did wield a kind of economic power, it is also true that the landlord was at the mercy of his tenants and their neighbours. Indeed, it was in the interest of the landlord to maintain a stable and sound class of peasant on his domaine. The sieur Métinville de Talhouet, the owner of a tenure in Arradon found that his agent, a certain Dubois, had leased one of his tenures under *domaine congéable* to Jean Hérve, a peasant, who sought to expel the occupant, Sébastien Hulbron. When the actual proceedings for expulsion got under way in 1783, Métinville intervened to stop them on the grounds that the lease was subject to his approval, which he had

[37] Above, pp. 210, 276 and H. du Halgouet, *Archives des châteaux bretons: iii Inventaire des archives du château du Grégo (1343–1830)* (St-Brieuc, 1913), 99–102; A.D. Morbihan, 47 G 7 (376): November 1773.
[38] Giffard, *Les justices seigneuriales*, 248 n. 2.
[39] Du Halgouet, *Château du Grégo*, 86, 98–100, 102.
[40] A.D. Morbihan, B: Largouet, minutes: sieur de Kermorin v. Jean Dréan, 1780.

never given; he pointed out to the court that Dubois had rented the land to unreliable tenants: 'Il est bien éloigné d'approver une baillée qui lui enlève des vasseaux riches pour y substituer d'autres peu aisés et hors d'état de rembourser de leurs propres deniers.'[41] The control of the seigneur over his tenants through the pressure he was able to exert as a landlord under *domaine congéable* was by no means absolute; it was subject to the willingness and ability of other peasants to co-operate with the landlord in expelling their own neighbours, and tempered by the landlord's unwillingness to lose money himself in a costly expulsion procedure.

Although the *domaine congéable* was the characteristic way in which the direct domain of the seigneurie was let out, it was not essentially a 'feudal' system of tenure—at least, if we adopt the final decision of the Revolutionary authorities—but rather a form of leasehold. This seems an appropriate point, then, to assess the benefits of the various forms of landed revenues, 'feudal' and otherwise, to the landlords and their weight on the people working the land.

Seigneurial revenues, as distinct from those of the *domaine congéable* and from simple land rents, were of two kinds, fixed and casual. Casual revenues consisted chiefly of the *lods et ventes* and *rachats,* levied on property transactions and successions on land which had been alienated from the seigneur, but on which he still collected *cens* and other feudal dues. These casual revenues were of no great importance to peasants in the Vannetais, for the simple reason that so few peasants were proprietors in the full sense. Neither land leased out as *métairies* nor even land subject to the *domaine congéable* was considered to have been alienated from the seigneur's domain and it was on these two types of holdings that the majority of peasants resided.[42]

A glance at the revenues of seigneuries such as Coëtcandec and La Chenaye, held by the La Bourdonnaye family, or the fief of the Chapter of Vannes in Grand-Champ, or the three seigneuries given as examples of noble holdings in Lower Brittany by Meyer, shows the small importance of fixed feudal dues in the total income of the seigneur. Similarly, the family of Châteaugiron, which held eight-

---

[41] A.D. Morbihan, 17 C 5322: fol. 100.
[42] 'Supplement de l'Usement de Brouërec. Extrait des mémoires du sieur Gatechair', in Sauvageau, *Coutumes de Bretagne,* i, 25–30; cf. Baudouin de Maisonblanche, *Institutions convenantières,* ii, 177.

een seigneuries scattered throughout Lower Brittany, obtained only about 13 per cent of its revenues from this source.[43] This, however, does not tell the whole story. Some of the higher fiefs such as that of Largouet, collected feudal dues from seigneurs such as the La Bourdonnaye family and the Chapter, and these dues were in turn passed on to the *tenuyers*. Thus on the one complete tenure belonging to the Chapter in Grand-Champ on which such rents were due, they amounted to one *perrée* of oats, worth about 5 lives in the period 1726–39 and 11 livres between 1773 and 1789, or about 19 per cent of the total rent which the peasant paid.

There were three other forms of dues and obligations which applied to virtually all peasants working the land. One was the *dîme inféodée*, tithes which had been taken over by nobles and levied in addition to the ecclesiastical tithe or in place of it; another was the seigneurial tithe, scarcely distinguished from the first. But as far as can be deduced from the surveys of church property which have been done for the region, *dîmes inféodées* were rare in the area about Vannes, except in the parish of Sarzeau and on some of the islands of the gulf of the Moribihan.[44] The second form of the seigneurial regime which applied to more than just the holders of land under *domaine congéable* was the obligation to perform *corvées* and make token payments symbolic of the seigneur's lordship; and the third was the requirement of 'following' the seigneur's mill.

If these dues were in theory distinguishable from the *domaine congéable*, they were in practice very closely tied up with it, since so many of the dues which are often thought of as 'feudal' were written into the lease: the annual delivery of fowl to the landlord, a small cash payment, the obligation to perform *corvées* and grind corn at the seigneurial mill (*suite du moulin*). During the eighteenth century the practice spread of compounding for these obligations with a cash payment, translated as a simple increase in the tenant's rent. Thus landlords in the parishes of Theix, Plaudren, Grand-Champ, Plescop and Ploeren had their tenants buy exemption from the *suite du moulin* for the price of one *perrée* (1.7 hl) of rye each year. Over

---

[43] A.D. Morbihan, E 2620: Largouet: rentier des terres de Couëtcandec et la Chenaye, 1754. The revenues of Coëtcandec came to 23½ *perrées* of wheat, 40½ *perrées* of rye, 813 l. 17 s. 0 d. in cash, and no 'feudal' dues at all; those of La Chenaye consisted of 41 *perrées* of wheat, 88½ *perrées* of rye, 34 *perrées* of oats, 390 l. 3 s. 6d. in cash, plus only 1 *perrée* of oats and 4 l. 11 s. 9 u. in cash from 'fiefs'; See also Table V-2 and Meyer, *La Noblesse bretonne*, ii, 653, 856, 859.

[44] Luco, *Pouillé: Le Mené Histoire archéologique, passim.*

the years these and other exemptions became accepted as part of the rent and continued to be considered in this way into the Revolution, and indeed the legislation of the Constituent Assembly favoured this attitude. So, although the pattern of landholding in the region gave the seigneurs some income which might be termed more or less accurately as 'feudal', most of it was absorbed in, and formed only a minor part of, the *domaine congéable*, the predominant form of tenure. The owners of most seigneuries were landlords rather than seigneurs.

Were they successful as landlords? The evidence of land sales in the eighteenth century suggests that they were at least not abandoning their land; quite the contrary. To judge their performance beyond this depends on what criterion of success is used. If we take a modern one, the rate of return on invested capital, they do not really appear as profit-minded entrepreneurs. Baudouin de Maisonblanche reckoned the capitalized value of the *fonds* at 4 per cent.[45] In reality, the return on capital seems to have been rather lower. If we take the average price paid for the *fonds* of tenures by nobles in the period 1773–89 (6,600 l.) or by bourgeois (3,900 l.), and compare it with average rents in Grand-Champ (around 100 l.) in the same period, we get an annual return of only about 2 to 3 per cent.[46] *Métayage* and *fermage* gained three or more times this amount, that is, upwards of 6 per cent. If the *tenuyer* had made the same calculation of the return in rent from a sub-tenant, to the capital he had paid for his edifices, the result might have been shocking: the average set of edifices went for 1,200 to 1,500 livres in the region in the period 1740–89 but even if we round this up as high as 2,000 livres to allow for the inevitable exceptions which pull an average down, an average subletting of these tenures at three times the rental value, or about 200 livres (300 livres less 100 livres to the landlord of the *fonds*), would have given them the prospect of a 10 per cent annual return! This is obviously a rough estimate,[47] but it gives an order of size, and it is clear that the *rentiers du sol* who

[45] Baudouin de Maisonblanche, *Institutions convenantières*, i, 215.

[46] Table XI-2 and A.D. Morbihan, 65 G 1–6 (491); E^n 1866, 3466, 4376; 17 C 5197–5335: Contrôle des actes; H 22–44; C: Subdélégation de Vannes, paroisse de Grand-Champ: vingtièmes, 1751–6, summarized in a table in Le Goff, 'Vannes', 439–40.

[47] The official of the *centième denier* reckoned it at a conventional rate of only 5 per cent, but this was still at least double the landlord's return. Baudouin de Maisonblanche recognized the anomaly in *Institutions convenantières*, ii, 172: 'L'estimation des droits reparatoires en congément n'a nul rapport avec leur revenu'.

depended on rents from the *domaine congéable* were being handily beaten by their own tenants in the race for landed revenues.

Why did they allow this situation to continue? For there were remarkably few attempts to convert the tenures into more profitable *métairies*, or combine them into larger and more economical holdings, though in law there was nothing to prevent the landlords from doing so. Indeed, some landlords changed *métairies* into *domaines*.[48] Several explanations can be advanced. One is that the landlords were being 'throttled' by the rise in prices and could not afford to expel their tenants. While this may have been true of some of the smaller landlords, it cannot have been true of all of them: the edifices on a tenure could be bought for 2,000 livres or so, sometimes less—half a year's benefices for a canon of the cathedral of Vannes.

Another explanation is that the landlords simply did not make the same calculations of profit and percentage returns to capital that we do. This is true, but only up to a point. No doubt, for the landlords, the tenures assured a comfortable income, and that was enough for most of them. Yet the landlords were not blind to the possibility, indeed the necessity, of increasing the income from their holdings. They reacted to the price rises of the eighteenth century as one might expect rational landlords to react: they raised the rents, even if they did not raise them as drastically as elsewhere in France, for they only just kept ahead of the rise in grain prices.[49]

In fact, there were at least plausible and sometimes quite solid economic reasons for a landlord's not transforming a *domaine congéable* into a *ferme* or *métairie*. The *domaine congéable* gave the landlord, first of all, a more stable tenant, from the better part of rural society, while the sharecropper or *fermier* was a potential drifter, without the means and the stake in his holding that the *tenuyer* had. Secondly, if the landlord bought out his tenant's edifices, he could look forward to the recovery of his 1,000 or 2,000 livres of scarce capital only after about ten years, assuming—and this was an unreasonable expectation—that his new sharecropper or *fermier* did not fall behind on his payments or simply steal away unnoticed at the end of a bad growing season, as at least two of the merchant Desruisseaux's sharecroppers did; the hope of gain was

---

[48] See below, p. 311.
[49] Below, pp. 298–9.

nullified by the cost of buying out the tenant.[50] But perhaps the most convincing explanation goes beyond these short-term consider-ations: the fact seems to have been that neither landlords nor peasants were able to conceive of changing the rules of the economic system in which they lived in order to increase their shares of the profits. So, if the landlords raised the rents to make up for the increased profits of the *tenuyer,* they did not make any move to get rid of the *domaine congéable* and replace it with tenant farms which might possibly have allowed for technical innovation and an im-provement in yield. Probably the idea never occurred to them. And then, even if it had, how many of that comfortable group of mid-dling peasants would have been ready or bold enough to come forward and be the agents of 'progress' by accepting to replace not one, but several of their neighbours as *gros fermiers,* paying higher rents but reaping economies of scale from a large holding on the English model? True, there were some wealthy and grasping men within the rural community. No doubt they would have had to face long struggles with their neighbours if they had co-operated in such a move. But would it have occurred to them to do so? And, if it had, how many could have afforded it? Many of the expulsions by which one tenant replaced another were only possible because they were carried out on credit. In the later eighteenth century, an unknown monk of the abbey of Lanvaux cast a rough account of the abbey's rent income from its tenures and concluded resignedly that there was no way of increasing the rents because, if they expelled their tenants, nobody else could be found in the parish to replace them.[51] Landlords and tenants, the tenants of the tenants, and, of course, the landless poor were locked in a cultural and economic system with no apparent way out; indeed, no means of changing it was found until the mid-nineteenth century or, some might say, the twentieth.

The existence of a link between the systems of land tenure, rural social structure, and a certain form of culture was perceived intuit-ively and violently attacked at the time of the Revolution by the more radical revolutionaries, men such as the future regicide J.-M. Le Quinio:

[50] A.D. Morbihan, E 2259¹, 1781.

[51] A.D. Morbihan, H 31: Abbaye de Lanvaux (unclassified): 'Livre assez instructif' [*c.* 1756].

Il n'est point en France de province où la féodalité ait conservé plus long-temps sa barbare domination [he wrote in 1790] qu'en Bretagne. Cette domination a conservé la servitude: la servitude a conservé l'abrutisse-ment: l'abrutissement, la misère et le défaut d'industrie. Toutes ces calamités sociales, soutenues par un idiôme particulier [the Breton language] jettent sur une moitié de cette grande Province l'empreinte de l'humiliation et la détresse. . . .

Je croirai que l'effet de ce régime [the *domaine congéable*] sera toujours de conserver les colons de la Bretagne dans l'état d'abrutissement, d'anéantisse-ment, de misère où tous les voyageurs l'aperçoivent.

Je croirai que l'effet de ce régime sera toujours l'étouffement des facultés intellectuelles, l'amortissement du zèle, la stagnation de l'industrie et la plus meurtrière indifférence pour une culture qui donnerait au-delà des besoins indispensables.[52]

The solution for this impasse, he thought, lay in two directions: economic—the abolition of the *domaine congéable,* and cultural—making the peasants like the 'laboureurs d'Angleterre et des environs de Paris'.[53]

For all his prejudices and bias, Le Quinio may have stumbled on the best explanation for the attitude of landlords and tenants in the Vannetais; assuredly he was wrong to put the blame on the *domaine congéable* for maintaining this system of which it was as much an effect as a cause, but he glimpsed the fact that it was part of a cultural complex which in its way functioned well enough; distri-buting profit, rewarding hard work—at least for those who had resources to work with—and in which the landlord intruded little. The landlords and the *tenuyers* were, in a way, partners in what prosperity there was in the countryside, although they probably did not realize it; they were also partners in maintaining the rigidity of its social structure.

However, it is unlikely that either *tenuyers* or landlords saw things this way. There were nobles who dwelt in the country, and when they did, they were capable of exercising some influence based on prestige, *bienfaisance* or coercion. But they were present in ever-decreasing proportions, and by the end of the century most landlords were absentees. The basic relationship of landlords,

---

[52] J.-M. Le Quinio, *Élixir du régime féodal,* 7–8, 45.
[53] *Idem, École des laboureurs; ouvrage dans lequel on explique . . . ce que c'est que la Révolution françoise . . ., ou lettre familière aux laboureurs de Bretagne* (2nd ed., Vannes, 1790), 4.

whether noble or bourgeois, with their tenants was an economic one, expressed in the *domaine congéable,* and occasionally by *métayage* and *fermage,* and that relationship was that of a landlord and tenant, not a seigneur and vassal, regardless of the terminology employed in the leases and despite the fossils of medieval feudalism which still survived in legal texts and in rural geography.

Yet the existence of this 'cash nexus' alone was not enough to transform the countryside. If a change in the rules of the economic game were to take place, it had to come from the side of the landlords, or perhaps from an injection of urban investment and a new group of landlords. That, and much more, depended in turn on the shifts and swings in the regional economy over the century, the subject to which we now turn.

CHAPTER XI

REGIONAL ECONOMY AND SOCIAL CHANGE, 1730–1789

Prices, wages, revenues, taxes and population rose throughout the Atlantic world during the eighteenth century. Their upward course was hesitant and unequal, but everywhere they rose, and in doing so played a major role in those social transformations which in France were already apparent before the end of the old regime.[1] It is not therefore an idle amusement to trace the flux of prosperity and penury, the possibilities and realities of economic development and the social consequences of economic changes for this particular corner of France.

Despite the importance which has been placed on grain production in the preceding chapters, it would be wrong to consider that the wealth of the Vannetais depended entirely upon it. There was some industry, as the eighteenth century understood the term (e.g. shipbuilding, textiles, leatherworking, the building trades) in and about Vannes; there were 'service' industries if one counts the little merchant fleets of the Île d'Arz, Sarzeau and the Île-aux-Moines. But the market for secondary production was largely local and, presumably, unchanging, given the stagnant local population. Shipbuilding was an exception, but the average annual production of ships in Vannes itself came to only 200 *tonneaux* or so a year during the two decades of its greatest development at the end of the old regime; this could have brought in a gross revenue of about 20,000 to 30,000 livres at most. The merchant fleet based in Vannes depended on the availability of exports and does not, as we shall see, seem to have known much consistently increased activity, though a larger number of sailors may well have gone to work for shippers in Nantes for longer or shorter periods of time. Nevertheless, when all these

---

[1] C.-E. Labrousse, *Esquisse du mouvement des prix et des revenus en France au xviiᵉ siècle*, 2 vols. (Paris, 1933) and *La Crise de l'économie française à la fin de l'ancien régime et au début de la Révolution*, i (Paris, 1944).

factors are taken into consideration, primary production seems to have accounted for most of the region's earnings from outside.

Even so, the primary production of the region was not limited to grain alone. Farms produced dairy products and hides for the tanneries of Vannes, and cattle, some of which were exported to Normandy and Poitou, as well as a wide range of sidelines, all of which helped the peasant get by. Hedgerows and seigneurial woods provided marketable wood for builders, shipwrights and for the fireplaces of rich and poor. The sailors of Arzon, St-Gildas and Sarzeau could try their luck at the sardine fisheries off Belle-Île. Yet grain dominated even such a varied primary sector as this and dependence on grain tied the region to the fluctuations of the French and Atlantic agricultural economy. In a middling year, it has been estimated, the port of Vannes exported about 4–5,000 *tonneaux,* or about 69,000 to 86,000 hectolitres of rye and wheat for an average value, by the 1780s, of, say, 800,000 to 1,000,000 livres; to this we can add a domestic consumption by consumers not living on farms of about 40,000 hectolitres, or another 465,000 livres' worth.[2] Even if we reduce these quantities a little, to take account of grain from adjoining regions re-exported through Vannes, they are impressive when set against rough estimates of the value of the other major forms of production of the town and its region. The total product of textiles and hides probably came to no more than 100,000 livres; marketed cattle, 150,000 to 200,000 livres at the most. The volume of wood put up for sale is simply incalculable, but to judge from Cassini's detailed late eighteenth-century map, from the activities of the merchants Danet and Jamet, and the accounts of royal forests subject to the *maîtrise des eaux et forêts,* there was only one stand of timber of any considerable size around Vannes by the end of the old regime, the 305 *arpents* of the royal forest of Lanvaux which earned about 4,000 livres a year. Most of the wood brought

---

[2] On grain exports, see above, Chapter I, pp. 14–16. The estimate of consumption by non-producers is based on an urban population of 11,000 in Vannes and Sarzeau plus about one-third of the rural population, or another 13,000. If they consumed the 'average' French ration of 3 hl/year of wheat per capita, they would have needed about 72,000 hectolitres, but because of the use of buckwheat and millet, we can reduce this to a very conservative equivalent of about 40,000 hl/year. Cf. Meyer, *La Noblesse bretonne,* i, 460; J.-C. Toutain, 'Le Produit de l'agriculture française de 1700 à 1958. I Estimation du produit au xviii\e siècle', *Cahiers de l'Institut de Sciences économiques appliquées,* série AF, 5 (juillet 1961) n° 1, 82; J.-J. Hémardinquer, *Pour une histoire de l' alimentation* (Paris, 1970), 60–7; J.-P. Aron, *Essai sur la sensibilité alimentaire* (Paris, 1967) for estimates of consumption.

down to the coast from farther in the interior went through Auray and Redon rather than Vannes. Small seigneurial woods about Vannes no doubt supplied some timber for construction, but trees in hedgerows, under *domaine congéable,* belonged to the tenant as long as their trunks were shorter than 5 *pieds* (1.6 metres); of course, as officials complained, tenants took care to see that they stayed at that height in order to keep a supply of firewood for themselves.[3]

Growth in the total wealth of the region, in the absence of significant increases in local population and levels of consumption, depended largely on the behaviour and circumstances of those peasants, perhaps a third of the rural population, who could produce more grain than they consumed, and of those landlords, clerics and lords who creamed off part of the regional production in the form of rents and tithes; it also depended on the state of the markets for which they produced. Inevitably, questions about the evolution of the regional economy are questions in the first place about the health of the grain-producing, agricultural sector.

Grain production in the Vannetais appears to have risen a little during the period from the 1720s to the 1780s. There was a little more land cleared—about 358 hectares were declared between 1768 and 1787 for the area comprising the District of Vannes after 1790—though this was a tiny fraction of the cultivated area; growth appears to have come as well from increased yields per unit of land and, perhaps, the sowing of extra crops.[4] Tithe yields give some reason to believe in a real, though limited, growth in the eighteenth century; records of tithes covering the seventeenth and eighteenth centuries indicate rises of the order of 0.3 to 0.4 per cent a year for the period 1718–89, though this increase was largely a recovery of seventeenth-century yields after a slump at the turn of the century rather than a new departure. Similarly, the growth of the local harvests, as measured by the estimates of the *subdélégués* from 1734

[3] See above, Chapter I, p. 15; the revenue from cattle is based on the cattle prices in post-mortem inventories summarized in Table XI-7 below, assuming an annual increase of 50 to 65 livres for the 3,000 households in the region with calves, yearlings and old cows and oxen to sell; on forests, M. Duval, *Forêt et civilisation dans l'Ouest au xviiie siècle* (Rennes, 1955), 94, 110–11, 151, 198–9, 247, 251, 270–1; 'Économie forestière et féodalité dans l'Ouest à la veille de la Révolution', *Annales de Bretagne,* lxiv (1957), 347–58; J.-D. Cassini, *Carte de la France, publiée sous la direction de l'Académie des sciences* (Paris, 1744–87), and see above, pp. 86–7.

[4] A.D. Morbihan, B 1378–80: Déclarations. . . . de défrichements ou dessèchements, 1768–89, the figures for 1768 include some clearing done before 1768; cf. also 30 G 1 (65): Mémoire des novales de la paroisse de Sulniac [c. 1760].

to 1788, was of the order of 0.4 per cent a year for rye and 0.5 per cent a year for wheat. It was no agricultural revolution, but the increase was comfortably greater than the rather limited population rise in western France, which ran at about 0.1 per cent a year between 1740 and 1789.[5] Had the region been isolated from the rest of the world, there might have been almost no price rise in the Vannetais.

But price rise there was. Between 1738 and 1789 wheat prices (*gros froment*) rose at an annual rate of 1.2 per cent; rye, at 1.5 per cent, oats at 1.6 per cent, and millet at 1.7 per cent. There was nothing unusual in this: it compared to the general rate for all of France in the same period. Pulled up by rising prices, leases, taxes and labour costs also rose. The reasons for this general inflation lay in the increase of the European population and the expansion of the monetary stock and instruments of credit and exchange, but the rates and the timing of the rises were everywhere different, and their effects depended on the enormously diverse social structures of each part of France.

The variation in the rates by which grain prices rose in each region were what permitted the Vannetais to export its produce towards the south, to its two major export markets, Bordeaux and the north-western Iberian peninsula. Although the profit margin on the sale of grain to these markets can be measured only for wheat, and although the advantages for Vannes merchants varied considerably from year to year, certain definite trends did exist. Thus, on the whole, the profit margin for Vannes grain on the northern Spanish market tended to get better and better from the 1720s to the mid-1760s. On the Bordeaux market, however, profits varied much more over the long run: the trend moved against exporters from roughly 1730 to 1737, favoured them increasingly until 1746, moved against them until 1753, favoured them again until 1768, and then moved against them more or less without a break until the Revolution. The periods in which grain from Vannes fetched its lowest profits in Bordeaux coincided closely with these years in which the general level of grain imports in that port was lowest: 1732, 1734–6, 1744–7, 1754–8, 1762, 1767–8. Although the Iberian market promised, on the whole, more steadily increasing profits than Bordeaux, whenever cheaper grain supplies were available from other areas, including Bordeaux itself, or even America, the chances for grain

5 Le Goff, 'Autour de quelques dîmes vannetaises'.

Table XI-1: Average yearly percentage increases of elements in rural income

Period	Rents (domaine congéable)	Commisns. (domaine congéable)	Rye prices	Wheat prices	Direct taxes	Gross tenant revenue (nominal value) (a) wheat	(b) rye	Net real tenant income	Index of expendi-ture	Expulns. (number) from centième denier	Value expulns. from centième denier	Value of expulns. from juris-diction of Largouet	Value of mortgages from juris-diction of Largouet
1728–43	—	—	1.8	1.7	—	—	—	—	—	3.0	2.5	—	—
1733–48	—	—	− 0.3	− 0.8	—	—	—	—	—	0.6	0.0	—	—
1738–53	1.2	1.7	1.2	1.2	0.2	− 4.5	− 4.2	− 5.3	1.0	− 0.9	− 0.9	—	—
1743–58	2.6	0.5	3.7	3.2	0.4	− 3.4	− 0.9	− 4.3	1.8	2.0	2.8	3.4	3.8
1748–63	2.7	1.6	0.1	− 0.2	0.4	3.9	4.1	3.5	0.5	− 1.7	− 2.1	− 1.1	0.2
1753–68	2.7	1.3	2.7	3.0	0.3	5.1	5.3	3.0	2.1	0.8	1.1	− 1.9	− 5.2
1758–73	4.3	− 0.2	5.1	3.3	0.6	3.5	4.7	0.5	3.3	1.2	2.1	0.5	− 7.6
1763–78	2.5	0.3	2.2	0.6	1.0	2.2	2.0	0.0	2.0	1.7	2.2	4.4	9.1
1768–83	0.2	0.5	− 1.5	− 1.2	1.2	3.1	0.2	1.5	0.4	− 0.1	0.9	3.5	15.1
1773–88	1.5	0.5	0.7	1.1	0.7	− 0.7	− 1.8	− 2.4	1.3	0.8	2.3	1.9	3.4
1738–89	1.8	0.8	1.5	1.2	0.6	0.6	0.5	0.5	1.5	1.2	0.8	—	—

from Vannes on the Spanish and Portuguese markets were reduced, so that the years in which the trend in profit margins for Vannes merchants in Bordeaux was downward tended to be chancy years for exporting to Spain, even if the trend there was moving in the opposite direction. This appears to have been the case particularly in the later 1770s. The market for grain from Vannes in Marseilles behaved in much the same fashion, with a long period from 1733 to 1768 in which shipments were advantageous, followed by a collapse, when rising Breton prices wiped out the hope of gains. In short, Vannes had a promising, though hazardous export market to the south, but the margins of profitability there were less wide in the 1730s, the mid-1750s, and especially after 1770.[6]

Not much is known of the functioning of the local grain market. Most of the cereals consumed in the region by non-producers were probably exchanged in the countryside, but the market in Vannes provided grain for local bakers, and for others who bought it in order to prepare dough which they took to local oven-tenders or no doubt used to make *crêpes* and porridge in the manner of the

[6] Annual percentage growth in profit margins on wheat shipments from:

	Vannes to Bordeaux	Vannes to Spain	Bordeaux to Spain
1728–43	− 0.9	1.4	2.4
1733–48	1.9	0.5	− 1.9
1738–53	0.0	0.9	1.1
1743–58	− 2.3	− 2.5	0.5
1748–63	0.0	0.4	0.4
1753–68	1.8	1.1	− 0.7
1758–73	− 0.5	0.1	0.6
1763–78	− 0.4	− 4.8	− 3.6
1768–83	− 0.3	0.3	1.0
1773–88	− 0.5	1.7	1.8

The profit margins were calculated annually by division of Bordeaux and Spanish prices by the Vannes price; an increase in this quotient over several years indicates an improvement in market conditions for Vannes producers. For Vannes prices, A.D. Morbihan B 1360–76 (1661–70 and 1739–89) and Mauricet, *Des anciennes mesures,* 45–8 (1671–1738); for Bordeaux, J. Benzacar, 'Le Pain à Bordeaux (xviiiᵉ siècle)', *Revue économique de Bordeaux,* xiv (1904), 54; for northern Spain, E. J. Hamilton, *War and Prices in Spain, 1651–1800* (Cambridge, Mass., 1947), 53, 77, 231, 242–57 (prices for Old Castile, converted to grams of fine silver). On shipments to Bordeaux and Marseilles, see P. Butel, *La Croissance commerciale bordelaise dans la seconde moitié du xviiiᵉ siècle* (Lille, 1973), ii, annexes, 125; Le Goff, 'An Eighteenth-Century Grain Merchant'; G. Rambert (ed.), *Histoire du commerce de Marseille,* vii (Paris, 1966), 150–67.

country folk. Grain sold for local consumption on the Vannes market went to feed not only townsfolk, but also people in the nearby countryside who had none of their own. As the population of the town remained rather stable, overall demand no doubt changed little; an equivalent of about 40,000 hl of wheat or rye a year does not seem an unreasonable figure. However, it is likely that in the later years of the century some local consumers shifted to buying more of the cheaper grains, as the prices of wheat and rye rose. At least, this shift is suggested by the way in which prices of the lesser grains (oats and millet), rose at a faster rate than wheat, and by the appearance of buckwheat on local market records, from which it had previously been absent, after the great price rise of 1765–72. However the recourse to cheaper grain was a response to rising prices, not falling production. There was nearly always enough grain of all sorts left on the local market at the end of each year to satisfy local needs: in the twenty-six years from 1762 to 1789, there were only four (1775, 1782, 1786, 1789) when shortages appear to have been a real problem for the town.[7] An export market was something of a necessity not only for the prosperity of local producers and shippers but for the region in general.

The social groups dependent on the production and sale of grain were variously affected by the fortunes of the grain market. In the Vannetais, those who got their income from tithes drew a double benefit from the rise in prices and the increase in production, with no more trouble than the occasional lawsuit to enforce their rights (which, to be sure, could take an exceptionally long time; the bishops of Vannes took the first half of the eighteenth century to impose their claims on all the parishioners of Theix) and the very rare incident of tithe strikes. A greater problem seems to have been the reluctance of tithe-farmers to bid for the lease when the *décimateurs* were too demanding. Those who employed salaried personnel in large numbers—such as the cathedral chapter, who had given increases to their choristers and *congruistes* in the 1760s—found themselves in some difficulty in the price slumps of the later 1770s and 1780s.[8] But even so, the tithe-holder had an enviable

---

[7] A.D. I.-V. C 1652–3: Observations sur le reste des précédentes récoltes and A.D. Morbihan, B 1370.

[8] A.D. Morbihan, 32 G 31–2 (131–3); 42 G 7 (376), March, 1778; C (unclassified): Commission intermédiaire de Vannes: Paroisse de St-Avé: État des personnes qui ont refusé de payer les prémices . . . 1771; examples of the failure to take up leases in 62 G 3 (476).

situation.

That other great rentier of the old regime, the state, had less luck than the tithe holders. In direct taxes, at least, its gross revenues were far outstripped in Brittany by inflation. For the period from 1738 to 1789, direct taxes rose on the average by only 0.6 per cent a year; only in the 1750s and the 1770s did rises catch up to the rate of price inflation which, measured by the rise of wheat and rye prices, was double or triple this rate during the same period.[9]

Those whose incomes came from rents had a much harder time meeting inflation, since they had to combat not only impersonal and irreversible general inflation, but also the natural reluctance of their tenants to pay more. Moreover, rents under *domaine congéable* tended to be treated as fixed dues because of their semi-feudal nature, even though the tenants could impose on their unfortunate sub-tenants three or more times the rent they themselves paid. It has been possible to construct several indices of rents for the region around Vannes. The first comes from a set of leases on tenures held under *domaine congéable* in the parish of Grand-Champ; since these rents are chiefly in kind, the rise in these has been calculated on the basis of average grain prices during two periods of complete grain price cycles, 1726–39 and 1773–89. The second is a set of rents, paid chiefly in kind, but for which only the money equivalent is known. These equivalents were estimated by the officials of the *contrôle des actes* and were based on an average of the grain prices of the ten preceding years. In these instances, the estimated rise in rents was 92 per cent in the first case and 56 per cent in the second (the latter, because of its basis of evaluation, is an underestimate). The rise in grain prices between the same two periods, based on 'cyclical' averages of grain prices, was 76 per cent for *gros froment,* 88 per cent for *petit froment,* 89 per cent for rye, and 116 per cent for oats. A third set of leases, calculated on a different basis by P. Thomas-Lacroix for the parish of Theix gave rises of about 40 per cent in rents between 1701 and 1779, as against rises of 40 per cent for *petit froment,* 22 per cent for rye and 50 per cent for oats.[10]

At first glance then, the race between rents and the general price rise looks as if it ended in a dead heat for the landlords, but, on closer examination of the relative rates of increase of wheat and rye

---

[9] See Table XI-1.
[10] See Table XI-1; Thomas-Lacroix, 'La Condition des terres', 348–54; Le Goff, 'Vannes' 401–2, 439–40, 452–6.

prices and rents during the period 1738–89, it appears clear that the landlords won nearly all the time. For the whole of the period, the average annual rate of increase in rents, based on an index derived from the Grand-Champ series, was 1.8 per cent a year; the rise in rye was 1.5 and that of wheat (*gros froment*), 1.2. When the chronology of the rise is examined, there emerge only two periods in which landlords' incomes rose at slower rates than grain prices: 1743–58 and 1753–68 or, roughly speaking, the 1750s and early 1760s, when grain prices had their great boom in France and momentarily caught the landlords unprepared; but the latter quickly made up for their negligence in the 1770s and 1780s, just at the time when grain prices were stagnating. In 1778, the grain merchant Desruisseaux wrote of 'nos propriétaires aiguillonés il y a plusieurs années . . . il n'est plus possible d'entrer en marché avec nos rentiers, les plus modestes exigent aujourd'hui 150 [livres le tonneau] peut être demain ne les voudrent-ils pas et le plus grande partie ne veulent vendre que cet hiver.'[11] Provided that they watched their own expenses—which of course could never be guaranteed—and had some resources to cushion themselves against a bad year —which not all had—they could not lose.

If rents won the race with inflation most of the time, those who paid them nearly always lost it. The landlords tied their rent increases closely to the price of grain and thus to the cost of living, but the tenants had at least two other variables to contend with: variations in production and increasing operating costs. If, as the tithe records suggest, production did rise across the century, there were many ups and downs in its course. The principal measure of these variations are the *états des récoltes*, approximate indicators of harvest volume, expected or attained, sent to the intendant each year by the *subdélégués:* there is a series for Vannes from 1754 onwards and regional estimates for Brittany from 1734. Although these are approximations, they were made by reliable witnesses, often men with experience in the grain trade.[12]

A calculation of gross real revenue from each unit of land from wheat and rye volumes suggests a marked deterioration of gross tenant income in the early 1740s, followed by a period in the 1750s and the early 1760s in which gross revenues increased faster than

---

[11] A.D. Morbihan, 11 B 56: Desruisseaux to Vignes, Bordeaux, 1778.
[12] A.D. I.-V., C 1652–3; Meyer, *La Noblesse bretonne*, i, 510–11 (for 1770–4), summarized in Le Goff 'Vannes', 452–6.

rents. This period of grace was followed by a slowing-down in the later 1760s and the 1770s during which the landlords were gaining the upper hand. A momentary recovery in the later 1770s was followed by a real regression of gross revenue in the crisis of the 1780s. The gross income of tenants, reckoned on this basis, fluctuated roughly as the inverse of landlords' incomes. But in the long run, from 1738 to 1789, gross revenues rose less than rents: 0.6 per cent a year for rye crops, 0.5 per cent a year for wheat as against 1.8 per cent for rents.

It is possible to take this analysis one step further by calculating an index of net real income for tenants under *domaine congéable*, based on indices of wheat and rye prices deflated by an index of expenditure and multiplied by harvest volumes; it could be expressed by the formula

$$\frac{\text{Index of grain prices } (1732\text{--}7 = 100)}{\text{Index of expenditure}} \times \begin{array}{c}\text{harvest} \\ \text{volume}\end{array} = \begin{array}{c}\text{net real} \\ \text{income}\end{array}$$

where the index of expenditure is formed from rents, commissions on leases and taxes, calculated on the basis 1732–7 = 100 and weighted in the ratio 8:1:3 respectively (changes in the weights, in fact, affect the results very little).[13]

Calculated on this basis, the index of real net income gives a slightly more optimistic view of the tenant's lot, the main reason being the sluggishness of direct taxes in the long inflationary cycle 1726–89. There is the same fall in real net revenues in the 1740s and 1750s as in gross revenues, but a distinct upturn in real revenue (3 to 3.5 per cent a year) in the 1750s and 1760s. The rise was then progressively squeezed to 0.5 per cent a year in the early sixties, and then to unity in the 1770s. It rose again briefly in the late seventies but then fell back in the later eighties to − 2.4 per cent a year. The overall growth rate in real net income, was 0.5 per cent a year for the period 1738–89, but this small though positive overall increase

[13] I wish to thank my friend Dr Neil Arnason, of the University of Manitoba, who developed this index from my data. A straightforward discussion of the statistical problems involved can be found in R. G. D. Allen, *Statistics for Economists* (London, 1966), 115–32, 150–2, T. Yamane, *Statistics, an Introductory Analysis* (New York, 1966), and R. Floud, *An Introduction to Quantitative Methods for Historians* (London, 1973).

hid larger gains in the 1750s and 1760s that were later reduced but never really wiped out until the crisis of the 1780s. Thus a small dose of expanding production, probably more the fruit of a series of good harvests than of any conscious and organized programme of investment, plus the relatively slow reaction of direct taxation to inflation, enabled those fortunate enough to rent their tenures under *domaine congéable* to face eighteenth-century inflation with a certain serenity.

Not all could do so, however, nor could they all bargain on terms so favourable with their landlords and the blind forces of nature and the economy. Those who rented as sub-tenants on tenures subject to *domaine congéable* or who were *métayers* seem to have experienced rent rises at least as great as tenants, but as these rents were as much as five times the value of the rent paid to the original landlord, they began the 'economic eighteenth century' under a severe handicap and were all the more susceptible to the occasional bad year.[14] If the lot of the simple tenant farmer was not enviable, and probably getting worse, that of men and women who depended on the sale of their labour seems to have worsened as well. Salaries paid in the rural Vannetais varied little, if at all, across the century. Rural day-labourers' wages seem to have remained fixed at around 8 sols a day through most of the century. Certainly rural artisans had very 'sticky' wages, which rose only after the great price boom of the 1760s. Rural roofers and masons, for example, seem only to have got permanently better salaries around 1778, and even then they were modest increases, compared with the long-term rise in living costs. The precarious existence of people living in pockets of poverty such as the peninsula of Rhuys and their plight in the bad years following 1770 can easily be imagined. Day-labourers and artisans in the towns as well, although they received wage increases better spaced across the century, did not increase their earnings sufficiently to make up for the rise in the cost of living.[15]

It is true that in the countryside and to some extent in the town such people had some degree of protection against the economic fluctuations that bedevilled the life of the merchant, the speculating landlord and the *laboureur,* but the margin of safety offered was thin. There were, to be sure, grains cheaper and sometimes with a higher nutritive value than wheat and rye. These had an added

---

[14] Thomas-Lacroix, 'La Condition des terres', 354–60; Le Goff, 'Vannes', 401–2.
[15] Le Goff, 'Vannes', 375, 474–5.

advantage: a bad harvest of the better quality cereals did not always coincide with bad harvests of millet, oats and buckwheat. There were the cows owned by the poorer folk in the countryside, whose milk eked out their meagre fare. But the prices of the cheaper grains tended in the long run to follow those of rye and wheat upward across the century, and in particularly bad years for wheat and rye, the prices of lesser grains shot up too, regardless of the quantities harvested (e.g. 1775, 1781, 1785). And cattle could be wiped out; probably the most tragic example of this was in 1785, when first the rigorous cold of the winter killed the new offspring and then the heat of the summer—the driest summer recorded before 1976—ruined the forage crops, forcing the peasants to butcher many of their cattle who had not already died of starvation. In that same year, grain prices were higher than they had been since the crisis of 1772, higher than they were to be in the year of Revolution, 1789. In 1785, as in the great crisis of 1770–2, the receiver of the Estates of Brittany pointed out that the general and extreme poverty of the countryside made it impossible to press for tax payments as in ordinary years: 'la misère est excessive dans les campagnes . . . Il y aurait de l'inhumanité à prendre des partis violents et nous serons forcés d'attendre que la prochaine récolte soit faite avant d'employer la rigueur.' In 1787, the same official claimed that, because of the 'misère affreuse' of the countryside, he had still some 82,000 livres to collect on taxes due in the terrible years of 1784 and 1785.[16] In this case, the defences of the poor as well as the rich collapsed simultaneously.

What, in these circumstances, happened to rural wealth and rural property, which have been depicted for convenience of presentation in previous chapters rather like still photographs of moments in a moving picture film? The struggle for land is best documented in the records of the *centième denier*, the tax imposed on real property transactions. Because the *centième denier* recorded all property transfers in a given area, and not just those which happened to be concluded within the region, it provides a reliable record of the flow of this resource from one social group to another.

For this study all the property transfers in ten of the rural parishes of the region outside the peninsula of Rhuys were examined. Because this work takes time, it was necessary to restrict part of it, and it was

[16] A.D. I.-V., C 1654–5; Rébillon, *Les États de Bretagne*, 613 n. 25.

decided to limit the complete study of all purchasers and sellers to the period 1772–89. However, the most important form of property transfer, the reimbursement of edifices held under *domaine congéable*, was studied for the period from 1726 to 1789, while simple sales of edifices under *domaine congéable* were enumerated from 1761 onwards.[17]

In all of these parishes, except for Séné, part of St-Patern and the Île-aux-Moines, the *domaine congéable* was the predominant form of tenure, and this predominance was accurately reflected in the proportion of the land changing hands in each of the categories of property transactions. There were four kinds of transfers. Three of them were basically alike, although kept distinct in the records of the *centième denier*: (1) the sale of property not held under *domaine congéable* (commonly called *héritages*), (2) the sale of *fonds* held under *domaine congéable* and (3) the sale of edifices held under the same system of tenure, and considered, like the *fonds*, to be real property. The fourth type of transaction was the act which marked the end of the expulsion of a tenant holding edifices under *domaine congéable*; the interested parties recorded either the value of the edifices and the share of the expelled tenant worked out by appraisers, or else the final payment of the value of the edifices to the expelled party.[18]

[17] A.D. Morbihan, 17 C 5351–5403: Bureau de Vannes, 1726–90 and 17 C 4786–4805: Bureaux of St-Jean-Brévelay and Plaudren, 1726–54: parishes of Arradon (with Île-aux-Moines) Grand-Champ, Meucon, Plescop, St-Avé, St-Nolf, St-Patern-les-Champs, Séné, Theix, Trefféan and Plaudren (the parish of Plaudren was dealt with by the bureau of Vannes after 1754; before that date, transactions from part of the parish were registered at St-Jean-Brévelay and Plaudren). On the critical problems posed by the use of the *centième denier* see above, Chapter VI, p. 199. For two examples of the treatment of this source, see P. de Saint-Jacob, 'Le Mouvement de la propriété dans un village bourguignon à la fin de l'ancien regime, 1748–1789', *RHES*, xxvii (1948), 47–52 and G. Béaur, 'Le Centième Denier et les mouvements de propriété. Deux exemples beaucerons (1761–1790)', *Annales: E.S.C.*, xxxiii (1976), 1010–33.

[18] Before mid-century, however, sales of *fonds* under *domaine congéable* were not always kept distinct from sales of *héritages*. There were other types of transfer of real property, chiefly *cessions* (the voluntary surrender of a share of land in a succession to one's co-heir), *subrogations* (installing a third party in one's right to real property), *afféagements* (the granting of land to a 'vassal' by a seigneur in return for a *cens* or similar token payment) and *ventes à réméré* (sales with an option for repurchase by [*p. 304 for n. 18 cont.*]

Of the four types of transfer, the last, the reimbursement of the value of the edifices after expulsion, was the most common. In the eighteen years running from September 1772 to August 1790, this form of transaction accounted for 44 per cent of the total number of acquisitions of land and 40 per cent of the value of transactions. The next most important in number were sales of edifices without expulsion: 41 per cent of the total of transactions which, however, represented only 21 per cent of the value of land sold, so that really the second most important form of exchange was the sale of *héritages* (31 per cent of the value of land exchanged and 11 per cent of the number of transactions, not including transactions below 300 livres value). The least frequent and least important form of land transfer was the purchase of *fonds* held under *domaine congéable* (4 per cent of the total number of transactions and 7 per cent of their value). Of the four types of transaction, the average value of sales of *héritages* is the greatest, but in reality this average is a compound of many small sales and a few big ones. The average value of sales of edifices was around 900 livres, while the reimbursement of edifices was a much more considerable enterprise, involving the payment of about 1,700 livres on the average. The average values of sales of *fonds* varied widely from year to year.[19]

A word should be said at this point about the method used in analysing these property transfers. In order to study the number of transfers to and from social groups, some working definitions suited to the information given in the documents had to be adopted. Thus 'bourgeois' have been considered to be all persons above artisan

the seller within a fixed period; this could conceal a mortgage or loan). These three forms of transfer were rare enough to be ignored, following the practice of P. de Saint-Jacob, 'Le Mouvement de la propriété'. The total value of *ventes à réméré* of edifices under *domaine congéable,* the most considerable of these lesser transactions, came to only 123,818 livres for the period 1772–89; cf. the figures in note 19 below. Collateral, but not direct, successions were also recorded in the *centième denier.*

[19] A summary of the totals of sales and their value for the harvest years 1772–89 inclusive is as follows:

	Value	%	Number	%
Sales of héritages ≥ 300 livres	671,822	31.2	136	11.3
Sales of edifices, *dom. congéable*	443,693	20.6	488	40.5
Payment of edifices (expulsions)	880,003	40.9	531	44.0
Sales of fonds, *dom. congéable*	157,074	7.3	51	4.2
Totals	2,152,592	100.1	1206	100.0

and shopkeeper status in Vannes or any other town such as Auray and Hennebont, with the exception, of course, of nobles and clergy. As well, persons with the title *sieur* but with no listed profession have also been considered as bourgeois. Because of the somewhat blurred limits of the 'rural bourgeoisie', a different procedure was adopted for the countryside: only people exercising liberal professions were considered to be part of the bourgeoisie. However, in the commentary on these statistics, an attempt has been made to single out other members, or possible members, of the 'rural bourgeoisie' when they have been counted among the peasants—which happens very seldom.

Two methods of tracing the direction of land transfers among social groups are possible. The first, pioneered by Pierre de Saint-Jacob, consists of counting all land transfers and their values. The second, more rapid, was used by Paul Bois; it requires only that transfers occurring between members of different social groups be counted; under this method for example, a land sale, no matter how large, between two *laboureurs* or two *bourgeois* would not be taken into account, because it does not change the economic position of the peasants or bourgeois considered as a group, but one made by a peasant to a bourgeois would be counted because it indicates that the bourgeoisie are impinging on the patrimony, as it were, of the peasantry.[20]

Of the two, the first method, rather than that employed by Bois, seems preferable, because what may show up in Bois's statistics as a monstrous dispossession of one class by another may well prove to be only a tiny loss when compared with the total turnover in land sales by a given class. In a region where, for example, nobles are the principal landed proprietors, most purchases of land by non-nobles will be at the expense of that class; but does this mean that the nobility were declining? It depends on how many other nobles held on to their land. It also depends on what was happening to the new purchasers: were they becoming nobles? Were they establishing new, rational forms of agriculture? Or were they merely replenishing the numbers of the landed nobility? Similarly, if the peasants of a region buy only 15,000 livres worth of land in a given period from bourgeois while the latter acquire land worth 50,000 livres

---

[20] Saint-Jacob, *Les Paysans de la Bourgogne du Nord,* 620–3 and *passim;* 'Le Mouvement de la propriété dans un village bourguignon', 47–52; Bois, *Paysans de l'Ouest,* 359–74.

from the peasants, one might conclude that the peasants were losing out to the bourgeoisie; but if it is known that peasants exchanged another 250,000 livres worth of land among themselves, then obviously this loss becomes more difficult to interpret.

Indeed, this is the sort of conclusion which emerges from an analysis (see Table XI-2) of the social origins of buyers and sellers of *fonds* between 1772 and 1789.[21] The market for *fonds*, to begin with, was extremely restricted: there were only 51 sales spaced irregularly over a period of eighteen years, for a total value of 157,000 livres. The 'winners', if they can be called that, are the bourgeois of Vannes; the 'losers', the nobility, for nobles sold a total of 27 tenures for a value of 124,335 livres and bought a total of 6 for 39,314 livres—a 'loss' of 85,021 livres; conversely, the bourgeoisie bought a total of 21 tenures and sold 13, but the value of their gains (81,504 livres) far surpassed their losses (20,675 livres). The principal purchasers of the nobles' *fonds* were the bourgeois, who bought over half of the value of the lands that the nobles sold during this period; they were followed in importance by other nobles (31 per cent of sale value), peasants, and one blacksmith (17 per cent of value). The bourgeois, like the nobles, found many customers among people of their own class—38 per cent of the total value of lands sold by the bourgeoisie went back to bourgeois. Peasants purchased 47 per cent of the value of sales by bourgeois; the negligible remainder went to one noble and one domestic servant in Vannes.

It is possible in this context to speak of the bourgeoisie eroding the landed wealth of the nobility, but only in a very limited sense. For the proportion of *fonds* actually sold was extremely small in comparison to the total holdings of the nobility. And only nine of the twenty-seven nobles who sold *fonds* during this period were living in the region. These local nobles sold 43 per cent of the total value of *fonds* which members of their class put up for sale, but two-thirds of this percentage went back to the nobility in sales to other local nobles. The nobility of the Vannetais kept a tight hold on their property.

[21] The 'harvest year' has been taken as beginning on 1 September, the feast of St Michael, when the annual prices for the major grains were recorded by the Présidial and when rents fell due. Thus 'harvest year 1788' means the twelve months from September 1788 to August 1789 inclusive. The peak months for the sales of *héritages* were May, December and November, in that order; for *fonds*, April, July and May; for edifices, January, May and December.

Table XI-2: Sales of *fonds* of tenures held under *domaine congéable* (harvest years 1772–89)

(1) Number of sales

Sold to / Sellers	Nobles	Bourgeois	Clergy	Urban 'petites gens'	Peasants	Total
Nobles	5	12[a]	—	—	10[b]	27
Bourgeois	1	5	—	1	6[c]	13
Clergy	—	—	—	—	—	—
Urban 'petites gens'	—	2	—	—	1	3
Peasants	—	2	—	1	5	8
Total	6	21	—	2	22	51

(2) Value of sales

Sold to / Sellers	Nobles	Bourgeois	Clergy	Urban 'petites gens'	Peasants	Total
Nobles	38014	64651[a]	—	—	21670[b]	124335
Bourgeois	1300	7950	—	1672	9843[c]	20675
Clergy	—	—	—	—	—	—
Urban 'petites gens'	—	6900	—	—	600	7500
Peasant	—	2003	—	300	2171	4474
Total	39314	81504	—	1972	34284	157074

[a] Includes 1 sale by a noble cleric.
[b] Includes 1 sale to a merchant in Grand-Champ.
[c] Includes 1 sale to a miller in Plescop.

Nevertheless, there were a few who succeeded in breaking into the charmed circle of owners of *fonds*. Thus, one of the richest merchants of Vannes, Gabriel Danet, bought the *fonds* of two tenures, one in St-Patern-les-Champs in 1773 and another in Theix in 1785, from Anne-Claude Bossard du Clos and Armand-Sébastien de Bruc for a total of 6,700 livres. A few other merchants of Vannes made similar purchases: Vincent-Joseph Macé and Antoine Léonard *dit* Champagne. So did attorneys and notaries such as P.-J. Perret, J.-B. Le Ridant, the barrister Mathurin Goujeon, F.-M. Bréville, a bourgeois from Auray, one widow in Vannes and a handful of the small class of 'rural bourgeois'—the enterprising notary of Grand-Champ, P.-V. Le Franc and Mathurin Cadoret, a merchant in Grand-Champ. But this list, short as it is, includes practically all the bourgeois purchasers.

A final feature of this particular class of transaction is the rather high proportion of peasants buying and selling *fonds*. They were their own best customers, but they bought as well from the nobility a total of ten *fonds* of tenures—more than the bourgeoisie bought from this class, though of less value. Most of these were purchases from distant landlords who had probably lost interest in the few isolated tenures they held, which represented more trouble than they were worth. Thus in 1775, Mathurin Coustic, a *laboureur* in Arradon purchased the *fonds* of a small holding from Toussaint de Francheville de Pellinec, who lived in Guérande, while in 1780, Pierre le Page, a *laboureur* in Plaudren bought the *fonds* of two small tenures there from Messire J.-R. Le Flo de Tremelin de Kerleau, who also lived in Guérande. But it would be pointless to go on with such examples. As with the purchases by and from bourgeois and nobles, although a definite trend in the direction of sales can be discerned, the total value of these transactions hardly amounts to a massive transfer of property from one class to another.

This trend appears again in the buying and selling of *héritages*[22] (see Table XI-3), though here, because of the larger sums and greater number of transactions involved, the movement of property is more significant. This is not apparent at first glance, for although the nobles put the largest amounts of land on the market (64 per cent of the total value sold) they themselves bought back very nearly half of that amount. This however is due to two very big estate sales by absentees in 1781, in which the maverick royalist parlementaire, R.-J. Le Prestre de Châteaugiron, and a local noble, P.-B.-L. Le Charpentier de Lenvos acquired the seigneuries of Beauregard (in St-Avé) and Limoges (in St-Patern) for 83,000 livres each. Without these, the nobles' purchases from other nobles would have been much smaller. Even as it was, bourgeois bought some 45 per cent of noble lands offered for sale. In the case of *héritages,* the amount of land bought by peasants from nobles is much lower, and closer to what we would expect it to be.

The bourgeoisie did not let many *héritages* go by sale in comparison to what the nobility lost, and it acquired much more new land than the nobles did. The bulk (75 per cent of value) of what the bourgeoisie sold went to other bourgeois; the nobility got 13 per cent, and urban artisans, shopkeepers, gardeners, peasants, rural artisans and merchants shared the leavings. Peasant holdings of *héritages* were nothing like as large as bourgeois and noble holdings, so it is not surprising that the volume of purchases and sales by

---

[22] Of a value of 300 livres or more; anything worth less has an infinitesimal surface and the number of such small purchases, mainly in the parish of Séné, slows research to a halt.

Table XI-3: Sales of *héritages* over 300 livres (harvest years 1772–89)

(1) Number of sales

Sold to / Sellers	Nobles	Bourgeois	Clergy	Urban 'petites gens'	Peasants	Rural artisans & shopkeepers	Unknown	Total
Nobles	8	11	1	1	4	—	—	25
Bourgeois	6	19	—	3	1	3[a]	4[b]	36
Clergy	—	1	1	—	—	—	—	2
Urban 'petites gens'	—	5	—	1	4	—	—	10
Peasant	4	10	—	2	33	2[c]	—	51
Rural artisan, etc.	—	5[d]	—	—	7[e]	—	—	12
Total	18	51	2	7	49	5	4	136

(2) Value of sales

Sold to / Sellers	Nobles	Bourgeois	Clergy	Urban 'petites gens'	Peasants	Rural artisans & shopkeepers	Unknown	Total
Nobles	209132	191463	7000	900	18150	—	—	426645
Bourgeois	22250	131186	—	10279	424	1849[a]	8259[b]	174247
Clergy	—	4200	600	—	—	—	—	4800
Urban 'petites gens'	—	6828	—	300	2375	—	—	9503
Peasants	9850	9667	—	600	27533	1575[c]	—	49225
Rural artisan, etc.	—	3130[d]	—	—	4272[e]	—	—	7402
Total	241232	346474	7600	12079	52754	3424	8259	671822

a Sold to 1 former sea-captain, 1 blacksmith and wood merchant, 1 miller.
b Sold to 2 on Île d'Arz, 1 on Île-aux-Moines. Seamen?
c Sold to 1 tavern-keeper, 1 sailor and 1 building contractor.
d Sold by 2 shoemakers, 1 tavern-keeper, 1 tailor, 1 innkeeper.
e Sold by 1 tavern-keeper, 1 fishmonger, 1 blacksmith, 1 baker, 1 former sea-captain, 1 tailor, 1 coasting captain, 1 weaver.

peasants should be slight. Nevertheless, the fact that a fifth of what the peasants sold (9667 of 49,225 livres) should have gone to bourgeois purchasers (the remainder being sold mainly to nobles and other peasants) shows that a demand for land certainly existed among the bourgeoisie.

Who were these bourgeois buying into the countryside? Much the same as those active in buying *fonds:* men and women like the goldsmith Tiret, the *négociants* Joseph Lallemand, Armand Serres, Dame Françoise Bertain, widow of the printer and bookseller Galles, Antoine Léonard *dit* Champagne, Jean-Joseph Danet and, especially, Gabriel Danet, who purchased a total of about 86,000 livres of rural land, or about a quarter of all the purchases made by the bourgeoisie, in the 'suburban' parishes of St-Patern-les-Champs, Séné and Theix alone. Over half of their purchases were from the nobles, 38 per cent from other bourgeois, and only 3 per cent from peasants, but this does not include the many tiny parcels bought up in Séné and costing less than 300 livres.

These merchants of Vannes appear as the most important single group of purchasers of *héritages* among the bourgeoisie of Vannes. With one exception, the lawyers were much less prominent, though a half-dozen were also buying up land, chiefly rural *métairies:* the notary Joseph Hervieu, the attorneys Pierre-Joachim Perret de la Lande, J.-B. Le Ridant, and Jacques Glais, the barrister Mathurin Goujeon and the *lieutenant* of the Présidial of Vannes, C.-L. Poussin. Only one made really notable purchases however: the attorney and rural notary Michel-Anne-Sébastian Le Monnier, who purchased a *métairie* and two seigneuries worth a total of 177,370 livres between 1784 and 1786 (although in the purchase of these two seigneuries he may well have been acting for others or indulging in short-term speculation).[23] The remainder of the purchases made by the bourgeoisie were limited to a few rentiers, such as the retired captain of the Company of the Indies, *noble homme* François-Marie Bréville, already noted above as a purchaser of *fonds,* who bought up rural land in Séné and St-Patern.

Once again, it is possible to speak, but this time with more certainty, of a drive by the bourgeoisie to take over the land. Yet even here, we must be cautious. It is not correct, for example, to conclude that the local nobility was being dispossessed by a jealous

---

[23] e.g. A.D. Morbihan, 17 C 5400: two sales to Le Monnier 'pour lui ou autres qu'il nommera', 19-10-1786

and pushing bourgeoisie. Jealous and pushing the bourgeoisie may have been, but they did not victimize the local nobles, at least in this. All of the nobles save one who sold *héritages* in this period lived elsewhere in the province, some even as far off as Poitiers and Paris.[24] The sale of their land left the local noblesse untouched. Moreover, much of the land purchased by the bourgeoisie—and most of that bought by the *négociants*—was in the three 'suburban' parishes of Theix, Séné and St-Patern; the extension of bourgeois ownership of *héritages* and *fonds* into the countryside did not go very far.

The fact was that the *domaine congéable* seriously limited the availability of land. The rate of return to the landlord on *métairies* and *fermes* was much higher than that on *fonds* leased under *domaine congéable*. Yet *fonds* and edifices covered most of the land. This increased the pressure of demand on *héritages,* which offered a much greater possibility for returns, and this pressure explains in part the tenacity with which respectable merchants and lawyers such as Guillo Dubodan and C.-L. Poussin carefully amassed a few furrows of land here and there, imitating the land-hungry peasants from whom they bought it. In fact, their avidity for such scraps is underestimated by the figures given here, since they do not record the scores of purchases of tiny plots worth less than 300 livres made by the bourgeoisie of Vannes in these years, nor purchases on the peninsula of Rhuys, where there was no *domaine congéable*.

As for the market in edifices under *domaine congéable,* it can be seen how closed and unattractive it was for people outside the rural world from the records of sales of edifices and expulsions of *tenuyers* from their holdings during this period (see Table XI-4). Over these eighteen years the total turnover in sales of edifices reached about 444,000 livres, but 60 per cent of this represented sales by peasants, rural artisans and the like to other peasants and rural artisans. Another fifth consisted of the creation of edifices by nobles and a few bourgeois out of what had been *héritages* by the legal device of selling the edifices by *premier détachement*. In all peasants were the great gainers in this sort of transaction; nobles and bourgeois 'lost', though that is not quite the right expression. Rural tradesmen lost

[24] M.-A.-J.-V. de Rossi, captain in the Royal Corsican regiment, detained in the citadel of St-Malo under the King's orders in 1784 but reported back in Vannes in 1787 (transactions of 1-4-1784 and 24-4-1787), J.-F.-S. Dondel Du Faouëdic (19-11-1774), J.-M. Le Sénéchal abbé de Kerguisé and his brother (8-4-1774).

Table XI-4: Sales of edifices under *domaine congéable* (harvest years 1772–1789)

(1) Number of sales

Sales to Sellers	Nobles	Bourgeois	Clergy	Urban 'petites gens'	Peasants	Rural artisans, etc.	Total
Nobles	—	1	—	1	27	1	30
Bourgeois	—	2	—	2	13	1	18
Clergy	—	—	—	—	2	—	2
Urban 'petites gens'	—	—	—	4	20	1	25
Peasants	1	7	1	7	310	30	356
Rural artisans, etc.	—	2	—	4	38	13	57
Total	1	12	1	18	410	46	488

(2) Values of sales

Sales to Sellers	Nobles	Bourgeois	Clergy	Urban 'petites gens'	Peasants	Rural artisans, etc.	Total
Nobles	—	1200	—	2224	72499	300	76223
Bourgeois	—	3793	—	4600	16338	2100	26831
Clergy	—	—	—	—	—	—	—
Urban 'petites gens'	—	—	—	1785	12848	72	14705
Peasants	160	13020	679	4040	247433	19034	284366
Rural artisans, etc.	—	1760	—	6465	26186	7157	41568
Total	160	19773	679	19114	375304	28663	443693

somewhat too, though they had not much to lose.

Bourgeois and other non-rural people did invest money in purchases of edifices held under *domaine congéable*, but their investments were quite small: three rural notaries, Le Franc, Le Thieis and Caris, of Grand-Champ, got four sets of edifices between them; two notaries of Vannes, Goujeon and Rostiel, the *valet de chambre* of the comte de Châteaugiron, an exciseman and a woman in Quimper, a goldsmith of Vannes, Tiret, and the ubiquitous merchant Léonard Champagne bought themselves holdings. A few artisans of Vannes also got some scraps of land this way, but clearly the market belonged to the peasants.

However, if one wanted to purchase the totality of the edifices of a tenure under *domaine congéable*, the normal way to go about it was to undertake to expel a tenant by prior arrangement with a landlord. There was much greater scope in this kind of transaction for town-dwellers since they did not have to deal with the peasants but could treat directly with the *seigneur foncier* or with his middle-man. And in fact a much larger amount of land came into non-peasants' hands in this way than by simple purchase of edifices—about 31,000 livres' worth. If the absolute figures were larger, however, the importance of these transfers in relation to the total turnover in expulsions was again not very high, for these trans-actions came to only about 4 per cent of the total of 880,000 livres turnover in the harvest years 1772–89.

Who were these men of the town, shouldering their way into the 'peasant' land market? Much the same as the bourgeois purchasers we have met already: three merchants of Vannes: Armand Serres, Laurent Le Goff and Jean Macé. Two were priests: one, the spiritual director of the Ursulines of Hennebont in partnership with his brother, perhaps a peasant; the other, the rector of Trefflean. Three were lawyers: the notaries Pierre Caris and his brother-in-law Jan Pouliquen, J.-B. Le Ridant, Mathurin Goujeon, and Pierre-Vincent Le Franc. The remaining three were a gardener, a tavern-keeper and one unidentifiable individual from Vannes.

Of course, expulsions of tenants under *domaine congéable* could work both ways, and there were non-rural tenants expelled as well. One anomalous expulsion was that of Marie-Julien-Louis de Robien, sieur de Trenlan, who, no doubt by some freak of the succession laws, had come to own the edifices of a tenure whose *fonds* be-longed to de Penhouet, another local noble; de Robien was expelled, perhaps by prearrangement, by one Yves Hemon, for 2,473 livres. One priest, one lawyer and one gardener from Vannes were re-lieved of a share of edifices with their rural relations in this way. But the total amount which reverted to the rural world in this way was small, and was far from balancing the amount which went in the other direction.

Thus it can be seen that although there was a certain demand for land by people who were not countrymen, it was not very great. It was limited first of all by numbers: the prosperous bourgeoisie of Vannes was small and the same group of *négociants* and lawyers appear again and again in the acts of sale: Danet, Guillo Dubodan, Champagne, Serres, Le Ridant, Goujeon, Le Franc. The clergy as individuals virtually do not count among the purchasers of land and as an institution the Church bought nothing and sold nothing. A few, but only a few, urban artisans bought land, the most notable being a small group of market-gardeners in Vannes. The nobility appear primarily as sellers.

The market was restricted as well by the nature of landholding in the Vannetais. If we look at the land market as a whole, the most common form of transaction was the expulsion of tenants under *domaine congéable,* followed in popularity by the sale of edifices of lands under *domaine congéable,* but these were the forms of investment least indulged in by non-rural groups, because of the complicated tenure system, the precariousness of holdings and possibly the low rate of return by comparison to what could be got by farming out a *héritage.* To be sure, the hunger of the urban bourgeoisie for land at the end of the century was such that a few went so far as to buy edifices or expel tenants, but compared to other forms of non-rural investment in the countryside, the effect of this was negligible.

If we examine instead the relative importance of purchases by non-rural buyers, we find an almost completely different set of preferences. During the nineteen years examined in detail in this study of the land market, non-rural buyers purchased 600,000 livres worth of *héritages,* 120,000 livres' worth of *fonds,* but obtained only 31,000 livres' worth of edifices by expulsions of tenants under *domaine congéable* and bought less than 40,000 livres' worth of edifices outright. The most popular form of investment among non-rural groups was therefore the purchase of *héritages,* and the land market appears curiously 'compartmentalized', with the bourgeoisie largely excluded from the trade in lands under *domaine congéable.* Although they did make inroads into the 'peasant' market, the dozen or so takeovers by bourgeois and other non-rural persons in these eighteen years cannot be classified as wholesale expropriation of the patrimony of the rural classes; far from it.

Nevertheless, with these reservations, one may correctly speak of the irruption of the bourgeoisie of Vannes into the countryside, for it is, after all, extremely significant that over half of the value of *héritages* worth 300 livres or more that were sold, went to bourgeois. Without the *domaine congéable,* the bourgeoisie might well have extended their mastery of the soil much further. But the *domaine congéable* erected a barrier against this extension in several ways. First, it provided for a solid, steady income for the landlords, derived from a stable class of tenant-farmers, an income which gave the nobility, who made up the bulk of this group, a hedge against the ruin which would have thrown their estates into the hands of the bourgeoisie and the wealthier peasants. At the same time, the restricted market in *fonds,* which usually went up for sale only when absent heirs of a few fragmentary holdings wished to be rid of their land, allowed a select portion of the bourgeoisie gradually to accede to the possession of *fonds* and that permanent landed property so necessary to a bourgeois who wished to live nobly. Secondly, the *domaine congéable* protected the status of the propertied peasant and the archaic social pattern which went with its preservation. Too precarious a form of tenure and exploitation for the bourgeoisie to purchase in any large proportion, the edifices were passed up by them in favour of *métairies* and small plots of land on the fringes of the town.

Did the new landowners bring a new mentality into the country-side, taking to 'improvements' after the manner of the eighteenth-century agronomists? Some did, and doubtless more would have liked to. The chief means which men at the time saw of improving agricultural production was by reclaiming wasteland, either on common or individual holdings. On the whole, little improvement of this kind did take place in the Vannetais: 190 hectares were cleared between 1768 and 1774, and another 168 between 1774 and 1787 in the area which was to become the District of Vannes in 1790, hardly an impressive total. In the parish of Surlniac only 83 hectares were cleared and put under the plough in the period from 1720 to 1760, of a total area of about 4,400 hectares.[25] Much of even this limited land clearing may have been merely the semi-regular clear-ing of temporary fallow peculiar to the region. But a few of the townsmen who had been buying land in one form or another were among those who cleared two or more hectares: Chanu de Kerhedin and Chanu de Limur, relatives who had offices in the Présidial of Vannes; the ambitious merchants, the Danets, father and son, whom we have seen buying up land in the 'suburban' parishes of Séné and Theix, cleared about 20 hectares between them. A few peasants and gardeners put in bids for exemptions as well. No doubt much more clearing would have been done if the rural communities had not been so firmly set against the division of land often con-sidered as common land—even if the seigneurs claimed it—and so ready to sabotage the efforts of entrepreneurs like the bishop of Vannes and Kermasson in Theix. The principal agricultural entrepreneurs in the area, however, were not the 'new men', but

[25] Note 4 above.

rather a handful of noble landowners who managed in one way or another to carry out some land clearance: Toussaint de Francheville de Pelinec, who held the record by far with 123 hectares of clearing between 1771 and 1787; two members of the Quifistre de Bavalan family, with 28 hectares between them. Most of this clearing of large tracts took place in the parishes to the south-east of Vannes, especially along the coast, where there were many marshes in the hands of seigneurs.

Here, as in the overall ownership of land, the local nobility held most of the economic trumps. But it may be doubted whether an obsession with economic expansion and innovation moved many of the bourgeois who scrambled for the few scraps of available land. The movement of the successful elements of the bourgeoisie towards the land was a constant in Breton history and represented a necessary step in the gradual ascent of a family into the nobility. 'En cette province, entourée des mers', wrote the *sénéchal* of nearby Quimperlé in 1789, in a burst of lyrical hyperbole:

la navigation et le commerce occupent les Bretons pendant les deux-tiers de leur vie. L'autre tiers, réservé à leur repos bien mérité, est terminé dans le bonheur champêtre, par leur plaisir et leurs soins à soigner, planter ou arrondir leurs propriétés héréditaires ou d'acquisition.[26]

It has been noted that Breton merchants showed this tendency to retire into gentility on the land in the fifteenth century,[27] and the merchants of Vannes, along with other members of the bourgeoisie, displayed the same dispositions in the eighteenth.

True, it is possible to see some zeal for agricultural improvement and a sense of the social changes which would (and should, they thought) follow it in 1789 and after in the pamphlets of J.-M. Le Quinio and in the petition of another radical, the rector of St-Patern, M.-G.-A. Le Croisier, who, like Le Quinio, denounced the power the *domaine congéable* gave the nobility ('La noblesse, intéressée à maintenir cet usement, ancien reste de la tyrannie féodale . . .') but was more interested in attacking the economic consequences of the *domaine congéable*, which, he believed, was the great obstacle to agricultural improvement. Besides the abolition of the *domaine congéable*, he also demanded the compulsory concession (*afféagement*) of wasteland in return for a token pay-

[26] 'Observations du sénéchal du roi à Quimperlé sur le domaine congéable' [21-9-1789] cited in Dubreuil, *Les Vicissitudes*, i, 354.
[27] Touchard, *Le Commerce maritime breton*, 371-6.

ment. Le Croisier's memorandum, presented to the King in January 1789 as the aspirations of his rural parishioners, is in fact a plea for the enterprising, capitalist-minded bourgeois or peasant who wanted to increase both his holdings and their productivity.[28]

Unluckily for men such as Le Croisier and Le Quinio, and for the Revolution in Lower Brittany, their appeals found little echo among the landed bourgeoisie in Vannes. Complaints against the *domaine congéable* seem to have been included in the *cahier de doléances* of the *sénéchaussée* only at the insistence of Le Quinio and some of the representatives of the rural parishes, and then only in a mild form.[29] Local bourgeois who had *fonds* under *domaine congéable* supported the *fonciers'* lobby in the Constituent and Legislative Assemblies, which helped prevent the government from introducing any real changes in the system until the autumn of 1792.[30]

This in its way was typical of the bourgeoisie of Vannes and the Vannetais. Once the political power of the nobility was broken, they had no desire to destroy the basis of noble wealth. So accustomed were they to considering the basic relationship of the *domaine congéable* as that of a landlord and tenant rather than that of a seigneur and vassal, that any attack on this local variety of 'feudalism', such as occurred in 1789 and after, was bound to threaten the whole system of private property in the eyes of noble and bourgeois proprietors and of many revolutionaries who themselves had no personal interest in the matter. A doctrinaire view might be that the local bourgeoisie did not recognize that their own interests, or their historical role, lay in breaking down the 'feudal' system; a less rigid view might be that they were themselves quite content with a stable

---

[28] Le Goff, 'Les Doléances des paysans du Vannetais', 31–50.

[29] Le Quinio, *Élixir du régime feodal*, 40 n. (g), 112; the cahier of the *sénéchaussée* of Vannes has been printed in *Archives parlementaires* vi, 107–12.

[30] Among those who contributed to Jollivet's mission (see above, pp. 64–5) were Danet *aîné* and his brother, Gildas Macé, Le Ridant, Le Gris (father and son), Duranquin, Lauzer Larmor and his daughter, Serres and his mother, Brulon, Le Petit, Champagne, Tiret, the children and heirs of Lallemand and Brunet, etc. The only notable refusal among the bourgeois landowners on Jollivet's list of prospective contributors was that of the Dubodan clan. A.D. Morbihan, E 1072 (Fonds Jollivet). See also 'Petition des propriétaires fonciers' [December 1790] and 'Nouvelle petition des propriétaires de Vannes [December 1790–January 1791] cited in Dubreuil, *Les Vicissitudes*, i, The legislation of September 1791, with the principle of 'reciprocity' according to which a *domanier* could claim reimbursement at any time for his edifices, did not touch the essential problem. That so few writers should have realized this is an interesting commentary on the kind of history which results when the principal sources are propaganda and the texts of laws.

rural society and a static economy, and neither desired social up-
heavals nor wished to undertake risky agricultural investment.
'Feudal' or not, the *domaine congéable* was part of a well-
established system for the economic exploitation of the country by
the town, a system into which they bought their way when they
could. If there was 'feudalism' in the Vannetais, the bourgeoisie had
no objection to it. The radicals might call it what they would; it was
still property.

Thus the limitations and limited means of the bourgeoisie and
nobles, the restrictions imposed by the system of tenure, and the
relative cohesion of rural society in the face of the town combined to
limit the incursion of new ways into the countryside. But what was
becoming of the distribution of land and wealth in the rural community itself?

To discover whether one group of rural people was amassing the
land of another is not easy. One thing is certain, the records of
transfer in the *centième denier*, quite useful for the study of transfers
into and out of the rural community, are much more reticent in
mentioning social distinctions based on wealth and occupation within
that community: for the clerks, all peasants were 'laboureurs', and
sometimes even this all-purpose description was omitted. Comparisons with *capitation* assessments such as were made in Chapter VI
for the study of rural social structure are almost impossible, because
of the rarity of tax records, and the difficulties of finding many of the
new owners, often young men previously not noted on the assessment records. Worse, there are simply not enough explusions in a
given year in any one parish to make the operation yield significant
results.

There are, however, several other ways of approaching the question. Since the most common form of landholding in the Vannetais
was the *domaine congéable,* and since the most common form of
land transfer by the end of the old regime was the expulsion of
tenants holding edifices under this system, one can isolate these
transactions and see what happens to them across the 'economic
eighteenth century', from the mid-1720s to the year of revolution,
1789.

What happened, first of all, to the number of expulsions through
the century? It is generally assumed that on the eve of the Revolution, the landlords of Lower Brittany were exercising their rights

of *congément* as they never had before; and looking at the *cahiers de doléances* and the revolutionary pamphlets against the *domaine congéable,* historians like Henri Sée thought they had good reason to arrive at this conclusion—but they never went beyond the claims of the *cahiers,* the publicists and the politicians to see what was really happening. Later, in an important article, Pierre Thomas-Lacroix suggested that, at least in the parish he studied, Theix, no such process was visible. No study has since attempted to resolve the question.[31]

The results of a count of expulsions in the registers of the *centième denier* between 1726 and 1790 in the same set of parishes studied above are shown in Table XI-5 and Graph 2. These figures do bear out Sée's conclusion for the Vannetais, but with several important nuances. The average number of expulsions per year in the region did rise, from 23 a year in 1726–41 through 26 in 1747–57, 27 in 1758–72 and 30 in 1773–89. In a large parish like Grand-Champ, this meant that around seven or eight families a year would be expelled from their lands, as opposed to four or five in the 1720s and 1730s. The increase, however, was not felt uniformly in each parish. Six of the twelve parishes studied attained their maximum number of expulsions in periods before 1773–89: of those six, four had their highest number of expulsions in the period 1758–72.[32]

There can be no doubt that expulsions were primarily the result of competition for land among rural people. This was something which, apparently, Henri Sée did not realize. Undoubtedly, the landlords profited from the situation to raise their rents and lent their name to expulsion proceedings, but they could not have done so without pressure on the land from the peasants themselves. The average price of an expulsion rose, albeit slowly, from 1740 to 1789 by something between 0.4 and 0.5 per cent a year, from 1,100–1,300 livres in 1740 to 1,400–1,600 livres in 1789—an increase which

---

[31] Sée, *Les Classes rurales,* 294; Thomas-Lacroix, 'La Condition des terres', 364. Le Floc'h, 'Le Régime foncier et son application pratique' does count the number of edifices *sold,* and his figures show an increase in the number of sales in the decade before the Revolution. However, unless it was the practice for expelled tenants in the region he studied to sell their edifices to the expelling tenants, Le Floc'h appears to have ignored expulsions, a more significant sign of competition for land than voluntary sales.

[32] The periods in which each parish attained its maximum number of *congéments* were: Arradon, 1726–41; St-Patern, 1742–57; Plaudren, St-Nolf, St-Avé, Theix, 1758–72; Grand-Champ, Île-aux-Moines, Meucon, Plescop, Séné, Treffléan, 1773–89.

Table XI-5: Expulsion of tenants under *domaine congéable*

Year (harvest year)	Expulns., according to the centième denier		Expulsions, jurisdiction of Largouet-sous-Vannes							
	Number	Value (livres)	Number of expulsions	With relaisse-ments	With mortgage	Total mortgaged	Value of mortgaged expulsions (livres)	Value of relaisse-ments (livres)	Value of mortgages (livres)	Total mortgaged value (livres)
1726	12	19209								
1727	18	27658								
1728	16	19013								
1729	27	44745								
1730	21	33644								
1731	20	28609								
1732	18	27147								
1733	22	32819								
1734	16	21065								
1735	20	24378								
1736	22	39730								
1737	30	41270								
1738	28	42798								
1739	25	33701								
1740	39	58081	30	6	12	16	36253	3050	8102	11152
1741	27	42589	27	0	7	7	39114	0	5896	5896
1742	26	34611	20	2	3	4	23320	252	4559	4811
1743	24	28303	14	3	3	5	18604	1940	1980	3920
1744	19	30881	12	1	5	6	18873	536	5934	6470
1745	16	24178	10	3	4	7	13449	1566	3040	4606
1746	12	15893	9	2	2	4	8089	1131	1320	2451
1747	34	44686	24	2	5	6	35144	494	3434	3928
1748	35	42062	25	2	7	7	23248	1623	4038	5661
1749	46	60604	27	5	6	10	26484	2669	3440	6109
1750	27	32996	22	4	8	10	23453	1446	5934	7380
1751	26	38292	19	3	3	5	24886	994	1620	2614
1752	14	26228	11	1	4	4	18012	300	4635	4935
1753	25	36780	17	3	7	8	28661	1149	4677	5826
1754	31	38056	23	6	8	11	31511	2193	6060	8253

Table XI-5: Expulsion of tenants under *domaine congéable* (*continued*)

Year										
1756	26	41024	22	3	10	13	33579	852	10482	11334
1757	31	41366	19	2	7	8	22765	1375	5337	6712
1758	33	51271	22	1	7	7	29868	642	6677	7319
1759	20	28083	18	5	4	8	20542	2070	3660	5730
1760	27	33965	20	2	9	10	26625	1864	8864	10728
1761	18	22959	13	3	5	7	15347	2050	2400	4450
1762	26	33240	21	4	6	10	19069	1927	2664	4591
1763	26	31997	19	1	8	9	23124	394	3720	4114
1764	20	30769	7		2	2	11769	844	2100	2944
1765	33	52727	19	6	7	12	28225	2756	5635	8391
1766	23	29006	14	1	4	5	14250	177	1860	2037
1767	37	64830	26	2	9	10	35331	1087	5625	6712
1768	26	39478	15	0	3	3	16857	0	2034	2034
1769	29	34482	11	1	0	1	12609	142	0	142
1770	28	41174	13	2	5	7	16189	1707	3772	5479
1771	30	45913	23	5	2	7	32391	2631	2940	5571
1772	25	38891	21	2	4	4	25535	551	2480	3031
1773	30	46648	19	2	3	5	29140	926	2100	3026
1774	27	44597	18	6	9	12	25570	3413	7380	10793
1775	27	38853	15	4	5	8	21189	3182	5550	8732
1776	29	48805	25	2	6	7	34706	345	7255	7600
1777	40	60030	25	2	10	12	39652	2083	10405	12488
1778	34	47326	24	8	6	13	30996	5361	5020	10381
1779	22	39257	17	3	7	9	21129	2585	5760	8345
1780	24	26934	16	2	4	6	18440	290	4648	4938
1781	16	28577	11	4	3	6	14192	2577	3700	6277
1782	25	43848	19	3	7	9	30170	1277	8250	9527
1783	45	78199	34	2	13	4	54151	1838	10670	12508
1784	33	49461	25	3	9	11	35464	1442	9033	10475
1785	48	84611	32	3	6	8	47833	2536	9800	12336
1786	36	77108	18	1	4	5	41717	2856	6750	9606
1787	30	57371	20	0	11	11	35586	0	14351	14351
1788	23	41881	15	3	5	7	21327	1888	5340	7228
1789	17	27606								

reflected continuous competition for land. Moreover, people had recourse to the procedure of the *congément* more and more as a means of acquiring edifices. Graph 2 shows how, from 1760 to 1789, the number of simple sales of edifices as a means of acquiring land declined. By the 1770s peasants were turning in greater numbers away from the ordinary and inexpensive exchange of land by simple sale of edifices to the aggressive, costly and elaborate ritual of the *congément*, with its expensive survey, visits to the seigneurial court and attendant attorneys' fees. That they were willing to pay more for the land they got this way suggests that the peasants were not at all sorry to play the landlord's game; at least, not those peasants who could afford to play it.

Yet this increased competition for land did not put larger shares of this resource in the hands of the richer tenants. Concentration or fragmentation of holdings ought to be indicated by an increase or decrease in the percentage of land value acquired by a fixed proportion of purchasers; for example the 10 per cent carrying out the most expensive expulsions in a given period compared with the same proportion of people in an earlier period. An analysis of the distribution of the value of expulsions among different categories of purchasers for ten-year periods across the century shows no variation in the percentage of the value of land acquired by the wealthier class of buyers. The chances were the same at the end of the century as at the beginning that the most expensive quarter of the total expulsions would constitute 44 per cent of the total expulsions, and so forth.[33]

A clue to solving this apparent paradox may lie in the mechanism by which expulsions were financed: by mortgaging part of the value of the tenure either to a third party or parties, or to one of the expelled tenants, themselves—usually a minor with a share in a holding. The proportion of mortgaged expulsions was quite high. Of the 1364 acts of expulsion in the period 1740–89, 936, or 69 per cent (62 per cent of total value), went before the jurisdiction of

---

[33] Percentage of value of expulsions carried out by:

	1730–9	1740–9	1750–9	1760–9	1770–9	1780–9
(1) Most expensive 10% of expulsions	20.6	20.6	18.4	20.6	19.7	19.6
(2) Most expensive 25% of expulsions	41.5	44.0	42.5	42.0	43.0	44.0

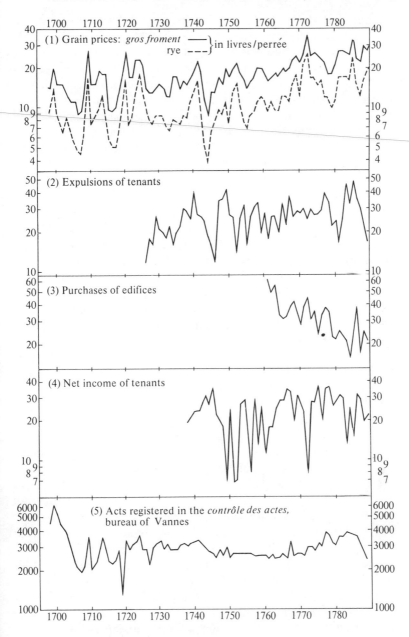

Graph II—Some indicators of economic activity

Largouet; of these, 287 (31 per cent) were financed with a mortgage and 133 (14 per cent) with a *relaissement*—that is, a guaranteed loan granted to the new tenant by one of the previous occupants—for a total of 26 per cent of the total value of holdings exchanged by expulsion.[34] Thus it was not just that those with a little wealth were using their surplus to acquire tenures—this they did—but they also used it to finance acquisitions by people with less resources.

Moreover, the tendency was for more and more of the value of expulsions to be covered in this way by mortgages. Between 1740 and 1788, in the jurisdiction of Largouet, the value of edifices acquired increased on the average by 0.5 per cent a year, but the value of mortgages increased by 1.2 per cent a year, or more than double the increase in the value of the edifices. This progress was not uniform throughout the half-century; in the 1750s and 1760s, when rural income progressed faster then rents and other expenses, the mortgaged value of expulsions fell, but after the mid-sixties, the mortgaged value of expulsions grew at a rate four times as fast as that of total value. Most of this increased mortgage borrowing took the form of outright loans, not the granting of a *relaissement* by the expelled tenant or tenants. Who accepted the mortgages? Friends, relatives, rich *laboureurs,* a widow or a minor who had come into an inheritance. No single individuals appear to have cornered any part of the mortgage market, and townsmen scarcely appear at all. The financial resources of the more prosperous sections of a predominantly rural community were tapped; the result was the increased indebtedness of *tenuyers* as a group. When the credit ran out, and the number and value of mortgages and *congéments* fell together, as they did after the crisis year of 1785, it was a sure sign that the prosperity of the rural community had been shaken.

Land and debt are one thing; wealth and the distribution of wealth sometimes another. The effect of these fifty to sixty years of inflation and debt on the wealth of families is not easy to measure, but one can make some attempt at approximation. One important element of rural wealth was the edifices on holdings under *domaine congéable,* and some indication has already been given of the rather slow increase in their value. The price of edifices does seem to have risen somewhat, but only as a result of inflation, not of improvements, for one of the most inhibiting aspects of *domaine congéable* was that the tenant could not demand reimbursement for the value

[34] A.D. Morbihan, B: Largouet, minutes: 1741–89.

of improvements upon expulsion. It is consequently not surprising that the value of edifices reimbursed should have risen by only 0.8 per cent a year for the period 1738–89, a time when rye and wheat prices rose at almost double that rate. Another element in rural wealth, personal property, can be studied in post-mortem inventories (*inventaires après décès*). The results of an examination of all the inventories made of the possessions of deceased persons in the countryside in the jurisdiction of Largouet in 1732, 1745, 1765, 1775 and 1780 are shown in Tables XI-6 and XI-7. These tables represent the wealth of the deceased as it appeared in *biens mobiliers,* to the exclusion of landed property, debts and credits, which are sometimes mentioned but not evaluated in the total. The overall worth of these possessions has been evaluated in two ways, by including and excluding the value of cattle and grain and by distinguishing those who were most likely to be actually getting all their income directly from a holding (those who had a pair of oxen in their byre) from those who were not.

Two conclusions emerge from these tables. The first is that there does not appear to have been overall enrichment of the rural population. Whether we take the median value or the mean value, whether we consider the group with draft oxen or the whole lot of inventories, whether we count grain and cattle or not, there appears to be a clear fall in the real value of personal possessions from the 1740s through the prosperous sixties and the uncertain seventies. Only at the end of the period did the value of personal property even catch up with inflation. To take another sign, the average number of cows in the byres and pastures and swine in the pigsties of ploughmen with a team of oxen did not change at all significantly. At the most, there was a slight increase in the average number of cows per owner from around 4 in the 1730s and 1740s to around 5 in 1775, followed however by a return to 4 in 1780. In part, it is true, this lagging response to the increased well-being of mid-century can be put down to the low marginal propensity of peasants to lay out money on the luxuries and even on the necessities of life.[35] Their responses to increasing income in the form of decisions to invest in land were, as we have seen, much more rapid, and it is perhaps significant that the livestock holdings, too, increased slightly by the seventies. But even if we admit that peasants preferred to put their

[35] The main sign of extravagance in the inventories of the rich is a profusion of linen sheets and shirts.

Table XI-6: Post-mortem inventories (i)

(1) Median values of inventories

	(a) Net value (excluding cattle and grain)				(b) Total value			
	Persons with oxen		All inventories		With oxen		All inventories	
	Value	Index (1732 = 100)	Value	Index (1732 = 100)	Value	Index (1732 = 100)	Value	Index (1732 = 100)
1732	173	100	112	100	526	100	240	100
1745	198	114	134	119	523	99	261	109
1765	158	70	104	92	371	104	197	82
1775	290	168	145	129	715	136	320	133
1780	294	170	198	176	784	149	355	148

(2) Mean values of inventories

	(a) Net value				(b) Total value			
	With oxen		All inventories		With oxen		All inventories	
	Value	Index	Value	Index	Value	Index	Value	Index
1732	225	100	173	100	526	100	357	100
1745	205	91	159	92	516	98	326	91
1765	225	100	162	94	524	100	309	87
1775	439	195	276	160	918	175	534	149
1780	383	170	246	143	932	177	521	146

Source: A.D. Morbihan, B: Largouet, minutes.
Inventories in which only the common property of married people was listed were not used.
Numbers of inventories: 1732: 29 with oxen, 24 without; 1745: 28 with, 38 without; 1765: 34 and 18; 1775: 39 and 31; 1780: 26 and 30.

Table XI-7: Post-mortem inventories (ii)

Year	Quartile	Number of animals	Average value (livres)	Animals/ owner	Number of owners
(1) Cows owned by persons with oxen					
1732	Lowest	21	11.9	2.6	8
	2nd	29	15.3	4.1	7
	3rd	35	17.1	5.0	7
	Highest	34	20.9	4.9	7
	Total	119	16.8	4.1	29
1745	Lowest	20	16.6	2.9	7
	2nd	24	21.4	3.4	7
	3rd	25	21.3	3.6	7
	Highest	37	21.0	5.3	7
	Total	106	20.3	3.8	28
1765	Lowest	7	15.1	1.8	4
	2nd	10	18.9	2.5	4
	3rd	10	22.8	3.3	3
	Highest	13	19.5	4.3	3
	Total	40	19.4	2.9	14
1775	Lowest	27	20.0	3.4	8
	2nd	27	20.4	3.9	7
	3rd	34	22.9	4.9	7
	Highest	65	27.1	9.3	7
	Total	153	23.8	5.3	29
1780	Lowest	17	29.6	2.4	7
	2nd	25	32.5	3.6	7
	3rd	26	35.9	4.3	6
	Highest	36	36.6	6.0	6
	Total	104	34.3	4.0	26
(2) Swine owned by persons with oxen					
1732	Lowest	6	8.3	0.6	8
	2nd	5	11.0	0.7	7
	3rd	6	14.7	0.9	7
	Highest	8	16.5	1.1	7
	Total	25	13.0	0.9	29

Table XI-7: Post-mortem inventories (ii)

Year	Quartile	Number of animals	Average value (livres)	Animals/ owner	Number of owners
1745	Lowest	4	9.0	0.6	7
	2nd	10	6.8	1.4	7
	3rd	6	15.0	0.9	7
	Highest	10	8.1	1.4	7
	Total	30	9.2	1.1	28
1765	Lowest	1	15.0	0.3	4
	2nd	4	7.2	1.3	4
	3rd	2	20.0	0.7	3
	Highest	3	25.7	1.0	3
	Total	4	6.8	0.3	13
1775	Lowest	6	6.7	0.8	8
	2nd	5	18.0	0.7	7
	3rd	9	20.3	1.3	7
	Highest	4	21.8	0.6	7
	Total	24	16.7	0.8	29
1780	Lowest	5	16.0	0.7	7
	2nd	8	15.5	1.1	7
	3rd	4	16.5	0.7	6
	Highest	9	22.1	1.5	6
	Total	26	18.0	1.0	26

Source: As in Table XI-6.

money into land and livestock rather than linen, it seems sure that on the whole the wealth of the countryside, as it showed in the objects of daily use, was at best stagnant.

However, within this pattern of stagnation in inflation there are signs of an increasing diversification of the economic hierarchy. This increasing inequality is shown by grouping the values of the various inventories from 1732 to 1780 about multiples of the mean value, in the manner proposed for tax assessments by Jacques Dupâquier and used above in Chapter II. The categories are rather fine and the numbers small, but if we pay attention to the lowest and highest groups, we find among the total mass of inventories a tendency for the proportion whose fortunes were less than one-quarter of the mean fortune to increase between 1732 and 1775–80 by, roughly, 30 to 50 per cent depending on whether we consider gross or net value.[36] This increase in the numbers of the poor seems to be at the expense of those with middling fortunes rather than the richest. Among those with a team of oxen, there was also increasing diversity, but this probably meant less within the boundaries of that group; it was a fairly substantial block of fortunes sitting firmly astride the mean value. The significant changes appear to have taken place rather between this set of men with oxen, which corresponded roughly with the *tenuyers,* and the 'others', who included a fringe of better-off millers and retired people and a much larger group of *laboureurs,* artisans and marginal tenants.

What changes occurred in other forms of economic activity which brought wealth into the region, and what effects did they have? The decline of the textile trade, whose fate, as far as Vannes was concerned, seems to have been sealed early in the century, has already been described. A brighter picture was offered by the notable shipbuilding industry within the Amirautés of Vannes and Lorient, and it seems that Vannes and Auray concentrated most of the production of the region. Total tonnage constructed increased more than eight times between 1714 and 1789, or about fourfold between the 1730s and the 1780s; average tonnage grew by about 70 per cent between 1714 and 1789 and by about 45 per cent between the 1730s and the 1780s. More and bigger ships were being constructed than ever before, and even though the average tonnage of ships built in the region remained modest, the aggregate tonnage of the ships built in the ports of the region between 1767 and 1787 was the fifth highest in France, greater even than commercial tonnage

---

[36] Percentage of inventories worth less than 25 per cent of the mean value (net values):

	People with oxen	All inventories
1732	8%	20.8%
1745	15.1	18.2
1765	7.7	11.5
1775	26.6	31.7
1780	28.5	28.6

built in the great ports of Toulon, Le Havre, Marseilles and Rouen.[37] This was a source, and almost the only source, of increased revenue for local industry in the century, and its effect on the economy of the town has been mentioned above in Chapters II and III. But somehow this activity merely served to keep the town of Vannes from disaster rather than promoting any real growth of the regional economy; probably this was owing to the relatively light weight it bore in the total value of regional output. Within its limits, however, shipbuilding was a considerable success and because it was relatively independent of the fluctuations of the local harvest cycle, it doubtless helped the region through the instability of the 1770s and 1780s.

Sardine fishing, if we follow the accounts of it given by the Ministry of the Marine, seems at first glance to have enjoyed a tremendous boom in the 1780s with two to three score boats drawing an average of 133,000 livres a year in the quarter of Vannes during the years 1783–7; again, not a very large proportion of local marketable production, but not inconsiderable either, and, to judge from these figures a five-fold improvement over the catches of the 1760s.[38] However, these statistics are fragmentary and probably misleading; the years 1783–8 were clearly record years, to judge from the number of boats for which licences (*congés*) were taken out in comparison to previous years, and the apparently record-

[37] Figures derived from the graphs in Thomas-Lacroix, 'Les Constructions et les ventes de navires', 71–11; Le Goff and Meyer, 'Les Constructions navales en France', 173–85.

[38] A. N. Marine, C^5 36 gives the following:

Year	Fresh sardines		Salted sardines	
	Quantity ('000)	Value	Quantity ('000)	Value
1751	4,354	8,708	1,085	2,177
1752	1,204	4,800	1,449	8,200
1753	1,498	7,000	1,393	5,560
—	—	—	—	—
1760	1,700	3,600	2,030	13,500
1761	1,200	8,400	2,975	23,375
—	—	—	—	—
1783	10,300	51,500	5,150	41,200
1784	10,666	74,662	5,333	53,330
1785	7,067	70,670	3,534	53,010
1786	11,954	95,632	5,976	65,736
1787	11,400	114,000	3,800	49,400

breaking catches of these five years are also exaggerated by an astronomical rise in the price of fish after 1783, a result no doubt of momentarily bad harvests. When the number of licences taken out during the whole period 1745–58 and 1770–90 is examined, we can see that the Ministry's figures put too optimistic a face on things and show neither the usual value and volume of catches nor the extremely chancy fluctuations between seasons. There is in fact no clear trend towards an increase in the number of fishing licences, and only a very small rise in the number of licences taken out—about 0.1 per cent a year.[39] Local shipping likewise appears to have known no expansion. Although it is hard to discern trends in a trade so subject to the caprices of weather, wars and prices, the general tendency of ship departures from the ports of Vannes and the gulf was stagnant or downward.[40]

Looking at all these series of prices, production, wages and rents, it is possible to break down the economic history of the Vannetais between 1726 and 1789 into four phases. The first runs to the late 1730s and early 1740s when prices reached hitherto unprecedented

[39] According to A.N., G⁵ 31: Amirauté de Vannes: comptes rendus par le receveur: Dépenses en congés et commissions yields the following averages for the ports of Auray, Locmariaquer, Redon, Vannes and Sarzeau:

1745–9	205 (average)
1750–4	212
1755–8	221
—	—
1770–4	246
1775–9	192
1780–4	173
1785–9	269

See also Ogée, *Dictionnaire*, 378–9 which speaks of years of poor catches before 1780.

[40] Licences for shipping (not including foreign trade or *expéditions en guerre et marchandises*) from the same source as in note 39:

	Brittany	France
1745–9	194	312
1750–4	191	332
1755–8	161	230
—	—	—
1770–4	189	302
1775–9	171	268
1780–4	173	205
1785–9	218	248

heights, crops failed, rents rose, and the chances of selling grain elsewhere diminished. Although prices in Spain generally rose in relation to those in Vannes during this time, it appears that southwest France was better placed to profit from this trade. This unhappy phase came to a climax in the great demographic crisis of 1741. The number of expulsions of tenants, one indicator of the prosperity of the wealthier part of the countryside, fell and did not recover until 1747.

If we are to judge the general level of economic activity by the number of transactions registered to the *contrôle des actes,* the year 1741 marked the beginning of a long period of stagnation stretching into the 1760s.[41] Certainly the 1740s began inauspiciously, with declining real revenues and rising rents for tenants under *domaine congéable,* but the terms of sale for grain in Spain, and Bordeaux and even Marseilles did begin to improve, and this encouraged the merchants of Vannes to export their grain at a profit, legally or surreptitiously. If the landlords, tithe holders and corn merchants were the immediate beneficiaries, the surge in grain prices in the war years 1745–9 seems to have extended a momentary prosperity to the countryside; it brought forth almost immediately an increase in long-term tenant expenditures in the form of expulsions, which began to rise in 1747, although net income took longer to recover, as rising costs ate up profits on the average holding until at least 1750.

In the early 1750s the advantage in the export grain trade was momentarily threatened, and the year 1751–2 was a crisis year in the region,[42] but the prospects for grain shipments began to improve around 1754, and it is from this point that we can date the boom of the late 1750s and 1760s when both tenants and landlords pros-

[41] A.D. Morbihan, 17 C 5156–341, which can be summarized as a series of averages:

1698–9	5540	1740–4	3147
1700–4	4166	1745–9	2734
1705–9	2495	1750–4	2654
1710–14	2721	1755–9	2657
1715–19	2252	1760–4	2548
1720–4	3317	1765–9	2767
1725–9	2886	1770–4	2810
1730–4	3092	1775–9	3419
1735–9	3105	1780–4	3563
		1785–9	3139

[42] A.C. Vannes, BB 18: 21-2-1752, 5-6-1752.

pered, tenants even more than the landlords. At least some shipments found their way southward on neutral ships during the Seven Years War, and a continuation of good harvests, strong external demand and 'sticky' operating costs allowed a rise in net income for tenants. This rise began to peter out around 1770, killed by rising prices in Vannes, which gradually destroyed the advantage in shipping grain to Spain, the south-west and Marseilles. The price increase on the local market, which began in earnest in 1765, continued until wheat prices reached a level in 1772 which was 30 per cent higher than their 1764 level. The prospects of sales stimulated once again peasant land hunger, probably encouraged already by the rise in the number of young adults during the 1740s and 1750s. Expulsions of tenants, which had proceeded in an upward but irregular path from the early 1750s got a new impetus, peaking in 1767–8, but remaining on a high level until 1777.

But in the meantime, rents and taxes had begun to catch up with the price rise, and by 1772 reached a kind of plateau. Meanwhile, producers lost their advantages on southern markets, for although their potential profit margins rose on the Spanish market, they never regained their edge in Bordeaux, and it would appear that other competitors, in south-western France, and even from as far away as America, were able to sell in Spain at a greater profit. And, except for a few isolated shipments, the Marseilles market remained inaccessible.[43]

There was an alternative, or rather a supplement to grain exports, however. There had always been some sort of market for local cattle, which were sold for meat and hides and also to itinerant merchants, mainly Poitevins and Normans. From 1764 onwards, cattle prices improved, partly because of occasional shortages of forage, partly because of demand in Normandy and Poitou (in 1768) and Bayonne (in 1775). In any event, prices held good for a long time, and from 1775 onwards, the intendant's *subdélégués* noted that the number of offspring was on the rise: 'Les bestiaux sont en bon état et se vendent bien. On a beaucoup emporté pour Bayonne. Ce qui a produit un bon effet, en mettant nos laboureurs dans le cas d'entretenir beaucoup d'élèves. Vraie richesse de la campagne' was the commentary in 1775; in 1780, the *subdélégué* wrote that cattle were 'en très bon état et depuis deux ou trois ans on les a bien multipliés, ce qui est un avantage pour le commerce vu les

[43] A.D. Morbihan, 11 B 53 (19) and above, p. 296 n. 6.

circonstances', and the next year he repeated that continued high prices offered for them 'fait qui les cultivateurs font beaucoup d'élèves', an observation repeated in 1783.[44] This period, in fact, marks the beginning of a slow conversion to a greater emphasis on cattle-raising in the region, but its impact, as the sizes of herds indicated in Table XI-7 show, was limited to a recovery of levels seen earlier in the century: the average number of cows per owner on a holding with a team of oxen was 4.1 in 1732, 3.8 in 1745, 2.5 in 1765, and 5.3 and 4.0 in 1775 and 1780. The most significant change seems to have been an increase in the size of the herds owned by the richest peasants.

Despite these encouraging signs, the transition was by no means smooth or easy, and the increase in herds was cut short by the hard winter and heat-wave of 1784–5. It was not until 1789 that the losses of that year were replaced, and then of course other troubles intervened. On the whole, although there were moments of euphoria in the last two decades of the old regime, the generally stagnant market for grain, still by far the most important element in the rural economy, and the fragile and limited character of the conversion to cattle-raising made it an awkward time. From the early 1770s the net real income of *tenuyers* became unsteady, declined in 1776, then fell rapidly from 1782. Dramatically, between 1774 and 1775, the percentage of value of expulsions financed by mortgages rose from 10 to 49 per cent, as the better-off began to feel the effect of a price recession at a time when costs had soared. By 1777, expulsions, financed or not by mortgages, began to fall, and although there was a brief recrudescence of expulsions from 1782 to 1785, after this point the lack of cash or credit in the countryside prevented any further speculation, while grain prices once again began the precipitous climb which marked the beginning of the revolutionary period.

So, if we look at the evolution of the region over the sixty-odd years from the beginning of the 'economic eighteenth century' from the point of view of tenants, one can say that the 1750s and the 1760s were the good years; from the point of view of the landlords, they were the 1740s the 1770s and the 1780s. Those at the bottom of the scale in town and country never knew good years; only ones which were less bad than others, depending on the chances of the harvest. The grain trade had come to be less and less a reasonable venture by the 1770s and 1780s and although local peasants drew the conse-

[44] A.D. I.-V., C 1652–5.

quences of this change and began to put more emphasis on raising cattle to take advantage of rising prices, the scale on which they operated, the limited time they had to carry out the conversion, and the terrible summer of 1785 still left them vulnerable to the vagaries of the grain economy. In town and country indebtedness and the gap separating rich and poor grew under the impact of sixty years of inflation which rewarded on occasion the wealthier tenant farmers but brought neither comparable benefits to sub-tenants and wage-labourers, nor structural transformations of a sort which might have lifted this rural economy to a different level of activity. Except for shipbuilding, manufacturing activities, which might have at least fed some of the increasing numbers of poor, declined.

Capital had nevertheless been generated during the period. In the years from 1772 to 1789 alone, half a million livres went into the expulsion of tenants by other tenants and their backers; another half a million was spent on land purchases by non-rural buyers. But this fund served only to keep the old economy turning over. Judged by utilitarian standards, the surplus skimmed from agricultural production by the Church in the form of tithes at least served to maintain some poor relief and a level of music, education and culture in the region; the state's diminishing share of local production did no good except inadvertently to provide a fund of specie which eased the credit arrangements of local merchants. Capital, then, did exist. But what could a man do with it in the Vannetais in the eighteenth century? Invest in colonial trade? After mid-century, the future in that line—and a dicey one at that—was in Nantes, where there were infinitely better facilities for supplies and more sophisticated, if precarious, credit arrangements. In shipbuilding? It had some future as the history of the region after 1815 was to show, but shipbuilding was not infinitely expandable, was closely tied to the progress of French shipping—highly vulnerable in wartime —and the influx of outside capital, and was hobbled by a small-scale form of production. Buy an office, whose value was declining? Buy land, which, under *domaine congéable,* was uneconomical to improve and which, if converted to *métairies,* would only find the most unfortunate sort of ploughmen for tenants? The chances of success, in theory, were greatest with landed investment, but the rigidity of rural social structure and the system of land tenure set definite limits to the profits and growth that could be achieved.

In the end, the chief resource of the region was its land and its people. The land had considerable though variable earning power, but too many people were trying to make a living from it, and from each other. That the land nearly always produced enough to feed its inhabitants was almost irrelevant; many of the poorest could barely afford a subsistence diet, while the revenues of the one-third or so, from whom any investment in development had to come, were, directly or indirectly, subject to the caprices of nature and markets far away, and too few of them were able to spend the little they did gain in any profitable fashion. As the *subdélégué* of Vannes wrote of the grain trade in 1758: 'Quand les débouchés manquent, les plus riches se trouvent dans une espèce d'indigence . . . car quoique le plus ou moins de production doive s'influer sur le prix de cette denrée, c'est moins cette circonstance qui y contribue que le plus ou moins d'exportation. . . .'[45]

In effect, although many of the rentiers of Vannes and its region in theory did well, or ought to have, during the last decades of the old regime, not all of them were equipped, as we have seen, to withstand several years in which they could not export their grain; nor were the merchants on whose services they depended much safer. It is perhaps this insecurity, in addition to inertia and fear of disorder, which explains the willingness of the local nobility to accept the municipal revolution of 1789 in the hope that business, that is, the free export of grain, would resume again. And when the local rentiers and the merchants were deprived of the income they drew from the countryside, the artisans and the poor in the town who depended on them were caught up in the crisis as well. A century-long stagnation, a difficult recession and a sharp crisis in the last four years of the old regime made it certain that the Revolution, when it came to the Vannetais, would have dramatic and unpredictable effects.

---

[45] A.D. I.-V., C 1652: 1758.

CHAPTER XII

EPILOGUE: THE REVOLUTION IN THE VANNETAIS

By 1792, even before, most inhabitants of the Vannetais had made their political choice, and the region was almost totally given over to the forces of counter-revolution. But when we consider the economic conditions on the eve of 1789, when we take into account what we know of the balance of poor and rich in town and country, and the impetus which rural and urban poor gave to the Revolution elsewhere in France, this political choice becomes less important as a fact than as a problem. In most of France, the peasants made the final and decisive attack on the old regime in the summer of 1789, and in many towns, the artisans, shopkeepers, labourers and lesser professionals later became the revolutionary social amalgam known as the sans-culottes. Why did the common people of Vannes and its countryside enroll under the wrong banner? What had gone wrong? The best way to begin answering these questions is to ask how the political changes of the Revolution affected these groups.

To most 'enlightened' outside observers, the answer was clear: it was put succinctly by the Directory of the Department of the Morbihan in February 1792: 'Les citoyens de ce département principalement ceux des campagnes bénissaient la révolution jusqu'au moment où les ecclésiastiques leur ont fait un crime des moyens qu'ils employaient pour la soutenir.'[1] Matters were a good deal more complex than this. What happened seems to have been that the political action taken by the common people never coincided very well with the course of the Revolution as it was seen from Paris and interpreted by the local bourgeoisie. And the changes which the Revolution brought, if they affected each section of local society differently, had one thing in common: few of them bettered the lot of the ordinary folk, and many of them brought drastic and unpleasant changes for their way of life.

[1] A.D. Morbihan, L 135: Directory of Department to the King, 7-2-1792.

Indeed few, if any, people had even a fleeting chance to 'bless' the Revolution, except for the small group of bourgeois who took power in 1789 and retained it for the duration of the Revolution and Empire. The first signs that the Revolution was for the few rather than the many came when the new regime had to face up to the problem of the food supply. Quickly, it showed itself just as incapable of reconciling the interests of consumers and shippers of grain as the old regime had been. The continuing problem of *subsistances*, which in many other regions of France gave edge to the revolutionary zeal of the common people, here simply proved at the very beginning of the Revolution that the new men in control had the same interests as the old oligarchy. Where the problem appeared at its most acute was in the areas with large concentrations of poor, the peninsula of Rhuys and in the town of Vannes. In Arzon, on the peninsula of Rhuys, in May 1789, a crowd stopped Brénugat de Kervéno, the receiver of the royal domain, from embarking a shipment of grain. It was a time of high prices and dearth, and the rumour circulated, rather like the tales which spread during the Great Fear elsewhere in France that year, that the grain was being transferred to an English vessel sheltering behind the island of Hoedic. The local rector and the excisemen stationed at Arzon gave the crowd their sympathy and support, but the judicial officers of Vannes, many of them patriots, did their ineffective best to seek out and punish the rebels. In December, grain was still being held back.[2]

In the autumn of the succeeding year, Brénugat tried, again without success, to ship grain from Sarzeau, this time for Lorient where it was intended, ironically, to keep down the discontent of the hungry townsfolk there. After an unsuccessful attempt by the local *maréchaussée* to get the Sarzeau National Guard to protect the shipment (the Guardsmen claimed their guns were too small for the ammunition provided) the administrators of the District, on 23 December, sent out an armed force made up of line troops and National Guards from Vannes and Lorient. In revenge, on Christmas Eve, a crowd stoned the houses of Thebaud, a notary, and Brénugat, both of whom it considered responsible for this invasion from outside. The report of the Departmental administrator who had led the force described the interests in conflict:

[2] A.D. I.-V., C 1712: Febvrier (Vannes) to de Rochefort (Rennes), 8-5-1790; C 1716: Brénugat de Kerveno (Rhuys) to de Linière (Paris), 13-5-1789, Limur to intendant, 20-5-1789, intendant to Limur, 29-5-1789; A.D. Morbihan, B 1342.

En général le peuple . . . est doux mais . . . la dernière des classes craignant pour sa subsistance dans une année où la récolte a été mauvaise, l'enlèvement des grains était pour elle un sujet d'alarmes et de murmures . . . il n'existait pas d'autres causes des oppositions faites jusqu'ici aux chargements; des menaces faites aux chargeurs, bateliers, charretiers et à eux-mêmes [the municipal officers]; de la grande fermentation dans les esprits qui effraie quiconque a des propriétés et quelqu'autorité . . . Le laboureur et quiconque a une propriété ont gémi de l'inconvénient, mais . . . ils ont été maîtrisés et intimidés par la populace.[3]

The fear of dearth and grain hoarders and tension between haves and have-nots in both country and town condemned from the beginning the chances of a revolutionary 'alliance' between bourgeois and the poorer folk in Vannes and around it. In Vannes itself, the fear of hoarders had given an impulse to the little municipal revolution of July 1789, when the poor had mobilized to demand an embargo on food exports. This fear persisted into 1790 and 1791, much to the chagrin of the revolutionary élite. All through the autumn and winter of 1789–90, the local bourgeoisie maintained their hold on municipal government at the price of maintaining this compromise. In December 1789, apparently under pressure from the common people of Vannes, the town council complained to the Controller-General that the merchants had caused a shortage in the town by buying up all available stocks in the countryside for shipment to Rennes, Nantes, Brest and Lorient. The knowledge that extraordinary demands were being made on the region was enough to freeze the local grain trade. In March 1790, in what appears to have been only one incident among many, a crowd composed mainly of day-labourers stopped three small grain merchants from passing beyond the commune of La Trinité-Surzur with the grain they had bought at Vannes for the nearby town of Muzillac.[4]

In Vannes itself, by the beginning of April, not only the common folk, but even what the council called 'reasonable people' believed the activities of merchants in the countryside were leading to famine. Unfortunately the council chose this moment to reaffirm their right to govern: on 5 March they re-established the institution of the

[3] A.D. Morbihan, Lz 272[7]: trial of L. Le Bodo *et al.*, 1790; L 252: declaration of Regnier, 23-12-1790; see also ibid., 9, 22-9-1790; L 134: 22-9-1790; L 1445: 28-9-1790.

[4] A.D. I.-V., C 1712: Petition of the commissioners of the municipality and commons of Vannes, 31-12-1789; Febvrier (Vannes) to de Rochefort (Rennes), 8-3-1790; Fréville, *L'Intendance de Bretagne*, iii, 313; A.C. Vannes, BB 29: 27-3-1790.

nightwatch, in which service was obligatory for all men under fifty and, far worse in the eyes of the ordinary people, on 29 March took the fatal step of asserting its right to collect the town's traditional excise taxes on drink. This meant that those paying less than three livres in *capitation* would be forced, as in the old regime, to obtain special permission from the judges of the *devoirs* when they wanted to store wine, beer or cider in their homes.[5]

The reply came quickly. On 3 April a crowd forced the council to release the prisoners arrested after the affair of La Trinité; on the 6th they met in large numbers in the courtyard of the town hall to demand an end to the excise and an embargo on grain shipments out of the town. The council yielded on the second demand by out-lawing grain purchases outside the town market and setting up a subsidized municipal granary for the poor. Having calmed the storm, the council then raised it again when they arrested two individuals who had attacked a countryman in the town market and cut open his sacks of rye. On the night of Sunday 11 April, a crowd, calling for the mayor and shouting 'Vive le roi, vive la noblesse, au diable le Tiers', besieged the town hall, stoned the *jeunes volont-aires* and the town militia, and fought a running battle with the forces of order in the pitch-dark streets. Charging that the mutineers had threatened to call in people from the surrounding country parishes, the municipality mustered its volunteer forces and the few regular troops on hand and proclaimed martial law.

Who were the crowds and individuals who carried out this classic *sàns-culotte* riot to counter-revolutionary slogans? The people arrested in the market incident on 4 April were a weaver, an oven-tender, a mason, a carpenter, a draper, a tanner, one man without a profession, and a woman. The men who had attacked the *laboureur* on 10 April were a draper and a tavern-keeper. All of those who gave a place of residence were from the quarter of St-Patern, around the parish church. This was apparently the place where the revolt of 11 April had started as well. According to one witness, the initiative in that movement had been taken by the drapers and wool-carders, both men and women, from the rue Gillard, near the church of St-Patern, a group from the class of persons 'connu sous la dénomination vulgaire de pis mignettes'. But in the crowd, the *jeunes volontaires* claimed to distinguish also a woman dressed in the manner of women from the French-speaking

5   A.C. Vannes, BB 29: 29-3-1790.

country parishes, to the south-east.

It was characteristic that the poor of Vannes should have felt themselves allied to the surrounding countryside, or at least to the poorer people there who, like them, had the most to fear from a sudden shortage of grain. The alliance, like the fear, appears to have been real: a year later, it became known that the people of Sulniac had planned to march on Vannes at that time. Characteristic too was the fact that the rural side of the agitation in the first part of 1790 took place in the less prosperous part of the region, to the south-east of the town, where the proportion of poorer people in each parish was highest. This alliance of rural and urban poor, reinforced no doubt by the links which many of the townspeople retained with the countryside, was to appear again, in graver circumstances, in 1791 and 1793.[6]

In the meantime, the lot of the poor in town and country alike did not seem to be improving. The town council's measures may have had some temporary effect in Vannes, but the flow of grain from the countryside remained in constant danger of interruption, especially around harvest time. In September 1790, rumours spread through the rural parishes of secret grain shipments by sea to La Roche-Bernard. In March 1791, there was another riot against corn merchants at Surzur. In September, the grain trade froze because peasants refused to accept the new assignats from bakers in Vannes. In the countryside, old sources of revenue and poor relief dried up: the people of Billiers in February 1791 planned to block a grain shipment from the abbey of Prières on the pretext that the alms they used to obtain from the monks there were no longer offered by the new regime. In September 1791, the poor of St-Avé were promising publicly 'que si on ne leur procurait pas des ressources honnêtes ils seraient obligés d'employer la violence pour s'en assurer'. The future member of the Convention, Le Quinio, accused the local nobles of deliberately refusing to buy goods in the countryside in order to provoke discontent; whether this was true or not, the economic crisis and general uncertainty undoubtedly reduced such expenditures by nobles. The poor relief that the country parishes had expected to receive after 1789 did not materialize fast enough, as the parishes which rose up in revolt in February 1791 were to complain. Not surprisingly, in this time of troubles, the number of

---

[6] A.C. Vannes, BB 29: 6, 11, 12, 15-4-1790; A.D. Morbihan, B 3703; B 1342: trial of J. Gaultier *et al.*, 1790; Lz 274: Interrogation of J. Le Bourhis, 1791.

vagrants and the danger they posed to order seemed to be on the increase, and probably was. At the same time, the new revolutionary authorities and their allies among the wealthier peasants tried clumsily to deal with these perennial problems by rounding up the local poor and other marginal people.[7]

In the circumstances, the attitude of those in the countryside who had a little wealth to defend and who might have hoped to benefit from the agrarian reforms of 4 August 1789 and after, was crucial. Such people were not lacking; the original electoral assemblies of 1789 and 1790, if they were dominated by townsmen, had nevertheless drawn on the élite of the countryside and of the seacoast. To some extent loyal partisans of the Revolution could still be found among that élite as late as 1791 and 1792; thus in 1791, sea-captains and *laboureurs* denounced counter-revolutionary priests in Arzon and Brandivy. In a handful of communes in the area—Ambon, perhaps the Île d'Arz and the Île-aux-Moines—they managed to keep the upper hand even beyond this date. The students of the College of Vannes, by and large the sons of the rural élite, were ardent supporters of the Revolution at its beginning, and probably joined the *jeunes volontaires* in the town; in the summer of 1789 the future Chouan leader Georges Cadoudal, then still a student in the college, seems to have taken the lead in signing a letter of support addressed to the young revolutionaries of Rennes. Even after the troubles in Vannes, at the local celebration of the Feast of the Federation in July 1790, the students showed, according to the official account, by 'l'ardeur avec laquelle ils prenaient leur serment qu'un jour la patrie n'aura pas de plus fidèlcs défenseurs. Ces mots nous le jurons formèrent un cri de joie qui attendrit tous les spectateurs.'[8]

But the enthusiasm of the *sanior pars* of rural society for the Revolution received little material reward. Thus, on the peninsula of Rhuys, nobody benefited for a long time from the decisions taken by the National Assembly on the night of 4 August 1789. Ecclesiastical tithes, as elsewhere in France, continued to be collected in

---

[7] A.C. Vannes, BB 29: 15-9-1790: A.D. Morbihan, Lz 273[8]: trial of J. David *et al.*, 19-3-1790: L 343: Municipality of Vannes to District, 3-9-1791; L 134: Directory of Department to District of La Roche-Bernard, 15-2-1791; Le Quinio, *École des laboureurs*, 52–3. On brigandage, several cases in A.D. Morbihan, B 1340; see also Le Goff and Sutherland, 'The Revolution and the Rural Community', 113.

[8] A.C. Vannes, BB 29: 14-7-1790; A.D. Morbihan, Lz 278[8]: trial of P. Levanteur, 1791; Lz 281: trial of F. Endoux, 1791; Cadoudal, *Georges Cadoudal,* 12.

the area in 1789–90, and the peasants of Theix and the rural part of St-Patern, where the bishop skimmed off part of the tithe, refused for a time to pay. The peninsula of Rhuys and the Île d'Arz were in turmoil for the opposite reason: the authorities of the District of Vannes decided that certain dues, considered up to then as ecclesiastical tithes usurped by the priory of Arzon, the monastery of St-Gildas and other seigneurs, were really *champarts,* so that under the legislation of 4–11 August 'abolishing' feudalism, they still had to be paid to their successor, the revolutionary government, until they were redeemed at a capitalized value. In addition, the peninsula, which had previously been exempt from the provincial tax called the *fouages extraordinaires* because of a special privilege, was now compelled to pay this tax until the new forms of land and personal taxes could be established. The poorer country people had gained nothing; the richer were disappointed. After the difficulties with grain shipments, it was not surprising that, by the beginning of 1791, the life of a *patriote* on the peninsula of Rhuys was cheap.[9]

Thus the revolutionary changes which in many other regions of France in one way or another won the support of the solider elements of the rural community by satisfying their economic grievances, did not take place around Vannes. It was not that there were no potential revolutionaries; it was simply that they had no chance to fit their aims into the course of the Revolution as it was evolving in Paris and elsewhere in France. This incompatibility was especially evident in the way the question of the *domaine congéable* was handled. Here, if anywhere, was an area for reform which would have gained the solid support of the rural élite for the new regime. And indeed, at the beginning of the Revolution, a few of the urban revolutionaries did make a considerable effort to win the countryside to their cause. In January 1789, the municipal council of Rhuys had begun to circulate the propaganda of the Third Estate in the countryside, and certain members of the Third Estate were denounced at the same time by De Lenvos, a noble of Vannes, for sending out anti-noble propaganda to the country rectors. In January as well, the rector of St-Patern, Le Croisier, claiming to speak for the *laboureurs* of his parish, sent a petition to the King in which the denunciation of the *domaine congéable* featured prominently. The

    [9] A.D. Morbihan, L 234: 27-7-1790; L 1445: 13-10-1790, 18, 20-11-1790, 17-10-1791; L 1446: 27-3-1792, 12-6-1792; L 134: 28-1-1791; L 261: Le Quinio (Sarzeau) to District, 31-1-1791.

cahiers de doléances of the rural parishes have been lost, but it appears that at least as far as the *domaine congéable* was concerned, articles 143 and 145 of the *cahier* of the *sénéchaussée*, like article 43 of the *sénéchaussé* of Auray and Article 181 of the *sénéchaussée* of Hennebont were put in at the insistence of the rural parishes.[10]

The *domaine congéable* certainly remained in the minds of the peasants. In June, the *laboureur* Le Floch of Elven, correspondent of the *commission intermédiaire* of the Estates of Brittany, took the trouble of painfully composing a letter to Necker to remind him that the *cahier* of the *sénéchaussée* had condemned this form of tenure: 'nous désirons d'être délivré de c'ete cruel cervitute, pour être pus [*sic*] utile à l'état'.[11] In the days following 4 August, the Breton Deputy, Coroller du Moustier, tried without success to have the *domaine congéable* included among the types of tenure to be abolished or declared redeemable. In February 1790, the question was opened again at the patriotic assembly of Brittany and Anjou, held at Pontivy. Among others, the deputies of Languidic asked 'Qu'on demande à l'Assemblée Nationale de supprimer le congément et tous les usements locaux et tous les abus qu'on voit en Bretagne parce qu'on a promis beaucoup aux domaniers; mais rien de bon ne vient pour eux, ce qui fait qu'ils sont hors d'eux-mêmes et en désolations.'[12] Gradually, the demands for the 'reform' or 'suppression' of the *domaine congéable,* probably watered down in the *cahier de doléances* of the *sénéchaussée* in 1789 and rather vaguely formulated at the Pontivy meeting, were made more specific in the course of the campaign for the election of the officials for the new Department of the Morbihan and the District of Vannes. Delegates from the rural communes of Bourg-Paul-Muzillac, Billiers, Noyal, Le Guerno, Arzal, Marzan, Péaule, Plaudren, Treffléan, St-Nolf, Theix, Noyalo-Muzillac, Surzur, La Trinité and Ambon met on 29 April in Muzillac to put pressure on the electors who were to set up the new Department; they endorsed the general condemnation of the *domaine congéable* by the Pontivy assembly and ordered their electors to obtain four concessions for them: (1) the 'restitution' to tenants of cutting rights on trees, (2) the abolition of the *commis-*

---

[10] *Archives parlementaires,* vi, lll, 115; Thomas-Lacroix, 'Les Cahiers de doléances de la sénéchaussée d'Hennebont'; Le Goff, 'Les Doléances des paysans du Vannetais', 40 n. 19.

[11] A.N., B^A 26 pc. 4: 8-6-1789.

[12] Dubreuil, *Les Vicissitudes,* i, 31-2, 190-1.

sions, or *pots de vin* paid at the beginning of the lease, which had been the principal way in which landlords had raised the rent during the eighteenth century, (3) an assurance of permanent occupancy for tenants as long as they paid their rent on the *fonds* regularly and (4) a fixed rate for those rents.[13] These were truly revolutionary proposals; they would have taken the remaining element of impermanence out of the *domaine congéable,* and entrenched the tenants, and therefore the wealthier peasants, on their lands even more firmly than they were already.

This was just what the local landlords feared. Forewarned by the resolutions of the Pontivy assembly, they had already begun in March to organize a lobby of the Constituent Assembly, which would have to make the final decision, and soon floods of pamphlets began to inundate the unsuspecting deputies of the Nation denouncing the evils or, alternately, extolling the virtues of this obscure form of landholding. On the local level, the tenants won a battle; in May, the electors of the Department voted to denounce the *domaine congéable* as feudal and demanded that rents paid on the *fonds* should be made redeemable; in July, the Administrators of the Department followed suit. The news of the struggle, the expectation of reform, some individual cases of scandalous rent rises and, it was alleged, threats of expulsion exercised against peasants active in local politics kept the tenants in a state of agitation throughout the remainder of 1790.[14] But the revolutionary politicians expressed a fervent desire that the Constituent Assembly would decide in the tenants' favour and their confidence that such a decision would commit the élite of the rural community to their side. 'Cinq à six mille paysans', wrote Rollin de la Farge, *procureur-syndic* of the District of Vannes

qui sont de très mauvaise humeur et qui se promettent bien de se refuser à tout, parce que jusqu'à present on n'a pas fait un mot de réponse à leurs pétitions sur les domaines congéables, feront tout, si l'on daigne enfin s'occuper d'eux sérieusement. Ils prendront les assignants, ils payeront les

---

[13] Dubreuil, *Les Vicissitudes,* i, 246–8.
[14] D. Jouany, *La Formation du département du Morbihan* (Vannes, 1920), 57, 60–1; A.D. Morbihan, E[n] 36: Minutes Josse: rise de deux tenues . . . au village de Kermur [Theix], 20-2-1790, which includes provision for a supplementary payment to the landlord if the tithe is abolished; Le Quinio, *Élixir du régime féodal,* iv–v; P. Sagnac and P. Caron, *Les Comités des droits féodaux et de législation et l'abolition du régime seigneurial 1789–1793* (Paris, 1907), 477–8; Dubreuil, *Les Vicissitudes,* i, 31–2, 240–8.

impositions, ils achèteront les biens nationaux, ils mettront toutes les terres en pleine valeur, et certes, tout cela peut et doit enfin provoquer un début favorable.[15]

The judgement of the Constituent Assembly, when it eventually came in August, 1791, was to be a disappointment to local politicians and tenants alike. In the meantime, when all over France peasants had already obtained by the legislation of 4–11 August 1789, changes in the system of land tenure not greatly different from those the tenants of Lower Brittany were now demanding, the delicate hesitation of the Constituent Assembly over the respective rights of *domaniers* and *fonciers* made it certain that the hopes of Rollin and others like him would be dashed even before a decision was reached.

An added inconvenience, with disastrous administrative and political consequences, during this time was that the uncertainty surrounding the status of the *domaine congéable* discouraged peasants and bourgeois alike from purchasing confiscated Church property, for most Church lands consisted of *fonds* under *domaine congéable*. In the first year in which *biens nationaux* were made available, peasants actually bought more *fonds* than the wary bourgeois, but neither group dared invest much until the status of land under *domaine congéable* was settled: 'Le colon se regardant presque déjà comme propriétaire du fond [wrote the Directory of the District of Vannes in October 1790], se croit dispensé d'en faire l'acquisition; et d'un autre côté le particulier qui serait disposé à acquérir craint d'acheter un bien dont la valeur peut être considérablement dimunée d'un moment à l'autre.'[16] The slow sale of confiscated Church property in turn meant that the Department had no funds to pay its priests and religious the pensions and salaries the new regime had guaranteed; 300,000 livres were due to be paid on 1 January, and the Department had only 50,000 to 60,000 livres on hand. Assignats could not be used, because they would not be accepted in the countryside.[17]

Unable to satisfy the hopes of the better-off citizens for material benefits which the fall of the old regime had seemed to announce, powerless even to feed, much less to control, the growing army of beggars in the countryside, to neutralize the rancour of rural and

[15] Sagnac and Caron, *Les Comités des droits féodaux*, 479–80.
[16] A.D. Morbihan, L 1445: 13-10-1790; Q 185.
[17] Sagnac and Caron, *Les Comités des droits féodaux*, 479–80.

urban consumers, or even to guarantee the safety of its own agents beyond the walls of Vannes except when accompanied by armed troops, the revolutionary authorities watched helplessly as the propaganda of their enemies began to take effect. The first protests in Vannes against the new order came from disgruntled nobles and their sympathizers in the wake of their local defeat and the reverses suffered by the nobility in Versailles: these were three canons of the cathedral; the brothers Le Charpentier, both nobles; a young noble, Denis de Robien; an obscure person, Juhé—all of them denounced by the *jeunes volontaires* to the town council in the second half of 1789. In May 1790, the council complained of incendiary pamphlets circulating in Vannes.[18] These were mere squibs, however; counter-revolutionary propaganda and this agitation seem to have had little impact on the region until the full import of the reorganization of the French Church dawned on people in the autumn of 1790.

The text of the Civil Constitution of the Clergy was published on 25 October; there was a flurry of complaints from the Chapter, from la Villeloays, the rector of the minuscule urban parish of St-Salomon, and from several other rectors and assistant priests, who refused to read the decrees of the Assembly from the pulpit. At the beginning of November, La Villeloays' parishioners took matters into their own hands and protested against the impending closure of their church. There were secret meetings in the house of a woman who lived near the church; she went from door to door, it was reported, saying, 'Comment abandonnerez-vous votre église, la laisserez-vous déserte?' Voices were raised in a meeting of vestrymen after High Mass on 1 November to say 'tenir bon et nous serons conservés, s'il faut répandre du sang nous en répandrons'; at another meeting that evening after Vespers a layman mounted the pulpit, announced that the bishop sympathized with them and read a similar protest from a church in Nantes. 'Nous sommes toujours sûrs de rester comme nous sommes jusqu'au premier avril prochain et alors nous verrons . . . Nous ne reconnaissons d'autre maître', he cried, pointing to the tabernacle, 'que celui-là.'[19]

---

[18] A.C. Vannes, BB 29: 15, 19-1-1790, 3-5-1790; A.D. Morbihan, K 1511: *Extrait des registres des délibérations de la ville et communauté de Vannes . . .* 5-1-1790; K 1543: *Arrêté des jeunes volontaires de la ville de Vannes*, 10-12-1789; 47 G 7 (376) fol. 205v–206v: 7-12-1789; Lz 272⁴: trial of de Robien, 1791.

[19] A.D. Morbihan, B 1342: Petition of Bachelot, attorney of the commune of Vannes, 8-11-1790; L 134: 26-10-1790; Cariou, 'La Constitution civile', 59–65; A.N., D xix (45) 704 bis: Directory of Department to Comité ecclésiastique, 23-12-1790.

Events such as these, and similar happenings elsewhere in the Department of the Morbihan, drove the revolutionary officials of the Department and District to despair. By the end of December, the new administrative machinery set up only that year started to break down. One after another, rural municipal officials sent in their resignations; complaints against the retention of the old taxes started to flow into the District of Vannes, and municipal officials, some of them churchmen, began to suffer for their services to the new regime. 'Nous sommes à la veille d'une insurrection générale,' wrote the Directors of the Department to the National Assembly at the beginning of 1791; 'Les campagnes sont en fermentation.' Everything, they said, was being used by the enemies of the Revolution to stir up the peasants, 'surtout le religion et les impôts.'

Religion and taxes were important issues, but only the most prominent of all the discontents that political changes since 1789 had aroused or exacerbated. The Civil Constitution of the Clergy provided the immediate cause of the revolt which broke out in February 1791: most of the rioters claimed that Bishop Amelot, who had refused the oath to the Civil Constitution, was in danger and had to be rescued, and the rising was only a final stage in a campaign of agitation which had got its start at least as early as December 1790. It is impossible to deny the partial responsibility of the local clergy for the increase of tension at the beginning of the year. The local priests had followed Bishop Amelot almost to a man in his rejection of the oath to the Civil Constitution, and even before the matter of the oath had come to a head in February, the bishop and his clergy had helped stimulate protests against the new legislation. In December, Amelot is supposed to have called a meeting of the faithful at Ste-Anne-d'Auray to invoke Divine protection against the new legislation; by the year's end, the *Exposition des principes des Évêques de l'Assemblée Nationale* and other anti-constitutional tracts were propagated in the diocese.[20]

Why should the lower clergy have rejected the Revolution in this fashion? It is a difficult question to answer if we look only at the motives of individuals. They had favoured the Revolution at first, and had a particular grievance against the nobles, whom they accused of monopolizing the higher benefices. Most of the rectors and

[20] A.D. Morbihan, L 134: 22, 28, 29-1-1791, 5-2-1791, 5-2-1791: L 73: 27-1-1791; L 1455: 26-12-1790; A.C. Vannes, D₁: 1-1-1791; Buléon and Le Garrec, *Sainte-Anne-d'Auray*, i, 367–9.

assistants stood to gain financially by the new arrangements for clerical salaries: eight of the twenty-one rural rectors of the District had received only a *portion congrue* in the 1780s, and only the rectors of the large parishes of Sarzeau, Grand-Champ and also Le Croisier of St-Patern, who received a large rural tithe, stood to lose clearly by the arrangement. It seems likely that their heavily local recruitment and their common background in the local college and seminary left them with a debt of loyalty to Amelot and, probably more important, to their ex-masters in the college who, after some hesitation, refused the oath. For some recusants, nevertheless, like Caradec, rector of Baud, whose brother Ambroise, a lawyer in Vannes, was a leading revolutionary figure in the area, it must have been a painful decision.[21]

The choice is understandable only when studied in the context of the people among whom the clergy lived and from which many of them came. As Father Cariou has established, in more 'progressive' parts of the diocese such as the District of Hennebont, which included the revolutionary town of Lorient, all of the 54 rectors and vicars took the oath; in the region around Le Faouet, also considerably less reactionary than the rest of the diocese, 17 of 33 rectors and vicars (9 of the 14 rectors) complied. In comparison, in the District of Vannes, only one of 67 rectors and vicars acquiesced; in the District of Auray, only two of 49.[21] The hapless plight of Morin, assistant priest and mayor of St-Avé, illustrates their plight perfectly. In mid-January 1791, he wrote that he was a prey to insults from the poorer people of his own parish as well as wandering drunkards from Vannes; he no longer dared come into the town; and now, since a troop of dragoons sent to Vannes from Lorient after the troubles of the previous spring had been withdrawn, his parishioners had become quite uncontrollable:

Pour moi il faut que je ne me mêle de rien, ou je serai brulé ou tué, au moins qu'il n'y ait une garde dans la paroisse, je n'ai fait que recevoir des menaces et des insultes depuis samedi au soir et dimanche par les personnes de la ville qui allaient et revenaient de Mangolerian [a place where fairs were held] ils prenaient des fruits tels qu'ils étoient ça et là en presence, ils jetaient sans cesse des pierres à ma portée, et lorsque je leur parlais, ils me menaçaient de m'en faire autant. . . . Lundi au soir je ne fus pas moins menagé par les

[21] A.N., H¹ 564: Livoys to Necker, 11-21-1788; Macé, 'Les Elections du Morbihan', 126–8; Cariou, 'La Constitution civile', 59–67; Archives de l'Évêché de Vannes: Paroisses, prêtres et fondations . . . 1784.

ivrognes de St-Patern qui revenaient de la foire . . . tout n'est plus qu'histoires et complots . . .[22]

Thus, if the clergy had, on the whole, reasons of principle for refusing the Civil Constitution, and perhaps a certain resentment of the new authorities who had yet to pay their salaries, they were also subject to local pressures and reflected in their decisions the general dispositions of their parishioners.

That disposition around Vannes was shown overtly in the rising of 14 February 1791. From early January onwards there took place a series of meetings and demonstrations in the area about Vannes, extending into the French-speaking regions as far away as Rochefort and Muzillac. In the region immediately about Vannes, protests to the National Assembly were prepared in the parishes of Sarzeau, Sulniac, Berric, St-Nolf, Molac and Theix. In some of these, it is possible to see at least the co-operation of the clergy and, perhaps, the hand of some prominent laymen, such as the comte de Serent in Sarzeau. Also in Sarzeau, a priest helped the municipality to draw up their protests, but he gave surprisingly little space to purely ecclesiastical problems. Most of the complaints in these petitions in fact summed up the economic failings of the Revolution. Rhuys complained about the temporary imposition of the *fouages,* about the stamp duties, the new forms of taxing land, houses and furnishings, and—shades of the insurgents of 1675!—expressed fears that a salt tax, called *cartage* might be established (there had never been a salt tax in Brittany); they protested against the lack of funds for poor relief in a bad year, and finally against the oath to the Civil Constitution. All parishes voiced their discontent over the failure to pay the parish priests their salaries. Berric asked for the suppression of the District. St-Nolf showed annoyance with the persistence of the *fouages,* echoed the fears of Sarzeau that the *gabelle* was on its way (in St-Nolf they called it a *salorge*), and asked for poor relief. Theix complained that one of the members of the Danet family of Vannes managed to avoid paying personal taxes in the parish by claiming his residence in Vannes. The local authorities received these complaints without sympathy; the National Assembly, with amusement.[23]

[22] A.D. Morbihan, L 255: Morin to Directory of Department, 12-1-1791; Cariou, 'La Constitution civile', 65–79.

[23] A.D. Morbihan, L 134: 8, 24, 26, 28-1-1791, 10-2-1791; L 1455: Letters and extracts from registers of Berric, St-Nolf, Sarzeau, Sulniac, Molac, January–February 1791; ibid., 8, 21-1-1791; 3-2-1791; Lz 278[11], Lz 272[7]; Collection Debauve: Comte de Serent to [?] 21-3-1791; *Archives parlementaires,* xxiii, 176–7.

The rising itself was prefaced by a meeting at Ste-Anne-d'Auray on 5 February and then, on 7 February, by a gathering at Bondon, just outside Vannes, led by a student from the College of Vannes. Manifestos were drawn up against the *domaine congéable* and the Civil Constitution; but nothing came of it. On the 12th, the barrister Le Monnier sent out a circular letter to the parish of Sulniac which warned that the Church had condemned the Constitution. It ended 'Faites part de toutes ces vérités, le plus qu'il sera possible, et surtout de l'activité. Faites passer de paroisse en paroisse et agir en conséquence.' Starting in the parishes of Sulniac and Berric, this is exactly what was done. Led, it seems, by a certain Le Mée, a blacksmith, and convinced that the bishop of Vannes was in danger, the peasants of a half-dozen parishes—Berric, Trefflean, Larré, Sulniac, St-Nolf and St-Avé—marched on Vannes, some armed with guns or cudgels, some unarmed. The rectors of St-Nolf and Sulniac approved the movement, though the rector of Sulniac wept when he saw the note; those of St-Avé and Elven spoke against it. Around 1,500 peasants descended on Vannes and were repulsed with a few casualties by troops sent out hurriedly. From the lists of those arrested it is quite evident that this was a rising representative of the rural population as a whole rather than the much younger bands which formed the 'troops' of the guerrilla warfare known as the *chouannerie*.[24]

No doubt it would have been too much to hope, as some continued to do even after the February rising, that the countryside could be reconciled to the new order by persuasion; in any case, the events of the succeeding two years had the opposite effect. The new friends the Revolution had in the rural municipalities either abandoned the cause or gave up their offices. Theirs was an unpopular task, even if they wanted to continue it. Not only were they classed by their neighbours as enemies of religion; they were also expected by the government to be responsible for assessing and imposing a reformed tax system, which was to include a new-fangled land tax, the *imposition foncière*. Taxes are never popular and this one seemed more iniquitous than most. The *tenuyer* and the tenant farmer were obliged to pay all of it, where under the old regime the *tenuyer* and *foncier* had each paid a share; and the *métayer*, nothing at all. True, the *tenuyer* and tenant were now authorized to deduct a

---

[24] A.D. Morbihan, L 1435; Lz 274[1–2]; A.N., F[7] 3682 (18): *Rapport présenté au Roi par MM Bertolio, Deléon et Daumesnil* (1791).

proportion of their rents equal to the percentage of net revenue which the new tax represented, but just how this was to be calculated was not immediately clear, and the administrators and the central government were themselves not sure how to determine that measure. Whether or not he paid more when the year's accounts were settled, it must have seemed to the *tenuyer* that he was being put upon to a degree unsurpassed by the old regime. Many municipal officials refused to help in the assessment, and had to be forced to do so.[25]

The *tenuyers* had a more serious reason for discontent. In August, 1791, the Constituent Assembly settled to its own satisfaction the question of the *domaine congéable*. The legislators made a few concessions to the tenants: 'feudal' remnants in the system abolished outright in 1789 were to be suppressed without compensation for the landlords, although *corvées* could still be required as long as they were stipulated in the lease; tenants could sell the edifices during the lease, or divide them among heirs, as long as the occupants remained collectively responsible for the rent; chestnuts and oaks were to be considered 'fruit' trees and therefore the tenants' property—unless specified otherwise in the lease. The tenants were given the hollow satisfaction of being able to claim reimbursement from the landlord for the edifices if they wanted to leave the holding at the end of their leases.[26] This was the famous principle of 'reciprocity', over which historians have spilled much ink; in fact, since purchasers were always ready to hand within the rural community, it made no difference at all to most tenants. At bottom, the law of 6 August 1791 was a victory for the landlords, for no concession was made on the basic principle which the tenants had demanded: the conversion to a fixed and redeemable *rente foncière* of the rent paid for the *fonds*. The revolution of the wealthy peasants had been blocked.

A year later, on 27 August 1792, the rump of the Legislative Assembly, with nothing to lose, tried to make amends by declaring the *domaine congéable* to be 'feudal' and the rent paid for the *fonds* redeemable; yet even here it bungled its task, for it shrank from outright abolition of the landlords' rights, at a time when it had extinguished virtually all the other remnants of 'feudalism' in

[25] A.D. Morbihan, L 1445: July–September, 1791, *passim.;* Dubreuil, *Les Vicissitudes,* i, 475–90.

[26] Dubreuil, *Les Vicissitudes,* i, 447–55.

France, and in addition, gave only the fruit trees in hedgerows to the tenants; other trees had to be purchased, surrendered to the landlords, or rented from them at 5 per cent of their value. Even this relatively radical measure was too much of a concession, and in October 1797, the Directory restored the legislation of 1791.[27]

The result of all this procrastination and foot-dragging, perhaps inevitable in a series of National Assemblies devoted to the principle of private property, was as Rollin de la Farge had foreseen in 1790: the stable, wealthy element in the countryside, already demoralized by the religious struggles of 1790—1 and threatened in its position of leadership in the rural world, lost whatever interest it had had in the Revolution; and the deathbed repentance of the Legislative Assembly on the question of tenures in August 1792 was less inadequate than simply too late to modify this state of affairs. Typical of the changed attitude of this class of peasant was Joseph Le Floch, the *laboureur* who had written to Necker in 1789 to complain of the *domaine congéable*; in the abortive rising of March 1793 in Elven, Le Floch announced to the local tax collecter that he intended to kill him, and shortly was reported to have taken the lead of a group of people bent on carrying out the threat. Not all prosperous *laboureurs* changed their views so decidedly as this, but in the course of 1791 and 1792, the supporters of the Revolution in the countryside, disappointed by their bourgeois sponsors and demoralized by their unpopularity among their own people, allowed the administration of the rural communes to break down. Some municipalities resigned as early as November 1790; in others the electors refused to name officials. From mid-1792 onwards, resignations flowed into the District. Long before then, however, the machinery of local government had ceased to operate; the administrators of the District complained at the end of 1791 that they had completely lost touch with most of the rural communes. Whatever remaining interest people might have had in the success of the new regime was certainly not helped by the distinction between 'active' and 'passive' citizens made by the Constituent Assembly. In Brittany this measure actually achieved what it was supposed to do everywhere in France: it reduced the number of voters in primary assemblies drastically—by 40 to 50 per cent in the District of Vannes. Even the select few active citizens were remarkably unenthusiastic; in the meetings of primary electoral assemblies held in August 1791, the participation rate lay

[27] Ibid., i, 518–23; ii, 168.

between 3 and 7 per cent of the *active* citizens eligible to attend. Indifference and hostility to the new regime were already assured.[28] The town of Vannes seems to have been little more enthusiastic for the Revolution than the countryside. The popularity of the non-juring priests stood high in the spring and summer of 1791, with non-jurors preaching and confessing openly and, said the revolutionary authorities, inflaming the people. Their services in the semi-rural chapels of St-Symphorien and Le Bondon, and in that of Le Féty, on the port, were well attended, and the annual retreat flourished, while the parish churches, when run by constitutional priests, stood deserted. The eccentric rector Le Croisier earned a last moment of glory when he preached a long and learned Lenten sermon in St-Patern on the themes of mortal sin, obedience to the Church, the respect due to true pastors, and the sin of simony—all (he claimed afterwards) without mentioning the problem of the Civil Constitution: a dialectical *tour de force* of which his judges, when he was taken to court, not surprisingly found him incapable. As in his previous quarrels with the bourgeoisie of Vannes, Le Croisier had popular support, and in general, the cause of the priests, if it had been left to the common people in Vannes ('la ville la plus superstitieuse peut-être de tout l'empire' according to the special commissioners sent out in March 1791), would have triumphed. In May, a drunken grain-porter, after announcing to his hearers that Le Croisier would get his tithe in the autumn and that the country folk would soon invade the town, worked up the courage to throw his hat down in front of the procession for the consecration of Bishop Le Mâle, shouting 'qu'il se foutait de ces bougres-là', 'qu'il voulait mourir dans sa religion et qu'il était bon chrétien'. Popular opposition to the new regime in the town never got much more space on official paper than this, but the ocassional comments made by officials in succeeding years left little doubt where the sentiments of the mass of the people in Vannes lay.[29]

The town was hostile to the Revolution, the countryside had already risen up in brief revolt by 1791, but it was finally the need to recruit men for the army and navy, as France slipped into war in

[28] A.D. Morbihan, L 834, pc. 44: 1-4-1793; L 1445: 9-12-1791 and *passim;* L 252: 26-11-1790; L 235: Elections, 1791.

[29] A.D. Morbihan, Lz 273[7]: trial of Laurent Raud, 1791; Lz 278[2]: trial of M.-G.-A. Le Croisier, 1791; L 134: Directory of Department to National Assembly, 9-6-1791; L 135: Directory to Municipality of Vannes, 24-4-1792; A.N., F[7] 3682 (18): Commissaires du roi, Vannes, to minister of the Interior, 23-3-1791.

1792 and 1793, which precipitated open rebellion and cut the links between country and town. Rural resistance to military recruitment did not date, as might be imagined, from the famous levy of 300,000 men for service on the frontiers in March 1793. Recruitment of a kind had begun as clearly as July 1791, when an appeal was made for volunteers for the ranks of the National Guard to serve in the army. None came forward from the countryside. The response of the commune of Séné was typical: 'Nous désirons fortement défendre la patrie; mais nous n'aimons pas la guerre et on craint de s'engager.'[30] This levy had been for service at home; in July 1792, an attempt was made to recruit volunteers for the National Guard and the army on the frontiers. A total of 58 National Guards and 33 regular soldiers were to be furnished from the District of Vannes, or about five to seven men from each rural canton. Again, there were no volunteers from the countryside. The parish of Ambon pointed out 'que cette paroisse fournit grand nombre de marins au service de la nation, ce qui la gêne beaucoup et que tous veulent profiter de l'avantage de la liberté decretée par l'assemblée nationale.'[31] The troops were raised only by threatening to quarter garrisons on the recalcitrant communes.

During the same period, naval administrators, with the reluctant help of local politicians, were busy trying to reimpose administrative controls on the seamen in the coastal parishes. For the sailors and captains of the coast, the 'liberté decretée par l'Assemblée Nationale' meant freedom from customs duties and inspectors and from military service. From 1790 onwards, they refused to purchase the *congés* required for shipping and fishing.[32] More serious than this insubordination was their response to levies of sailors for service in the Royal Navy. In response to the demands of pamphleteers and a few of the *cahiers de doléances,* the National Assembly decided to alter the *classes,* the regime of compulsory registration of seamen for service on the King's ships established by Colbert and hardly changed since. Though not so brutal as the English methods of impressment, the *classes* had been a harsh system, run by firm administrators backed up by the possibility of armed force. Although the losses incurred in the recent War of American Independence

[30] A.D. Morbihan, L 1445: 26-8-1791; L 255: 2-9-1791; L 1446: 14-5-1792.
[31] A.D. Morbihan, L 554, 14-10-1792.
[32] A.N., G⁵ 5¹ dossier 8: 28-7-1791.

had been dramatic,[33] there seemed remarkably little overt resentment of the system, possibly because it had been established long enough to be accepted as a kind of national service, and a coming-of-age for the younger men; possibly because in peacetime it affected mainly the youngest sailors.

When the National Assembly came to deal with the system, it found that it dared not abolish it completely, but it tried all the same to make it more democratic by having the local recruitment officials, the *syndics,* elected; a clever device designed to permit the seamen to enforce their own oppression. As a result of this dose of manipulative democracy, the system nearly collapsed.[34] The correspondence of Jouany and Pellegrin, the two officials in Vannes charged in succession with co-ordinating and transmitting orders to the *syndics,* makes melancholy reading. In July 1791, there were still no *syndics* elected in the region, either because of refusals, delays or deliberate absenteeism. By November most had been elected, but could get no assistance from the local municipalities to back up their orders. In the meantime, with the troubles in the West Indies and then the threat of war, the government was beginning to demand levies. Incompetence and bad faith, according to Pellegrin, characterized the responses of nearly all the *syndics,* except those at Vannes and Ambon; in Sarzeau, the sailors simply refused to elect anyone at all. Further demands for sailors came: 110 men in April 1792, 244 in May—apparently only partly satisfied, for no men came from Auray, Arzon, Sarzeau or the previously faithful Ambon. Another levy of 162 men in October 1792 was more successful, thanks to the intervention of the Department, which sent troops to Arzon and Sarzeau. Finally came an order for 1,200 men for Lorient in January 1793. Pellegrin continually denounced the insubordination of the sailors, influenced by 'fanatical priests', and also by their women, who made it their job to warn off ships when the levy was due. Even when a levy was successful, there was no guarantee that the men would reach the arsenals: in December 1792, only 32 men out of a levy of 80 showed up in Brest; the rest had disappeared along the road.[35]

---

[33] Goubert, *Maladies et médecins en Bretagne,* 23–4, 428.

[34] N. Hampson, *La Marine de l'An II. Mobilisation de la flotte de l'Océan 1793–1794* (Paris, 1959), 45–6, 209–10.

[35] A.D. Finistère, 100 J 1650–1653: Letter-book of citizen Pellegrin, 1787–Year IV.

Comment se fait-il, Messieurs [wrote the departmental authorities in 1792] que ces marins qui sous l'ancien régime marchaient au 1er ordre refusent maintenant d'obéir? L'amour de la patrie devrait les engager à aller s'offrir d'eux mêmes et à ne pas attendre qu'on exige leurs services.[36]

It was a good question. Part of the answer may be that the sailors had not been quite so eager to serve under the old regime as the administrators imagined. Part of the answer, too, was furnished by a memorandum from nearby Port-Louis. Until recently, they said, the recruiting officials had never taken the captains of fishing boats, but only the common sailors: 'on savait que le maître restant il trouverait assez de matelots'; now the navy took both masters and men.[37] But what the men complained of most was the favouritism shown by the *syndics* towards the older sailors, who were not being taken in even the modest proportions customary in levies in the past: 'les jeunes sont dégoûtés du service'.[38] Such were the difficulties of reconciling national security with a token democratization of military structures in the navy. Like the old regime navy, the new was slow in paying its men; but at least the old navy had paid advances in hard cash before ordering them to the arsenals. Now they were paid in assignats which the innkeepers along the road to Brest refused. But the local receiver in Vannes had trouble in providing even assignats: Paris preferred to remit only large bills to him without the means of breaking them into smaller sums. Since Pellegrin and the treasurer in Vannes did not want to purchase specie, already at a discount of 15 per cent in November 1791 and 45 per cent five months later, the sailors had to wait: 'tous les jours je suis assailli par les marins . . . que me representent leurs besoins en larmes.'[39] Bad enough in normal times, such meanness and mismanagement had harsh consequences in the increasingly gloomy economic conditions of 1791–3. 'La plupart d'entre eux sont dans la dernière misère,' wrote Pellegrin of the sailors in March 1793, 'ils murmurent avec raison: ventre affamée n'a point d'oreilles.'[40]

To the difficulties caused by the inefficiency of the new navy were added the effects of economic collapse. The coasting trade had certainly declined since 1789 as commerce everywhere in France

[36] A.D. Morbihan, L 135: 18-6-1792.
[37] A.N., F^{12} 1836: 1-11-1790.
[38] A.D. Finistère, 100 J 1651: 30-5-1792.
[39] A.D. Finistère, 100 J 1650: 26-4-1792, 11-5-1792; 100 J 1651: 30-5-1792.
[40] A.D. Finistère, 100 J 1651: 9-3-1793.

slowed to a standstill; the slump in the fisheries continued; at the end of 1790, the rector of Arzon noted in his parish register that

la récolte a manqué, le commerce de sardines a été ruineux et a occasionné plus de 12,000 livres de pertes réelles dans la paroisse. La misère est à son comble; plus de cinquante familles sont sans pain . . . Le commerce est tout-à-fait mort . . . il semble que tout le numéraire a disparu avec les troubles du royaume; tous les jours on n'entend parler que de meurtres ou vols.[41]

In March 1792, the District of Vannes reported that the parishes of the coast were particularly subject to dearth; and with the outbreak of war with Britain and Holland, an embargo was placed in February 1793 on virtually all coastal shipping, a measure which extended even to fishing vessels.[42] The effects of the economic crisis were thus exacerbated for the seamen by war and bureaucracy. Then there were the petty inventions of the new administrators. In October 1792, on the initiative of the Minister of the Marine, Monge, the government demanded that pensioned seamen should take an oath of loyalty to the Nation in order to be able to claim their pittances. In the region of Vannes, few did. In November, the oath was required even from their widows, and this by Monge's express orders. In February, the government took the unprecedented action of submitting men previously declared unfit for naval service to a re-examination by a surgeon.[43]

It is against this background that the protest of one *syndic* who resigned his post must be seen:

Mais à mis

je suis né françois: sugete du fils ainé: de liglis catolique apostolique et Rommen je suis libre: jeme ma liberté: et pour en donnere une preuve palpable jabdique la plasse de Caindicate [= syndic] de janse de mere de Lomariaquer:

je ne pui en meme temps oublier que je suis Chretien: je Cherise ma Religion. C'Est Celle de mes pere C'est la seule veritable je n'en veux point dunotre; je suis né dans le sein de cette Eglise Catolique apostolique Et Romanne Et paisen que je suis je veux vivre Et mourire avecque la grasse de dieu:

Jean Philiberte comis[44]

[41] A.C. Arzon, GG 4 cited in Rosenzweig and Estienne, *Inventaire sommaire* . . . *Série E*, 264.

[42] A.D. Morbihan, L 1446: 29-3-1792, 2-2-1793; L 78: 2-2-1793; L 590: 4-3-1793; A.D. Finistère, 100 J 1651: 8-2-1793.

[43] A.D. Finistère, 100 J 1651: 6, 30-10-1792, 13-11-1792, 21-2-1793.

[44] A.D. Morbihan, L 590: 8-12-1791.

If Philiberte was sincere in his devotion to 'liglis catolique apostolique et Rommen', there were also other discontents of the seamen which found their outlet and expression in complaints about the changes in the Church.

Finally, and perhaps most important of all, the Revolution represented a far-reaching and generally unwelcome threat to a certain pattern of life, a kind of *laissez-faire* in which the old regime town and its officials had largely left people to run their own affairs. The Revolution changed all that: it brought national politics to the village level, gave the force of the law to attempts by the minority of better-off people in the rural community to impose their way of life on the mass, helped arrest beggars, and generally tried to enforce the writ of undoubtedly more enlightened but none the less unwelcome bourgeois morality on a countryside where it had been hitherto unknown. This happened in a score of different ways: take, as one example, the opinion of the Directory of the Department on the subject of village fairs: 'la multiplicité de ces établissements est contraire aux vrais intérêts des laboureurs les enlevant trop souvent à leurs travaux, leur donnant le goût des voyages, de la dissipation et de la vie de cabaret, d'où dérivent les querelles, la perte du temps, de l'aisance, de la santé et des bonnes mœurs.' Rural fairs were accordingly declared suppressed through the Department. For the townsmen it was only a small matter to abolish them with a flourish of the pen; for countrymen, their disappearance was both a blow to the rural economy and an insult to their way of life. But the decision of the authorities proved to be a blunder, because such events could not be put an end to by a bureaucrat's whim, and fairs continued to be held and even became political gestures against the new regime, as when the fair of Keralier in Sarzeau was held under the counter-revolutionary auspices of the comte de Serent. Or consider the remarks of the Directory of the Department of the Morbihan, when, in January 1791, they began to doubt the wisdom and loyalty of the electors to whom they owed their own nomination only a few months before, when they found that they were not behaving like the docile *administrés* they had bargained for: 'Les cultivateurs dominent dans les assemblies primaires, moins instruits qu'ailleurs, et par conséquent plus susceptibles de mauvaises impressions, il est peut-être dangereux de les assembler.'[45] Acts like

---

[45] A.D. Morbihan, L 134: Directory of Department to President of National [*p. 360 for n. 45 cont.*]

these were symptomatic of the gap between revolutionaries and those they ought to have been leading, a gap which few had the wit or ability to try and bridge.

Thus the whole of the countryside had been cut off from the new regime by the autumn of 1792, when the Convention began seriously to enforce measures against the refractory clergy, who until then appeared to have been tolerated by the local authorities in the Vannetais. By the end of that year, the countryside was like a tinderbox. It was set ablaze, as in the Vendée, by the famous decree levying 300,000 men for the army on the frontiers in March 1793. In response to this decree, the whole countryside to the south and west of Vannes erupted in a fortnight of violence, looting, and marches on Vannes, Rochefort, Sarzeau, and Muzillac. Some leadership was provided by local nobles: Francheville in Sarzeau and de Silz in Muzillac; a coincidence which led some historians to infer that this was part of a larger plot led by the adventurous marquis de la Rouerie before his death, but this connection has never been proven. Certainly, local nobles like Le Charpentier and Serent had no need of outside organization to encourage their hostility to the Revolution; they had campaigned against the Revolution in town and countryside since its beginning.[46] What matters however is not that the revolt broke out at this particular moment, but that in these conditions which had slowly developed since 1789, a revolt could have taken place at virtually any time after 1790. By then the Revolution had established itself as a harsher—and yet weaker—master of the countryside than the old regime had been; after that date, the sullen and continual hostility of the peasants and other country folk to the Revolution was guaranteed—a climate which was to foster sporadic and often continuous guerrilla warfare which ended only after the *débâcle* of the Hundred Days.

Assembly, 29-1-1791; to Department of Ille-et-Vilaine, 8-9-1791; to District of Vannes, 12-5-1791, 21-6-1791; L 135: 22-5-1792; Le Goff and Sutherland, 'The Revolution and the Rural Community', 112–13.

[46] Certainly the departures of some of the local nobles, including Francheville, from Vannes on the eve of the rising were suspicious; see A.D. Morbihan, L 1446: 2-3-1793, 4-3-1793. But no direct connection between this rising and the plots of La Rouerie has been established; cf. A. Goodwin, 'Counter-revolution in Brittany: the Royalist Conspiracy of the Marquis de la Rouerie, 1791–1793', *Bulletin of the John Rylands Library, Manchester*, xxxix (1957), 326–55; on Le Charpentier, see Le Goff. 'Les Doléances des paysans du Vannetais', 36, n. 13, and on Serent, Le Quinio, *Élixir du régime féodal*, 67–8 and Collection Debauve, Serent to [?] 21-3-1791. The account of the rising given here is based principally on A.D. Morbihan, L 136, L 1455, Lz 834–7 and R 201: *Précis des événements désastreux qui ont affligé le département du Morbihan . . .* (Vannes, 1793).

CONCLUSION

This description of the immediate origins of the counter-revolution in the Vannetais throws several sidelights on the reasons for the hostility and resentment which the Revolution provoked through most of western France. The first is that there was much that was not inevitable in the way that the West turned against the Revolution; the enmity which came about was the result of the confusion surrounding the first couple of years of revolutionary government; the difficulty of making new and uniform laws for a country which had previously known only regional usages; a certain political inexperience on the part of the revolutionaries, the most notable example of which was the way the reform of the Church was bungled; and the fact that all of this was taking place in a time of profound economic instability and social disorder. In these conditions nobody could expect the deputies in the National Assembly to understand the complexities of obscure questions like the *domaine congéable*—especially when presented by such consummate sophists as there were on both sides of the controversy; nobody could have foreseen that some priests would express the discontents of their region by rejecting the Civil Constitution of the Clergy.

A second feature of the outbreak of the counter-revolution is the diversity of its origins. Even within a small area like the District of Vannes, three distinct types of society—the smallholders and day-labourers of Sarzeau, the seamen, and the rural society of the mainland where the *domaine congéable* predominated—reacted differently to the Revolution, at different times, though undoubtedly the climate of one area had its effect on those of its neighbours. If this remark holds true of the region of Vannes, it is true *a fortiori* of the whole of western France.

Nevertheless, the question remains why the choices made by the Revolutionary assemblies in Paris should have been received in the west with such hostility. Not all areas took up arms against them, to be sure, and not all risings were equally violent; the Breton risings of 1791 and 1793 and the subsequent *chouannerie* pale by comparison with the Vendée. Indeed, in many parts of the west, the main obstacle to the Revolution was sullen resistance rather than active rebellion; and, of course, there were islands of Republican fervour scattered throughout the region which remained untouched by the counter-revolutionary tide.[1] In these enclaves, and in the rest of France, too, there had also been requisitions and conscription; new taxes were imposed and collected and non-juring curés expelled, and yet these areas remained loyal to the Republic. By contrast, most of the west, then and subsequently, soon rejected the Revolution and its works by either active or passive resistance, and the Vannetais was at one with its neighbours.

But in reality, the search for the reason why certain areas broke into open revolt is of secondary importance to the question of why the west should have been characterized for so long afterwards by a certain conservative social structure, a rather stagnant economy and constantly conservative political behaviour. When viewed in this light, actual outbreaks of counter-revolutionary violence seem more or less ephemeral. Their explanation may well lie in the presence of large numbers of poor in the areas of insurrection, people inclined to adopt the predominant allegiances of their society and apt to precipitate the rest into violent action.[2] Conversely, the presence of troops undoubtedly had a dampening effect on counter-revolutionary activity. Because of the strategic importance of the Breton coasts to national defence both before and after 1789, garrisons tended to be concentrated on the coastline, and the proximity of strong contingents in places like Brest and Lorient undoubtedly helped at least to neutralize the coastal regions of Brittany, if not to eliminate passive resistance and guerrilla activity. There seems to be little need to elevate these statements to a further remove from reality by claiming that the outbreak of counter-revolution had something to do with 'urbanization' or 'modernization'.[3] The presence of the poor and the absence of troops made counter-revolution, like revolution, a possibility, but not a necessity. What happened then depended on the temper of the larger rural community.

This is why historians must look beyond the immediate events of risings and guerrilla warfare to the larger question of the distinctive structure of rural society in western France. One hesitates on the

[1] R. Dupuy, *La Garde nationale et les débuts de la Révolution en Ille-et-Vilaine* (Rennes, 1972), 108–54, 274.

[2] See, in particular, M. Faucheux, *L'Insurrection vendéenne de 1793. Aspects économiques et sociaux* (Paris, 1964), 193–260, 369–83.

[3] Tilly, *The Vendée*, 9–37 and *passim*.

basis of a limited study such as this, to advance general explanations for the behaviour of one-quarter of France, but one theme which has been dwelt on in this work does suggest a key to the unique character of that region. That theme is the link between land tenure, rural social structure and political behaviour. West of an irregular line running from Caen to Poitiers, lies one of the conservative bastions of France. It is also the area in which a large mass of peasants, poor and rich, enjoyed land in the eighteenth and nineteenth centuries under various systems of precarious tenure; leasing, sharecropping and *domaine congéable*.

What we know of the mood of these regions at the beginning of the Revolution suggests that, though they may not have been carried forward on a tide of insurrectionary fervour, they were by no means hostile to the Revolution.[4] However, as they were not touched as closely by the seigneurial system as those areas in which peasant-owned property prevailed, they had less to gain from its abolition. In all parts of France, it is becoming increasingly apparent, the poorer sort of peasant benefited little from the Revolution.[5] The difference in the west may well be that there was also a large class of middling peasants dependent on rented land for a living, who did not benefit either. These were the men who set the political temper of rural society. Their attitude seems to have been one of caution and hestiation in the first year of revolution, though some, like Le Floch, Necker's correspondent, appear to have been genuinely enthusiastic, and in the meeting of February, 1790, in which the abolition of the *domaine congéable* was requested, it was clear that a good fraction of the better-off peasants looked to the Revolution for a solution of some of their problems. This 'middle class' of peasants themselves had little to gain from disorder and much to lose, but they were given few tangible results to encourage them to defend the Revolution in their own communities when the Parisian assemblies began to impose measures which flew in the face of local desires and to interfere in the internal life of the rural world. Sometimes the pressure and resentment of the poor, as in the Vendée or, in this study, on the peninsula of Sarzeau seems to have

---

[4] Bois, *Paysans de l'Ouest*, 167–87; Faucheux, *L'Insurrection vendéenne*, 243–62; Tilly, *The Vendée*, 177–86.

[5] See, for example, G. Lefebvre, 'La Révolution française et les paysans,' *Études sur la Révolution française* (Paris, 1954) 246–68; *Questions agraires au temps de la Terreur* (La Roche-sur-Yon, 1954), 1–132; A. Cobban, *The Social Interpretation of the French Revolution* (Cambridge, 1964) 107–19, 132–44.

sufficed to bend their will; sometimes it was simply an extraordinary affront to the way of life of the community, as was the imposition, by the revolutionary townsmen in the administration of the District of Vannes, of their own version of ecclesiastical polity in 1791, and of military conscription in 1793. And all this took place, it must be remembered, in an economy tried by twenty years of uncertainty and five years of crisis, where practically all exchanges had broken down, where the very act of transporting grain to the town market had become a sort of treason against poorer fellow-countrymen. Had they taken a strong stand, the more prosperous *tenuyers* might, possibly, have been able to influence their fellow parishioners to accept the Revolution and all its works, but what incentive had the new regime given them to do so by 1793?

The appreciation of these conditions depends on an understanding of the social structure of the old regime in all its complexity, and it is above all as a modest contribution to this understanding that this book has been written. From it, there emerge several features of rural and urban society which can be considered significant for the region, and which may well be applicable to other adjoining parts of Lower Brittany. The first of these is the relationship, both complementary and opposed, between the town of Vannes, the creation of trade, administration, the Church and the law, and the countryside. Doubtless the antithesis goes back to the Middle Ages, though the extension of the grain trade in the seventeenth and eighteenth centuries helped emphasize that the principal link with the town was the economic bond forged by the grain trade and the collection of rents in kind.

No doubt the situation of Vannes was like that of many, perhaps most, other small-to-middling French towns of the old regime. Vannes was an administrative, market, religious and service centre for its region, and this combination of functions made it an attractive place for nobles to foregather. The limited, and diminishing, extent of its manufacturing made it, economically at least, something of a parasitic growth on the surrounding area, though the metaphor is perhaps of limited value if it causes us to forget how many of the men and women of the area, rich and poor, depended on the town at one time or another for employment, career advancement, education, devotion and entertainment. But in a century in which significant urban expansion in France depended on economic development based on overseas commercial expansion or the growth of the more modern aspects of the State's administrative apparatus, the advantages appear to lie with larger urban centres like Rennes and Nantes. The seventeenth and eighteenth centuries sorted out the large French towns from the small, and Vannes was a small town, in the process of becoming smaller, in both a relative and absolute sense, within the Breton urban network. The Revolution, when it came to Vannes, was the local outcome of tensions within the urban élite, an active minority of which had been drawn into the issues of provincial and national politics as a natural outcome of their interest in town business and their frustration with interference by the privileged in their affairs. Paradoxically, the Revolution, despite all the hardships it brought on the region, arrested the decline of the town: if the politicans who drew up the new administrative map in 1790 had not been such traditionalists and not merely placed the *chef-lieu* of their Department where administration had always been situated, instead of in its more important economic centre, Lorient, or in Pontivy, the centre of its road network, Vannes would today be no more than a sleepy *sous-préfecture*. As it was, it remained, down to the twentieth century, the diminutive capital of one of France's most unchanging departments.

The source of that permanence must be sought, less in the town than in the countryside, and chiefly, as the preceding chapters have argued, in the fact that Lower Brittany, and to some extent all of western France, had a rural society which differed in many important respects from the classic models drawn from north-east France with which the great studies of Georges Lefebvre and Pierre Goubert have made us familiar. Its predominant feature was the existence of a larger group of middling peasants, which seems to have been extraordinarily stable. Personal tragedies and bad harvests might eliminate some of them, but as a group, the *tenuyers* showed a remarkable resistance and indeed a capacity to adapt to changes in the demands made by their markets. None of the crises of the seventeenth or eighteenth centuries really affected their predominance. Their presence, and the system of landholding on which they depended, did not prevent them from being surrounded by larger numbers of the poor and insecure, but at least what wealth there was in the rural community was spread about among a larger group of people.

Whether this prosperous layer of rural society was a closed world is a question difficult to answer, since the fate of those younger sons and daughters who survived into adulthood but did not inherit a holding is not easy to determine, but it does seem that, as much as they could, better-off parents saw to it that their children married people of comparable wealth and expectations. However the ambiguities of the *domaine congéable* seem to have helped prevent a radical estrangement of rich and poor in the countryside during the course of the eighteenth century. Given the extent of absentee landlordism, the influence of the nobles, or of any other landlords, over this peasant 'middle class' was, with some notable exceptions, bound to be minimal. The clergy, itself increasingly rural in background as time went by, seems to have reflected the general temper of the countryside as much as it led it.

What preoccupied the countryside was largely its own business. It was not however by any means a place in which people shut themselves up in their hamlets and holdings, only to emerge for Sunday mass at the parish church. Family, hamlet and parish formed the basic units of loyalty; the tavern, the *veillée,* the fair and Sundays in the *bourg,* the occasions on which people met and reinforced those loyalties by habit. In the universe of country folk, a town like Vannes, while somewhat different, was not unfamiliar, for it was inhabited by people in many ways like themselves, and a place they went for business, devotion or pleasure, but it did contain some people whose income, occupation, education, way of life and even language were different from their own. It was the presence of this element, not the physical fact of walls or paved streets which set the town apart, and which made it seem that the principal link of the countryside with the town was the relation between exploited and exploiters. The complex mass of economic discontent, misery and wounded dignity which men at the end of the eighteenth century summed up as 'feudalism' was closely associated with this economic link, and the *domaine congéable* was its most important expression. Given the interests involved, it is doubtful whether this system of tenure, any more than simple leaseholding, could have been reformed by a revolution based on respect for private property. Certainly the failure to do so in the early stages of the Revolution ended the popularity of the new regime in the Vannetais; and the region, along with most of Lower Brittany, entered the nineteenth century virtually unchanged for better or worse by the greatest political upheaval of modern times.

APPENDIX I

A PROCEEDING FOR EXPULSION UNDER
DOMAINE CONGÉABLE

The following documents are intended to give an idea of the steps involved in the expulsion of one tenant by another from a tenure held under *domaine congéable*.

(1) Lease granted to a new tenant with the power to expel, 8-7-1782:

8 juillet 1782

Baillée par Monsieur Le Comte
du Nedo d'une tenue du Quenihoet
en Plaudren à Joseph Renaud
fils de feu Julien

Devant nous notaires royaux de la sénéchaussée de Vannes soussignés, fut présente Demoiselle Yvonne Thimony, veuve de noble maître Augustin Symon vivant avocat en parlement et sénéchal des regaires, demeurant carroir et paroisse Saint Pierre dudit Vannes, laquelle faisant pour Messire Claude-François Gicquel, chevalier comte du Nedo, seigneur dudit lieu, de Kerdrean, Kcrouricc, Couetcourso et autres lieux, capitaine aux gardes françaises, chevalier de l'ordre royal et militaire de St-Louis et Brigadier des armées du Roi, a baillé, pour neuf ans qui commenceront le vingt-quatre decembre mil sept cent quatre-vingt-trois, à Joseph Renaud laboureur, fils de feu Julien Renaud demeurant au village du Quenhoet, paroisse de Plaudren, aussi présent, et acceptant la jouissance, à titre de convenant à domaine congéable suivant l'usement de Brouerec de la tenue où il demeure, appartenances, servitudes et dépendances; à la charge à lui d'en jouir en bon père de famille, sans pouvoir rien dégrader, délmolir, ni innover, couper aucun arbre par pied ni tête, pas meme émonder ceux qui ont pris vent, ni ceux qui sont ou seront destinés à le prendre; construire aucuns nouveaux édifices, ni changer la forme des anciens, sous prétexte de réparation ni autrement, ni subroger personne au tout, ni partie du présent bail, le tout sans l'exprès consentement, par l'écrit dudit seigneur comte du Nedo, à peine de nullité des subrogations, pure perte des nouveaux édifices, et de tous dépenses, dommages et intérêts; de payer et acquitter toutes les rentes et charges auxquelles cette tenue peut être assujettie, sans que cette clause soit l'approbation d'aucune; de suivre le moulin de la seigneurie, à la manière accoutumée, de faire les corvées et obéissances suivant l'usement; de fournir, au premier réquisitoire dudit seigneur foncier, déclaration et description, par tenants et aboutissants, des fonds et des édifices de ladite tenue, et d'y comprendre les différentes espèces d'arbres y étant, et de payer pour prix de jouissance, en nature de rente foncière et convenancière chaque année, au jour Saint Gilles, audit seigneur comte du Nedo, en la ville de Vannes quitte de frais de port, quatre lives quatre sous en argent, deux couples de chapons, et cinq perrées de seigle bon grain, net, sec et marchand, mesure du marché de Vannes; à commencer à Saint-Gilles mil sept cent quatre-vingt-cinq, et au surplus il a été convenu qu'aux fins de la présente le preneur pourra congédier tous autres détenteurs de ladite tenue en les remboursant du prix de leurs droits convenanciers aux termes dudit usement; partant fait et passé, audit Vannes en l'étude et au rapport de Goujeon, dits notaires, sous le seing de Mademoiselle Symon, et celui du sieur Mathurin Riallan prud'homme présent dudit Vannes, pour et à la requête dudit Joseph Renaud qui a affirmé ne savoir signer, de ce interpellé, et lecture a été donnée avant sa signature, ce jour huitième de juillet mil sept cent quatre-vingt-deux après midi.

Thimony veuve Symon   Riallan
Menard   Goujeon
    no^{re}. royal   no^{re}. royal
Contrôlé à Vannes le 10 juillet 1782
R. trente sous.   Priaud
                    p^r le C^r

(2) Judgement by the court of the Jurisdiction of Largouët, 12-1-1786.
Messire Claude François Gicquel, chevalier comte du Nedo seigneur de Kerdrean, Kerouriec, Couetcourzo, le Hincouet et autres lieux, maréchal des camps et armées du Roi, chevalier de l'ordre royal et militaire de Saint-Louis demeurant en son hôtel rue Saint-François paroisse Saint-Pierre de cette dite ville de Vannes demandeur en congé aux fins d'assignation du seize novembre dernier signifiée par Le Marec contrôlée le dix-sept, Goujeon procureur, Le Claire substitut.

Joseph Le Martelot laboureur et Marie Renaud sa femme demeurant au village de Renal, Laurent le Martelot et Louise Renaud sa femme demeur- ant au bourg paroissial de Plaudren, Jean le Petit, meunier et Perrinne Renaud sa femme demeurant au Moulin de Keryzac, trève de Loqueltas, Jeanne Renaud, et Guillaume Renaud, mineur emancipé demeurant à Botera et Pierre le Brun, demeurant à la métairie de Kerbolher, son curateur pour l'autoriser défendeurs audit congément. Jehanno procureur.

Nous ouï Le Claire procureur substitut et du consentement de Jehanno pour ses parties, qu'il signera avons jugé au profit du demandeur le congé des édifices et tous autres droits convenanciers d'une tenue située au village de Quenihoet en la susdite paroisse de Plaudren relevant à domaine congéable suivant l'usement de Brouerec de la seigneurie du Nédo pour ledit congé être executé par provision aux termes dudit usement, et à cet effet avons ordonné aux parties de convenir d'experts priseurs et arpenteurs pour procéder aux mesurage et prisage des dits droits faute de quoi il en sera pour les défailleurs nommé et donné d'office avec un tiers et au surplus ordonné aux experts qui vaqueront aux mesurage et prisage desdits édifices de les priser comme s'ils étaient en bon état de réparations.

D

no. p^r.

(3) Nomination of experts, 25-1-1786

Du vingt-cinq janvier mil sept cent quatre-vingt-six huit heures du matin. Devant nous Ignace Pierre Jacques Duliepvre, avocat en Parlement Sénéchal et seul juge des juridictions du comté de Largouët, Baronnie de Quintin et de Lanvaux sous Vannes y annexées ayant avec nous pour adjoint Louis Joseph Allanic commis greffier,

Messire Claude Francois Gicquel chevalier comte du Nedo, seigneur de Kerdrean, Kerouriec, Couetcourzo, le Hincouët et autres lieux, maréchal des camps et armées du Roy, chevalier de l'ordre royal et militaire de Saint Louis demeurant en son hotel rue Saint François paroisse Saint Pierre de cette ville demandeur en congé Goujeon procureur

Joseph Le Martelot et consorts défendeurs audit congé Jehanno procureur Maître Maturin Goujeon procureur dudit demandeur a remontré que par sentence du douze de ce mois il a fait juger le congément des édifices, superfices, stucs, engrais et droits de labourage d'une tenue située au village de Quenihoet en la paroisse de Plaudren, qu'en conséquence il demandait acte de la déclaration qu'il a faite à l'endroit de convenir pour sa partie de la personne de Maître Pierre Vincent Le Franc demeurant au bourg paroissial de Grand Champ et sommait celles de Jehanno de convenir de leur part d'un autre expert priseur et arpenteur pour procéder aux mesurage et prisage de la tenue dont est cas et a ledit Maître Goujeon signé

Goujeon

A l'endroit ledit maître Jehanno procureur des dits défendeurs au congé a declaré convenir pour sa partie de la personne de maître Vincent Joseph Pocard demeurant près la Place du Marché au Seigle, paroisse Saint Salomon, et a ledit Maître Jehanno procureur signé

Jehanno

Nous, juge, avons donné acte des déclarations des dits Goujeon et Jehanno procureurs de convenir pour leurs parties des dits Le Franc et Pocard, et avons nommé d'office pour tiers Pouliquen demeurant au bourg de Baud pour procéder aux mesurage et prisage de la tenue dont est cas, et a cet effet avons ordonné que les trois experts priseurs et arpenteurs seront assignés de

moment à autre pour prêter devant nous le serment requis fait et arrêté au greffe les dits jour et an que devant
Duliepvre   Allanic
V.ᵃⁿ [vacation] trois livres
Reçus

(4) Swearing-in of surveyors, 26-1-1786
Du vingt six janvier mil sept cent quatre-vingt-six deux heures de relevé
   Devant nous Ignace Pierre Jacques Duliepvre, avocat en Parlement, sénéchal et seul juge des juridictions du comté de Largouet, baronnies de Quintin et de Lanvaux sous Vannes y annexées ayant avec nous pour adjoint Louis Joseph Allanic commis greffier
   Messire Claude François Gicquel chevalier comte du Nedo Seigneur de Kerdrean, Kerouriec, Couetcourzo, Le Hincouet, et autres lieux, maréchal des camps et armées du Roy, chevalier de l'ordre royal et militaire de Saint Louis demeurant en son hôtel rue Saint François paroisse Saint-Pierre de cette ville demandeur en congé, Goujeon procureur

   Joseph Le Martelot et consorts défendeurs audit congé Jehanno procureur
Maître Maturin Goujeon procureur du dit seigneur demandeur a remontré avoir, par exploit de ce jour signifié par Giron, donné assignation à maîtres Pierre Vincent Le Franc et Vincent Joseph Pocard experts respectivement convenus des parties et à maître Pouliquen demeurant au bourg paroissial de Baud tiers nommé et donné d'office aux fins de la convention du matin de ce jour à comparaître à ces jour lieu et heure pour prêter devant nous le serment de se bien et fidèlement comporter en leur commission et a le dit maître Goujeon signé
                                                                     Goujeon
A l'endroit le dit maître Jehanno procureur a declaré assister à la prestation de serment des dits experts y consentir pour ses parties et a signé
                                                                     Jehanno
A l'évocation sont aussi comparu les dits Le Franc, Pocard et Pouliquen lesquels priseurs ont la main levée promis et juré de se bien et fidèlement comporter en leur commission et ont signé
   Pocard   Pouliquen   Le Franc
Nous juge susdit avons donné acte des dires des dits Goujeon et Jehanno procureurs pour leurs parties de la présence des dits experts, et de leur serment ordonnons à ceux-ci de vaquer de moment à autre aux mesurage et prisage de la tenue dont est cas, pour leur rapport être par nous statué ce qui sera vu appartenir. Fait et arrêté au greffe les dits jour et an devant
   Duliepvre   Allanic

(5) Survey of the edifices

Mesurage et prisage d'une
tenue située au village
du Quenihoet en Plaudren.

Mesurage et prisage afin de congément des édifices, superfices, stucs, engrais et droit de labourage d'une tenue située au village de Quenihoet en la paroisse de Plaudren, relevant à domaine congéable suivant l'usement de Brouerec de la seigneurie du Nedo, faits à requête de Joseph Renaud fondé pour un sixième en ladite tenue et demandeur audit congé pour les cinq autres sixièmes contre Guillaume Renaud son frère et autres consorts défendeurs audit congé, jugé par sentence de la juridiction de Largouet à Vannes du douze janvier dernier, convention et prestation de serment d'experts du vingt cinq même mois, auquel mesurage et prisage a été vaqué par nous Pierre Le Franc, Vincent Joseph Pocard et Jean Pouliquen, priseurs et arpenteurs convenus des parties et données pour tiers comme suit ce jour treizième février mil sept cent quatre-vingt-six suivant la montrée nous faite par les parties.

Et premier
Un cour de logement construite de massonne et couverte de paille contenant de long à deux longères cinquante-trois pieds, de franc par le dedans à trois pignons dix-sept pieds et de hauteur de longères dix pieds le tout reduit prisé avec les espèces et en raison considerées la somme de sept cent soixante un livres huit sols cy .... 761 l. 8 s.

2° Une loge à charette accolée à la longère du nord de ladite maison contenant de long à une longère dix-huit pieds, de franc par le dedans à une arras sept pieds et demi et de hauteur de la dite longère quatre pieds prisée en l'état qu'elle est la somme de douze livres cy .... 12 l.

3° Une chambre vers levant et midi des dits logements construite de massonne et couverte en ardoises contenant de long à deux longères vingt-huit pieds et demi, de franc par le dedans à deux pignons dix-sept pieds et de hauteur de longères dix pieds et demi le tout reduit, prisée avec les espèces et curaisons la somme de six cent six livres cy . . 606 l.

4° Le puits dudit village prisé pour une moitié la somme de trente-six livres cy .... 36 l.
Trois cordes de fossés sur le jardin derrière la maison nommé Liorh bihan prisées avec les bois et fruitiers la somme de neuf livres cy . . 9 l.

5° Dix-huit cordes et demi de talus et fossés sur autre jardin nommé Liorh Brase prisées égard aux bois et fruitiers la somme de cent quatre-vingt livres cy .... 180 l.
La nuit survenue nous nous sommes retirés et renvoyés à demain pour la continuation des présents et avons signé

Pocard   Pouliquen   Le Franc
Advenu ce jour quatorzième février mil sept cents quatre-vingt-six

nous dits experts nous sommes transportés jusqu'au dit village du Quenihouet pour la continuation du présent, ce que nous avons fait comme suit suivant la montrée nous faite par les mêmes parties

6° Quatre-vingt-neuf cordes de talus et fossé sur un parc en labeur nommé le Grand Clos prisées égard aux bois et fruitiers et rue batterie y étant la somme de deux cents dix livres cy .... 210 l.

7° Six cordes de talus et fossés sur un jardin nommé Raquerebihan prisées avec des bois et fruitiers la somme de dix livres cy .... 10 l.

8° Onze cordes de talus et fossé sur un autre jardin nommé Liorh frehe, prisées avec les bois et fruitiers la somme de trente livres cy ..... 30 l.

9° Quarante cordes de talus et fossés sur un clos en labeur nommé Parc Moigne prisées avec les bois et fruitiers la somme de soixante-huit livres cy .... 68 l.

10° Trente-deux cordes de fossé sur le grand pré prisées egard aux bois et fruitiers même le long du ruisseau la somme de quatre-vingt livres cy .... 80 l.

11° Dix-huit cordes de fossés sur un petit clos en labeur nommé le petit pré prisées avec les bois et fruitiers la somme de trente-sept livres cy   37 l.

12° Trente cordes de talus et fossé sur un autre parc en labeur nommé Parc Cohgarhen prisées avec les bois et fruitiers la somme de soixante-quinze livres cy .... 75 l.

13° Dix-huit cordes de talus et fossés sur un jardin à chanvre nommé Liorhfourne prisées avec les bois et fruitiers la somme de soixante livres cy .... 60 l.

   Trente-six cordes de talus et fossés sur un clos en labour nommé parc Raguere prisées avec les bois et fruitiers la somme de quatre-vingt-un livres cy .... 81 l.

   Procédant au calcul du present cahier de mesurage et prisage, il s'est trouvé monter sauf erreur de gilt [?] et calcul et les stucs non compris, à la somme de deux mille deux cent cinquante-cinq livres huit sols cy .... 2255 l. 8 s.

   Les stucs de ladite tenue au nombre de douze journeaux soixante cordes prisées suivant l'usement la somme de soixante-seize livres dix sols cy .... 76 l. 10 s.

Fait et arreté sous nos seings les dits jour et an

Pocard	Pouliquen	Le Franc
vacation vingt-quatre livres serment compris	vacation trente-deux livres, prestation de serment, et retours compris	vacation vingt-quatre livres

(6) Continuation de payement
2 mars 1786
L'an mil sept cent quatre-vingt-six le jeudi deux mars audience tenue par monsieur le sénéchal des juridictions du Comté de Largouet Baronnie de Quintin et de Lanvaux sous Vannes y annexées.

Messire Claude François Gicquel chevalier comte du Nedo seigneur de Kerdrean, Kerouriec, et autres lieux, demandeur en congé aux fins d'assignation du seize novembre dernier signifiée par Le Marec contrôlée à Vannes le lendemain. Goujeon procureur, Le Ridant procureur substitut.

Joseph Martelot, et Marie Renaud sa femme, Laurent Le Martelot et Louise Renaud, sa femme, Jean Le Petit et Perrinne Renaud sa femme, et Jeanne Renaud et Guillaume Renaud mineur sous l'autorité de Pierre Le Brun son curateur défendeurs, Jehanno procureur
intervient
Joseph Le Falher, Le Ridant procureur
Nous, ouï Le Ridant substitut de Gourjeon, avons continué au payement et distribution du prix des édifices dont il s'agit à demain trois du présent mois et avons donné acte de l'intervention dudit le Ridant pour ledit Joseph Le Falher

Duliepvre

(7) Reimbursement of the former tenants
3 mars 1786   Payement d'une tenue située au village de Quenihoet en Plaudren par Joseph Renaud et sa femme sur Joseph Le Martelot et femme

Devant nous Pierre Jacques Ignace Duliepvre avocat en Parlement, sénéchal et seul juge des juridiction du Comté de Largouet, Baronnie de Quintin et Lanvaux sous Vannes y annexées, ayant avec nous pour adjoint Allanic Le Perderel commis greffier

Messire Claude François Gicquel, Chevalier Comte du Nedo Seigneur de Kerdrean, Kerouriec, Couetcourzo, Le Hincouet et autres lieux, maréchal des camps et armées du Roy, chevalier de l'ordre royal et militaire de Saint Louis, demeurant en son hotel rue Saint François paroisse Saint Pierre de cette ville de Vannes, demandeur en congé Goujeon procureur, lequel a déclaré que sa partie a fait juger le congé de la tenue dont il sera ci-après parlé pour tourner au profit de Joseph Renaud, aux fins d'acte de baillée du huit juillet mil sept cent quatre-vingt-deux, controlée à Vannes le dix, au rapport de Goujeon no^re royal et a le dit Goujeon signé

Goujeon

Contre

Joseph Le Martelot et Marie Renaud sa femme, Laurent Le Martelot et Louise Renaud sa femme, Jean Le Petit et Perrinne Renaud sa femme,

Jeanne et Guillaume Renaud mineurs émancipés sous l'autorité de Pierre Le Brun, leur curateur, défendeurs Jehanno p^r.

Ledit Joseph Renaud et Jeanne le Moel sa femme de lui autorisée, assistés dudit Goujeon leur procureur, ont remontré que les experts et tiers respectivement convenus et nommés d'office ayant par procès-verbal des treize et quatorze fevrier dernier, procedé aux mesurage et prisage des droits convenanciers de la tenue où ils demeurent au village de Quenihoet, paroisse de Plaudren, relevant à domaine congéable de la seigneurie du Nédo, ont porté les édifices à somme de deux mille deux cent cinquante-cinq livres huit sols, et que par jugement du jour d'hier, il a été pris continuation, à ces jour, lieu et heure pour le payement et distribution de la dite somme; pourquoi les dits Renaud et femme ont demandé acte de la réprésentation de la susdite somme, et qu'il fut ordonné aux défendeurs en congé de la recevoir, et qu'après cette réception ils fussent jugés quittes du prix des dites édifices (quoique ce soit pour le tiers et les cinq sixièmes des deux autres tiers, parce que les demandeurs retiennent par mains, la somme de deux cent cinquante livres, douze sols pour le sixième revenant auxdits Renaud ès dits édifices) et que les libres proprieté et jouissance de ladite tenue leur fussent adjugées et que les défendeurs fussent condamnés de la vider de leurs personnes, familles et biens, et qu'à défaut, il fut permis de les en expulser à leurs frais et par provision; à l'endroit lesdits Renaud et femme ont déclaré que pour faire le présent payement ils ont emprunté, savoir de Jean Le Roux de Norbrat en Meucon, tuteur des enfants mineurs d'autre Jean Le Roux et de Marguerite Allanic de Dolan en Sené quatre-vingt livres, de Mathurin Lotodé, de Kergourio en Plaudren, tant en privé nom qu'en qualité de tuteur des enfants de feu Jacques Daniel la somme de trois cent soixante livres et de Julie Le Calonec, veuve de Jean Le Moel du Cosquer en Monterblanc la somme de treize cent quatre-vingt livres, le tout à titre de constitut, aux fins d'actes au rapport de Goujeon que seront contrôlés dans les délais; et au surplus les dits Renaud et femme ont déclaré consentir à payer pour l'année courante les mêmes prestations que les années précédentes aux défendeurs en congé, les dites prestations consistant dans le tiers et les cinq sixièmes des deux autres tiers de dix perrées de seigle, pour demeurer quittes vis à vis des dits défendeurs en congé de pareilles portions leur revenant dans lesdits stucs et a le dit M^e. Goujeon signé et sur ce que les dits Renaud et femme ont declaré ne savoir signer, de ce interpellés pour eux et à leurs requêtes ont signé, savoir pour le dit Joseph Renaud, le sieur Oliver Burnolle, et pour la dite Jeanne Le Moel, le sieur Mathurin Riallan présents

    Riallan   Burnolle   Goujeon

Est aussi comparu Jacques Le Falher, lequel par M^e. Le Ridant son procureur a demandé à toucher sur la somme représentée celle de sept cent cinquante-un livres, seize sols, pour un tiers lui revenant dans lesdits édifices aux fins d'acte de vente du neuf mars, mil sept cent soixante-deux au rapport de Lezot no^{re}. de cette cour, réferé, contrôleé, insinué à Vannes le dix-huit du même mois, lui consenti par Julien Renaud et Perrinne Conan, auteurs communs des Renaud ci-devant dénommés, declarant abandonner ses stucs au demandeur en congé, par ce qu'il il [*sic*] lui payera à la St-Gilles prochaine, conformément à ses offres, trois perrées un tiers de seigle, mesure de Vannes, réservant seulement le droit de revue et a ledit Le Ridant signé et sur ce que le dit Jacques Le Falher a déclaré ne savoir signer de ce interpellé pour lui et à sa requête a signé Le Sieur Louis Joseph Allanic présent

Le Ridant   Allanic

Sont aussi comparus Joseph Le Martelot et Marie Renaud sa femme de lui autorisée, Laurent Le Martelot et Louise Renaud sa femme, de lui autorisée, Jean Le Petit meunier et Perrinne Renaud sa femme de lui autorisée, lui-meme assisté et autorisé de Gildas Le Petit son père, Jeanne Renaud fille majeure, et Guillaume Renaud mineur assisté et autorisé de Pierre Le Brun présent son curateur, lesquels assistés de M^e. Jehanno leur procureur ont dit n'avoir moyen empêchant de recevoir chacun leur part et portion dans lesdits édifices, montant chaque part à deux cent cinquante livres douze sols, à l'exception dudit Guillaume Renaud, lequel sous l'autorité dudit Pierre Le Brun son curateur a déclaré relaisser ladite somme de deux cent cinquante livres douze sols montant de sa part et portion au demandeur en congé pendant l'espace de quatre ans pour lui en payer les intérêts au taux de l'édit et ont de plus declaré accepter pour payement des stucs la rente accoutumée payable à St-Gilles prochaine, à la déduction néanmoins de la portion demandée par Jacques Le Falher, réservant leur droit de revue à la coutume et a ledit Jehanno p^r. signé et sur ce que les parties ont déclaré ne savoir signer, de ce interpellées pour elles et à leurs requêtes ont signé savoir pour ledit Joseph Le Martelot le sieur Yves Giron, pour ladite Marie Renaud, le sieur Joseph Le Gal, pour ledit Laurent Le Martelot le sieur Julien Glais, pour la d^e. Louise Renaud le sieur Joseph Marie Jouhanic, pour ledit Jean Le Petit, le sieur Jean Le Quillo, pour lad^e. Jeanne Renaud le sieur Mathurin Rouxel, pour ledit Guillaume Renaud, le sieur Olivier Evaux, et pour ledit Pierre Le Brun le sieur Antoine Bizard présents

Giron   Le Gal   Glais   Clement   Jouhanic

Rouxel   Bizard   Lemaréchal   Evaux   Le Quilo   Jehanno n^{re}.

Desquels dires, déclarations, consentements et réservations nous avons donné acte ensemble de la représentation faite à l'endroit par lesdits Joseph Renaud et femme de la somme de deux mille quatre livres seize sols pour le prix du tiers et des cinq sixièmes des deux autres tiers de ladite tenue, même de la reprise par eux faite à l'endroit de la somme de deux cent cinquante livres douze sols pour la portion revenant audit Guillaume Renaud, à la charge à eux de lui en payer les livres pendant les quatre ans portés en son plaidé.

Et procédant au payement et distribution du surplus qui est la somme de dix-sept cent cinquante-quatre livres quatre sols, nous l'avons adjugée, savoir, audit Joseph Le Falher, la somme de sept cent cinquante-un livres, seize sols, auxdits Joseph Le Martelot et femme, deux cent cinquante livres douze sols, auxdits Laurent Le Martelot et femme pareille somme, auxdits Jean Le Petit et femme, sous lesdites autorités même somme, et à Jeanne Renaud égale somme de deux cent cinquante livres douze sols, lesquelles sommes ont été prises et emportées par les susdits comparants dont quittance et sur ce que lesdits Joseph Renaud et femme et les autres comparants ont d'abondant déclaré ne savoir signer, de ce interpellés pour eux et à leurs requêtes ont signé

Au moyen duquel payement nous avons jugé quitte lesdits Joseph Renaud et femme des sommes par eux ci-dessus payées et en conséquence nous leur avons adjugé les libres disposition, propriété et jouissance des droits convenanciers de lad^e tenue, et condamné les défendeurs de la vider de leurs personnes, familles et biens dans quinzaine et à faute de ce permettons de les en faire expulser par provision et à leurs frais et au surplus avons décerné acte de la répétition de la déclaration desdits Joseph Renaud et femme d'avoir emprunté pour faire le present payement, les sommes mentionnées en leur plaidé, et en conséquence avons adjugé aux dits Jean Le Roux, Mathurin Lotodé et Julie Le Calonec l'hypothèque spéciale et préférable sur lesdits droits convenanciers pour sûreté des principaux et des intérêts des sommes par eux prêtées conformément au plaidé des demandeurs en congé.

Et ont été les vacations du present taxées savoir à nous vingt livres, pareille somme au greffe papier outre et les deux tiers de notre vacation à chacun des dits Goujeon et Jehanno procureurs.

Fait et arrêté lesdits jour et an

Duliepvre	Jehanno	Goujeon
Vacation vingt	Reçu moitié	R. moitié
livres reçus		

Contrôlé à Vannes le 10 mars 1786 reçu quinze livres quinze sols insinué ledit jour reçu trente livres un sou cinq deniers

De la Chauvelays

(8) The costs of the operation
Du 3 mars 1786
M. le chevalier du Nedo demandeur en congé
Joseph Le Martelot et consorts defendeurs

Sentence cy	1 l.	4 s.
Convention et prestation de serment cy	11.	10
Mesurage et prisage	2.	10
Continuation cy..................................	. 7.	6.
à M. Le Sénéchal cy	20.	. .

au greffe et papier cy .... 20. 10.   .
A M. Goujeon .... 13. 6. 8.
A Monsieur Jehanno cy .... 13. 6. 8.
Contrôle et insinuation .... 46. 15.   .

Total cy .... 1291. 9 s. 10 d.

Sources: (1) A.D. Morbihan E^n 65: Minutes Goujeon, 1782;
         (2–7) B: Juridiction de Largouët, 1786.

APPENDIX II

A SUMMARY OF THE CONTENTS OF SOME *INVENTAIRES APRÈS DÉCÈS*

(1) Inventory of the effects of a relatively prosperous *tenuyer*: 24/25-4-1780.

Inventaire, prisage et estimation fait d'autorité de la juridiction des Regaires de Vannes au village de Keriben paroisse de Surzur, ce jour vingt-quatre avril mil sept cent quatre-vingt, des meubles et effets mobiliers dépendants de la succession de Louise Le Pahun, veuve Jean Le Louërec decedée audit village de Keriben . . .

Dans la cuisine: 1 trépied 2 livres 5 sols — 1 banc près le feu 1.10.0 — un lit près ledit banc garni d'une couette de balle, deux draps de réparation et une bonne 9.0.0 — 1 petite armoire à un battant sans fermeture 2.10.0 — 1 mauvais banc 1.0.0 — 1 couchette garnie d'une couette de balle, deux draps, et deux bornes 7.0.0 — 1 poele grasse 1.0.0 — 1 dressoir 1.0.0 — 1 lit mode de campagne garni d'une couette de balle, deux mauvais draps de réparation et une bonne 14.0.0 — 1 table mode de campagne et un couteau crochu 2.5.0 — 1 escabeau près de la table 15 s. — 1 autre escabeau 5 s. — 1 marmite 3.0.0 — 1 casserole 4.10.0 — 1 grand bassin 36.0.0 — 1 autre moyen bassin 16.0.0 — 1 autre bassin 4.10.0 — 1 autre bassin 3.0.0 — 1 autre bassin 2.0.0 — 1 couloir 10 s. — toute la poterie 15 s. — 1 assiette de faïence et un plat de terre 10 s. — 1 volet de bois et deux poteaux de faïence 9 s. — 3 planches prisées avec une mauvaise chaise de bois 15 s. — 1 scie 8 s. — 1 panier d'oisier 5 s. — 1 paire de tenailles et 1 petit marteau 6 s. — 1 herminette 5 s. — 1 tarier 6 s. — 1 percevin et une lame de percevin 6 s. — 1 coniq de fer 4 s. — 2 faucilles 15 s. — 3 autres faucilles 10 s. — 4 autres faucilles 6 s. — 2 pillesvoisin 12 s. — 2 grands couteaux 2 s. — 9 écuelles de bois 1.0.0 — 1 écuelle de terre, 1 soucoupe et 6 cuilliers de bois 2 s. — 1 pendule de bois avec ses poids de plomb 3.0.0

Dans la chambre: 1 grand coffre 9.0.0 — 1 autre mauvais coffre 2.10.0 — 1 panne 2.0.0 — 2 broies 3.15.0 — 4 fûts de barriques 4.0.0 — 2 travoirs 5 s. — ce qu'il y a de cuir 15 s. — 6 fléaux 12 s. — 1 mée 15 s. — 1 armoire à deux battants fermant à clef, sur laquelle était apposé le scellé que nous avons trouvé non altéré 27.0.0 — 1 autre armoire à 4 battants et deux tiroirs 10.0.0 — 1 petit coffre fermant à clef 1.0.0 — 1 autre coffre 1.5.0 — 1 autre coffre 1.10.0 — 1 mauvaise table 5 s. — 1 lit complet 6.0.0 — 2 grands rangeots avec leurs couvertures de paille 1.4.0 — 1 rangeot 8 s. — 1 autre petit rangeot 5 s. — 1 mauvais charnier de terre 10 s. — 6 ruches de paille 16 s. — 9 autres ruches de paille 8 s. — 5 autres ruches 9 s. — 2 rouets 1.0.0 — 1 mesure de demi quart 12 s. — 2 sas 8 s. — 2 cribles 6 s. — tout ce qu'il y a de vieilles ferrailles 1.0.0 — la meilleure pelle 2.0.0 — une autre pelle 1.0.0 — la meilleure étreppe 2.10.0 — la meilleure fourche de fer 1.10.0 — 1 autre fourche 1.5.0 — 1 autre fourche 1.4.0 — 1 autre fourche 5 s. — le meilleur croc 1.7.0 — le petit croc 15 s. — 1 autre croc 8 s. — 3 rateaux ferrés 12 s. — l auge de pierre 7.10.0 — 1 vache rouge 27 l. — 1 autre vache gare blanche 36 l. — 1 autre vache gare rousse 36 l. — 1 vache noire 27 l. — 1 autre vache rouge 20 l. — 1 autre vache noire 39 l. — 1 vache rouge 24 l. — 1 genisse noire 15 l. — 1 autre génisse noire 13.10.0 — 1 jument rouge 90 l. — *Dans la loge à charrettes*: la meilleure charrette ferrée 48 l. — l'autre charrette ferrée 40.10.0 — de quoi faire une charrette 3 l. — 5 morceaux de bois 1 l. — 4 rateaux et 12 fourches de bois 15 s. — 2 mauvais cables 6 s. — 2 planches, 1 broie et timon à charrette 15 s. — la meilleure charrue, le meilleur et une autre charrue [*sic*] 3 l. — une autre charrue et 2 socs 1.12.0 — 2 paires d'étriers 13 s. — 1 bride 1 l. — 1 panneau et 2 sangles 1.10.0 — les traits du cheval 10 s. — la meilleure fane 1.10.0 — l'autre fane 1.5.0 — 3 courroies 18 s. — le meilleur joug, un atelloire de fer et un cable 1.5.0 — 2 mauvais jougs 8 s. — l'auge de bois et . . . [?] à boeufs et 4 mats à piller lande 10 s. — l'échelle 10 s. — l'autre échelle 6 s. — 200 de bois 16 l. — ce qu'il y a de viande de porc avec le charnier 31 l. — 1 tourte de saindoux 6.10.0 — 1 fusil 2.10.0 — 1 peseau 5 s. — 30 pièces de fil réparation 12 l. — 14 pièces de fil brin 7 l. — 1 marteau 5 s. — 2 faux avec leurs équipages 3.10.0 — 2 poches 14 s. — 2 autres poches 14 s. — 2 autres poches 14 s. — 3 autres poches 14 s. — 2 couvertures à boeufs 12 s. — 1 plat d'étain 5 s. — 1 manteau de drap bleu 14 l. — 1 manteau noir à femme 5.10.0 — 1 drap brin lin 2.5.0 — 1 autre pareil 2 l. — 1 autre drap 1.17.6 — 1 autre drap 2.1.0 — 1 demi-drap 1.4.0 — 1 serviette 8 s. — 1 autre serviette 12 s. — 1 autre serviette 15 s. — 1 autre serviette 6 s. — 1 demi douzaine de coiffes et 4 collets 3 l. — 1 demi douzaine de coiffes et 7 collets 3 l. — 1 paire de souliers 16 s. — 1 jupe de drap brune 5 l. — 1 autre jupe noire 2 l. — 1 paire de manches noires 3 l. — 1 jupe de toile 2 l. — 1 tablier noir 2.10.0 — 1 tablier de toile 15 s. — 1 paire de manches noire 1.5.0 — 1 paire de manches brunes 12 s. — 1 paire de manches blanches 1 l. — 1 autre paire de manches de toile 1 l. — 1 paire de manches blanches 2 l. — 1 jupe de drap brun 2 l. — 3 perrées de froment 60 l. — 3 perrées de seigle 25.10.0 — 4 perrées de mil 40 l. — 1 godelée de graine de lin 12 s. — 3 poules 15 s. — 2 civières 4 s. — *Argent monnayé*: 1506 l.

Papiers: Acte de vente de la moitié des édifices de la tenue Le Louerec de Keribeau en Surzur, faite par François Crossin et Jeanne Coleno sa femme au profit de Vincent Le Louerec pour la somme de huit cent quarante livres (Le Monnier, notaire, 17-1-1749).

Acte de la baillée de ladite tenue de Keribeau en date du 19-1-1771 (Le

Monnier), consentie par le seigneur de Rosmadec à Jean Le Louerec sous l'obligation annuelle de trois perrées, 1 quart de seigle, et une demie perrée de froment.

Acte de constitution portant la somme de 60 livres de principal, passé entre Jacques Le Mercier débiteur, laboureur demeurant au village du Baro paroisse de Surzur et Vincent Le Louerec autre laboureur en son vivant audit village de Keribeau, 17-10-1761 (Desalleurs, notaire).

Valeur totale des meubles et effets mobiliers et argent monnayé:

2448 l. 0. 6.

(2) Inventory of the effects of a rural artisan: 3-4-1781

Inventaire fait par moi soussigné Louis Jegat commis greffier de la juridiction du comté de Largouet . . . des meubles et effets mobiliers restés après le décès de Jean Brien vivant tisserand au village de Loperhet, paroisse de Grand-Champ . . .

1 table close 2 l. 10 s. — 2 pots à lait et 1 écuelle de terre 2 s. — 1 poteau gris 1 s. — 1 petit bassin 2.10.0 — 1 passoir d'airain 1.5.0 — 3 écuelles de bois 6 s. — 1 petite casserolle de cuivre 1.5.0 — 1 rangeot et 1 sceau 10 s. — 1 marmite, sa cuillière et son couvert 2 l. — 1 poele grasse 1.10.0 — 1 moyen bassin 4.10.0 — 1 petit trépied 15 s. — 1 mauvaise chaise et 1 escabeau 5 s. — 3 mauvaises buches 3 s. — 1 lit clos près le feu garni 12 l. — 1 mée auprès 1.10.0 — 1 autre lit au-dessous pareil 15 l. — le banc auprès et foncé 1.10.0 — 1 couchette garnie près la fenêtre 5 l. — 1 armoire à deux battants 15 l. — 1 petite armoire à battant sur laquelle était un scellé à bande non vicié 11. — 1 vache noire 30 l. — 1 mauvais coffre 10 s. — 1 autre coffre 3 l. — 1 grand rangeot 10 s. — 5 echeux de fil d'étoupe 1.5.0 — 11 ruches pour des abeilles 1.4.0 — 1 charnier de bois 15 s. — 1 petite scie 6 s. — 1 bedane 2 s. — 1 petit beurrier 2 s. 6 d. —

Hardes du défunt: 1 habit de burle blanc 1.10.0 — 1 mauvaise veste rouge sans manche 10 s. — 1 autre habit 2 l. — 2 gilets 10 s. — 1 paire de culottes bleues 1 l. — 1 mauvaise paire de souliers et une paire de bas 5 s. — 1 chapeau 10 s. — les 4 meilleurs chemises 4.5.0 — . . . [?] mauvaises chemises 5 s. —

Hardes de la veuve: 1 chemisette bleue 1.10.0 — 1 paire de manches vertes et un mauvais tablier brun 10 s. — 3 chemises 1.10.0 — 3 coiffes 10 s. — 1 croc à peser 3 l. — les meilleurs des métiers de tisserant et 5 harnais 24 l. — l'autre métier et quatre harnais 15 l. — 1 boite 10 s. — la boite aux plotons 1.10.0 — 1 bâteau de tisserand et deux cordes 15 s. — 1 mauvais faucillon et 1 petite hache 10 s. — 1 mauvaise faucille 2 s. — 2 poches 1 l. — six ruchées d'abeilles vivantes et une morte 27 l.

Valeur totale des effets: 77 l. 7 s. 0 d.

A l'endroit le tuteur m'a représenté une grosse de vente de la maison où demeurait le défunt consentie par lui audit Jean Brien son fils passée au rapport de Le Franc notaire de Largouet dûment contrôlée et insinuée à

Vannes le vingt mars 1775 ledit acte du douze aussi de mars . . .
A l'endroit ladite veuve nous a declaré avoir en argent monnayé la somme
de quatre-vingt-sept livres dix-sept sols six deniers dont ledit tuteur s'est
emparée et emportée
que Yves le Drean a payé pour pension qu'il a touché pour la mineure de
Perichot de laquelle somme ledit Jean Brien fils et tuteur s'est saisie.

(3) Inventory of the effects of a tenant subletting a tenure under *domaine
congéable*. Le Falher paid 1 l. 17 s. *capitation* in 1782:
29-12-1783
Inventaire fait par moi Jean Baudou commis greffier des juridictions du
comté de Largouet de Vannes . . . des meubles et effets restés après le décès
de Pierre Le Falher vivant laboureur au village du Reste paroisse de Grand
Champ et veuf de Julienne Allanic . . .
1 trépied 15 s. — 1 marmite 1.10.0 — 1 bassin 3.10.0 — 1 autre bassin 1.0.0
— 1 autre plus grand 2.10.0 — 1 petite marmite 10 s. — 1 grand bassin 15 l.
— 1 couloir 12 s. — 1 petit bassin 8 s. — 1 râteau 12 s. — 1 autre 10 s. — 1
autre 7 s. — 1 fourche de fer à trois doigts 18 s. — 1 autre 15 s. — 1 étrepe 1 l.
— 2 mauvaises étrepes 4 s. — 1 tranche 1.10.0 — 1 pelle de fer 2 l. — 1 petite
pelle 2 s. 6 d. — 1 piquette 2 s. — 2 bûches à lande 6 s. — 1 grand croc 1.5.0
— 1 autre petit 1 l. — 1 autre 3 s. — 1 charrue 3 l. — 1 charrue les rouelles et
la corde 15 s. — l'équipage du cheval 15 s. — 3 barriques 2.5.0 — 3 brouettes
1 l. — 1 charrette ferrée 30 l. — 1 autre de bois 24 l. — 3 civières 10 s. — 1
braye 1.5.0 — 1 autre braye 1.0.0 — tout le chanvre tant en filasse qu'en
bois 10.0.0 — l'équipage des boeufs 1.0.0 — 1 grand landier 8 s. — 2 autres 6
s. — 1 marteau 3 s. — la hache 5 s. — 1 faucillon 5 s. — 1 fane à charrette 10
s. — 1 scie 10 s. — 1 verloupe 5 s. — 5 fléaux 10 s. — 2 feuilles 1 l. — 3 autres
5 s. — 1 basset et 1 pesseau 4 s. — 1 brouette 5 s. — 4 bûches à pain 10 s. — 2
dévidoirs 6 s. — 1 tierçon 8 s. — 1 table à menuisier 10 s. — 2 petits bassets 4
s. — 3 autres 3 s. — le rangeot et son couvert 15 s. — 1 autre rangeot et son
couvert 10 s. — 2 rangeots 10 s. — 1 grande bûche 10 s. — 1 mesure de quart
1 l. — 1 dévidoir 6 s. — 1 autre 4 s. — 1 ruche à miel 5 s. — deux ruches 3 s.
— 1 couverte de paille 3 s. — 5 cercloirs 12 s. — les écuelles et les écullières
16 s. — le panneau et la sangle du cheval 8 s. — la gavidelle 2 s. — 1 buie 5 s.
— tous les pots 9 s. — les fuseaux 2 s. — le foin 45 l. — la paille d'avoine 9 l.
— 1 lit clos complet 15 l. — 1 autre lit clos complet 15 l. — 1 autre lit clos
complet 18 l. — 1 autre lit 4 l. — 1 banc 2 l. — 3 quarts d'avoine 4 l. — 1
perrée de blé noir 11 l. — 1 autre banc près le lit clos 2 l. — un mauvais coffre
5 s. — 1 buffet 1.10.0 — 1 petite armoire 10 s. — 1 armoire 27 l. — 1 armoire
30 l. — 1 ventoire 10 s. — 6 poches 2 l. — 1 seau 1 s. — 1 vache gare jaune 24
l. — 1 génisse 15 l. — 1 cochon 20 l. — 1 chèvre 4 l. — 1 mauvaise table 5 s.
— la graine de chanvre 2.10.0 — toutes les hardes 4.5.0
Valeur totale 371 l. 8 s. 6 d.

Sources: (1) A.D. Morbihan: Juridiction des Regaires: Minutes, 1784.
(2) A.D. Morbihan: Juridiction de Largouët: Minutes, 1781.
(3) A.D. Morbihan: Largouët: Minutes, 1783.

APPENDIX III

SEIGNEURIES OF COËTCANDEC ET LA CHENAYE: REVENUES

	Wheat (perrées)	Rye (perrées)	Oats (perrées)	Cash (livres)
Seigneurie de Coëtcandec:				
Pourpris de Coëtcandec		0.50		425.10
Métairie de Coëtcandec		13.00	3.00	35.25
[Domaines congéables:]				
Tenue Coparco		1.75		1.50
Parc Jagu		4.25		8.00
Talnay		2.75	1.00	20.95
Penerstang		0.25	1.00	7.00
Kerolivier	1.75	1.75	1.00	11.14
Boetmadec	1.00	0.50	1.50	6.70
Pratelmat			2.00	6.30
,,	0.50		1.00	6.30
Locmeren des Bois	0.50	0.25	0.50	4.80
,,	1.00	0.50	1.50	6.60
,,	0.50	0.50	1.00	7.80
Kermenezy	1.00	0.75	2.00	9.90
Talnay	1.50	0.50	1.00	9.00
Goxverte	1.00	0.25	1.00	5.25
,,	1.00	0.25	1.00	8.10
Kerolivier	1.00	1.75	1.00	15.00
,,	0.50	0.25	0.50	3.75
Botnotaire		0.50	1.00	3.50
Gliscouet		1.75	1.00	6.30
Boutonio		1.75	1.00	4.55
Les Saints	1.00		1.00	7.32
Bourg de Grand-Champ	0.50		1.00	7.20
,,	1.00		1.50	4.30
,,		0.50		19.80
,,				2.40
,,	0.50		1.00	6.07
,,	0.50		2.00	4.55
,,	0.50			11.05
,,	0.50		1.00	10.00
,,	0.50	1.00	1.00	5.15
,,	0.50		1.50	6.01
La Madelaine 'une pièce de terre'		0.50		1.80
,,	0.50			1.80

Keranscoet		0.50	1.00	9.00
Kermeneach			1.00	5.40
Traincher	1.00	1.00		4.50
Bourg			1.00	4.80
Moustoir	0.25			8.25
Clos Lanitrec en Plumergat				3.00
Kerthuet 'une prairie nommée des grenouilles en St-Jan'				15.00
Kermenezy '2 petites maisons domaine congéable'				3.00
[Miscellaneous rents:]				
Kermenezy 'apartenante au sr des Ruisseau rente foncière'				3.75
Maison de la Croix Verte à Vannes rente foncière				0.60
Clos en la lande talhouec en Meucon				3.00
Bois Keribio en Grand-Champ arrentement				6.00
Les bouchers de Grand-Champ				0.77
Loqueltas en Plaudren rente				2.40
Locmeren des Bois ferme d'une maison et jardin				10.00
Bourg de Grand-Champ métairie des salles	1.00	1.00	1.00	5.70
Sous le domaine du Roy à rachat [Domaine congéable:]				
Locpabu	2.00	2.00	2.00	9.00
,,	0.50		1.00	7.80
,,	1.00		1.00	7.80
,,	0.50		0.50	5.30
,,	0.50		0.50	4.80
Seigneurie de la Chenaye:				
Pourpris de la Chenaye				108.00
Métairie	2.00	25.00		5.60
Moulins à eau, La Chenaye	12.00	31.00		
Moulins Toulnay afféagés				100.00
Pièce de terre au dessous des moulins de La Chenaye [Domaine congéable:]				
Kerret	1.50		1.00	6.30
,,	1.00		1.00	6.30
,,	1.00		1.00	6.30
,,	3.00	6.00	3.00	7.80
Guenfrout	0.50	0.50		7.50
,,	0.50		0.50	10.50
Lesulit	0.50	1.00	1.00	6.60
Guerno	3.50	4.00	6.50	1.50
Bremenit	0.50		1.00	7.05
,,	0.50	1.00		7.05
Toulnay	5.00	8.00	5.00	0.70
,,	1.00	1.50		9.00

Tregonderf	0.50		1.00	6.30
Kerevalan	0.50	1.50		4.50
Verger		1.00	1.00	7.50
Moustoir	0.50	0.50		4.70
,,	1.00		1.00	12.60
Kerscot en St-Jan		1.00	2.00	1.70
Kerguillerme (St-Jan)	0.50		1.00	1.80
Collehaut ou Coelan (St-Jan)			1.00	4.50
Kermartré (St-Jan)		1.00		1.20
,,			1.00	1.30
Veahouet	5.50	5.50	6.00	2.70

[Rentes féodales, etc.:]
Loperhet suite de moulin
Le Graguen: 'une pièce de terre à l'usement par
   Silvestre Coech depuis par Guillame Pratelmat'
Prathenri: 'une pièce de terre ½ journal'
Boiscasio ou Bois Segalo, tenue
Kerral, manoir et metairie au Chapitre de Vannes

Famenen, métairie au même Chapitre	1.15
Rescourlais, au Chapitre 4 tenues (rente fèodale)	0.10

Penprat
Kerhouarn

Coulac, une tenue au Sr. Le Goff		0.02
Les Saints, au Prieur des Saints		0.36

Lesmeuly, à Mr de Penhouet
La pièce de l'étang des moulins de La Chenaye à
Mr de Penhouet nommé au-dessus
Tetenio, au mème
Kerdelan, à Mr de Lesquen Kerruzeaic

Trehorno, pièce dependant de la maison Kerrio		0.17
Loperhet, 2 maisons et jardin au sr Keraudrain		0.20
Erzellec, tenue boquentan à la veuve Gouarain	0.50	0.30

Couetlagon, à Mde. de la Grandville

Couetqueneach, à la même		0.05
Porcher, une tenue â la même		0.05

Coulac, à Mr DuPargo
Couetqueneach, aux Religieux de Lanvaux
Kerdual, sous St-Nerven

Lesquinino, sous St-Nerven		0.05

Kerluden ou Kerloeden, sous St-Nerven
Rohello, sous St-Nerven

Nizelec, 5 tenues sous M. de Penhouet	0.50	0.30
Kerroperts, métairie au même		0.05
Kerimout, tenue à la dlle le Nevé		0.05

Famenen, au sr Lucas de Vannes

Kerribert, tenue aux dlles Gouisac		1.50

Seigneurie de Chenaye Tregonleau et du Sonnant ('en fief et justice sous le duché de Rohan à son héritage à l'exception de la maison de Kerjagu et de Colpo relevant de la vicomté de Tribemoet à foi homage sans rachat')

	Wheat (perrées)	Rye (perrées)	Oats (perrées)	Buck-wheat (perrées)	Cash (livres)
Pourpris de la Chenaye Tregonleau en St-Jan	2 V	8 V	4 V	1 V	67.25
Moulins de Sonnant					230.00
[Domaines congéables:]					
Kerguen	0.25 V	0.50 V			18.60
Sonnant			1.00		3.90
Kerrouy	1.50 L				7.00
,,	1.50 L				3.00
,,	1.50 L				2.40
,,					3.00
Kervequin en Bignan					8.40
Prairie à domaine au dessous du Pont Sonnant					7.00
Kebernard en St-Jan	1.00 L		1.00 L		6.00
,,	0.50 L		1.00 L		4.26
,,					2.50
,,	1.00 L		1.00 L		6.00
Keraudrain	1.00 L	1.00 L			6.00
,,	1.00 L				4.00
Bas Moulac					2.70
Penhouet en Bignan					2.95
Kerdrizen en St-Jan					2.70
Colpo en Bignan	1.00 L		1.00 L		6.90
,,	1.00 L		1.00 L		4.90
,,	1.00 L		1.50 L		12.60
,,	1.00 L		1.00 L		5.48
,,			1.00 L		4.30
,,	0.50 L		1.00 L		4.50
Josseau en St-Jan	0.50 L		1.00 Por		6.00
Clos Du Gal					0.30
Kerrouy					5.10
Kebernard, prairie					3.00
,,					1.05
Kerman en St-Jan	0.50 L		0.50 L		3.05
Kerivalin en Lominé					10.00
Kerdramel en St-Jan	0.50 V				
,,	0.50 V				
Kermarquer, métairie			1.00 L		1.75
Kerbernard					4.50
Colpo, pièce de terre en Bignan					3.00
Colpo, tenue	1.00 L		1.00 L		5.50
Colpo, pâture					3.00
Prairie Leovet (?) en St-Jan					1.20
Kerguillerme en St-Jan					0.05

Colpo une maison en Bignan					3.00
Tenue au village du Sonnant en St-Jan	1.00 P	1.00 P	3.00 P		8.40
Tenue proche Kerjagu en Pontivy					2.00
Maison du Mené en St-Jan					0.05
Maison de Kerjagu en St-Jan					300.00
Sur les Moulins le Lay en St-Jan (rente foncière)	2.50 Por	5.00 Por			
Récapitulation Totale					
Coetcandec	23.50	40.25	42.00		813.85
La Chenaye sous Largouet	41.00	88.50	35.00		394.71
Le Chenaye Tregonleau sous Rohan	22.25	15.50	20.00	1.00	790.16
Total	86.75	144.25	97.00	1.00	1998.72

Evaluation

Les 86 Perrées $^3/_4$ à 12 l.	1047
Les 144 Perrees $^1/_4$ à 8 l.	1154
Les 97 Perrées avoine à 4 l.	388
Une perrée ble noir	6
	2595 l.
En argent	1998.72
	4593.72

* A.D. Morbihan, E 2630 'Rentier des terres de Couëtcandec et La Chenaye' [1754] and 'Extrait du nouvel aveu de Mr de la Bourdonnaye de Couëtcandec presenté par luy le 14 juin 1754' [simplified].

V = mesure de Vannes, L = mesure de Locminé, P = mesure de Pontivy, Por = mesure de Porhoet.

BIBLIOGRAPHY

PRIMARY SOURCES

1. Manuscript

Most of the material used for this study came from local archives, mainly the Archives départementales du Morbihan and the Archives départementales d'Ille-et-Vilaine. However, some useful documents were found in Paris as well. In addition to the general inventories and catalogues published for the Archives nationales and the Bibliothèque nationale, a useful general guide for research on Brittany is H. Du Halgouet, *Répertoire sommaire des documents manuscrits de l'histoire de Bretagne antérieurs à 1789 conservés dans les dépôts publics de Paris. Tome I. Bibliothèque nationale et Archives nationales* (St-Brieuc, 1914).

(i) Archives nationales

B^A 26	Elections aux États-Généraux. Minutes
B^III 37	Elections aux États-Généraux. Copies
BB^18 551	Ministère de la Justice. Situation politique de l'arrondissement du tribunal correctionel de Vannes, 1797
D xix 17 (260), 45 (740 *bis*)	Comité ecclésiastique
E 2051 fols. 70–4	Conseil d'État
F^1 C^III Morbihan 7	Esprit public
F^1 C^V Morbihan 2	Esprit public. Prefectoral reports
F^7 3682 (18)	Police générale
F^12 555, 1344, 1347, 1370, 1418, 1464, 1596, 1680^A, 1836, 1838	Commerce et industrie
F^20 229, 361	Statistique
G^5 5, 31	Amirauté et conseil des prises
H^1 419, 480, 538–9, 563–4, 591	Généralités du Royaume: Bretagne This series contains the correspondence of the intendants with the central administration, principally with the Controller-General.
K 1151 n° 13	Observations sur la dépopulation de la Bretagne [n.d.]

(ii) Archives de la Marine

Detailed repertories of this extremely rich collection are gradually appearing in print; the general guide for the pre-Revolutionary period is the *État sommaire des archives de la Marine antérieures à la Révolution* [by D. Neuville] (Paris, 1898), so far the only inventory available for the series consulted for this book:

C⁴ 170, 175, 208	Classes, amirautés, police de la navigation
C⁵ 21, 35, 36, 49–51, 53–5	Pêche, etc.

(iii) Archives des Colonies

E 159	Dossiers personnels: Dossier Dupleix Silvain

(iv) Bibliothèque nationale

500 Colbert 259	Offices
Fonds français	
5463	Mémoire sur l'état présent de la province de Bretagne [n.d.]
8149	Mémoire sur la province de Bretagne dressé par l'ordre du Roy en 1698 par M. de Nointel
8753	Mémoire de l'intendant des Gallois de la Tour, 1731
18598	Blés, 1643

(v) British Library

Add. MS. 8759	Situation actuelle des provinces de France en l'année 1746

(vi) Archives départementales d'Ille-et-Vilaine, Rennes

The residence of the intendant of Brittany was in Rennes, as were the seats of the *commission intermédiaire* of the Estates and the Parlement of Brittany; the Estates of Brittany held most of their sessions there during the eighteenth century. The Archives départementales in Rennes received the bulk of the records from these bodies. A good general guide to the collection is H.-F. Buffet, *Guide des archives d'Ille-et-Vilaine*, i (Rennes, 1965), which lists the available inventories. Most of the documents used for this book came from series 1Bᵍ and 1Bⁿ, which group the criminal cases heard on appeal from lesser jurisdictions, and from series C, which contains the correspondence between the intendant and his *subdélégués* and other officials in Vannes, statistical reports, the records of the Estates of Brittany, audits of municipal accounts, etc.

B: Cours et juridictions

1Bᵍ 274, 280, 303–4, 313, 316–17, 319, 321, 329–30	Arrêts criminels ou de la Tournelle

1B^n 1133, 1178, 1290,   Chambre de la Tournelle. Audiences, regis-
1374, 1662, 1776, 1799,   tres d'ordre, dossiers de procedures
1801, 1863, 1924, 2069,
2085, 2138, 2192–3, 2215,
2226, 2287, 2299, 2310,
2367, 2385, 2424, 2580,
2585, 2725, 2829, 2916,
2935, 2970, 3043, 3119,
3390bis, 3433, 3516, 3519,
3615, 3818
1B^h 14   Requête de Laurent David, adjudicataire
                          des fermes royales, 1776

C: Intendance de Bretagne et États de Bretagne
688–704   Ville de Vannes: Correspondence and ordinances of the intendant
1289   Mendicité et vagabondage
1400–37   Population, 1770–87
1447   États de la situation des corps d'arts et métiers, 1750–5
1451   Suppression des maîtrises et jurandes, 1776
1594–6   Pêche maritime, 1727–86
1651–3   États des apparences des récoltes, 1735–77
1654–5   États des produits des récoltes, 1778–90
1666–9   Correspondence with the Controller-General on grain exports, 1757–8, 1761–4
1680–2   Enregistrement des déclarations d'embarquement et des acquits à caution, 1773–4
1690–2   Marchés aux grains, 1716–90
1693–1709   Prix des grains, pain et fourrages, 1748–90
1712   Correspondence concerning grain shortages and relief measures, 1766–90
1714, 1716 Grain riots, 1788–9
1747   Secours destinés aux pauvres vieillards, aux enfants et aux infirmes, 1786
1772   Miscellaneous correspondence
1804   Correspondence concerning the last meeting of the Estates of Brittany, 1788–9
1807   Correspondence with the *subdélégué* and others on the preparation of the elections of 1789
1825   Sièges d'Amirautés de la Bretagne
1944   Afféagements et arrentements, 1718–88
3932   Villes et communautés: correspondence of the *commission intermédiaire,* 1697–1790
3934   Octrois des villes, 1697–1790

3982	Capitation, évêché de Vannes, 1737–90
4134–43	Capitation, évêché de Vannes, 1738–90
4272–4	Capitation de Messieurs de la Noblesse, 1735, 1760, 1783
4364	Capitation, etc. Dégrèvements, diocèse de Vannes, 1780–2

(vii) Archives départementales du Morbihan

| 8 A 1 | Domaine. Petition to the Princesse de Conti, 1730, etc. |

B: Cours et juridictions

There are some printed inventories for the Présidial of Vannes and the *sénéchaussées* of Auray, Belle-Île-en-Mer, Gourin and Hennebont: M. Rosenzweig, *Inventaire sommaire des archives départementales antérieures à 1790. Morbihan . . . Série B* (Paris, 1877), with manuscript supplements in the Archives; P. Thomas-Lacroix, *Répertoire numérique de la Série B. 8–14 B—Juridictions d'attribution* (Vannes, 1941) covers the Admiralty, the *consulat, maîtrise des eaux et forêts* and *traites,* and has a concise introduction. There is no printed repertory for the other jurisdictions, but their minutes and registers are classed chronologically, so that it is relatively easy to find one's way. The documents consulted were

| B 1–1383 | Présidial de Vannes |

especially:

309, 407	Ventes et provisions de charges judiciaires, 1708–13, 1777–9
412–13, 415, 419	Tutelles et curatelles, 1780–90
432, 435–6, 438	Police: réception de maîtres, tarifs des denrées, des journées d'ouvriers, etc., 1753–90
648–52	Inventaires après décès, 1730–3
740	Succession de Nicolas Viel, 1778
751–6	Inventaires après décès, 1783–5
782	Accounts of the association of Danet *aîné* and J.-L. Jamet, 1777–87
862	Audition d'expertz . . . sur l'uzement du trafiq des marchandises . . . au païs d'Espaigne, 1657
1137–44, 1172–9, 1266–9	Crime, 1730–5, 1760–4
1270–2	Troubles et séditions à Vannes au sujet de l'exportation des grains, 1763–6
1279–80	Mendiants et vagabonds, 1768
1313	Procédure criminelle contre des individus accusés d'avoir mis le feu . . . sur plusieurs points du bourg de Theix, 1780
1340–2	Crime, 1789
1345–53, 1359	Offices et maîtrises: réceptions, 1641–89
1360–76	Apprécis des grains, 1674–1790

The data from before 1740 are fragmentary, and it was necessary to use the *mercuriale* published in Mauricet, *Des anciennes mesures,* 47 for the period 1671–39. Up to 1749 and from 1754 to 1757, only the prices for the feast of St Giles, 1 September, remain. For the period 1749–54 and 1757 onwards, there are two quotations a week. Throughout this work the 1 September figures have been used, since they were employed at the time to evaluate the cash value of rents and represent the price at the time most peasants had to sell.

1378–80	Déclarations de défrichements et dessèchements, 1768–90
3431 (Lz 1699)	Registre d'écrou
3703	Crime, 1789–90
5804	Présidial, minutes, 1759
9 B: Amirauté de Vannes	
56–63	Déclarations de construction ou d'achat de navires, 1714–35, 1746–An 5
82	Rapports des capitaines, 1780–6
11 B: Consulat de Vannes	
23	Audiences, 1752–4; registre du greffe, 1753–4
42–63	Faillite Advisse Des Ruisseaux, 1723–81
75–8, 119	Faillite Granger, 1777–83

12 B: 2: Consulat de Lorient: Création du consulat, 1781
B: Unclassified sub-series

Sénéchaussée de Rhuys:	Minutes, 1730–2, 1760–3, 1771–89
Régaires de Vannes:	Minutes, 1730–4, 1762–6, 1775–80, 1783–5
Largouet-sous-Vannes:	Minutes, 1740–89

C: Administration provinciale
This series has not yet been permanently classified.
Commission intermédiaire de Vannes

273,280 (temporary classification)	Correspondence concerning tax assessments, demands for remission, etc.
4 Paroisses de Vannes	Capitation for 1733, 1760, 1765, 1783; vingtième d'industrie, 1783; vingtième, 1783; capitation de MM de la Noblesse, 1781
Arradon	Capitation, 1779
Grand-Champ	Capitation, 1747, 1770, 1778

Ploeren	Capitation, 1770
St-Avé	Capitation, 1774
	État des personnes qui ont refusé de payer
	les prémices aux fermiers des dîmes, 1771
St-Nolf	Capitation, 1774
Sulniac	Capitation, 1786–8
Domaine	Petition of the inhabitants of Séné [1763]
Subdélégation de Rhuys	
Sarzeau	Vingtième, 1751–4
Subdélégation de Vannes	
Grand-Champ, Surzur	Vingtième, 1751–4

17 C: Domaines et droits joints

There is a printed inventory for this sub-series: P. Thomas-Lacroix, *Répertoire numérique de la série C. 17 C—Domaines et droits joints* (Vannes, 1932), with a useful introduction. Two types of documents were of prime importance: the registers of the *Contrôle des actes,* which recorded all notarized acts; and of the *centième denier,* which summarized, but in greater detail, acts concerning the transfer of real property. They help fill the gaps in the notarial collections for the region and are the source for the study of property transactions. The series used were

3808–24	Contrôle des actes, bureau de Pluvigner, 1763–91
3866	Table des contrats de mariage, bureau de Pluvigner, 1764–1822
4474	Contrôle des actes, bureau de Questembert, 1757
4789–805	Centième denier, bureau de St-Jean-Brévelay et Plaudren, 1726–54
5156–341	Contrôle des actes, bureau de Vannes, 1698–1791
5351–403	Centième denier, bureau de Vannes, 1726–90
5406	Centième denier des biens réputés immeubles, 1748–50
5452–64	Baux: table alphabétique des bailleurs, bureau de Vannes, 1722–An VI

E: Féodalité, notariat, corporations, confréries, etc. État-civil.

There is no printed inventory, except for part of series E^c (see below under Archives communales); manuscript inventories and calendars of varying detail are available in the Archives.

1040	Communauté des maîtres cordonniers de la ville de Vannes
1062–72	Papiers de famille: fonds Jollivet. The business and personal papers of one of the more active notaries
2259	Papiers de famille: Advisse Desruisseaux. Completes the collection in 11 B, above
2620	Juridiction de Largouet. Rentier des biens de Couetcandec et La Chenaye, 1754, etc.

E^c: Registres de baptêmes, mariages, sépultures
These registers are also classified as series GG of the Archives communales; see under this heading for the registers from Vannes. Other registers consulted were those of Grand-Champ (1747–65), Arzon (1778–80), St-Gildas-de-Rhuys (1781–5), Sarzeau (1781–31), Surzur (1771–9)
E^s: Registres de baptêmes, mariages, sépultures
Duplicates submitted to the *sénéchaussée* of Vannes. After 1770, the clerks of the court noted on the flyleaf the vital statistics for each year, and these eventually were grouped in the provincial statistics assembled for the Controller-General. Parish records were consulted for Elven, Arradon, Theix, St-Pierre, St-Patern, Notre-Dame-du-Mené, St-Salomon.

E^n: Fonds des notaires

21–9	Buisson, 1755–65
33–6	Josse, 1782–90
51	Josse, 1761
66	Goujeon, 1783
636–40	Fabre, 1756–67
692–6	Perrigaud, 1726–62, 1785
772–8	Jarno, 1781–3
1866	Desalleurs, 1732–46 (répertoire)
3443–68	Le Ridant, 1769–84
4376	Pihan, 1739
4403	Hervieu, 1766

The *fonds des notaires* is quite ample from mid-century onwards, but rather thin for the earlier part of the century.

G: Clergé régulier
There are two excellent printed repertoires for this series: C. Estienne, *Inventaire sommaire des archives départementales antérieures à 1790 . . . Archives ecclésiastiques Série G. Clergé séculier—Évêché de Vannes* (Vannes, 1901) and J. de la Martinière, G. Duhem and P. Thomas-Lacroix, *Inventaire sommaire . . . Série G. Clergé séculier. Fonds du Chapitre* (Vannes, 1940). There is a *répertoire numérique* which serves for most of the rest of the series, J. de la Martinière, *Répertoire numérique de la série G. Clergé séculier* (Vannes, 1914), and manuscript inventories for subsequent additions.

30 G 1 (65)	Paroisse de Sulniac, pièces diverses, 1524–1775
31 G 35–6 (100–1)	Dîmes de Surzur
32 G 30–2 (131–3)	Dîmes de Theix
40 G 2–8 (301–7)	Ordinations, 1633–1793
40 G 3–25 (311–33)	Insinuations ecclésiastiques, 1692–1791. Contains the *titres cléricaux* discussed in Chapter IX
43 G 1–3 (324–3)	Domaine des gens de main-morte

47 G 5–7 (374–6)   Délibérations capitulaires
52 G 4 (380)   Personnel du chapitre: scolastique
54 G 1 (369)   Questions de préséances
62 G 3–4 (493, 476)   États de revenus du chapitre
65 G 1–6 (491)   Seigneuries de Couetergraff et de Queral,
                          1617–1770
77 G 6 (519)   Baux des annates
190 G 12 (1044)   Mémoire pour le général [of St-Patern]
                          contre messire Le Croisier, recteur, 1785.

H: Clergé régulier
There is no full calendar for this series. The only documents used extensively were those concerning the lands of the abbey of Lanvaux.
22–44   Abbaye de Lanvaux
J: Private collections of documents, etc.
412   Papiers Lallemand. Autobiographie de Jacques Glais
L: Administration et juridictions de l'époque révolutionnaire
There is a manuscript inventory in the Archives which is generally adequate, since the documents are classed chronologically and by content. The principal ones consulted were:
72–8   Département: Lois et décrets
116   Département: Traitement du clergé régulier et séculier,
               1791
134–6   Département: Correspondance générale, 1790–3
233–49   Département: Élections-Affaires générales, 1790–An VII
252–75   Département: Police générale et administrative, 1790–An
               III
337–8   Département: Secours aux indigents, colons et réfugiés,
               1790–1800
339–46   Département: Subsistances, 1790–An V
349–50   Département: Mercuriales, 1790–An II
355   Département: Population, 1789–An VI
357–62   Département: État-civil, 1790–An VIII
437–82   Administration et comptabilité générale: contributions,
               1790–An IV
553–6   Guerre et affaires militaires; recrutement, 1790–3
590   Guerre et affaires militaires: Marine, 1790–An VII
850   Culte: correspondance, 1790–1
864   Culte: circonscriptions paroissiales, 1791–3
1420–2   District de Vannes: délibérations et arrêtés du directoire du
               district, 1790–6
1445–6   District de Vannes: correspondance générale, 1790–4
1455   District de Vannes: Police générale et administrative, 1790–3
1460   District de Vannes: Subsistances, 1790–4
1463   District de Vannes: Divisions administratives, population,

état-civil, 1793

1464	District de Vannes: agriculture, industrie et commerce, 1790–5
1465	District de Vannes: santé publique, 1790–5
1466–71	District de Vannes: contributions directes, 1789–An VII
1472–3	District de Vannes: contribution patriotique, 1790–8
1572–80	Comité de surveillance, Vannes
1646	Clubs: Vannes, Société des Amis de la Constitution (transcription by the abbé Luco)
1676	Département: organisation des districts
1730	Direction du Département

L$_z$: Justice: période révolutionnaire

272–83	Tribunal du district de Vannes
517	Tribunal criminel du département
830–1, 834–7, 849	Comités de surveillance
1699 (B 4313)	Registre d'écrou

M: Personnel et administration générale

1242	Agriculture
1317	Statistique agricole, 1841–79
1657	Population, An VIII–1831

Q: Domaine

27	Répertoire des minutes des actes de vente des biens nationaux de première origine
28	Répertoire des minutes des actes de vente des biens d'émigrés
185–6	Minutes des actes de vente, District de Vannes, 1790–An III
205–25	Minutes des actes de vente, Département du Morbihan, préfecture du Morbihan

(viii) Archives départementales du Finistère, Quimper

100 J 1650–3	Copie-lettres du citoyen Pellegrin, 1790–An IV

(ix) Archives départementales de la Gironde, Bordeaux

7 G 1268	Correspondence of David (Bordeaux) with Bellefontaine Jan (Vannes)

(x) Archives communales de Vannes

A useful guide to all the parish records of the Morbihan prior to 1790 is M. Rosenzweig and C. Estienne, *Inventaire sommaire des archives départementales antérieures à 1790. Morbihan . . . Série E, supplément* (Vannes, 2 vol., 1881–8), with manuscript supplements. As some of the archives from which Rosenzweig and Estienne give excerpts have (as in Sarzeau) since disappeared, this inventory sometimes has the value of a primary source.

The documents consulted were

BB 15–29	Délibérations de la Communauté de Ville, Vannes, 1735–90
CC 1–2	Capitation de Vannes, 1703–9
7	Rôle des ci-devant privilégiés [1789 or 1790]
15	Capitation, aides, fouages, etc., 1567–1789
GG 4–8, 16–23, 46–63, 67–9	Baptêmes, mariages, sépultures: Notre-Dame-du-Mené, St-Pierre, St-Patern, St-Salomon, 1700–90
D₁	Municipalité de Vannes: délibérations, 1791

(xi) Other collections

Archives de l'Évêché de Vannes
  Paroisses, prêtres et fondations du diocèse de Vannes, 1784
Bibliothèque municipale de Rennes
MSS. 309–11   Mémoire du président de Robien [c. 1730]
Bibliothèque municipale de Vannes
R 52   Petition of the demoiselles Bonamy [n.d., probably from the 1780s]
Collection Debauve, Paris
    Letter of J.-A. Dubodan to J.-B. Roux & Cie., Marseilles, 30-11-1734
    Letter of the comte de Serent to . . ., 23-3-1791
Service départementale du cadastre, Vannes
    Grand-Champ: matrice du cadastre de 1856

2. Printed documents

(i) Treatises and manuals

Argouges, François d', *Ordonnances de Monseigneur François d'Argouges, Évêque de Vannes. Publiés au synode tenue à Vannes, le 22 septembre 1693* (Vannes, 1693).

Baudouin de Maisonblanche, M., *Institutions convenantières ou traité raisonné des domaines congéables en général & spécialement à l'usement de Tréguier & Goëlo* (St-Brieuc, 1776).

  The most comprehensive treatment of the system by one of its most ardent defenders. Like all legal treatises it must be carefully compared with what is known of daily realities. Baudouin was more familiar with the practice of the northern part of the Breton peninsula than the Vannetais, as his title indicates.

Potier de la Germondaye, *Introduction au gouvernement des paroisses suivant la jurisprudence du Parlement de Bretagne* (St-Malo–Rennes,

1777).

Poullain du Parc, M., *La Coutume et la jurisprudence de Bretagne* (Rennes, 1778).

Savary des Bruslons, J., *Dictionnaire portatif de commerce, contenant la connoissance des marchandises de tous les païs* (Bouillon–Liège, 1770).

—— *Dictionnaire universel de commerce*, 6th ed. (Geneva, Copenhagen, 1750–65).

Sauvageau, M., *Coutumes de Bretagne* (Rennes, 1737).
   Vol. 1 contains the text of Gatechair's commentary on the usement of Brouerec.

(ii) Descriptions, travel literature, memoirs, folklore

Bérenger, J. and Meyer, J. (eds.), *La Bretagne de la fin du xviiᵉ siècle d'après le mémoire de Béchameil de Nointel* (Paris, 1976).

Cassini, J.-D. *Carte de la France, publiée sous la direction de l'Académie des sciences* (Paris, 1744–87).

De Morval, 'Lettres morbihannaises', *Lycée armoricain*, x (1827), 259–67, 395–407, 431–40.

Description abrégée du Département du Morbihan (Paris, An VII).

Desjobert, L., 'Notes d'un voyage en Bretagne effectué en 1780 par Louis Desjobert', *Revue de Bretagne*, xlii (1909), 190–200, 250–9; xliii (1910), 38–47, 94–101, 143–57, 221–4, 318–20.

Grand Moulin, 'Mœurs et usages des Bretons du département du Morbihan', *Mémoires de la Société royale des sciences, arts, belles-lettres et agriculture de la ville de Saint-Quentin*, iii (1841), 113–23.

Jouvin, S., *Le Voyageur d'Europe . . .* (Paris, 1672).

Kerh'en, Y., 'Moez er botou koed', *Revue de Bretagne, de Vendée et d'Anjou*, xxii (1899), 223–7.

La Vallée, J., Biron, L. (*père*), Biron, L. (*fils*), *Voyage dans les départemens de la France enrichi de tableaux géographiques et d'estampes* (Paris, 1794).

Le Goff, P., *Proverbes bretons du Haut-Vannetais* (Vannes, 1912).

Mahé, J., *Essai sur les antiquités du département du Morbihan* (Vannes, 1825).

Ogée, J., *Dictionnaire historique et géographique de la province de Bretagne. nouvelle édition revue et augmentée par MM. A. Morteville et P. Varin* (Rennes, 1843–53).

Piganiol de la Force, J.-A., *Nouvelle description de la France . . . Seconde édition, corrigée et augmentée considérablement* (Paris, 1722).

Rio, A.-F., *La Petite Chouannerie ou histoire d'un collège breton sous l'Empire* (London, 1842).

—— *Épilogue à l'art chrétien* (Freiburg-im-Breisgau, 1870).

Young, A., *Travels during the years 1787, 1788 and 1789* (Bury St Edmunds, 1792–4).
—— 2nd ed. (London, 1794).
No proper English annotated edition of Young's *Travels* exists. The second edition of the original must be consulted in addition to the Bury St. Edmunds edition, because it contains several additional notes. The best annotated edition is
Young, A., *Voyages en France en 1787, 1788 et 1789,* ed. and tr. H. Sée (Paris, 1931).

(iii) Statistical and economic documents (nineteenth century and later)

Carte géologique de la France (1/80,000), feuillets 89 and 105: La Roche-Bernard, Vannes.
Cayot-Délandre, F.-M., *Annuaire statistique, historique et administratif du département du Morbihan* (Vannes, 1843–57).
Du Chatellier, A., *L'Agriculture et les classes agricoles de la Bretagne* (Paris, 1863).
Glais, J., *Manuel élémentaire des poids et measures redigé particulièrement pour le département du Morbihan* (Vannes, 1807).
Huët de Coëtsilan, J.-B.-C.-R., *Recherches statistiques sur le département de la Loire-Inférieurè pour l'an XI* (Nantes, An XI).
Kuntz, J., *Monographie agricole du département du Morbihan* (Vannes, 1937).
Ministère de l'Agriculture et du Commerce—Direction de l'Agriculture. Bureau des Subsistances, *Récoltes des céréales et des pommes de terre de 1815 à 1876* (Paris, 1876).
Ministère du Travail et de la Prévoyance sociale. Statistique générale de la France, *Statistique de la France* (Paris, 1835–52).
—— *Statistique de la France. Deuxième série* (Paris, Strasbourg, 1855–73).
Ministère des Travaux publics, de l'Agriculture et du Commerce, *Archives statistiques* (Paris, 1837).

(iv) Cahiers de doléances

For the *cahiers de doléances,* the two essential guides are:
Hyslop, B. F., *Répertoire critique des cahiers de doléances pour les États Généraux de 1789* (Paris, 1933).
—— *Supplément au répertoire critique des cahiers de doléances pour les États Généraux de 1789* (Paris, 1952).
The cahiers of the *sénéchaussées* of Vannes and Auray and of the deputies of the merchants of Vannes can be found in:
Archives parlementaires de 1787 à 1860 . . . première série (1787 à 1789) 2ᵉ éd., ed. J. Madival and E. Laurent (Paris, 1879), 107–17.
The missing cahier of the *sénéchaussée* of Rhuys was located in 1977 by J.

Danigo, and published as 'Le Cahier des plaintes et demandes de la ville de Rhuys aux États généraux', *BSPM*, cv (1978), 77–88.

No rural cahiers from the Vannetais have survived; the only document of this type purporting to come from a rural milieu dates from January 1789 or earlier, and is largely if not entirely the work of the rector of St-Patern, Le Croisier; the text is published in:

Le Goff, T., 'Les Doléances des paysans du Vannetais à la veille de la Révolution', *BSPM* (1969), 31–50.

These may be compared with the general cahier of the nearby *sénéchaussée* of Hennebont and with the two complete edited series of cahiers for Brittany:

Thomas-Lacroix, P., 'Les Cahiers de doléances de la sénéchaussée d'Hennebont', *MSHAB*, xxxv (1955), 51–104.

Savina, J. and Bernard, D., *Cahiers de doléances des sénéchaussées de Quimper et de Concarneau pour les États Généraux de 1789* (Rennes, 1922).

Sée, H. and Lesort, A., *Cahiers de doléances de la sénéchaussée de Rennes pour les États Généraux de 1789* (Rennes, 1909–12).

There are also a certain number of rural cahiers reproduced in the works of Corgne and Le Falher, listed below. The nobility of Brittany did not meet to prepare cahiers or elect deputies; the clergy of the diocese of Vannes met, but failed to draw up a cahier.

(v) Controversies, tracts, propaganda

A good selection of the polemical literature on the *domaine congéable* is contained in:

Dubreuil, L., *Les Vicissitudes du domaine congéable en Bretagne à l'époque de la Révolution* (Rennes, 1915).

but Dubreuil's collection should be complemented and compared with the original pamphlet literature, especially the tracts by the local Jacobin, Le Quinio, on this and other subjects:

Le Quinio, J.-M., *Dernières réflexions sur les domaines congéables* (Paris, 1791) (B.L., F.R. 250 [20]).

—— *École des laboureurs; ouvrage dans lequel on explique . . . ce que c'est que la Révolution françoise . . . ou lettre familière aux laboureurs de Bretagne* (2nd ed., Vannes, 1790) (B.L., F 488 [2]).

—— *Les Élections ou lettre familière aux laboureurs de Bretagne* (Rennes, 1790) (B.L., R 237 [16]).

—— *Élixir du régime féodal autrement dit domaine congéable en Bretagne* (Paris, 1790) (B.L., F 380 [3]).

—— *Mes Doléances* (Paris, 1791) (B.L., F.R. 250 [19]).

—— *Suppression des religieux, extinction de la mendicité* (Rennes, 1789) (B.L., F 108 [6]).

For Jansenism in the diocese of Vannes, besides the thesis of Fr Mahuas (see below), a few hours spent with the vituperative reports in the *Nouvelles ecclésiastiques* (1728–93) are useful for gaining the right tone of ecclesiastical politics in a small town.

On public education, there is a proposal of the comte de Serent, reproduced in:

Thomas-Lacroix, P., 'Mémoire inédit sur l'instruction populaire avant la Révolution', *BSPM* (1936), 87–96.

Considerable information on the events of the 'pre-revolution' and of 1789 in Vannes can be gleaned from pamphlets, which somewhat make up for the laconicism of the town council's minutes, and the mutilation by an unknown hand of some of the council minutes for 1789:

Extrait des registres de délibérations de la ville et communauté de Vannes du vendredi 3 octobre 1788 [includes report of the session of 10 November as well] (Nantes, 1788) (A.D. Morbihan, bibliothèque, K 1538; B.L. 911 c 4 [2]).

Remontrance de M. Caradec, avocat de la communauté de ville de Vannes [10-11-1788] (Nantes, 1788) (B.L. 911 c 4 [6]).

Extrait des registres des délibérations de la ville et communauté de Vannes [6-12-1788] (Nantes, 1788) (A.D. Morbihan, bibliothèque K 1536; B.L. 911 c 4 [19]).

Lettre écrite de Vannes, à MM. le Menez de Kerdelleau, Poussin & Bourgerel Lucas, premier député & aggrégés de Vannes, aux États de la Province de Bretagne & à MM. les députés des communes de Nantes, le 8 janvier 1789 [Vannes, 1789] (A.D. Morbihan, bibliothèque, K 1534).

Extrait des registres des délibérations de la ville & communauté de Vannes [7-1-1789 and 23-1-1789] (Vannes, 1789) (A.D. Morbihan, bibliothèque, K 1537).

Extrait du registre des délibérations de la ville et communauté de Vannes, en Bretagne [23-1-1789]; *Requête des notables bourgeois & autres habitans de la ville de Vannes, en Bretagne au Roi* [January 1789] [Vannes, 1789] (A.D. Morbihan, bibliothèque, K 1535).

Procès verbal des séances tenues par l'assemblée de la municipalité & des communes de la ville de Vannes [31-7-1789 to 23-8-1789] (Vannes, 1789) (A.D. Morbihan, bibliothèque, K 1544).

Précis des évènements désastreux qui ont affligé le département du Morbihan (Vannes, 1793) (A.D. Morbihan, bibliothèque, R. 201).

(vi) Other collections of printed documents

Aulard, F.-A., *L'État de la France en l'an VIII et en l'an IX, avec une liste des préfets et des sous-préfets au début de Consulat* (Paris, 1897).

Chassin, C.-L., *La Vendée et la Chouannerie* (Paris, 1892–1900).

Du Halgouet, H., *Archives des châteaux bretons: iii Inventaire des archives du château du Grégo (1343–1830)* (St-Brieuc, 1913).

Esmonin, E., 'Statistiques du mouvement de la population en France de 1770 à 1789', *Études et chronique de démographie historique* (1964), 27–130.

Galles, R., 'Pages inédites d'un philosophe vannetais du xviiiᵉ siècle', *BSPM* (1882), 161–5.

Isambert, F.-A., *Recueil général des anciennes lois françaises* (Paris, 1821–33).

Laigue, R. de., *La Noblesse bretonne aux xvᵉ et xve siècles. Réformations et montres. Tome 1: Évêché de Vannes* (Rennes, 1902).

Lockroy, E., *Une Mission en Vendée, 1793* (Paris, 1893). The correspondence of the *représentant* Jullien, who visited Vannes during the Terror.

Reinhard, M., *Étude de la population pendant la Révolution et l'Empire. Instruction, recueil de textes et notes* (Gap, 1961).

Sagnac, P. and Caron, P., *Les Comités des droits féodaux et de législation et l'abolition du régime seigneurial 1789–1793* (Paris, 1907).

SECONDARY WORKS

(i) Reference

Arkin, A. and Colton, R. R., *Tables for Statisticians* (New York, 1963).

Berthe, L.-N., *Dictionnaire des correspondants de l'Académie d'Arras au temps de Robespierre* (Arras, n.d.).

Brette, A., *Atlas des bailliages* (Paris, 1904).

—— *Les Constituants. Liste des députés et des suppléants élus à l'Assemblée constituante de 1789* (Paris, 1897).

Frotier de la Messelière, H., *Filiations bretonnes, 1650–1912* (St-Brieuc, 1912, rpt. Mayenne, 1965).

Gille, B., *Les Sources statistiques de l'histoire de France: des enquêtes du xviiie siècle à 1870* (Geneva–Paris, 1964).

Guiffrey, J., *Les Conventionnels. Listes par départements et par ordre alphabétique des députés et des suppléants à la Convention nationale* (Paris, 1889).

Kerviler, R., *Répertoire général de bio-bibliographie bretonne . . . livre 1. Les Bretons* (Rennes–Vannes, 1886–1908) [not completed].

Kuscinski, A., *Les Députés à l'Assemblée législative de 1791. Liste par départements et par ordre alphabétique des députés et des suppléants, avec nombreux détails biographiques inédits* (Paris, 1900).

—— *Dictionnaire des Conventionnels* (Paris, 1920).

—— *Les Députés au Corps Législatif, Conseil des Cinq-Cents, Conseil des Anciens, de l'an iv à l'an xviii. Listes, tableaux et lois* (Paris, 1905).

Levot, P.-J., *Biographie bretonne* (Vannes, 1852–7).

Luco, *Pouillé historique de l'ancien diocèse de Vannes, bénéfices séculiers*, 2nd ed. (Vannes, 1908).

Marion, M., *Dictionnaire des institutions de la France aux xvii* et xviii* siècles* (Paris, 1923).

Mauricet, A., *Des anciennes mesures de capacité et de superficie dans les Départements du Morbihan, du Finistère et des Côtes-du-Nord* (Vannes, 1893).

Rosenzweig, M., *Dictionnaire topographique du Morbihan* (Paris, 1870).

Saulnier, F., *Le Parlement de Bretagne, 1554–1790* (Rennes, 1909).

Van Gennep, A., *Manuel du folklore français contemporain* (Paris, 1937–43).

(ii) Works on Brittany: Institutions, general history, political history to 1787

Bernard, D., 'Essai historique sur la poste aux lettres en Bretagne depuis le xve siècle jusqu'à la Révolution', in *Mémoires et documents pour servir à l'histoire du commerce et de l'industrie en France*, ed. J. Hayem, 12e série (Paris, 1929) 73–222.

Bernard, M., *La Municipalité de Brest de 1750 à 1790* (Paris, 1915).

Chenon, E., 'L'Ancien Droit dans le Morbihan', *Revue morbihannaise,* ii (1892), 321–9, 363–96; iii (1893), 24–48, 65–86.

Delumeau, J. (ed.), *Histoire de la Bretagne* (Toulouse, 1969).

Dupuy, A., 'L'Administration municipale en Bretagne au xviiie siècle', *Annales de Bretagnè,* iii (1887–8), 299–370, 541–611; iv (1888–9), 66–102, 234–94, 553–84; v (1889–90), 3–80, 153–89, 662–91; vi (1890–1), 179.

Durand, C., *Les Milices gardes-côtes en Bretagne de 1716 à 1792* (Rennes, 1927).

Espinay, G. d', 'L'Ancien Droit successoral en Basse-Bretagne', *Nouvelle revue historique de droit français et étranger,* xvii (1895), 136–297.

Fréville, H., *L'Intendance de Bretagne (1689–1790). Essai sur l'histoire d'une intendance en pays d'états au xviii* siècle* (Rennes, 1953).

Giffard, A., *Les Justices seigneuriales en Bretagne aux xvii* et xviii* siècles (1661–1791)* (Paris, 1903).

Gourvil, F., *Langue et littérature bretonnes* (Paris, 1960).

Guillou, L., *Essai sur l'organisation et le fonctionnement de l'administration des domaines en Bretagne (1759–1771)* (Rennes, 1904).

Kerviler, R., *Armorique et Bretagne* (Paris, 1892–3).

Le Guiner, M., 'Le Bail à domaine congéable des origines à la Révolution', *École nationale des Chartes, position des thèses* (Paris, 1949), 111–13.

Le Moyne de la Borderie, L.-A., *Essai sur la géographie féodale de la Bretagne avec la carte des fiefs et seigneuries de cette province* (Rennes, 1889).

—— and Pocquet, B., *Histoire de Bretagne* (Rennes, 1905–14).

Léna, Hervé, 'La Communauté de ville d'Hennebont au xviiie siècle (1689–1789). Essai sur l'organisation municipale en Bretagne' (Thèse de droit, Univ. de Rennes, 1964).

Macé, A., 'La Réforme des présidiaux au xviiⁱᵉ siècle', *BSPM* (1890), 127–37.

Marion, M., *La Bretagne et le duc d'Aiguillon* (Paris, 1898).

Pocquet, B., *Le Pouvoir absolu et l'espirit provincial. Le duc d'Aiguillon et La Chalotais* (Paris, 1890–1).

Rébillon, A., 'Les États de Bretagne', *Conférences universitaires de Bretagne (1942–43)* (Paris, 1943), 201–23.

—— 'Les États de Bretagne et les progrès de l'autonomie provinciale au xviiⁱᵉ siècle', *Revue Historique*, clix (1928), 261–90.

—— *Les États de Bretagne de 1661 à 1789* (Paris–Rennes, 1932).

—— *Histoire de Bretagne* (Paris, 1957).

(iii) Breton economy and society

Blayo, Y. and Henry, L., 'Données démographiques sur la Bretagne et l'Anjou de 1740 à 1829', *Annales de démographie historique* (1967), 91–171.

Bourdais, F. and Durand, R., 'L'Industrie et le commerce de la toile en Bretagne au xviiⁱᵉ siècle', *Comité des travaux historiques et scientifiques. Section d'histoire moderne et contemporaine*, vii (1922), 1–48.

Bourde de la Rogerie, H., 'Étude sur la réformation de la noblesse en Bretagne (1668–1721)', *MSHAB*, iii (1922), 237–312.

—— 'Les Voyageurs en Bretagne: le voyage de Mignot de Montigny en Bretagne en 1752', *MSHAB*, vi (1925), 225–302.

Brekilien, Y., *La Vie quotidienne des paysans en Bretagne au xixᵉ siècle* (Paris, 1966).

Canal, S., 'La Bretagne au début du gouvernement personnel de Louis XIV', *Annales de Bretagne*, xxii (1906–7), 393–441.

Croix, A., 'La Démographie du Pays nantais au xviⁱᵉ siècle', *Annales de démographie historique* (1967), 65–90.

—— *Nantes et le pays nantais au xviⁱᵉ siècle. Étude démographique* (Paris, 1974).

Delumeau, J. and collaborators, *Le Mouvement du port de Saint-Malo, 1681–1720. Bilan statistique* (Paris, 1966).

Dubreuil, L., 'Le Paysan breton au xviiⁱᵉ siècle', *RHES* (1924), 478–92.

—— 'Une Tenure bretonne: le domaine congéable', *La Révolution française*, lviii (1910), 481–501; lix (1910), 24–51.

Du Halgouet, H., 'Gentilshommes, commerçants et commerçants nobles aux xviiⁱᵉ et xviiⁱᵉ siècles', *MSHAB*, xvi (1935), 147–88.

Dupuy, A., 'Les Épidémies en Bretagne au xviiⁱᵉ siècle', *Annales de Bretagne*, i (1886), 115–40, 290–308; ii (1886–7), 20–49, 190–226.

Durand, R., 'Le Commerce en Bretagne au xviiⁱᵉ siècle', *Annales de Bretagne*, xxxii (1917), 447–69.

Duval, M., 'Économie forestière et féodalité dans l'Ouest à la veille de.la Révolution', *Annales de Bretagne,* lxiv (1957), 347–58.

—— *Forêt et civilisation dans l'Ouest au xviiᵉ siècle* (Rennes, 1955).

Flatrès, P., 'La Structure rurale du Sud-Finistère d'après les anciens cadastres', *Norois,* iv (1957), 353–67, 425–53.

Gaston-Martin, *Nantes au xviiᵉ siècle. L'administration de Gérard Meillier* (Paris, 1928).

—— *Nantes au xviiᵉ siècle. L'ère des négriérs (1714–1774)* (Paris, 1931).

Goubert, J.-P., *Malades et médecins en Bretagne 1770–1790* (Rennes, 1974).

—— 'Le Phénomène épidémique en Bretagne à la fin du xviiᵉ siècle (1770–1787)', *Annales: E.S.C.,* xxiv (1969), 1562–88.

Goubert, P., 'Dans le sillage de Henri Sée. L'histoire économique et sociale des Pays de l'Ouest (Bretagne, Maine, Anjou) du xviᵉ au xviiiᵉ siècle', *Annales de Bretagne,* lxxi (1961), 315–28.

—— 'Recherches d'histoire rurale dans la France de l'Ouest (xviiᵉ–xviiiᵉ siècles)', *Bulletin de la Société d'Histoire moderne,* 13ᵉ série no. 2, 64ᵉ année (1965), 2–9.

Guilcher, J.-L., *La Tradition populaire de danse en Basse-Bretagne* (Paris–The Hague, 1963).

Guyot, J., 'Étude démographique de la paroisse d'Allaire de 1693 à 1789' (Faculté des Lettres, Rennes, mémoire for the D.E.S., 1966).

Le Floc'h, V., 'Le Régime foncier et son application pratique dans le cadre de la paroisse de Plonivel (Finistère) au xviiiᵉ siècle', *Bulletin de la Société archéologique du Finistère,* xcii (1969), 117–205.

Le Goff, T., 'La Construction navale en Bretagne de 1762 à 1788', *Annales de Bretagne,* lxxv (1968), 345–69.

—— and Meyer, J., 'La Construction navale en Bretagne de 1762 à 1788', *Annales de Bretagne,* lxxvi (1969), 433–43.

Le Guen, G., 'Types régionaux d'évolution démographique en Bretagne', *Norois,* xii (1960), 389–405.

Lemoine, J. and Bourde de la Rogerie, H., *Inventaire sommaire des archives départementales antérieures à 1790. Finistère. Archives civiles—série B. Tome iii* (Quimper, 1902).

Contains an Introduction by Bourde de la Rogerie which was the first serious discussion of the economic history of Brittany.

Letaconnoux, J., 'La Construction des grands chemins et le personnel des Ponts et Chaussées de Bretagne au xviiiᵉ siècle', *Annales de Bretagne,* xlviii (1941), 63–113.

—— 'Les Grands Chemins de Bretagne', *Revue du xviiᵉ siècle,* iv (1917), 220–34.

—— 'Note comparative sur la distance en temps entre l'intérieur de la Bretagne et la mer aux xviiiᵉ, xixᵉ et xxᵉ siècles', *Annales de Bretagne,* xxiii (1907–8), 305–21.

—— 'Le Régime de la corvée en Bretagne au xviiiᵉ siècle', *Annales de*

Bretagne, xxi (1905), 144–59, xxii (1906), 271–93, 453–66, 592–627.
—— *Les Subsistances et le commerce des grains en Bretagne au xviiie siècle* (Rennes, 1909).
Meyer, J., 'L'Armement nantais au xviiie siècle, d'après les registres des classes. La période 1735–1748: comparaison avec la deuxième moitié du siècle', *Actes du quatre-vingt-onzième congrès des Sociétés savantes, Rennes, 1966. Section d'histoire moderne* (Paris, 1969), i, 143–53.
—— *L'Armement nantais dans la deuxième moitié du xviiie siècle* (Paris, 1969).
—— 'Le Commerce négrier nantais', *Annales: E.S.C.,* x (1960), 120–9.
—— 'Structure sociale des villes bretonnes à la fin de l'ancien régime', *Actes du quatre-vingt-seizième congrès national des Sociétés savantes. Toulouse, 1971. Section d'histoire moderne et contemporaine,* ii (Paris, 1976), 483–99.
—— *La Noblesse bretonne au xviiie siècle* (Paris, 1966).
—— *et al., Histoire de Rennes* (Toulouse, 1972).
Meynier, A., 'Champs et chemins de Bretagne', *Conférences universitaires de Bretagne (1942–43)* (Paris, 1943), 161–78.
—— 'La Genèse du parcellaire breton', *Norois,* xiii (1966), 595–610.
—— 'Pseudo-pratiques communautaires en Bretagne méridionale', *Chronique géographique des pays celtes. Annales de Bretagne,* lii (1945), 92–6.
Nières, C., *La Réconstruction d'une ville au xviiie siècle: Rennes 1720–1760* (Paris, 1972).
Rébillon, A., 'Nécrologie et bibliographie des travaux de Henri Sée', *Annales de Bretagne,* xlii (1936), 2–33.
Sée, H., 'L'Administration de deux seigneuries de Basse-Bretagne au xviiie siècle: Toulgouët et Le Treff', *Annales de Bretagne,* xix (1903–4), 285–320.
—— *Les Classes rurales en Bretagne du xvie siècle à la Révolution* (Paris, 1906).
—— 'Les Classes sociales et la vie économique dans une ville de l'ancienne France (Rennes au xviiie siècle)', *MSHAB,* iv (1923), 89–136.
—— 'Le Commerce maritime de la Bretagne au xviiie siècle', *Mémoires et documents pour servir à l'histoire du commerce et de l'industrie en France, 9e série,* ed. J. Hayem (Paris, 1925), 1–270.
—— 'L'Enquête sur les clôtures en Bretagne (1786)', *Annales de Bretagne,* xxxviii (1928–9), 752–67.
—— 'L'Enquête sur les messageries en Bretagne de 1775, *Mémoires et documents pour servir à l'histoire du commerce et de l'industrie en France,* 12e série, ed. J. Hayem (Paris, 1929), 222–32.
—— *Études sur la vie économique en Bretagne, 1772–an III* (Paris 1930).
—— 'Études sur le commerce en Bretagne', *Mémoires et documents pour servir à l'histoire du commerce et de l'industrie en France,* 10e série, ed.

J. Hayem (Paris, 1926), 81–158.

—— 'Études sur le commerce maritime au xviiie siècle', *Mémoires et documents pour servir à l'histoire du commerce et de l'industrie en France*, 10e série, ed. J. Hayem (Paris, 1926), 159–204.

—— 'Les Forêts et la question du déboisement en Bretagne à la fin de l'ancien régime', *Annales de Bretagne*, xxxvi (1924), 1–30, 355–79.

—— 'L'Industrie et le commerce de la Bretagne dans la première moitié du xviiie siècle, d'après le mémoire de l'intendant Des Gallois de la Tour [1733]', *Annales de Bretagne*, xxxv (1921–3), 187–208, 433–55.

—— 'Notes sur les assurances maritimes en France et particulièrement à Nantes au xviiie siècle', *Revue historique de droit français et étranger* xxvii (1927), 287–311.

—— 'Notes sur les travaux dans les ports bretons au xviiie siècle', *Annales de Bretagne*, xl (1932–3), 412–19.

—— 'Quelques aperçus sur les métiers urbains en Bretagne au xviiie siècle', *RHES*, xiii (1925), 409–17.

—— 'Remarques sur la misère, la mendicité, et l'assistance en Bretagne à la fin de l'ancien régime', *MSHAB*, vi (1925), 105–32.

Sée's work was immense, and only those works directly relevant to this book have been cited here; a full bibliography is to be found in the necrology by Rébillon, cited above. His work, especially *Les Classes rurales,* is still the best introduction to Breton society of the eighteenth century, although the rural society Sée knew best was that of Upper Brittany, and he tended to take the *cahiers de doléances* of 1789 at their face value.

Tanguy, J., *Le Commerce du Port de Nantes au milieu du xvie siècle* (Paris, 1956).

—— 'La Production et le commerce des toiles "Bretagnes", du xvie au xviiie siècle. Premiers résultats', *Acts du quatre-vingt-onzième congrès national des sociétés savantes. Rennes, 1966. Section d'histoire moderne et contemporaine,* i (Paris, 1969), 105–41.

—— 'Les Révoltes paysannes de 1675 et la conjoncture en Basse-Bretagne au xviie siècle', *Annales de Bretagne et des Pays de l'Ouest,* lxxii (1975), 427–42.

Touchard, H., *Le Commerce maritime breton à la fin du Moyen Âge* (Paris, 1967).

Vallaux, Camille, 'L'Évolution de la vie rurale en Basse-Bretagne', *Annales de Géographie,* xiv (1905), 36–51.

(iv) Works on Vannes and the Morbihan: Economic and Social History

Allanic, J., 'Histoire du Collège de Vannes', *Annales de Bretagne,* xviii (1902–3), 59–105, 234–75.

André, J. and Thomas-Lacroix, P., 'Les Grands Itinéraires de la Bretagne méridionale (de la Vilaine à la Laita)', *BSPM* (1953–4), 23–55.

Battifol, L., 'Une Émeute de consommateurs jadis à Vannes', *Le Temps* (30-1-1912), 4–5.

Cariou, A., 'Les Arzonnais et Sainte Anne. La bataille de Schooneveldt (7 Juin 1673)', *BSPM*, cii (1975), 44–91.

—— 'L'Instruction dans le département du Morbihan à la veille de la Révolution de 1789', *MSHAB*, xxxv (1955), 39–50.

Cestari, C., 'La Ville de l'Orient et les classes sociales au xviiie siècle selon les rôles de capitation' (*Mémoire* for the D.É.S., Faculté des Lettres, Université de Poitiers, 1967).

Choveaux, A., 'L'Influence des engrais marins sur les rives du golfe du Morbihan', *Annales de Géographie*, xxix (1920), 417–25.

Closmadeuc, G. de., 'Autobiographie d'un ancien procureur du présidial de Vannes [Jacques Glais]', *BSPM* (1890), 26–33.

—— 'Un Coup de poing malheureux—Procès criminel devant le siège de l'ancienne Amirauté de Vannes, en 1720', *BSPM* (1886), 73–83.

—— 'Un Recueil manuscrit du xviiie siècle. Le Père Pierre de Vannes: Capucin, poète', *BSPM* (1889), 198–259.

Corgne, E., 'Essai sur les classes sociales et la vie économique de Pontivy à la veille de la Révolution', *Commission de recherche et de publication des documents relatifs à la vie économique de la Révolution. Assemblée générale . . . 1939. Tome I* (Besançon, 1942), 145–70.

Danigo, J., 'Le Mil dans le Morbihan, Culture et préparation', *BSPM* (1955–6), 125–34.

Debauve, J.-L., 'Deux aspects du commerce à Vannes à la fin du xviiie siècle', *BSPM* (1957–8), 65–79.

—— 'Documents nouveaux sur l'histoire de l'imprimerie à Vannes', *BSPM* (1951–2), 109–19.

—— 'Notes sur les chambres de lecture de Lorient et Vannes', *BSPM* (1955–6), 93–8.

—— 'Verlac et l'école de marine de Vannes', *BSPM* (1951–2), 66–8.

Du Halgouet, H., 'Commerce de Vannes avec les îles d'Amérique', *BSPM* (1940), 1–12.

Duval, M., 'Les Forêts royales de la maîtrise de Vannes sous l'ancien régime', *BSPM* (1957–8), 95–127.

Faye, S., 'La Société patriotique bretonne 1780–1790', *BSPM* (1942), 92–108.

Gueguen, E., 'La Mendicité au pays de Vannes dès la 2e moitié du xviiie siècle', *BSPM* (1970), 105–34.

Guillou, L., 'André Vanderheyde, courtier lorientais et ses opérations (1756–1765)', *Annales de Bretagne*, xxxiii (1918–19), 13–38, 189–202, 379–404, 536–7.

Guyot, J., 'Étude démographique de la paroisse d'Allaire de 1693 à 1789' (Faculté des Lettres, Rennes, *mémoire* for the D.É.S., 1966).

Guyot-Jomard, A., 'La Ville de Vannes à la fin du xviiiᵉ siècle', *BSPM* (1890), 34–60, 123–248.

—— 'La Ville.de Vannes et ses murs; revue des archives municipales, départementales, etc.', *BSPM* (1887), 26–75, 129–76; (1888) 37–84, 219–46.

—— 'La Ville de Vannes pendant la deuxième moitié du xviiiᵉ siècle', *BSPM* (1889), 91–128.

Guyot-Jomard's antiquarian studies are useful for his descriptions of the town in the old regime, for urban topography, and for the numerous documents he published.

Josso, A., 'La Corporation des barbiers-chirurgiens de Vannes', *BSPM* (1943–5), 26–52.

La Borderie, A. de, 'Le Baron de Kerker [the comte de Serent] et son château', *Revue de Bretagne et de Vendée*, n. s., ii (1887), 337–54.

Lallemand, A., *Les Origines historiques de la ville de Vannes*, (Vannes, 1858).

Lallemand, L., 'Le Corsaire l'Hermine de Vannes', *BSPM* (1892), 47–61.

La Martinière, J. de, 'Le plus ancien manoir de Vannes, Château-Gaillard', *BSPM* (1916), 93–153.

—— 'Vannes dans l'ancien temps', *BSPM* (1913–14), 5–48; (1915–16), 111–13.

Le Cam, L., 'Le Problème de l'openfield sur les rives du golfe du Morbihan', *Chronique géographique des pays celtes. Annales de Bretagne*, lviii (1951), 164–70.

Le Goff, A., 'Auray au xviiiᵉ siècle (vers 1740–1789) Étude sociale, économique et démographique', *École nationale des Chartes, Position des thèses soutenues par les élèves de la promotion de 1973* (Paris, 1973), 139–44.

—— 'Bilan d'une étude de démographie historique: Auray au xviiiᵉ siècle (vers 1740–1789)', *Annales de Démographie historique* (1974), 198–229.

Le Goff, T., 'Autour de quelques dîmes vannetaises' (xviiᵉ–xviiiᵉ siècles)', paper presented to the Colloque d'histoire rurale, École des hautes Études en Sciences sociales, Centre de recherches historiques, Paris, 2 July 1977.

—— 'An Eighteenth-Century Grain Merchant: Ignace Advisse Desruisseaux', in Bosher, J.F. (ed.), *French Government and Society 1500–1850. Essays in Memory of Alfred Cobban* (London, 1973), 92–122.

—— 'A Social and Economic Study of the Town of Vannes and its Region in the Eighteenth Century' (University of London, Ph.D. thesis, 1970).

Leguay, J.-P., 'Vannes au xvᵉ siècle', *BSPM*, ciii (1975), 45–120.

Le Lay, F., *Histoire de la ville et communauté de Pontivy au xviiᵉ siècle (Essai sur l'organisation municipale en Bretagne)* (Paris, 1911).

—— *Le Paysan et sa terre sous la seigneurie de Coetanfao, paroisse de*

Séglien au xviiᵉ siècle (Vannes, 1911).

Lesage, P., *Étude historique et critique du bail à domaine congéable dans le département du Morbihan* (Rennes, 1932).

The best study of the legal aspects of the *domaine congéable*, founded on a knowledge of the countryside as well as of the legal texts.

Lespagnol, A., 'A propos des élites urbaines dans l'Ancien Régime: l'exemple de Saint-Malo au xviiiᵉ siècle', *Bulletin de la Société d'histoire moderne*, 15ᵉ série, lxxiii (1974), 2–12.

Martin, É., *Une Grande Fortune bourgeoise à Vannes au xviiᵉ siècle. Olivier Delourme (1660–1729)* (Vannes, 1921).

—— 'La Population de la ville de Vannes au début et à la fin du xviiiᵉ siècle', *Annales de Bretagne*, xxxv (1921–3), 610–26.

—— 'Vannes aux xviiᵉ et xviiiᵉ siècles', *BSPM* (1917–19), 3–48.

A description of the physical aspect of the town.

Mauricet, A., 'Le Ménage de Lestrenic. Gestion d'une propriété rurale au milieu du xviiiᵉ siècle', *BSPM* (1890), 150–7.

The *ménage* of Lestrenic was run directly by the College of Vannes, and its account books provide information on salaries. It was situated just outside the town.

—— 'Le Collège de Vannes', *Revue de l'enseignement secondaire et de l'enseignement supérieur*, vi (1889), 393–410.

Nicolle, L., *Apothicaires et pharmaciens du Morbihan* (Vannes, 1962).

Raut, E. and Lallemant, L., 'Une Page peu connue de l'histoire du Collège de Vannes, actuellement "Collège Jules Simon": l'École de la Marine (1786–1791)', *BSPM* (1930), 58–77.

—— 'Vannes autrefois. La traite des nègres', *BSPM* (1933), 53–74.

A good description of the trade in mid-century, with a long account of the luckless voyage of the *Marguerite*, outfitted by the merchant Desruisseaux.

Rosenzweig, M., 'Quelques ordonnances de police à Vannes (1650–1785)', *BSPM*, xv (1859), 15–36.

Thomas-Lacroix, P., 'Les Constructions et les ventes de navires dans les amirautés de Vannes et de Lorient au xviiiᵉ siècle', *MSHAB*, xlix (1969), 71–111.

—— 'La Condition des terres et les modalités du domaine congéable dans le pays de Vannes, au xviiiᵉ siècle', *Commission de recherche et de publication des documents relatifs à la vie économique de la Révolution. Assemblée générale . . . 1939. Tome 1* (Besançon, 1942), 341–68.

An extremely important study; the first to establish the existence of sub-tenants under *domaine congéable* and to study the relative importance of the rents of *tenuyers*, *métayers* and *fermiers* and their evolution through the eighteenth century.

—— 'La Guerre de course dans les ports de l'Amirauté de Vannes et de Lorient', *MSHAB*, xxvi (1946), 159–215.

—— 'Les Listes électorales censitaires de la Restauration dans le Morbihan',

Actes du quatre-vingt-quatrième congrès national des Sociétés Savantes.
Dijon, 1959 (Paris, 1960), 471–9.
—— *Vannes* (Paris, 1949).
—— 'La Vie économique et sociale à Ploërmel avant la Révolution',
MSHAB, xliv (1964), 149–62.
—— *Le Vieux Vannes* (Vannes, 1975).

(v) The Church, principally in Vannes and the Morbihan

Berthelot du Chesnay, C., 'Le Clergé diocésain français au xviiie siècle et les
registres des insinuations ecclésiastiques', *RHMC*, x (1963), 241–96.
Buléon, J. and Le Garrec, E., *Sainte-Anne-d'Auray, histoire d'un village*
(Vannes, 1924).
Dubreuil, L., *La Vente des biens nationaux dans le Département des Côtes-
du-Nord, 1790–1830* (Paris, 1912).
Guillemot, A., 'Fondation de l'Hôpital de Sarzeau par Marie-Pierre de
Francheville', *BSPM* (1967), 13–20.
Join-Lambert, M., 'La Pratique religieuse dans le diocèse de Rouen de 1707
à 1789', *Annales de Normandie,* v (1955), 37–49.
Julia, D., 'Le Clergé paroissial dans le diocèse de Reims à la fin du xviiie
siècle', *RHMC,* xiii (1966), 195–216.
Langlois, C., *Le Diocèse de Vannes au xixe siècle. 1800–1830.* (Paris, 1974).
   Contains much valuable information on the eighteenth century as well as
the nineteenth, and a full bibliography.
—— 'Jésuites de la province de France, Jésuites de Bretagne vers 1750',
Dix-huitième siècle, viii (1976), 77–92.
—— and Wagret, P., *Structures religieuses et célibat féminin au xixe siècle*
(Lyon, 1971).
Le Bras, G., 'La Vitalité religieuse de la Bretagne depuis les origines
chrétiennes jusqu'à nos jours', in *Études de sociologie religieuse* (Paris,
1955), i, 72–84.
Le Mené, J.-M., *Histoire archéologique, féodale et religieuse des paroisses
du diocèse de Vannes* (Vannes, 1891–4).
—— *Histoire du diocèse de Vannes* (Vannes, 1889).
—— 'Abbaye de la Joie', *BSPM* (1903), 123–84.
—— 'Abbaye de Langonnet', *BSPM* (1904), 11–37.
—— 'Abbaye de Lanvaux', *BSPM* (1902), 203–55.
—— 'Abbaye de Prières', *BSPM* (1903), 8–80.
—— 'Abbaye de Rhuys', *BSPM* (1902), 26–119.
—— 'Abbaye de Saint-Jean-des-Prés', *BSPM* (1904), 30–7.
—— 'Capucins', *BSPM* (1906), 199–209.
—— 'Les Capucins de Vannes', *BSPM* (1899), 21–34.
—— 'Carmelites de Ploërmel', *BSPM* (1906), 210–19.
—— 'Les Carmelites de Vannes', *BSPM* (1897), 76–9.
—— 'Carmes d'Hennebont', *BSPM* (1905), 343–64.

—— 'Carmes de Josselin', *BSPM* (1906), 34–46.

—— 'Carmes de Ploërmel', *BSPM* (1905), 300–22.

—— 'Carmes de Sainte-Anne', *BSPM* (1906), 13–38.

—— 'Chartreux d'Auray', *BSPM* (1905), 247–99.

—— 'Communautés situées hors Vannes', *BSPM* (1905), 4–48.

—— 'Cordelières d'Auray', *BSPM* (1907), 12–20.

—— 'L'Évêché de Vannes', *BSPM* (1900), 45–112.

—— 'Hôpital-général de Vannes', *BSPM* (1899), 144–75.

—— 'Hospice de la Garenne', *BSPM* (1899), 78–108.

—— 'Mineurs de l'observance', *BSPM* (1906), 169–98.

—— 'Prieuré de Saint-Guen, à Vannes', *BSPM* (1899), 176–83.

—— 'Prieurés de diocèse', *BSPM* (1904), 41–92, 167–249.

—— 'Ursulines d'Hennebont', *BSPM* (1907), 153–64.

—— 'Ursulines de Josselin', *BSPM* (1907), 21–30.

—— 'Ursulines de Malestroit', *BSPM* (1907), 173–7.

—— 'Ursulines de Muzillac', *BSPM* (1907), 178–97.

—— 'Ursulines de Ploërmel', *BSPM* (1907), 31–42.

—— 'Ursulines de Pontivy' *BSPM* (1907), 43–59.

—— 'Ursulines du Faouët', *BSPM* (1907), 165–72.

—— 'La Visitation de Vannes', *BSPM* (1897), 179–85.

Mahuas, J., 'Le Concours pour l'obtention des cures dans le diocèse de Vannes, au xviiie siècle', *MSHAB*, xlv (1965), 41–58.

—— 'Le Jansénisme dans le diocèse de Vannes, au xviiie siècle' (Faculté des Lettres, Rennes, *doctorat de troisième cycle,* 1966).

Marsille, H., 'Note sur les origines de l'école spirituelle vannetaise au xviie siècle', *MSHAB,* xxxv (1955), 31–7.

—— 'Prêtres vannetais du xviie siècle', *BSPM* (1964), 31–45.

—— 'Vannes', in Delattre, P. (ed.), *Les Établissements des Jésuites en France depuis quatre siècles* (Paris, 1949), v, 15–67.

—— 'La Retraite de Vennes', *BSPM* (1951–2), 127–51.

McManners, J., *French Ecclesiastical Society under the Ancien Régime* (Manchester, 1960).

—— *The French Revolution and the Church* (London, 1969).

Moisan, J., *La Propriété ecclésiastique dans le Morbihan pendant la période révolutionnaire* (Vannes, 1911).

Not up to the standard of the works by Rébillon and Dubreuil.

Nèdelec, Y., 'Aperçus de sociologie religieuse du xviiie siècle, d'après les titres cléricaux. L'exemple coutançais', *Revue historique de droit français et étranger,* 4e série, xl (1962), 500.

Perouas, L., 'Le Nombre des vocations sacerdotales est-il un critère valable en sociologie religieuse historique aux xviie et xviiie siècles?', *Actes du quatre-vingt-septième congrès national des sociétés savantes. Poitiers, 1962 Section d'histoire moderne et contemporaine* (Paris, 1963), 35–41.

Plongeron, B., *Les Réguliers de Paris devant le serment constitutionnel*

(1789–1801) (Paris, 1964).

—— *La Vie quotidienne du clergé français au xviiᵉ siècle* (Paris, 1974).

Raut, E. and Lallemant, L., 'Missire Jean-Marie-Vincent Touzée de Grand'isle, Recteur de Sarzeau (1710–1785)', *BSPM* (1936), 68–86.

Rébillon, A., *La Situation économique du clergé à la veille de la Révolution dans les districts de Rennes, de Fougères et de Vitré* (Paris, 1912).

St Thomas d'Aquin, sœur Marie de, 'Les Dominicains de Vannes sous la Révolution', *BSPM* (1955–6), 5–45.

Tackett, T., *Priest and Parish in Eighteenth-Century France* (Princeton, 1977).

(vi) Works on the Revolution in Brittany, principally in the Morbihan

Bliard, P., 'Un Club de province au début de la Révolution 1791–1793', *Revue des questions historiques,* n.s., xxvii (1902), 490–537.

—— *Le Conventionnel Prieur de la Marne en mission dans l'Ouest (1793–1794), d'après des documents inédits* (Paris, 1906).

—— 'Idées politiques et religieuses d'un club de province au début de la Révolution (1791–1793)', *Études,* xciii (1903), 313–38.

—— 'L'Organisation d'un club de province, au début de la Révolution (1791–1793)', *Études,* xciii (1902), 165–85.

Cadoudal, G. de, *Georges Cadoudal et la Chouannerie* (Paris, 1887). By Cadoudal's nephew. Fascinating, but cites no sources.

Cariou, A., 'La Constitution civile du clergé dans la Département du Morbihan', *MSHAB,* xlv (1965), 59–88.

Closmadeuc, G. de., 'Débuts de la chouannerie dans le Morbihan, 1793–1794. Le capitaine J. Defay, officier des armées vendéennes', *La Révolution française,* xl (1901), 330–52.

—— 'Le 1ᵉʳ Bataillon des volontaires nationaux du Morbihan, 1791–1795', *Annales de Bretagne,* xix (1903–4), 409–27, 601–28.

Cobban, A., 'The Beginnings of the Channel Isles Correspondence', *EHR,* lxxvii (1962), 38–52.

Cochin, A., *Les Sociétés de pensée et la démocratie* (Paris, 1921). The preface to the better-known study of the pre-Revolution in Brittany:

—— *Les Sociétés de pensée et la Révolution en Bretagne (1788–1789)* (Paris, 1925).

Corgne, E., *Les Revendications des paysans de la sénéchaussée de Ploërmel d'après les cahiers de doléances de 1789* (Rennes, 1938).

—— *Pontivy et son district pendant la Révolution. 1789—germinal an V* (Rennes, 1938).

Debauve, J.-L., *La Justice révolutionnaire dans le Morbihan, 1790–1795* (Paris, 1965).

Thorough and learned; a mine of information on the notables of the Vannetais.

Dubreuil, L., 'Essai sur l'administration générale d'un district pendant la

Révolution. Le district de Redon. 1ᵉʳ juillet 1790—18 ventôse an IV',
    Annales de Bretagne, xix (1903–4), 115–32; xx (1904–5), 63–115, 520–
    33; xxi (1905–6), 90–110, 222–39, 521–50; xxii (1906–7), 93–147.
—— *Histoire des insurrections de l'Ouest* (Paris, 1930).
    The best general narrative treatment.
Du Chatellier, A.-R., *Histoire de la Révolution dans les départements de
    l'ancien Bretagne* (Paris–Nantes, 1835–6).
    The best of the early studies. Du Chatellier was a friend of the former
    représentant en mission Guezno, whose papers he inherited.
Dupuy, R., *Le Garde nationale et les débuts de la Révolution en Ille-et-
    Vilaine* (Rennes, 1972).
Egret, J., 'Les Origines de la Révolution en Bretagne (1788–1789)', *Revue
    historique,* ccxiii (1955), 189–215.
    A useful antidote to Cochin.
Erlannig [Marquer, F.], *Le Général Louis-Charles-René de Sol de Grissoles,
    1761–1836, frère d'armes et successeur de Georges Cadoudal* (St-Brieuc,
    1966).
Goodwin, A., 'Counter-revolution in Brittany: the Royalist Conspiracy of
    the Marquis de la Rouërie, 1791–1793', *Bulletin of the John Rylands
    Library, Manchester,* xxxix (1957), 326–55.
Jouany, D., *La Formation du département du Morbihan* (Vannes, 1920).
Kerrand, H., 'René Marie Gaillard de la Touche 1751–1838. Administrateur
    breton' (Faculté des Lettres, Rennes, *doctorat de troisième cycle,* 1967).
Le Falher, J., *Le Royaume de Bignan* (Hennebont, 1913).
Le Goff, T. J. A. and Sutherland, D. M. G., 'The Revolution and the Rural
    Community in Eighteenth-Century Brittany', *Past & Present,* lxii
    (1974), 96–119.
Macé, A., 'Les Affaires de Bondon et de Liziec (7–13 février 1791)', *BSPM*
    (1890), 181–97.
    Rather superficial.
—— 'Les Élections du Morbihan de 1789 à 1800', *BSPM* (1890), 74–110;
    (1891), 115–32.
    Unfinished; does not go beyond 1789.
Marsille, L., 'L'Affaire du Préclos', *BSPM* (1911), 34–58.
    An antiseigneurial riot at Tréal, in the east of the Département, in June
    1791.
Martin, E., 'La Contribution patriotique de 1789 dans le Département du
    Morbihan', *MSHAB,* iii (1922), 333–71.
Pocquet, B., *Les Origines de la Révolution en Bretagne* (Paris, 1885).
Pommeret, H., *L'Esprit public dans les Côtes-du-Nord pendant la Révolution*
    (St-Brieuc, 1921).
Queverdo, E., 'Le Club des Jacobins de Lorient' (Faculté des Lettres,
    Rennes, mémoire de D.E.S., n.d.).
Sageret, E., *Le Morbihan et la Chouannerie morbihannaise sous le Consulat*

(Paris, 1911–18).

Sée, H., 'Le Rôle de la bourgeoisie bretonne à la veille de la Révolution', *Annales de Bretagne,* xxxiv (1919–20), 405–33.

—— 'Les Troubles agraires en Haute-Bretagne (1789–1792)', *Commission de recherche et de publication des documents relatifs à la vie économique de la Révolution, 1920–21* (Paris, 1924), 231–373.

(vii) Also consulted

Abel, W., *Crises agraires en Europe (xiiie–xxe siècle)* (Paris, 1973).

Allen, R. G. D., *Statistics for Economists* (London, 1966).

Andrews, R. H., *Les Paysans des Mauges au xviiie siècle* (Tours, 1935).

Aron, J.-P., *Essai sur la sensibilité alimentaire* (Paris, 1967).

Béaur, G., 'Le Centième Denier et les mouvements de propriété. Deux exemples beaucerons (1761–1790)', *Annales: E.S.C.,* xxxiii (1976), 1010–33.

Benzacar, J., 'Le Pain à Bordeaux (xviiie siècle)', *Revue économique de Bordeaux,* xiv (1904), 41–57, 81–97, 113–27, 149–53, 181–98.

Bloch, M., *Les Caractères originaux de l'histoire rurale française* (Paris, 1952).

Bois, P., *Paysans de l'Ouest: des structures économiques et sociales aux options politiques depuis l'époque révolutionnaire dans la Sarthe* (Le Mans, 1960).

—— 'Réflexions sur les survivances de la Révolution dans l'Ouest', *Annales historiques de la Révolution française,* xxxiii (1961), 177–86.

—— 'Structure socio-professionnelle du Mans à la fin du xviiie siècle. Problèmes de méthode et résultats', *Actes du quatre-vingt-septième congrès national des Sociétés savantes. Section d'histoire moderne et contemporaine. Poitiers, 1962* (Paris, 1963), 679–709.

Braudel, F. and Labrousse, C.-E. (eds.), *Histoire économique et sociale de la France,* ii (Paris, 1970).

Butel, P., *La Croissance commerciale bordelaise dans la seconde moitié du xviiie siècle* (Lille, 1973).

Cavignac, J., *Jean Pellet, commerçant de gros 1694–1772* (Paris, 1967).

Chayanov, A. V., *The Theory of Peasant Economy* (Homewood, Ill. 1960).

Cobb, R., *Les Armées Révolutionnaires. Instrument de la terreur dans les départements, avril 1793 – floréal an II* (Paris–The Hague, 1961).

Cobban, A., 'British Secret Service in France, 1784–1792', *English Historical Review,* lxxix (1954), 226–61.

—— *The Social Interpretation of the French Revolution* (Cambridge, 1964).

Coornaert, E., *Les Corporations en France avant 1789* (Paris, 1941).

Danière, A., 'Feudal Incomes and Demand Elasticity for Bread in Late Eighteenth-Century France', *Journal of Economic History,* xviii (1958), 317–44 [includes a reply by D. S. Landes and subsequent controversy].

Dardel, P., *Navires et marchandises dans les ports de Rouen et du Havre au xviiᵉ siècle* (Paris, 1963).

Daumard, A., 'Une Référence pour l'étude des sociétés urbaines en France aux xviiiᵉ et xixᵉ siècles', *RHMC*, x (1963), 185–210.

Daumard, A. and Furet, F., 'Problèmes de méthode en histoire sociale. Réflexions sur une note critique', *RHMC*, xi (1964), 291–8 [a reply to J.-Y. Tiret, cited below].

—— *Structures et relations sociales à Paris au milieu du xviiᵉ siècle* (Paris, 1961).

Dawson, P., *Provincial magistrates and Revolutionary Politics in France, 1789–1795* (Cambridge, Mass., 1972).

—— 'Sur le prix des offices judiciaires à la fin de l'ancien régime', *RHES*, xlii (1964), 390–2.

Dehergne, J., *Le Bas-Poitou à la veille de la Révolution* (Paris, 1963).

Delumeau, J., 'Le Commerce extérieur français au xviiᵉ siècle', *XVIIᵉ siècle*, lxix (1965), 81–105.

De Roover, R., *L'Évolution de la lettre de change, xivᵉ–xviiᵉ siècles* (Paris, 1953).

Dion, R., *Essai sur la formation du paysage rural français* (Tours, 1934).

Dupâquier, J., 'Problèmes de mesure et de représentation graphique en matière d'histoire sociale', *Actes du quatre-vingt-neuvième congrès national des sociétés savantes, Section d'histoire moderne et contemporaine, Lyon, 1964* (Paris, 1965), t. 2, i, 77–86.

Du Puy de Clinchamps, P., *La Noblesse* (Paris, 1962).

Faucheux, M., *L'Insurrection vendéenne de 1793. Aspects économiques et sociaux* (Paris, 1964).

Floud, R., *An Introduction to Quantitative Methods for Historians* (London, 1973).

Friedmann, G., *Villes et campagnes. Civilisation urbaine et civilisation rurale en France* (Paris, 1953).

Galbraith, J. K., *The Scotch* (Toronto, 1964).

Garden, M., *Lyon et les Lyonnais au xviiiᵉ siècle* (Paris, 1970).

Gazely, J. G., *The Life of Arthur Young* (Philadelphia, 1973).

Gille, P., 'Jauge et tonnage des navires', in *Le Navire et l'économie maritime du xvᵉ au xviiiᵉ siècle* (Paris, 1957), 85.

Godechot, J., *La Contre-révolution: doctrine et action. 1789–1804* (Paris, 1961).

Goubert, P., *L'Ancien Régime* (Paris, 1969–73).

—— *Beauvais et le Beauvaisis de 1600 à 1730* (Paris, 1960).

—— *Familles marchandes sous l'Ancien Régime: les Danse et les Motte, de Beauvais* (Paris, 1959).

Greer, D. M., *The Incidence of the Emigration during the French Revolution* (Cambridge, Mass., 1951).

—— *The Incidence of the Terror during the French Revolution. A statistical interpretation* (Cambridge, Mass., 1935).

Hamilton, E. J., *War and Prices in Spain, 1651–1800* (Cambridge, Mass., 1947).

Hampson, N., *La Marine de l'An II. Mobilisation de la flotte de l'océan, 1793–1794* (Paris, 1959).

Hare, J., 'La Population de la ville de Québec, 1795–1805', *Histoire Sociale/Social History,* vii (1974), 23–47.

Hémardinquer, J.-J., *Pour une histoire de l'alimentation* (Paris, 1970).

Hufton, O. H., *Bayeux in the late eighteenth century. A social study* (Oxford, 1967).

Kaplow, J., *Elbeuf during the Revolutionary Period: History and Social Structure* (Baltimore, 1963).

Katz, M. B., *The People of Hamilton, Canada West* (Cambridge, Mass., 1975).

Knights, P. R., *The Plain People of Boston, 1830–1860* (New York, 1971).

—— and Thernstrom, S., 'Men in Motion: some Data and Speculations about Urban Population Mobility in nineteenth-century America', *Journal of Interdisciplinary History* (1970), 9–35.

Kordi, M. el, *Bayeux aux xviie et xviiie siècles. Contribution à l'histoire urbaine de la France* (Paris–The Hague, 1970).

Labrousse, C.-E., *La Crise de l'économie française à la fin de l'ancien régime et au début de la Révolution. I Aperçus généraux, sources, méthode, objectifs. La crise de la viticulture* (Paris, 1944).

—— *Esquisse du mouvement des prix et des revenus en France au xviiie siècle* (Paris, 1933).

—— 'Voies nouvelles vers une histoire de la bourgeoisie occidentale aux xviiie et xixe siècles (1700–1850)', *Relazioni del X Congresso Internazionale di Scienze Storiche* (Rome, 1955) iv, 365–96.

Landes, D. S., 'The Statistical Study of French Crises', *Journal of Economic History,* x (1950), 195–211.

Lebrun, F., *Les Hommes et la mort en Anjou aux 17e et 18e siècles* (Paris–The Hague, 1971).

Lefebvre, G., *Études orléanaises* (Paris, 1962–3).

—— *La Grande Peur de 1789* (Paris, 1932).

—— *Les Paysans du Nord pendant la Révolution française* (Paris–Lille, 1924).

—— 'La Révolution française et les paysans', in *Études sur la Révolution française* (Paris, 1954), 246–68.

—— *Questions agraires au temps de la Terreur* (La Roche-sur-Yon, 1954).

Le Goff, T. and Meyer, J., 'Les Construction navales en France dans la seconde moitié du xviiie siècle, *Annales: E.S.C.,* xxvi (1971), 173–85.

Lennard, R., 'The Alleged Exhaustion of the Soil in Mediaeval England', *The Economic Journal,* xxxii (1922), 12–27.

Letaconnoux, J., 'Les Voies de communications en France au xviiie siècle',

Vierteljahrschrift für Social- und Wirtschaftsgeschichte (1909), 94–141.

Leuillot, P., 'Réflexions sur l'histoire économique et sociale à propos de la bourgeoisie de 1789', *RHMC,* i (1954), 131–44.

Levasseur, E., *La Population française* (Paris, 1889).

Lévy-Bruhl, H., *Histoire de la lettre de change en France aux xvii͏ͤ et xviii͏ͤ siècles* (Paris, 1932).

Ligou, D., *Montauban à la fin de l'ancien régime et aux débuts de la Révolution 1787–1794* (Paris, 1958).

Louchitsky, J., 'Régime agraire et populations agricoles dans les environs de Paris à la veille de la Révolution', *Revue d'histoire moderne,* n.s., ii (1933), 97–142.

Lüthy, H., *La Banque protestante en France de la Révocation de l'Édit de Nantes à la Révolution* (Paris, 1959).

Martin, G., *Les Associations ouvrières au xviii͏ͤ siècle (1700–1792)* (Paris, 1900).

Martin-Saint-Léon, É., *Le Compagnonnage* (Paris, 1901).

—— *Histoire des corporations de métiers depuis leurs origines jusqu'à leur suppression en 1791* (Paris, 1922).

Massé, P., 'Survivances des droits féodaux dans l'Ouest (1793–1902)', *Annales historiques de la Révolution française,* clxxxi (1965), 270–98.

Mendras, H., *Sociologie de la campagne française* (Paris, 1965).

Merle, L., *La Métairie et l'évolution agraire de la Gâtine poitevine de la fin du Moyen Âge à la Révolution* (Paris, 1958).

Meyer, J., 'Une Enquête de l'Académie de médecine sur les épidémies (1774–1794)', *Annales: E.S.C.,* xxi (1966), 729–49.

Meynier, A., *Les Paysages agraires* (Paris, 1958).

—— 'Problèmes de structure agraire', *Annales: E.S.C.,* ix (1955), 27–36.

Michelet, J., *Le Révolution française,* ed. Walter, G. (Tours, 1952).

Mitchell, H., 'Resistance to the Revolution in Western France', *Past & Present,* lxiii (1974), 94–131.

—— 'The Vendée and Counterrevolution: a review essay', *French Historical Studies,* v (1967–8), 405–29.

Perrot, J.-C., *Genèse d'une ville moderne: Caen au xviii͏ͤ siècle* (Paris–The Hague, 1975).

Peter, J.-P., 'Malades et maladies à la fin du xviii͏ͤ siècle', *Annales: E.S.C.,* xxii (1967), 711–51.

Plessix, R., 'Une Paroisse angevine au xviii͏ͤ siècle, Mouliherne', *Revue du Bas-Poitou* (1969), 52–68.

Rambert, G., 'La France et la politique commerciale de l'Espagne au xviii͏ͤ siècle', *RHMC,* vi (1959), 269–88.

—— (ed.), *Histoire du commerce de Marseille,* vii (Paris, 1966).

Sachs, W., 'The Business Outlook in the Northern Colonies, 1750–1775', (Columbia University, Ph.D. thesis, 1957).

Saint-Jacob, P. de, 'Le Mouvement de la propriété dans un village bourguignon à la fin de l'ancien régime, 1748–1789', *RHES,* xxvii (1948–9), 46–52.

—— *Les Paysans de la Bourgogne du Nord au dernier siècle de l'ancien régime* (Paris, 1960).

—— 'La Propriété au xviiiᵉ siècle. Une source méconnue: le contrôle des actes et le centième denier', *Annales: E.S.C.,* i (1946), 162–6.

—— 'Une Source de l'histoire sociale au xviiiᵉ siècle; la table des contrats de mariage dans les fonds du contrôle des actes', *Actes du quatre-vingt-quatrième congrès national des Sociétés savantes. Dijon, 1959. Section d'histoire moderne et contemporaine* (Paris, 1960), 415–18.

Sée, H., *Histoire économique de la France* (Paris, 1939).

Siegfried, A., *Tableau politique de la France de l'Ouest sous la Troisième République* (Paris, 1913).

Taylor, G. V., 'Noncapitalist Wealth and the Origins of the French Revolution', *American Historical Review,* lxxii (1966–7), 469–96.

—— 'Types of Capitalism in Eighteenth-Century France', *English Historical Review,* lxxix (1964), 478–94.

Temple, N., 'The Control and Exploitation of French Towns during the Ancien Régime', *History,* n.s., li (1966), 16–31.

—— 'Municipal Elections and Municipal Oligarchies in Eighteenth-Century France', in Bosher, J. F. (ed.), *French Government and Society 1500–1850* (London, 1973), 70–91.

Tilly, C., *The Vendée* (London, 1964).

Tiret, J.-Y., 'Problémes de méthode en histoire sociale', *RHMC,* x (1963), 211–18.

Tocqueville, A. de, *L'Ancien Régime et la Révolution française,* ed. Mayer, J.-P. (Paris, 1952).

Toutain, J.-C., 'Le Produit de l'agriculture française de 1700 à 1958. I Estimation du produit au xviiiᵉ siècle', *Cahiers de l'Institut de sciences économiques appliquées,* série AF, 5 (juillet 1961), nᵒ 1.

Usher, A. P., *The History of the Grain Trade in France, 1400–1710* (Cambridge, Mass., 1913).

Vidal de la Blache, P., *Tableau de la géographie de la France* (Paris, 1903).

Vovelle, M., 'Formes de dépendance d'un milieu urbain. Chartres, à l'égard du monde rural, de la fin de l'ancien régime à la Restauration', *Quatre-vingt-troisième congrès national des sociétés savantes. Section d'histoire moderne et contemporaine. Aix–Marseille, 1958* (Paris, 1959), 483–512.

—— 'Problèmes méthodologiques posés par l'utilisation des sources de l'enregistrement dans une étude de structure sociale', *Comité des travaux historiques et scientifiques. Section d'histoire moderne et contemporaine. Bulletin,* fasc. 3 (1961), 49–104.

—— 'Structure et répartition de la fortune foncière et de la fortune mobilière d'un ensemble urbain: Chartres, de la fin de l'ancien régime à

la Restauration', *RHES*, xxxvi (1958), 385–98.
Yamane, T., *Statistics, an Introductory Analysis* (New York, 1966).

INDEX

affaire de Bretagne, 117, 120, 128, 130
afféagement, defined, 303 n. 18
agriculture, cattle and livestock, 9, 169, 173 n. 26, 176, 189, 190–2, 202, 292, 293 n. 3, 302, 325–9, 333–5, 378–81; communal usages, 151, 166–8, 203; crops, 5, 14–15, 95, 151, 168–9, 172, 293; crop rotation, 151, 166, 168; grain prices, 16–17, 89, 103, 287, 294–6, 302; methods of cultivation, 6, 168–70, 241, 276; production of grain, 15, 16–17, 103, 293–7, 299; profit margins, 171–5; second occupation, 7; seed:harvest yields, 171, 293; tenant income, 299–301; see also *bocage,* economic fluctuations, *fermage, domaine congéable, ferme générale, métayage,* peasants, rural community, wasteland
aiguillaneuf (forfeits), 222 n. 46
Aiguillon, Emmanuel-Armand de Vignerot du Plessis de Richelieu, duc d', 74–5, 119, 120, 124, 129, 130
Allaire (Morbihan), 12, 211–12
Allanic, Julienne, wife of P. Le Falher, 381; Louis-Joseph, *commis greffier,* 369–70; Marguerite, lender, 374
Allano, François, 235; Jean, 235; Louise, 235
Ambon (Morbihan), 3, 87, 170 n. 25, 177 n. 2, 208–9, 242, 258, 275, 277, 342, 344, 355, 356

Amelot, Sébastien-Michel, bishop, 147, 264, 348, 349, 351
Amirauté of Vannes, 11, 32, 68, 78, 329
Angers (Maine-et-Loire), 31, 267
Anjou, 8, 12, 173, 196, 344
Anne, saint, 245
anoblis, see bourgeoisie
apothecaries, *see* medical profession
apprentices, 37
Argentré-du-Plessis (Ille-et-Vilaine), 196
Arradon (Morbihan), 22, 87, 179, 208, 221, 225, 283, 303 n. 17, 308, 319 n. 32
arrière-ban, 273–4
arson, *see under* crime
artisans and shopkeepers, in countryside, 178, 187, 190–1, 232, 233, 250, 301; in town, 33, 38–9, 46–8, 54, 58 n. 6, 59–61, 91–106, 250, 336; *see also* apprentices, guilds, land transfers, Revolution
Artois, 243
Arzal (Morbihan), 344
Arzano (Morbihan), 5 n. 1
Arzon (Morbihan), 146, 186 n. 10, 203 n. 59, 212, 218, 219, 247, 292, 342, 343, 356, 357–8
assemblée générale, of parish, 217
assignats, 341, 346, 357
attorneys, *see* notaries and attorneys
Aubry, Jean-Charles-Gilles, physician, laureate of Royal Academy of Medecine, 91, 201; widow, wine merchant, 84
Augustinians, 266